This work of creative non-fiction was written from existing letters and the memories they triggered. Scenes and dialogue are true to the circumstances but may not be word for word, due to our flawed memories. After all, it's been fifty years!

Other than immediate family members, names of characters have been changed to protect the privacy of the individuals. Some locations and timeframes were also adjusted. Excerpts of the letters are verbatim, with minor editing for clarity.

Copyright © 2017 by **Carolyn L. Wade**

All rights reserved. No part of this publication may be reproduced, distributed or transmitted in any form or by any means, without prior written permission.

In some cases, sources for sidebar information gave conflicting "facts." I've double-checked everything, but there may still be some discrepancies. Sources for sidebars include: www.history-world.org/vietnam, www.onthisday.com, www.mrpopculture.com, www.historyorb.com, www.thepeoplehistory.com, www.google.com, www.grammy.com, www.oscars.org, www.billboard.com, The Oregonian; Vancouver, WA phone book.

Book Layout © 2017 BookDesignTemplates.com
Cover Design: Rebecca Malmin
Author Photo: Michelle Schmitz, Hello Photography

Five Hundred Letters/Carolyn L. Wade -- 1st ed.
Version 11.3
ISBN-13: **978-1545343081**

To my beloved Larry,
without whom there would be no book;
and
to our Heavenly Father,
who made it all happen.

Trust in the LORD with all your heart,
And lean not on your own understanding;
In all your ways acknowledge Him,
And He shall direct your paths.
Proverbs 3:5-6 NKJV

Chapter 1

Carolyn

My feet were barely across the threshold of my sister's house when she greeted me. "Guess what?" Emily's blue eyes sparkled excitedly beneath her bouffant brown hair. Before I could respond, she continued. "Larry Wade will be in church on Sunday. He and his mother are driving up for the July 4th weekend."

"Are you kidding? This Sunday, like the day after tomorrow?" I wasn't sure I shared her excitement, and the sudden flutter in my stomach was disconcerting.

"Yes, this Sunday. Mrs. Wade's letter was here when I got home from work. They'll leave Hanford early tomorrow and stay at the parsonage tomorrow night."

> **Current Culture**
> **July 1966**
>
> - New government program, "Medicare," goes into effect
> - Racial violence erupts in sixteen cities nationwide
> - President Lyndon Johnson signs the Freedom of Information Act, allowing release of previously controlled government documents
> - Average annual household income, $6,900

"Wow, that's...interesting, I guess." I headed for the guest room at the back of the house. "I'm going to change and unpack. Let me know if I can help get dinner on the table."

I was 19 years old, trying to figure out my life. During the week, I lived with my parents. Their ranch in the foothills of Mt. Hood east of Portland, Oregon was close to my summer job as a tutor for adults in the small logging town of Sandy. Most weekends, I drove an hour to the other side of Portland to Emily's house. Even with our ten-year age difference, Emily and I had a

1

special connection, and time with her family was a welcome break from my tense relationship with my mother.

Although I'd lived away from home at college for two years, Mom often treated me like an adolescent, and I reacted with barely concealed irritation. I loved my parents and knew they loved me, but I was the youngest of their six children, and they were reluctant to let their "baby" grow up.

In the small bathroom next to my room at Emily and Paul's, I stared at the blue eyes in the mirror. *Why does the thought of meeting Larry make me feel so vulnerable, like I'm at the edge of a cliff?*

I'd heard about him for years, ever since Paul and Emily had lived in Hanford, California, pastoring the church Larry and his mom attended. Emily had corresponded with Mrs. Wade ever since their assignment in Hanford ended. She frequently shared Mrs. Wade's return letters with me, including news and occasional photographs of Larry as he finished high school and college. I didn't think he was my type—too serious and stuffy-looking. *Now I'll finally get to meet him...*

Making a wry face at my reflection, I ran my fingers through my short sun-streaked hair. My parents had left that morning on a road trip, and I planned to drive back to the ranch after church on Sunday. My brother was coming home for a short break from his summer Forest Service job. *Whatever happens, I plan to enjoy the Independence Day weekend.*

I heard Emily call out the back door to her two sons. "Dinner's almost ready, boys. Come in and wash up!" I quickly stepped out of my summer dress and put on a cotton blouse and capris before heading to the kitchen.

Paul, slim and energetic, joined us from his study as the boys scrambled to their seats at the table. "Nice to see you, Carolyn. How was your week?"

"Pretty good, Paul. How about yours?"

"It was fine; I had lots of sales for a change." Paul supplemented his ministerial income by selling Fuller Brush products in local neighborhoods. He was ten years older than Emily, and always treated me with fatherly concern and kindness.

"It was good weather for you," I replied. "No rain and not too hot."

Paul directed his attention to the boys. "Time to pray, settle down now." Gary, age nine, tugged at the hand of five-year-old Jimmy. I bowed my head, trying to keep from chuckling as I heard muffled kicks from under the table.

My first forkful of oven-fried chicken was on the way to my mouth when Emily brought up the topic that seemed at the front of her mind. "Mrs. Wade and Larry should be here about this time tomorrow night. I hope they enjoy the drive."

"So you'll finally get to meet Larry!" Paul smiled at me. "Em's been trying to get you two together for years."

Emily shrugged and smiled. "I just think they might enjoy each other's company, that's all."

"Who's Larry?" asked Gary.

"He's a nice young man we met when we lived in California," Em said. "He'll be in church Sunday morning and Aunt Carolyn will get to meet him."

"Then will he be her boyfriend?" Gary got right to the point.

"I guess that's up to Carolyn," Paul chuckled.

I was annoyed to feel a blush rise in my cheeks; I needed to change the subject. "How was work this week, Em?" Her outgoing personality and attention to detail made her an efficient secretary.

"Stressful," she replied. "I'm glad it's Friday and Monday is a holiday. Did Dad and Mom get off okay?"

"Yes, they stopped by the Migrant Center office to tell me goodbye about 10:00. It's a long drive to Los Angeles, but they're really looking forward to seeing John and Fran and meeting the grandkids for the first time."

"I hope they're settling in okay," Em said. "It's hard to adjust coming back from the mission field. The kids haven't known any life but Nigeria." Emily spoke from experience. After their year in California, she and Paul and the boys had spent a year in Africa working with my oldest brother John.

"I'm sure John will have plenty of interesting stories," Paul added.

The conversation continued in a safe direction, but my mind ran on another track. Indistinct images from photos floated through my head. I vaguely remembered one of Larry in his high school football uniform looking tough and determined. Thinking about meeting him on Sunday made me suddenly feel like one of our horses shying away from being maneuvered into our corral.

After dinner I washed the dishes and tidied the kitchen while Paul and Emily read to Gary and Jimmy. When the boys were tucked into bed, Emily and I caught each other up on the week's events. Eventually we joined Paul in the living room.

Paul and Em sat close on the couch holding hands, while I lounged in a chair nearby. A welcome breeze drifted through the open window. Paul's snorts of laughter over Johnny Carson's antics on *The Tonight Show* raised Em's eyebrows, but we all enjoyed the hilarious comedy.

Later, as I stretched out under a sheet in the stuffy bedroom, I tried to sort my thoughts about Sunday. *Could Larry be someone who might share my goals?* Since early childhood, my parents had taught me that God had a unique plan for my life. In their minds, that meant being a missionary or a pastor's wife. Mom and Dad had allowed me to leave home to study at Oregon College of Education in Monmouth, a small town two hours away, because they believed teaching could fit with either of those options.

After lonely high school years living at the end of the school bus route, I loved the fun and activity of college life. Singing in the top-ranked college choir was exhilarating, and working on the yearbook provided new avenues for my creativity. It was exciting to feel my mind being stretched in classes, and there was always someone around to talk to or have fun with.

I'd tried my wings a bit in my first year, taking a dancing class I knew my parents would disapprove of, and even briefly dating a non-Christian boy. But over the months, I gradually realized that what I thought were just my parents' convictions had become truly my own.

None of the boys I'd met at college had come close to having the character and values I was looking for. The dedicated Christian guys seemed pious or pedantic, and apparently believed that zeal made up for lack of manners. Others were church-goers, but focused on their careers or making money. I hadn't found anyone who would accept me, could make me laugh, and who also put God first. After a couple of unsatisfactory relationships, I'd recently given up, telling God: Y*ou know the right man for me. I'm tired of looking; you'll have to bring him to me.*

Restless, I turned over in bed again, wishing that sleep would quiet my rambling thoughts. Eventually I succumbed to fitful dreams, and suddenly Gary and Jimmy were at my bedroom door arguing over who would tell me that breakfast was ready.

After breakfast, Em and I hurried through our Saturday chores before heading out for our weekly shopping trip. As she backed the car out of the driveway, I waved to Paul, who was bending over to start the lawn mower. Heading down the hill, Em said, "Do you want to stop by Jennie's Yardstick before we get groceries?"

"Silly question," I replied. "When do I ever turn down a chance to shop for fabric?"

"We might have some time to sew this afternoon. The boys are going to a friend's house, and Paul will be studying for tomorrow's sermon." We were silent for a few minutes before my sister brought up the subject on both our minds. "You don't seem very excited about meeting Larry tomorrow."

"I'm sure he's a very nice person, but a long-distance romance doesn't sound like much fun."

Hearing the wariness in my voice, Emily glanced at me before continuing. "He graduated from Fresno State last month. Mrs. Wade's letter says his degree is in English, with a minor in history."

"Well, that might give us something in common," I conceded. I had recently finished my second year studying secondary education with a minor in English and literature. "Maybe we've read some of the same books."

"The letter also said that he's been preaching at church occasionally." Em gave me another sidelong glance, wondering how I might receive that bit of news. We'd had many late-night conversations about my goals in life.

"What's he been doing since he graduated?"

"Job hunting. Hanford's a pretty small town; it may take time with his English degree."

"Not exactly the most marketable field of study. And there's the Draft to worry about now that he's out of college. I don't envy any guy right now." I thought of friends who were trying to stay alive in the jungles of Vietnam, and some who hadn't made it back. "I'm glad the Draft doesn't include women."

Emily pulled into the parking lot of Jennie's Yardstick, and our thoughts turned to sewing. Although she dressed for an office job and I shopped for college, our tastes were similar and we often traded clothes. After a happy hour browsing through fabric and pattern books, we headed to Fred Meyer to buy groceries. By the time we drove home, it was time to prepare lunch, and the afternoon passed quickly with our new sewing projects.

When dinner was over, Paul and Emily headed out the door to visit with friends, while I herded the boys to the bathroom and started filling the ancient claw-foot tub. An extra squirt of bubble bath provided them with piles of foam. The variations of soapy beards, mustaches and hairdos kept us all giggling as I frequently mopped up spills on the linoleum floor.

"Ok, guys, that's enough. Time's up!" I held up a towel to deflect another splash from the tub, warning the boys that my patience was dwindling. I wrestled them into their pajamas, promising stories as soon as their teeth were brushed. I was anxious to get them settled and have the rest of the evening to myself.

Once the boys were in bed, I got out the ironing board and my navy crepe dress. I was glad I had brought it for this weekend; the ruffled neckline and sheer sleeves were flattering. My patent leather shoes and matching handbag were ready with a quick swipe of a damp cloth. I tried on the new lipstick I'd bought that morning, squinting in the bathroom mirror to get the full impact. On the chance that Larry might be someone special, I wanted to look my best.

After watching some television, I set my hair in rollers before going to bed with a book. It was difficult to concentrate as my mind created possible scenarios of my first meeting with Larry. *Will he be interesting, or smug and opinionated? If I don't like him, at least he's only here for a weekend. And what if I do like him? How could that possibly work?* The problems of a long-distance relationship suddenly made my head hurt.

As I turned off the light, I heard Paul's car pulling into the carport. The last image in my mind as I drifted off to sleep was the photo of an intent young man with dark-rimmed glasses and crew-cut black hair.

Chapter 2

Larry

The pavement of Interstate 5 disappeared beneath the car like a retractable power cord. Mom and I had been on the road since shortly after dawn to drive nearly eight hundred miles from Hanford, our hometown in the San Joaquin Valley of Central California, to Portland, Oregon. As the mileposts flashed by, my thoughts flew ahead to our destination, and what I hoped might be there.

> **Current Culture**
> **July 1966**
>
> - US planes bomb the demilitarized zone in Vietnam
> - Alabamans burn Beatles products after John Lennon says that the Beatles are more popular than Jesus
> - Jim Ryun sets new record for running the mile in 3 m 51 s
> - Baskin-Robbins ice cream: 35 cents a scoop

Several weeks earlier, Mom brought up the idea at the dinner table. "What would you think about going to Portland over July 4th? I could take a couple of vacation days, and we could go for a long weekend. I'd like to see the church there and visit the Muellers."

"Oh, Midge, why d'ya want to do that?" Dad said gruffly. "You won't get me in a car all those hours just to go to a church service."

"I'll go with you, Mom," I said. "I wouldn't mind getting away from Hanford for a few days. I need a break from my job hunt, and it would be nice to go somewhere a little cooler."

Even if Dad wasn't coming, he still voiced his opinion. "Where would you stay? It'll be expensive."

I said, "Jesse usually stays in the parsonage next to the church. He says there are extra bedrooms. I'll ask him to call the caretakers and check for us." Jesse Black had grown up in church with me. His dad, the former pastor of our small non-denominational church near Hanford, had recently purchased a church in Portland. His weekly radio broadcast drew people from the West Coast for teaching and inspiration.

Mom added, "And I'll write to tell the Muellers that we're coming." I could hear the happy excitement in her voice as she started clearing the dinner table. Paul and Emily Mueller, our interim pastors several years earlier, were now living in Portland, and Paul had been installed as the resident minister by Rev. Black.

"I still think it's a long way to drive for church," Dad grumbled, heading to the living room for his nightly television shows.

We were well on our way north when Mom reached over to turn off the radio at the end of one of her favorite gospel programs, signaling that she wanted to talk.

"It's too bad that you haven't found a job yet. It must be frustrating to fill out applications for jobs that don't really fit you."

"Yes, it is," I replied, "but something will turn up."

"I'm really proud of you, Larry. It's a big thing to be the first in our family to get a college degree."

"It wasn't easy, and I'm glad I'm finished."

"I know you missed a lot of fun by living at home, commuting and working part-time."

"True, but I finished without any debt. That's worth a lot to me."

"I'm sorry that Dad and I couldn't help you. It was just bad timing with him losing his job a couple years ago."

"But I made it, Mom, and I'll find a decent job eventually. The other day someone suggested that I check at the county offices. I'll apply there when we get back from this trip."

"I'm glad you were willing to come with me," Mom said.

"It gave me a chance to get out of the house," I chuckled. "I'm looking forward to being in a big city for a change. Besides, who knows, maybe God will talk to me when I'm up there."

"I hope so," Mom said. She leaned back against the headrest with a sigh. "I think I'll close my eyes for a little while. Last night's shift at the hospital was a rough one."

As Mom dozed, my mind moved ahead to Portland. I couldn't avoid thinking about the possibility that I might meet Emily's sister Carolyn this weekend. A couple years earlier, Emily had sent Mom one of Carolyn's high-school graduation pictures, which of course, Mom had shown to me. Emily had written that her sister had graduated near the top of her class, and was planning to be a teacher. While Carolyn looked reasonably attractive, I wasn't interested in just a pretty girl, but one who truly loved God. If she was willing to consider being a pastor's wife, that would be even better.

But if she's as smart and capable as Emily's letters said, why would she be interested in some guy from a hick town in the middle of California?

At mid-day we were in Northern California, and the scenery began to change. One of the first dramatic landmarks was Mt. Lassen, its black cinder cone poking up from the scrubby, flat landscape. A little further north, we got our first views of Mt. Shasta, with snow still showing on its broken peaks. The smell of water relieved the car's stuffiness as the road wound above man-made Lake Shasta, with clumps of houseboats clinging to wooden docks. We stopped for lunch at a roadside rest area and stretched our stiff legs.

Back on the road, Mom turned the on radio to catch the news. As usual, the Vietnam War was the headline story, with reports of the latest battle and casualties. My hands tightened on the steering wheel—Chuck, my older brother, was somewhere in Vietnam. Desperate to get away from Hanford, he had lied about his age to enlist at sixteen, and military life suited him. *Is he okay?*

Echoing my thoughts, Mom said, "I hope Charles isn't near there. We never know exactly where he is."

"Career Sergeants like him end up in tough places. His letters probably give us only half the real story."

"It may be a good thing that we don't know all the details."

"I'll be glad when his tour is finished and he can be state-side for a while," I said.

"But you know Charles; he always wants to be in the thick of things."

"True enough. It's definitely not what I want to do with *my* life."

"If you took over our church, would you be safe from the Draft?" Mom asked anxiously.

"It's a possibility, but there are no guarantees. When I graduated, my student exemption expired."

"I don't think I could handle having two sons in Vietnam." Mom stared out the window, twisting her wedding ring.

"Even if I get drafted, there's always a chance I wouldn't go to 'Nam. No point worrying ahead of time, Mom." I tuned the radio dial until I found another preacher to distract her, and soon she seemed to relax.

As the highway climbed into the forested Siskiyou Mountains of southern Oregon, I reflected on my spiritual journey. From my earliest years, Mom had taken me to church with her weekly, but during my ninth summer, I committed my life to Christ at a vacation Bible school.

On a sweltering summer day three years later, I had a life-changing experience. Mom and Dad were at work, and without other kids in the neighborhood, I was bored. I finished the last of my weekly stack of library books and wandered out the back door. The screen door slammed behind me, and I could hear the distant growl of a tractor. Odors from the dairy down the road hung heavily in the air, combining with the acrid pesticide residue left by the crop-duster on the cotton field across the road earlier that morning.

I wandered aimlessly in the back acre, kicking dirt clods and throwing green peaches at a fencepost. Dad had hauled the frame of an old car to the back of our lot, planning to modify it into a trailer. The rusty hulk was a magnet for me, and I pushed and shoved at it for a while, testing my strength, before climbing into the corroded framework. Bits of the dashboard and steering wheel were all that was left of the interior, but in my imagination, I was speeding around a racetrack.

Suddenly it seemed that the rusty car and field beyond it peeled away. I saw a mental movie of myself as an adult, standing on a platform with others, teaching God's Word to a crowd of people. The picture was clearly defined, and I somehow sensed that God was speaking to me as He had to people I'd read about in the Bible. At that moment I knew I would dedicate my life to serving Him and His people.

From then on, that sense of destiny gave me a single-minded purpose that often made me feel isolated from classmates who were living carefree teenage lives. Now, as a young adult, I was looking for the key that would open the door to the future God had shown me.

How do I get there, God? Hanford is such a small place--I need to broaden my horizons. I like preaching when Rev. Black is gone, and the congregation seems to enjoy it, but I don't want to be stuck in a cow town for the rest of my life.

We passed a road sign indicating that we were nearing the town of Salem; Portland was less than fifty miles ahead.

Am I crazy, or is there a divine purpose to this trip?

Daylight was fading when Mom and I finally reached the outskirts of Oregon's largest metropolis. Rounding a long curve of the highway, we saw the city spread out before us.

"Look at the mountain!" Mom exclaimed. The centerpiece of the view was snow-covered Mt. Hood, its pristine glaciers tinted pink by the sinking sun. "And look at the river, and the bridges. What a wonderful view!"

The Willamette River lay below us, crossed by numerous bridges. Beyond the river, light industrial areas melded into residential neighborhoods, the terrain dotted with forested hills. Compared to the flat farmland around Hanford, it seemed like a paradise. *I wonder what it would be like to live here?*

We followed a map to our destination, turning off a busy street into a quiet residential neighborhood. Instead of the dusty stucco houses of Hanford, Craftsman-style homes lined the tree-shaded streets. Cedar-shingled roofs and spacious porches gave them a substantial, gracious appearance.

Across the street from the church a large traffic circle was planted with dozens of blooming rose bushes. We inhaled their heady fragrance as we got out of the car and stretched our tired legs.

"You finally made it!" said Mrs. Smith, the church caretaker, in response to our knock. "Come on in. Sandwiches are on the table. Your beds ready; I'm sure you're tired."

"We really appreciate being able to stay here," said Mom.

"That's what this place is for," said Mr. Smith, coming into the kitchen. "We always keep rooms ready for people who visit the church."

After a brief meal and conversation with the Smiths, we headed upstairs, grateful for comfortable beds after our fifteen-hour drive. Sleep came quickly, but not before I said a prayer.

Lord, if you want to talk to me, I'm here to listen.

Chapter 3

Carolyn

Birdsong from the backyard apple trees floated through the open bedroom window; the morning air was fresh and cool. I raised the roller blind and stretched the night's kinks out of my muscles. *Another sunny day, perfect for a significant encounter.*

Not wanting to put too much importance on meeting Larry, I tried to discipline my thoughts as I got ready for church. My emotions flopped between curiosity and irritation at feeling somehow manipulated.

I just don't think he's my type.

> **Current Culture**
> **July 1966**
>
> - Martin Luther King, Jr is pelted with stones during Chicago demonstration
> - "California Dreamin'" by the Mamas and the Papas is at the top of the charts
> - British band Herman's Hermits signs million-dollar movie deal with MGM
> - Jello advertised at 12 boxes for $1.00

The argument in my head continued as I applied makeup and fixed my hair. Leaving my bedroom, I was glad for the distraction of family breakfast. Gary and Jimmy were eating cereal at the kitchen table, already dressed in their Sunday best—slacks, white shirts and small clip-on ties. Their miniature sport coats, Bibles and Sunday School offerings were on the hall table ready to grab on the way out the door.

A quick cup of coffee washed down my toast before I finished dressing and headed for the full-length mirror in my sister's bedroom to make sure there wasn't a dangling thread or spot on my dress.

"Yes, you look great," added Em, giving me a hug and conspiratorial smile as we headed for the cars. I returned her hug gratefully, and our eyes locked for a moment. "I'll be praying for you today," she said, squeezing my hand briefly.

Driving their second car, I had a conversation with my Heavenly Father as I made my way across town to church.

If Larry is just another guy, why does this meeting feel so significant? There was no answer.

You know I'm not interested in just another boyfriend, especially one who lives eight hundred miles away. Still no response.

Father, you'll have to make it very obvious if your hand is in this.

The quaint stone church was tucked among stately homes on a side street. Mature trees lined the streets, shading wrap-around porches and second-story balconies. I parked beside a manicured rose garden and bent to sniff a large yellow bloom before crossing the street.

The lobby was cool when I walked through the carved wooden doors with their heavy iron hinges. Morning sun filtered through the stained glass windows, and a slight breeze from an open window stirred the smell of old hymnbooks, perspiration, and varnish from the worn pews.

Emily was already sitting at the organ bench, and I quickly took my place at the piano on the other side of the platform. Paul stood in the lobby to greet the congregation, while Gary and Jim checked between the pews for stray debris. Em and I played through a few songs before the first members arrived.

Glancing up from the keyboard, I noticed Paul talking with a young man in a dark suit. *That has to be Larry!* The crew cut from the graduation picture had grown out, but the face was unmistakable. A diminutive older woman with auburn hair stood beside him. *She must be Mrs. Wade.*

I concentrated on the music for a few minutes, and when I looked up, Larry was escorting his mother to a seat, his hand under her elbow. There was something about his touch and the angle of his head toward her that conveyed respect and affection. *Hmmm, I like that.*

As he took his seat, our eyes met briefly, and I was startled by my sudden desire for Larry to like me. Then the hands of the big clock in front of the balcony moved to eleven and Paul started the service with a prayer. For the next hour, I struggled to keep my mind on the music and the sermon. I was intensely aware of the young man seated in the middle of the sanctuary, and waited impatiently for the final "Amen."

In the lobby, I introduced myself to Larry and his mother.

"I've heard a lot about you," he said.

"I've heard a lot about you, too." We both grinned sheepishly, aware that we'd used the most cliché lines.

Mrs. Wade said, "I'm glad to finally meet you. Emily often mentions you in her letters."

"She's spoken of you as well," I replied. "She and Paul were very grateful for your friendship and faithful church attendance when they were in Hanford."

"That was a high point for our congregation. We were all sorry to see them go."

"They told me how well they ate when you butchered a calf," I smiled.

"We all ate well," Larry said with a chuckle.

I took advantage of the convenient opening. "Speaking of eating well, I'd like to invite you to a picnic tomorrow at my parents' ranch. Since it's a holiday, Paul and Emily will be coming, and other family and friends as well. We'd love to have you join us."

"That sounds nice," said Mrs. Wade. "What do you think, Larry?"

"I think it's a great idea, Mom. We've heard so much about the ranch; I'd like to see it."

"Then it's settled," I said quickly. "We'll plan to eat around noon, and you don't need to bring anything. Between my sisters and I, we'll have plenty of food. I'll have Paul give you directions."

On my drive to the ranch that afternoon, I had plenty of time to think about my brief meeting with Larry. In just a few minutes of conversation and my surreptitious observation from the piano bench, I had glimpsed sincerity and character that intrigued me. While he seemed as serious as his photographs, when we talked his gaze had been warm and engaging. He had looked at me as if he were interested in the *real* me, not just evaluating my physical appearance like most guys.

Maybe there is potential here after all!

I turned off the Mt. Hood highway and crossed the Sandy River onto Marmot Road. White-painted wagon wheels leaned against smooth river stones at the base of the log arch that held our sign: *The Ernest Cooke Ranch*. Parking beside my brother's car, I got out and stretched after my one-hour drive. As I patted Lady, Dad's collie-mutt, I heard the gurgle of the river across the road from the house. A light breeze carried the smell of sun-warmed grass and the faint whinny of one of the horses in the pasture.

My older brother Roger sauntered out the back door. "Hi, Rog," I said.

"Howdy, Sis. Nice to see you."

"I'm glad you made it over the mountain. By the way, we're having company tomorrow."

"So who's coming besides family?" he asked.

"Some people from California who were at church this morning."

"Not the folks from Hanford, by any chance?" Roger gave me a sidelong glance, one eyebrow raised.

"Yes, it's Mrs. Wade and Larry." I said nonchalantly. Roger could be a merciless tease, and I tried not to give him ammunition. Fortunately, as the years passed, his teasing had moderated from torment to affection, and we had become good friends.

"Well, this should be interesting," he said with a grin.

"I stopped at the store on the way home. Could you bring in the groceries for me?" As he reached for the paper bags, I took my overnight case through the back door.

The house was empty and quiet with Dad and Mom in California. My bedroom was stuffy, and I opened a window before changing into slacks and blouse. It was already late afternoon, and I had a lot to do to prepare for the holiday picnic.

I grabbed an apron off a hook in the hallway before unloading the bags Roger had put on the kitchen table. "Would you bring another picnic table and benches to the side yard while I start cooking?"

"Sure, Sis," he said. "How many are you expecting? Are Priscilla and Lauren coming?"

"I think so. We'll have at least a dozen—you'd better set up for fifteen to be safe." If our other sister came with her three small children, there would be nine family members coming from Portland, plus anyone they might bring, and the visitors from California.

A huge, mossy-trunked maple tree shaded the grassy strip between the driveway and the horse corral. It was a perfect location for a picnic, with a swing set to keep young visitors happy within view of their parents. Even on the hottest summer day, it was a cool and pleasant spot.

Roger arranged tables and chairs under the maple before heading through the back gate into the barnyard. While I cooked, my thoughts returned to Larry Wade. *Yes? No? Maybe...*

Eventually, I heard Roger's footsteps on the porch, and glanced at the clock--it was after 7:00 p.m.

"I saddled Spice and Pet," he said, coming through the kitchen door. "Do you want to go for a ride?"

"Oh, I'd love to! Just let me put the dressing on this potato salad. I can finish the rest when we get back."

The west woods were cool in the lowering sun as the horses walked along the narrow trail between alders, firs and hemlocks. Small birds exchanged evening news in the undergrowth of rhododendrons, salmon berry, and salal. I took the lead on my horse, Spice, since Pet was nasty-tempered and prone to kick at other horses. We rode quietly, enjoying the forest sounds. I loved the creak of saddle leather and the rhythm of the horse's gait. A covey of quail flew up ahead of us in the underbrush, and Pet jumped sideways, nearly unseating Roger. He settled her with a stern rebuke and tightened his reins.

Where the trail left the woods and entered the pasture, we startled a pair of deer. Reining in the horses, we watched as they bounded over the tall pasture grass and into the old pioneer orchard below the ridge. The gnarled, lichen-spotted trees provided perfect camouflage, and the deer were quickly out of sight.

I looked questioningly at Roger; he grinned back. "Let's go!"

We kicked our horses and galloped toward the barnyard, pulling up as we splashed through the shallow creek near the stable. We were both breathless and laughing when we slid out of our saddles.

"I'll take care of the horses, you finish your cooking." Roger was already pulling at the cinch strap of Pet's saddle, avoiding her teeth as she swung her head around.

I stood for a moment leaning against the top rail of the fence, looking back at the pasture, the woods, and the dark forested ridge rising steeply from the edge of our property.

What a gift to live in such a wonderful place.

Then another thought came. *I'll bet Hanford doesn't look like this!*

That night, I dreamed it was Sunday morning at church again. I somehow knew that one of the visitors in the lobby was Larry. I walked toward where he stood with his back to me, talking to a faceless female figure. As I approached, I heard them laugh together before walking away. I stood watching Larry's retreating back, feeling confused, bereft, and alone.

Chapter 4

Larry

When Mom and I walked into the sunlit lobby of the church on Sunday morning, my expectations were high. After my early-morning prayer time, I'd gained confidence that something good was going to happen.

Paul Mueller greeted us warmly. "I'm so glad to see you both. How was the drive from Hanford?" A small boy peered around Paul's legs, and I realized that he must be their son Jimmy, born during the Mueller's stay in Hanford.

> **Current Culture**
> **July 1966**
>
> - 16 killed and 31 wounded by a sniper at University of Texas, prompting gun control debates
> - South African government bans Beatles records
> - Frank Sinatra's new hit is "Strangers in the Night"
> - Dishwasher costs $119

"We had a good trip," Mom replied, "and we're looking forward to hearing you preach again."

"I hope I won't disappoint you." Paul laughed, turning to speak to others entering the lobby.

When we entered the sanctuary and moved down the aisle to find seats, I looked toward the platform and saw Emily Mueller playing the organ. From the photos I'd seen, I guessed that the young woman at the piano was Emily's younger sister, Carolyn. Our eyes met, and I was startled to feel a flash of connection.

Although I didn't want to be distracted from focusing on God, for the rest of the worship portion of the service my eyes were frequently drawn to the pianist. Dark blonde hair curled softly around her face, and her dark blue dress seemed to ruffle below her neck. When she left the platform as the sermon started, I glimpsed a trim, shapely figure and graceful walk. She took a seat on the front row, and with only the back of her head visible, it was much easier to concentrate on Paul's sermon.

I enjoyed his message, but by the time he gave the final prayer, I hadn't gotten the kind of confirmation or direction I had hoped for. *Was this trip in vain, Lord? Or was it just for Mom, and not for me?*

After the service, Paul introduced us to several people in the lobby, and we answered their polite questions about our visit. I waited impatiently until the girl from the piano finally walked toward us.

"You must be Mrs. Wade," she said to Mom, smiling as she extended her hand. "I'm Carolyn, Emily's sister."

"I recognized you from the pictures Emily sent," said Mom.

Carolyn turned to me with a dazzling smile. "And you're Larry." Her eyes sparkled with amusement. "I've heard a lot about you."

The blue of her eyes made me think of a deep clear pool. After only a few minutes of conversation, I had an astonishing thought: *I'm going to marry this girl!*

As the three of us chatted about ordinary subjects, my mind whirled. *Where would I get such a bizarre idea? I didn't come to Portland looking for a wife.* At the same time, I wanted to prolong the conversation, hoping to see her smile and hear the musical laughter that seemed to punctuate every other statement. I was mesmerized as I watched the interaction between my mother and Carolyn. I suddenly regained my voice when she invited us to a holiday picnic the following day. "We'd love to," I heard myself say. I hoped my voice didn't betray the eagerness I felt. *I'll take any opportunity to be around this girl!*

After getting details of the picnic, we walked outside into the early afternoon sunshine. The light seemed brighter, and the rose garden across the street was even more beautiful than I remembered. I couldn't wait for the next day, when I would learn more about the girl who had suddenly captured my mind and my heart.

That afternoon, Mom and I explored Portland. Our favorite spot was the International Rose Test Gardens in Washington Park, in the hills above the downtown core. Acres of manicured lawns and abundant rose beds basked in the summer afternoon. From this vantage point, Mt. Hood was a majestic sentinel behind the Portland skyline, framed by roses and fir trees. We were fascinated by the variety of color, shape, and size of the hundreds of fragrant blooms. But as I bent over a soft-ball-sized flower, instead of deep red velvety petals, I saw smiling blue eyes framed by blonde hair.

My mind brought up all sorts of arguments. *What if she doesn't feel the same way? And there's the little matter of living more than eight hundred miles apart.*

In spite of my mental turmoil, and in spite of the fact that I had previously persuaded myself that I should live a solitary life serving God without distraction, I had a deep and unexplainable conviction that Carolyn Cooke would one day become Carolyn Wade.

Chapter 5

Carolyn

I was already in the kitchen Monday morning when Roger strolled in for breakfast. He fixed himself eggs and toast while I prepared chicken for the oven and put the finishing touches on two pies.

> **Current Culture**
> **July 1966**
>
> - US troop levels in Vietnam exceed 250,000
> - A mob attacks the Beatles in the Philippines after they insult First Lady Imelda Marcos
> - Major hit song: "The Ballad of the Green Berets," by Sgt. Barry Sadler
> - Cost of first class postage stamp is 5 cents

The chicken was golden brown and I was putting paper plates on the picnic table when I saw Paul and Emily's car come around the curve of Marmot Road. My heart sank when I saw the third passenger in the back seat with my nephews. Hank was an older single man from church who hovered desperately around any eligible young woman. Paul and Emily kindly included him in social events; I was polite to him, but did my best to stay out of his range.

Gary and Jimmy were out of the car before Paul had turned off the key. One ran for the swings, the other for the Shetland pony Roger had saddled. Lady barked excitedly, and Gary stopped to give her a hug. "Whew," he said, "this dog has bad breath!"

"She's a farm dog, what do you expect?" said his dad.

"Keep her away from me," warned Emily, never an animal lover.

I helped take her food into the kitchen, peeking under the aluminum foil covering plates and bowls. "Yumm. This looks good. Priscilla and Lauren should be here soon," I added. "And I told the Wades we would eat at noon."

"So what did you think?" Emily asked.

"What did I think?" I said, straight-faced. "About what?"

"Oh, Carolyn--about Larry, of course."

"He seemed very nice, but you already knew that. Actually," I admitted, "he was easier to talk to than I expected."

"Well, you should have plenty of time to talk today."

"Don't get your hopes up, Em. He'll only be here for a few hours. It's not like we can start some heavy romance or something in one day."

"You never know. Stranger things have happened." With that arch comment, she headed outside to sit in a lawn chair under the maple tree.

Just before noon, two more cars pulled into the driveway and parked by the barnyard fence. My sister Priscilla and her family tumbled out of their turquoise and white Ford Fairlane; Larry and his mother got out of the other car. He looked relaxed in khaki slacks and a short-sleeved plaid shirt. Paul and Emily greeted them; Mrs. Wade embraced Emily. Larry walked over to the swing set where I was pushing Jimmy.

"Hi," I said. "Did you enjoy your tour of Portland yesterday?"

"Yes, we did," Larry replied. "Mom especially loved the rose garden at Washington Park. We can't grow roses like that in the San Joaquin Valley."

"I guess it is a little different up here, isn't it?"

"Not a little, a LOT different," he said. "Everything in Oregon is so lush and green, it's like paradise." His glance traveled from the shady yard to the picturesque barns, the pastures and the high forested ridge brushing the sky.

"I'm not sure about paradise," I said, "but I really love it here." I excused myself and joined my sisters putting food on the picnic table.

"Lunch is ready!" Emily called, and as people gathered, she introduced our guests to everyone. I sat next to Larry's mother, and he sat across from us beside Roger.

"How long have you worked in a hospital?" I asked Mrs. Wade.

"Too many years," she smiled. "I like the work, but it's exhausting, especially when I have rotating shifts."

"Mom's going back to school now." Larry's tone showed obvious pride in his mother's determination to advance her education. "Things have been tight since Dad lost his job at the Safeway creamery a few years ago. When Mom gets her LPN certificate, it will help."

"That must be a challenge," I said, turning back to Mrs. Wade. "You're working full time and going to school as well?"

"Yes, that's why it's good to get away from Hanford once in a while. I need a break from the routine. And Oregon reminds me of Illinois, where I grew up."

As the meal progressed, I learned more about the Wade family. Larry's sister JoAn lived in Pasadena with her husband and three young children. His brother Chuck was with the U.S. Army in Vietnam.

"So what are your chances of being drafted?" I asked Larry.

"About as good as anyone's, I guess, now that I'm out of college. But I have one thing in my favor," he laughed. "I have flat feet."

"I guess there's a positive side to everything," his mother smiled ruefully. Larry reached for a second helping of my potato salad, but I noticed he didn't have any chicken on his plate. I handed the platter to him, but he politely passed it on without taking any.

"He doesn't care for chicken," explained Mrs. Wade. Seeing my dismayed expression, she added, "Don't take it personally, he won't eat mine either."

As plates emptied and picnickers began to sit back with satisfied smiles, Roger asked, "Anyone want to take a trip to the top of the ridge?" He pointed to the summit of the dark green mass that rose steeply behind the pastures. "We found a way to get to the rocky ledge near the top, and the view is fantastic."

"I'll come," said Paul enthusiastically. "You've told us how beautiful the view is; I'd like to see it for myself."

"How would we get there?" Emily cautiously asked.

"I'll hitch the trailer to the back of the tractor, and you can all pile in."

"Count me out," said Em. "I'll be happy to sit here in the shade while you rough it."

Mrs. Wade added, "I think I'll stay here and catch up with Emily."

I glanced at Larry. He looked at the ridge and then at me. "I'm game," he said.

"Okay, let's do it." I smiled.

We joined half a dozen others and walked through the gate to the barnyard where Roger was hooking the trailer to the tractor. Out of the corner of my eye, I saw Hank heading my way, a grin on his face.

"Larry, would you do me a favor?" I tipped my head in Hank's direction. "Would you sit next to me in the trailer?" He glanced at Hank, then back at me.

"Of course, it would be a pleasure," he said. From the smile in his eyes, I knew he meant it.

When everyone was in the trailer, Roger drove through the barnyard and splashed across the creek. The dirt road through the pasture was rutted, and we laughed as we hung on to the sides of the bouncing trailer.

Leaving the flat pastures, the tractor put-putted up a winding gravel logging road through dense woods. In the dark shade, the air was cool and fresh. After about twenty minutes, Roger turned onto a bare track carpeted with fir and cedar needles, and shut off the tractor. The sudden silence was startling.

Roger led us down a faint path to a rocky outcropping a thousand feet above the ranch, and a spectacular view spread out in front of us. Larry joined me on some bare sun-warmed rocks near the edge of the cliff, and we sat quietly, absorbing the beauty before us, the pure sunshine, and the scent of the warm forest behind us.

The Sandy River wound along the valley floor like a tarnished silver chain. Beyond the river, row after row of wooded hills rippled south, a nearly unbroken forest extending hundreds of miles. The ranch looked like a toy farm far beneath us. We could faintly hear Lady barking as a lone hawk spiraled in the air currents below us.

"I could stay here all day." Larry quietly broke the silence. "It's so peaceful."

"I know," I replied. "It's one of my favorite places."

"The whole ranch is special. I hate to head back to dry, dusty California tomorrow."

"You should come back when you have more time." I glanced over to see his reaction. His eyes flashed a message, *"Try and stop me!"*

On the way back to the ranch, Larry sat beside me again and I learned more about him. He was the first in his family to earn a college degree. By commuting from home and working after classes, he had graduated debt-free. He loved listening to classical music; we liked the same movies and television shows. As English majors, we had read many of the same books, and our reactions to the books were very similar.

Larry told me about his church and also about some missionary friends in Mexico, where he hoped to visit them later in the summer. The way he talked about the needs of the people and his friends' lifelong commitment revealed his own passion for serving God. I felt a deep gravitational pull toward him.

This is who I've been looking for, Lord. We have so much in common and he's so easy to talk to. But he lives in California! How would that ever work out?

When we arrived at the tables under the maple tree, Emily and Mrs. Wade had set out the picnic leftovers. As we snacked, the fading sun headed toward the tops of the trees in the west woods. Our guests reluctantly started packing their cars, collecting cranky children, and saying goodbye.

Emily hugged Mrs. Wade. "It was so nice to spend time with you again, Mildred."

"If you ever come through California, you know where we live," she smiled. "Monk would love to see you again, Paul."

"Please tell him hello for us." Paul replied.

Larry walked over to where I stood near the maple tree. "Thanks for all you did to make this a wonderful day."

"I enjoyed talking with you. I'm glad we finally met," I said. I wanted to say, "Will you write to me?" but I could hear my mother's voice in my head. *Don't be forward; let him make the first move.*

He hesitated, looking at me uncertainly, before turning to open the car door for his mother. We all waved goodbye, and in a few minutes their car was out of sight around the bend in the road. I gave Priscilla a farewell hug, and Emily and I walked into the kitchen.

"I'd love to hear some details," Em said, "but we need to head home. Will you stay with us next weekend?"

"Yes, of course." I knew I'd tell her everything--what Larry said, what I said, what I felt.

When the dishes were washed and the kitchen in order, I sat down at the piano. Nothing sounded right until I pulled Beethoven's "Moonlight Sonata" off the stack of sheet music. In the fading evening light, the minor key and the moody, haunting notes seemed a perfect expression of my tumultuous emotions.

Later I sat in bed with pillows at my back and started a letter to my best friend at college.

July 4, 1966
Dear Tricia,
Guess what? I've met my man...

Chapter 6

Larry

The scenery that had captured my attention on the way to the Cooke Ranch now passed unnoticed as I drove back toward Portland. Nothing seemed to register in my mind, not the clear rushing river, the rustic log church, or the views of Mt. Hood in my rear-view mirror. All I could think of was the girl back at the ranch, and the overwhelming sense that my destiny was tied to her.

> **Current Culture**
> **July 1966**
>
> - All US airlines go on strike, grounding planes nationwide
> - Spaceflight Gemini 10 is launched, setting altitude record of 474 miles
> - *The Newlywed Game* premieres on ABC television
> - Hospital wage for a Licensed Practical Nurse: $2.00 / hr.

"Well, that was a nice day," Mom said as she settled into her seat.

"I'm glad you enjoyed it," I replied, startled out of my reverie.

"It was so good to visit with Emily again, and to meet people I've only heard about in letters. Did you have a good time?"

"Of course. Being in such a beautiful setting is always enjoyable."

"It seemed like you and Carolyn hit it off."

I felt her questioning gaze, but I kept my eyes focused on the road. "We actually have quite a bit in common," I said neutrally.

"Too bad it's so far between Portland and Hanford," Mom mused. "She seems like a girl you might enjoy spending time with."

"Maybe. But seven hundred miles is a long way."

"Who knows what might happen, Larry? God seems to find ways to overcome obstacles when He has a plan in mind."

"I guess we'll just have to wait and see, won't we?" I replied, giving her a skeptical grin. Mom leaned her head back and closed her eyes, giving me the chance to let my mind focus fully on the events of the day.

Emily and Paul's older son was the first to greet me at the ranch. "Hey Larry, look at me!" I turned toward the voice and saw Gary coming around the corner of the house on a Shetland pony. "This is Golden Boy," he said proudly. "You're too big for him, but there are other horses you could ride if you want to."

"I'm not much of a horse person," I replied, "but I'm glad you're having fun."

"Welcome to the ranch," said Paul, walking toward us with Emily at his side.

"Your timing is perfect, lunch is just about ready," Emily added.

"So this is the famous ranch we've heard so much about," I said. "You didn't exaggerate--it's a beautiful place."

"We'll give you the grand tour after lunch," said Paul. "But let's eat first."

On the way to the tables, I stopped to greet Carolyn. As she laughingly pushed a toddler on a swing, I couldn't help noticing the shapeliness of her legs in cropped pants.

At the picnic tables, Emily made introductions. I'd already met their friend Hank at church the day before, but hadn't met Paul's mother. Emily also introduced us to her sister Priscilla, brother-in-law Lauren, and their small children. A lanky young man came through the gate from the barnyard, and was introduced as Roger, the youngest of the Cooke brothers.

When everyone gathered at the table, I watched to see where Carolyn would sit. When she sat down next to my mother, I moved to a space opposite them. Paul blessed the food, and we began to fill our plates. I was dismayed to see that the main dish was fried chicken, something I'd never been able to stomach. I tried to be unobtrusive as I took potato salad and coleslaw.

At my left, Roger filled his plate as he asked me about California and talked about his work with the U.S. Forest Service. I was grateful that Carolyn took the initiative in conversing with my mother, who was not always comfortable in new settings. As they talked about Mom's work and our family, it was inevitable that mention of my brother would bring up the subject of the Vietnam War.

"Chuck has always wanted to be where the action is," I said. "I'm not as excited as he is about being in a war zone. I'd be very happy if my number didn't come up any time soon." Then, changing the subject, I said to Carolyn, "This potato salad is great. Did you make it?"

"Yes, it's my Mom's recipe," she admitted. I smiled inwardly. *She's not only pretty, she can cook!*

After enjoying a delicious concoction that Carolyn called raspberry chiffon pie, we pushed away from the table. I was definitely interested when Roger asked if anyone wanted to go to the top of the ridge behind the ranch. I looked at the steep, dark-forested mountain and then at Carolyn, who smiled and nodded. "I'm game," I said. When Carolyn asked me to sit next to her in the trailer, I jumped at the opportunity.

The route to the top of the ridge led through a flat pasture of golden stubble, then up a rocky track. "Is that an orchard?" I asked, pointing to rows of gnarled trees between the pasture and the edge of the forest.

"Yes," said Carolyn. "When we moved here the trees had been neglected for decades. A few of them still bear fruit, mostly apples and pears, and one plum. It's a favorite hangout for bears in the fall."

"Bears?" said Hank from the other side of the trailer. "Really?"

"Yes, black bears." Carolyn replied. "Roger shot one last fall in another orchard on the east end of the ranch. He had the skin made into a rug."

"That I would like to see," I said.

"He'd be glad to show it to you," Carolyn laughed. "He's very proud of it!"

At the edge of the pasture, she jumped out of the trailer to open a barbed-wire gate so that Roger could steer the tractor and trailer onto a gravel road. I admired the easy relationship I saw between brother and sister, and Carolyn's readiness to do things that other girls I knew would avoid.

"A few years ago, we wouldn't have risked driving up here," said Carolyn, settling back into the trailer beside me. "When the back of the ridge was being logged, the log truck drivers thought they owned the road. But now almost no one comes up here." We were silent for a while, enjoying the views of pastures and forest as the road wound up the side of the ridge. I suddenly realized that it was a comfortable silence, without the awkwardness I had felt with other girls.

Carolyn broke the silence. "Did you enjoy attending Fresno State?"

"Yes and no," I answered. "I was a commuter, and spent a couple hours in a car every day. It didn't leave a lot of time for fun."

"That's a shame," she said. "Living in a dorm has been a great experience for me." For the next half hour, we exchanged stories about classes, professors, part-time jobs, and our likes and dislikes. Somehow I wasn't surprised to learn that we liked the same books and classical music. Time flew by as the tractor strained and sputtered up the steep grade.

After half an hour, Roger turned off the gravel logging road and stopped the tractor on a dirt track. "Here we are, folks," he said. "Pile out, and I'll lead you to the rocks."

We followed him single-file down a spongy path through tall trees and low underbrush, surrounded by the deep quiet of wilderness. Suddenly there was a break in the trees, and we were at the edge of the cliff. We all stood silently for a few minutes, marveling at the limitless vista before us.

"How did you ever find this place?" I finally asked Roger.

"Well, I followed my nose up the logging road one day, and looked around until I found the rocks."

"That's pretty amazing." I couldn't imagine being able to pinpoint this particular spot in all the miles of forest, but Roger obviously had outdoorsman's instincts. I sat down beside Carolyn on a warm rock and took a deep breath of the still, forest-scented air.

"I love coming up here," she said quietly. "It's so peaceful."

I'd rarely seen such a vast expanse of untouched timberland. Layers of deep green hills swelled beyond the Sandy River valley beneath us, with little evidence of human habitation. The forest at our backs seemed even more mysterious.

"Since the sun is on our right, I'd guess we're facing south. What's behind us?" I asked.

"There's nothing but wilderness until you get to the Columbia River, ten miles north as the crow flies."

Carolyn pointed out ranch buildings, but there was little conversation as we sat at the edge of the hushed forest. My concerns about finding a job and my questions about the future seemed to shrink before the majesty of the view and the quiet presence of the girl beside me.

Eventually Roger said, "I guess we should head back."

Seated together in the trailer, Carolyn turned to me and said, "Tell me about your church."

"What do you want to know?" I asked.

"Well, what kind of people are there, and what is God doing in their lives."

"They're plain, down-to-earth folks," I replied. "Most of them have been in the church for years. They love God and are faithful attenders. I'd love to see God stir things up a bit and bring in more people. Years of prayer have gone into that congregation." Carolyn's sympathetic gaze prompted me to say more. "I know God has called me to the ministry. This church is a great place to get experience."

"I feel a call also," she said. "I'm not sure what it will mean, maybe missionary work. I know there's a need for teachers on the mission field." I told her about my friends in Mexico, and she talked about her family members' ministry in Ghana and Nigeria. With every shared story and insight, I felt a deeper connection with her.

When the tractor stopped in the barnyard, I helped Roger unhitch the trailer as Carolyn walked back toward the house. Roger said, "Let's stroll up to the fishpond. Do you like to fish?"

"Sorry, I'm not much of an outdoorsman. We'd have to drive a long way from Hanford to find a nice fishing hole," I replied. We walked through another gate, along the barnyard creek and up a small rise. On the opposite bank of the creek were huge tangles of wild blackberries, covered with white blossoms and tiny green fruit. As the path leveled out, we startled a pair of ducks. They rose quacking from cattails at the far edge of a large pond, and flapped away over the pasture. A stenciled sign at the water's edge read, "Rainbow Trout, 10¢ per inch."

"Do people really come here to fish?" I asked.

"Yep," said Roger, "Especially when they're headed home after a weekend fishing trip without catching anything. They know they can come here and have at least one fish to take home." A trout jumped for hovering insects, leaving glistening ripples as it fell back into the pond.

As we walked back to the house along a rippling creek, the cool water smells mingled with pungent barnyard odors. Near the house, I saw Carolyn at the picnic table, passing out snacks to her small nieces and nephews. I watched her for a few minutes. She seemed to tune in to the needs of others, anticipating desires and making them comfortable. *She'd definitely make a good minister's wife.*

She must have felt me watching her, because she glanced up and flashed me a smile as I walked through the barnyard gate toward her.

"Thanks for inviting us," I said. "It's been a wonderful day."

"I'm glad you came," she said. Our eyes locked, and I wanted to say more, to ask her if she would write to me, and to tell her that I wanted to get to know her better. But I felt awkward and self-conscious. There were too many miles, too many unknowns between us.

Mom said her farewells, and I walked to the car and opened the door for her. As I drove out of the driveway Carolyn's smile looked wistful.

Now as we neared Portland, the day seemed almost too perfect. *I can't believe how easy it was to spend time with her!* Somehow Carolyn had made me feel that I could trust her fully. She didn't display the flirty, insincere manner of the man-hungry girls I'd met in college. I hadn't felt a need to guard my words or try to impress her--I could be totally myself. *She's even more than I thought she would be. Would a girl like her want to be with someone like me? And would she want to leave a wonderful place like this for Hanford?* Doubts argued with yesterday's convictions. As the negative thoughts flooded my mind, a quiet voice overrode them.

Wait and see. Trust Me.

Chapter 7

Carolyn

"How was the Fourth of July picnic?" asked Mom, pulling clothes out of her suitcase. She and Dad had just returned from visiting my oldest brother in California. I sat on the edge of her bed, knowing she would want to hear everything that had happened during their absence.

> **Current Culture**
> **July 1966**
>
> - National Guard troops are deployed for riots in Chicago and told, "Shoot to kill"
> - Eric Clapton records guitar tracks for George Harrison's song, "While My Guitar"
> - Major daily newspaper sells for 10 cents

"It was good. The usual family members came, and we had some visitors."

"From church?" She wanted more details.

"Out of town, actually. Some people from California came for the weekend."

"Not the Wades, by any chance?" Mom's eyebrows went up. She knew that the Wade family had been favorites in Paul and Emily's Hanford congregation.

"Yes, it was Mrs. Wade and Larry."

"Didn't Mr. Wade come?"

"Apparently he doesn't like to travel, and they came mainly to attend a church service. He's not particularly interested in that."

Mom paused to tighten a hairpin in the gray coil at the nape of her neck. Her pale blue eyes looked tired, and the wrinkles in her 63-year-old face seemed more pronounced. "So what was Mrs. Wade like?" she asked.

"She's shy but very pleasant. She said she enjoyed hearing Paul preach again and being here at the ranch."

"What about Larry? Did he live up to Emily's glowing reports?"

"He was nice enough. He seems very dedicated to the church in Hanford."

Mom looked at me speculatively, as if trying to decide how far to push the conversation. "And...?" she asked. I shrugged nonchalantly. As I weighed the risks of telling her what I really thought about him, she said, "I hope you didn't throw yourself at him."

"Mom!" I glared at her, shaking my head, her negative assumptions renewing tension between us. I swallowed and took a deep breath. "I have too much self-respect to throw myself at anyone, much less someone like Larry Wade." Tears obstructed my voice.

"I'm sorry, Carolyn. I shouldn't have said that." Mom tried to give me a hug, but I shrugged away.

"You haven't really made any effort to know who I am after living at college for two years," I said, my voice shaking.

"You don't come home often enough for me to know you," she countered. Several retorts floated through my mind, but I had no taste for battle. Mom continued with a warning tone. "You may be growing up, but I'm still your mother. Be careful how you speak to me."

I took the path of least resistance. "Yes, Mom." Blinking back my tears, I walked to my bedroom and fell across the chenille bedspread. *There's no way I'll tell her how I really feel about Larry!*

Later Mom knocked on the door to tell me lunch was ready. "I'm not hungry, Mom," I said. "I have a headache."

"You need to eat, Carolyn." I didn't reply, and after a pause, I heard her walk away.

By mid-afternoon, I was calm enough to venture to the kitchen and put a piece of bread in the toaster. Mom was at her desk, occupied with ranch business. I heard tires on gravel and glanced out the window. The mailman's car was at the letterbox beside our driveway. "Mail's here," I said, heading out the door. I was disappointed that there was nothing for me in the box. Larry hadn't said he would write to me, but I could always hope.

"You were in a hurry to get the mail," Mom said as I came into the kitchen. "Expecting something?" I couldn't tell if she was teasing or irritated.

"You never know, I might win the sweepstakes someday." I hoped my joke would mask my disappointment.

Even with the activity of Dad and Mom's return and my routine at work, Larry was often on my mind. I kept replaying parts of our conversation, especially what we had shared about our dreams and hopes for the future. The similarity of our ideas and goals amazed me.

Walking emptyhanded to my bedroom, I tried to visualize his face. Even after more than a week, I was still stirred by the memory of the intent gaze in his deep brown eyes.

What I felt wasn't like crushes in the past, with the giddy, superficial emotional high. Instead, I had a peaceful certainty that my life was linked with Larry Wade. The prospect both thrilled and frightened me. *I don't really know him...*

There was tension in the office when I got to work a few mornings later. Through the college, I'd landed a great summer job teaching reading to itinerant farm workers through Valley Migrant League, part of President Lyndon Johnson's "War on Poverty." Oregon's Willamette Valley was a popular destination for families who drove up from Mexico for summer work picking berries, beans, hops, and other commercial agricultural crops.

"What's going on?" I asked John, my co-worker.

"Scotty just found out we have visitors coming. We'll have to look busy."

I put my purse in the drawer of my desk, next to John's in the common room of the converted church building. Mr. Scott, our diffident middle-aged director, came out of his office.

"Good morning, Carolyn," he said. "Some VISTA workers are arriving this morning. They want to tour some of the camps, and look over our program. Would you make sure there's plenty of coffee ready?" He looked around nervously, and then headed back into his office.

"Volunteers in Service to America," or VISTA, was the domestic version of the Peace Corps, federally funded like our agency. Mr. Scott's anxiousness showed his apprehension about any scrutiny of our work.

When the boss's door closed, John chuckled. "Well, this should stir things up a bit! We won't be so bored this week." He rubbed his hands together expectantly, emphasizing the stork-like appearance of his thin, six-foot-five body. His grin stretched the freckles on his cheeks, and his eyes twinkled behind the tortoise-shell glasses. I could imagine the wheels turning in his bright mind. While not close friends, we shared many classes at our small college, and I enjoyed his quick wit. "We can always ask the VISTA workers to give us some new ideas for wasting time at government expense."

I said, "It's not our fault that the farm workers are too tired at the end of the day to come to the center. Someone really didn't think things through when they planned this program. At least Maria comes when she can." My star pupil was the one bright spot in an otherwise frustrating job.

Our conversation was interrupted as the front door opened and three women filed in. "We're from VISTA," said the oldest of the trio. "We're supposed to meet Mr. Scott."

John's reply was drowned out by the roar of a motorcycle. A young man strutted through the door and joined the women. "Quite the small town you have here," he said.

"Where else did you expect to find migrant field workers?" John bristled.

As Mr. Scott joined us, Katherine, petite and gray-haired, introduced herself, then Mary, in tie-dye, and Barbara, in a linen blouse and preppy pleated skirt. "And that's Buzz." Katherine nodded affectionately at the motorcycle rider, who was already helping himself to coffee.

Mr. Scott introduced himself and gave a little speech about our center. Our guests shifted restlessly. "I'm anxious to see an actual migrant camp," said Katherine. "So far we've only seen urban projects."

Buzz cut through the polite interchange to get to the facts. "How many students do you have?"

"It varies, of course," replied Mr. Scott. "People come and go with the crops, and only a small number stay through whole the summer."

"So how many students do you have right now?" Buzz persisted.

"Fewer than twenty," Mr. Scott admitted reluctantly.

"For three of you?" Buzz was incredulous. "What do you do with the rest of your time?"

"We do a lot of recruiting in the camps," John interjected. "Maybe you'd like to help us. You seem to have a lot of energy." Buzz ignored John's barb.

Mr. Scott cleared his throat. "The van is ready, we can give you a tour. Carolyn, would you lock up?"

When I got to the van, Katherine had taken the front passenger seat next to Mr. Scott. John was between Mary and Barbara in the back seat, which left the space beside Buzz empty.

"So what's a pretty girl like you doing stuck out in the middle of nowhere?" Buzz leered at me.

I stared back at him, saying "I happen to like living in the middle of nowhere. We're close enough to the city, but have the benefits of fresh air and beautiful scenery. What about you? Where's home?"

"New Jersey. Do you know where that is?" I ignored his implied insult, and turned to talk with the girls in the back seat.

"We'll start at Modern Farms, one of the largest employers in the area. It's typical of camps around here." Owners of large farms typically provided temporary housing for workers. Much of it was sub-standard, violating health and safety codes, and often the topic of critical news articles.

"What crops are they picking now?" asked Barbara.

"Cane berries are just coming into season," I said.

"Cane berries? I don't think I've ever had those," said Mary.

"It's a term used to describe fruit like raspberries and boysenberries," explained John patiently. "The long thorny stems are called canes."

Mr. Scott pulled off the pavement onto a pot-holed dirt road and we braced ourselves for the bumps. Our visitors were silent when the van stopped at the camp. Getting out, Barbara wrinkled her nose.

"Sorry, we're down-wind from the latrines," I said. "It takes a little getting used to."

"I didn't expect to find *this* in such a beautiful setting," Barbara said. "It's worse than what I've seen in the news."

Glancing around, I tried to see the squalid surroundings through her eyes. Unpainted one-room cabins clustered around a central area of packed dirt, with a single water faucet in the center. Broken windows were patched with cardboard; empty cans and other garbage cluttered doorways. Behind it all, in stark contrast, was a view of pristine Mt. Hood.

John stepped over an oily puddle by the faucet and greeted a couple of small children peeking around a doorway. "Hi, kids. Is your mom around?" His question was met with silence, but fingers pointed toward the berry field. "Okay, I guess we'll have to wait." It would soon be lunch-time, and we hoped to invite some of the residents to our reading classes.

A couple of battered cars pulled up to the cabins, and tired workers stumbled out for a short mid-day break. In spite of the July heat, they wore long-sleeved shirts to protect their arms from the sun and sharp berry thorns. With no time to cook, their lunch consisted of cold beans in a tortilla or peanut butter on white bread, washed down with tepid water from the communal tap.

"Hola," said Mr. Scott. The only response was a few grunts and tired glances. A newer pickup truck pulled up in a cloud of dust.

"Saw your van. Whaddaya want?" We had met the camp foreman on earlier visits; he obviously resented our presence.

"We're just giving some visitors a tour. I have the owner's permission," said Mr. Scott defensively.

The foreman eyed the well-dressed visitors. "Just what we need, more bleedin' hearts around here," he growled. "Don't keep my crew from gettin' back to the field on time." The VISTA quartet shrank together to avoid his obvious antagonism.

"We won't stay long," John assured him.

Back in the van, we headed down the road to the next camp. "What are their working hours?" Katherine asked me.

"Generally sunrise to six o'clock, with a break during the hottest part of the day," I said.

"And what are your hours?" asked Buzz.

"We're open from nine to five, and Thursday until eight," replied John.

"So how does that work?" Barbara turned from the window.

"Not very well," admitted Mr. Scott. "Most of them are too tired to come in the evening, and they're in the fields when we're open."

"No wonder you don't have many students," said Katherine.

Mr. Scott shrugged resignedly as he paused before turning onto a dirt road marked by a hand-lettered sign. "This is a smaller camp," he said. "Usually it's the late-comers who end up here."

Our visitors stared silently at the assortment of broken-down travel trailers that provided seasonal shelter, and didn't move to get out of the van. "I think I get the picture," said Buzz. "I've seen enough."

Back at our office, Mr. Scott said, "John and Carolyn, why don't you show our guests our curriculum materials. I have some phone calls to make."

We pulled an assortment of adult literacy booklets from our shelves and passed them around. After glancing through them, Katherine shook her head in dismay. "Did these come straight from Washington bureaucrats? How do migrant workers relate to these?"

"They don't," I said. "That's why we started creating our own materials." I opened a drawer and pulled out some worksheets and flashcards. "I made these specifically for Maria, using things familiar to her."

"Has that made a difference?" Barbara riffled through the cards with simple words and drawings on them.

"Yes, she is making good progress since I've been using these. You should have seen her face when she read her daughter's name for the first time!"

"That must have been rewarding." Mary had been silently observing most of the day.

"What projects has your team worked on?" John asked our visitors. For the rest of the afternoon, we shared plans, ideas, and stories of successes and failures, all reflecting our common desire to help people in need.

It was nearly five when Buzz said, "Is there any good food around here? Let's all go out for dinner."

"There's a decent Chinese place at the other end of town," said John, getting nods and smiles.

"I'll have to pass," said Mr. Scott. "I have prior plans." He turned to John and me. "But I think it would be nice if you hosted our guests." We exchanged resigned looks and I mentally adjusted my evening plans. John gave the others directions to the restaurant, and as they left, I called Mom.

"I won't be home for dinner tonight," I said when she answered. "John and I are going to get Chinese food with some out-of-town visitors to the office."

"Do you have enough money? Is your boss going to be there?" Mom didn't sound happy. "I don't like you driving home after dark."

"I'll be fine, Mom," I replied. "It won't be dark until late, and I do know the way."

"There's no need for sarcasm, young lady," Mom scolded.

"Sorry, Mom," I said. "I'll see you later tonight."

At the Imperial Palace, Buzz moved to the seat next to me. I saw a knowing glance pass between Mary and Barbara. Through the afternoon, I'd gotten the impression that Buzz had previously worked his charm on the two girls, and his attention to me was standard procedure with a new female.

"So, how about coming to our motel after dinner? I've got some drinks on ice."

"Like Coke?" I asked. He stared at me, apparently trying to figure out if I was teasing or just dumb.

"Actually, something a little stronger," he said.

"Sorry, I'm under age," I said, smiling sweetly, "and besides, my parents are expecting me home by nine."

"You're kidding, right?" His uncertainty made me want to laugh.

"No, actually, I'm really not interested." My direct stare and tone of voice must have convinced him, because he turned his back on me, and started a conversation with Katherine. Across the table, John winked at me.

I couldn't help comparing Buzz's aggressive come-on with the respectful and considerate way Larry had treated me. Larry won, hands down. I appreciated being treated like a lady, not a potential conquest. There was a small envelope on the kitchen table when I got home that evening. The Hanford postmark made my heart skip a beat. *Great timing, Lord.*

"Did you see your mail?" Mom came out of the bedroom.

"Yes, thanks."

"How was your evening?" she persisted.

"It was okay, but I'm tired. I think I'll head for bed."

"Have fun reading your mail."

I closed the bedroom door and ripped open the envelope.

July 23, 1966

Dear Carolyn,

Thank you for your hospitality at the ranch on July 4th. I really enjoyed being there and getting to know you a little.

I hope your work is going well. I may be going to Mexico soon to spend time with the missionaries I told you about. It should be an interesting time.

Thank you again for the wonderful picnic and afternoon at the ranch.

Sincerely yours,

Larry Wade

I read the note twice, and turned it over to see if I'd missed something. *That's all? No mention of more letters or a return to Portland?*

At midnight I was still awake, staring into the darkness, confused and disappointed. *I thought I saw some signals. Did I just imagine a connection between us?*

Chapter 8

Larry

"Well, what do you think, Mom?" I wiped the sweat off my forehead with my sleeve, hoping I hadn't smeared paint on my face or glasses.

My mother stood in the doorway in her hospital whites, ready for swing shift. "It looks wonderful, Larry. I can't believe the difference!"

Painting was my least favorite chore, but I'd spent most of two days working on our screened-in back porch. It was a catch-all space, with cupboards for lawn furniture, a croquet set, Mom's canning, and a cot for Dad's afternoon naps. Mom thought a coat of paint and some comfortable furniture would make it an inviting space to relax and enjoy morning or evening breezes. She also hoped to persuade Dad to smoke there instead of in the living room.

> **Current Culture**
> **July 1966**
>
> - The nation is horrified by the brutal murder of eight student nurses by drifter Richard Speck in Chicago.
> - Beatles release "Yesterday & Today" which stays #1 for five weeks
> - One gallon of gas costs 30 cents

Mom's choice of a deep rusty red wasn't my favorite, but I had to admit that it looked a hundred times better than the bare wood. While I painstakingly painted a window frame, my thoughts returned to Oregon. *Does Carolyn ever think about me? Did she feel the same connection that I felt that day we spent together?*

Other than my trip to Portland, this seemed like a wasted summer. I had needed a break after four years of commuting to college, working part-time and being involved with the church. But with little to do, I felt bored and restless. I'd been looking for a full-time job, but had yet to be called for an interview.

After I put away the drop cloths and cleaned the brushes, I changed my clothes and poured a glass of cool water. I picked up two books from my nightstand, an enjoyable and engrossing political novel, *Advise and Consent*, and my Thompson Chain Reference Bible. I'd been asked to preach at church again on Sunday, and somewhat reluctantly put the novel aside. As I opened the Bible, Carolyn's image floated over the page. *Is she teaching today? I wonder if she's at the office, or at one of the camps to recruit students.*

We'd been together for only a few hours, yet in my mind our future together was an established fact. I was normally very rational and self-disciplined, so these thoughts were out of character. My heart had been totally captured by her blue eyes and welcoming smile. Her direct gaze, easy manner of communicating, and obvious heart for God had shattered my previous ideas of living a solitary life. She haunted my waking moments and visited my dreams.

My musing was interrupted by the ringing telephone; it was my friend Jesse. In spite of attending school and church together for years, we had little in common. He was an indulged only child, and seemed to be more interested in pleasure than serving God. While our friendship was more habit than depth of relationship, I felt a responsibility to him as a brother in Christ.

"So what time do you want to leave on Monday morning?"

"How about seven? I'd rather drive when it's cool." Robert and Martha Graham, missionary friends in Mexico, had invited the two of us to join them for a couple of weeks, and I was grateful for the diversion the trip would provide.

"That's a little early for me. How about I pick you up at 8:30?" Jesse had a newer car than my '58 Chevy, and there was no question which we'd use for the trip.

"Make it eight?"

"Okay, I guess so. You doing anything this afternoon?"

"Just studying."

"I'm bored. Let's shoot some pool. Meet you in town in an hour?" I still had a few more days to prepare before Sunday's sermon, and it would be good to get out of the house.

"Okay, see you soon."

In the early afternoon a few days later, we stopped to visit a pastor friend of Jesse's in Palm Desert. Later we passed the Salton Sea before crossing into Mexico. We reached the Graham's home in Mexicali at dinnertime, and spent a pleasant evening together. I was intrigued and impressed by the dedication to ministry that had brought them from Alaska to Mexico in their sixties, a time when most people were looking for an easier life.

The next morning, the four of us left their house after a simple breakfast. Turning off the highway, Mr. Graham followed a two-lane paved road for more than an hour before turning off on a barely visible dirt road. This desolate part of the Mexican state of Sonora gave me a whole new understanding of desert. Conversation was difficult as we braced for potholes in the rattling vehicle, but at various crossroads, Mrs. Graham pointed towards villages we might visit another day.

Near the mountains, a small settlement slowly became visible. There was no store or cantina, just small adobe houses clustered around a well. Robert stopped in front of one of the houses, and as the dust settled, we were surrounded by smiling faces.

"Hola, señores y señora, ¡bienvenida!" Toddlers peered shyly around skirts, and people came from neighboring houses to welcome us. Older children ran to the more distant homes and fields calling, "Señor y Señora Graham están aqui." I tried my halting Spanish on a cluster of kids gathered excitedly around the car, and was answered with giggles.

We were ushered into the dim and surprisingly cool interior of the house. Our hostess shooed out several chickens, while neighbors brought hand-hewn chairs for us. A girl offered us water, poured from a clay pitcher into random containers. I accepted gratefully, refusing to worry about its purity.

As the Grahams asked about village events since their last visit, I tried to keep up with the conversation. More people joined us until the small room was packed. Everyone seemed glad to see us, and I was struck by the happiness that seemed to radiate from these isolated people.

When the room was full, Mrs. Graham opened her Bible. "God loves us all so much," she began. "But He is holy, and our sin keeps us separated from Him."

She continued to speak a simple but enthusiastic message about God's love and what it meant to follow Jesus, God's only Son. The people gave her their total attention and there were many rapt expressions. Some nodded as though they were familiar with the message, others looked more uncertain. After she had spoken for about ten minutes, Mr. Graham ended by encouraging them to become followers of Christ, to receive forgiveness and freedom from the burden of sin. As they bowed their heads for a prayer, several wiped tears from their cheeks.

During the shared meal of beans and tortillas, there was eager conversation about Jesus. Their earnest questions were answered by verses pointed out in a Spanish Bible. Mr. Graham wanted them to know that God's Word was the basis of the good news they had shared.

On our way back towards the main road, I reflected on this first encounter. These people had so little—barely enough to sustain life—yet they seemed happy, cheerful, and uncomplaining. Not once had anyone asked us for anything; instead they had joyfully offered hospitality from their meager provisions. They seemed thrilled that we had taken the time to visit them.

Each day for two weeks we visited villages, traveling hours over dirt tracks. Invariably we were received with warm smiles and cheerful hospitality. For these people, the simple message brought by the Grahams was truly good news, received with joy and thankfulness. I couldn't help contrast that response with the apathetic reaction common in my over-religious hometown. I was deeply stirred to see first-hand that in its simplest form, to those who hadn't heard, the message of Jesus' love was life-changing.

Just after I finished my Sunday sermon several weeks later, several of the most faithful members approached me. "Larry, we think you should take over as our pastor. We know you, we like your preaching, and you've already been taking good care of us. Please say yes so we can make it official."

I was startled, but somehow not surprised. "Are you sure that's what you want?"

"Yes, we've prayed and discussed it for a couple of weeks, and believe it's the right thing."

"If you're certain, I'd be honored."

"Why don't you call Rev. Black tomorrow and let him know that we talked to you. He can call any of us to confirm our decision."

"Okay, I'll do that. Thank you for your support; I'll do my best to be a good pastor for you."

As I drove home, I looked forward to telling Mom when she came home from work. In her quiet way, she had been encouraging me toward this outcome. Turning onto our street, I was struck by a sudden thought. *Ministers can get a deferment from active military duty.* Could this be God's way of keeping me out of Vietnam? Then I considered something else. *What would Carolyn think of this development?* I had a sudden compulsion to tell her, and as soon as I got home, I found my stationery and wrote her a short note.

August 8, 1966
Dear Carolyn,

Could you write and let me know what type of weather to expect in Portland? I may come to the conference at the end of the month, and would like to know whether to bring a swimsuit or parka.

Please tell Paul and Emily that I am about to have my turn at Grace Chapel, as I have been asked to be the pastor. That really ends any ideas I had of moving to Portland.

I hope to see you on the 28th.
Sincerely,
Larry

I put the pen down and stared at the wall for a while before sealing the envelope.

Please, Lord, I'd really like a chance to get to know her better.

Chapter 9

Carolyn

I was playing the piano the first night of the conference when I saw Larry walk into the sanctuary with Jesse Black. I couldn't help comparing the two: Larry was dressed neatly in suit and tie, with a look of anticipation on his face; Jesse was also in suit and tie, but slightly disheveled and looking as if he really wanted to be somewhere else. There was no question which of them drew my attention.

Several weeks earlier, I'd gotten a second note from Larry, saying that he had been asked to be the pastor of the church in Hanford, and mentioning that he might come

> **Current Culture**
> **August 1966**
>
> - A firecracker causes chaos at a Beatles performance in Memphis
> - Blockbuster novel *The Source* by James Michener tops best-seller lists
> - Movie *Who's Afraid of Virginia Woolf* continues as box office hit
> - US Treasury stops printing of $2 bills

to a conference scheduled at the Portland church at the end of August. My dreams were rekindled when I read the line, "I hope to see you…"

Fortunately, my job had ended, so I was free for the whole week. In spite of my bias against long-distance romance, I had frequently found myself daydreaming about the earnest young minister with the dark brown eyes.

From the piano bench, I could unobtrusively observe the congregation, including Larry. His strong baritone rose above the other voices, and his obvious enjoyment of singing was very appealing.

Is he aware of me? He barely glanced my way when he came in. Has he met someone else since he was here?

I had to consciously pull my thoughts back to my hands on the keyboard. I didn't want to attract his attention with a sour note. He played piano also, and would hear mistakes. I was relieved when I could take my place on the front row and listen to the sermon undistracted.

During the closing prayer, I left the auditorium to prepare refreshments in the fellowship hall. The pies and cakes were sliced and coffee brewed when I heard the clatter of footsteps on the stairs, and people started filling up the seats at the long tables. The mint green walls and bare basement windows of the fellowship hall reverberated with lively conversation, drowning out the noise of metal folding chairs on painted concrete. Out of town visitors were excitedly renewing friendships and talking about what they were hearing from the Lord at the conference.

I stayed busy at the refreshment table until someone vacated a chair across from Larry. As I sat down, he looked startled, then pleased. I hoped the person next to me couldn't hear my heart pounding.

"Welcome back to Portland. How was your trip?" I hoped my smile covered my nervousness.

"It was good. The drive seemed shorter than our trip in July."

"I'm glad you were able to make it to the conference."

"Are you?" His intent look caused a blush to rise in my cheeks.

"Yes, I've looked forward to seeing you again." I returned his gaze and our eyes locked. Again I felt the current between us, and my heart soared.

I haven't imagined it all, there is something between us!

"So what have you been doing since July?" His question quickly pulled me back to earth.

"Mostly work and babysitting for my sisters. How's your job hunt going?"

"Things are finally looking hopeful. I had an interview earlier this week." Our conversation was interrupted when someone came to tell me that the coffee pot was empty. As I stood to go back to the kitchen, disappointment flashed across Larry's face.

"I hope you enjoy the conference," I said. "Maybe we can talk more tomorrow."

"I'd like that."

Somehow in that brief encounter, the warmth in his eyes had rekindled my hope for a future together. I scooped coffee grounds from the red can of Folgers with new enthusiasm. *It's going to be a great week!*

"Do you have plans for this afternoon?" Larry suddenly appeared beside me while I washed dishes after lunch on Monday.

"Not really. I need to finish up here, then there's a break in the schedule until this evening."

"If I help you finish, could we take a walk? You might want to stretch your legs, and I'd like to see more of the neighborhood."

"That would be great. The dish towels are on the rack over there." We quickly dried and stacked the dishes, and I smiled at him as I took off my apron. "Let's go!" Larry opened the door to the outside stairway, waiting for me to go through first. His good manners made me like him even more.

As we walked slowly along the shady sidewalk, I felt suddenly awkward. After all my daydreams, being alone with him was both intimidating and exciting.

"So you're a pastor now," I said. "How does that feel?"

"I'm enjoying it. I'm doing the same things as before, but now that I have the official title, it feels a little different. More weighty, somehow…"

"I'm sure you're doing a good job. What do you enjoy most about it?"

Larry considered for a few moments. "Probably studying for sermons, finding nuggets of truth, and then seeing the responses on people's faces when something registers. That's very rewarding."

"Will this make a difference in your draft classification?"

"I hope so! I'm applying for a ministerial deferment."

"What about the job interview you mentioned?"

"It's for a position as a social welfare worker for Kings County. Apparently they don't care that my degree isn't in social work."

"That might work well with your pastoral duties." I paused before asking a more personal question. "Do you think you'll stay in Hanford for a while?" As we crossed a busy street, he put a protective hand on my elbow.

"The church and job would probably keep me there, but I'd rather move here." He turned and looked at me with a frank smile, making my pulse jump. "This city is more attractive to me than ever, since I've met you." I sensed this wasn't just a come-on, and I wasn't sure how to respond. I decided to be neutral.

"Portland has a lot to offer. I think you'd enjoy living here. There are good libraries, a symphony orchestra, theater, museums. We even have lots of parks, like this one." I gestured toward an inviting space across the street where large firs shaded manicured grass, benches, picnic tables and play equipment.

"I was thinking something a little more personal," he said with another meaningful glance. "Let's stop for a while. That bench looks inviting."

We sat silently for a few minutes, hearing children's laughter from the other side of the park. "Does Hanford have parks like this?" I finally asked.

"Not exactly. There are a couple, but they aren't shaded by fir trees, that's for sure."

"What was it like growing up there?"

"I was a latch-key kid from kindergarten on," he chuckled ruefully. "It wasn't exactly an ideal childhood." As Larry revealed more of his life, my respect for him increased. I was impressed that he hadn't allowed isolation, loneliness or lack of affection grow into bitterness or cynicism. After a pause in our conversation, he looked at me intently.

"So what are your plans for the future, Carolyn?"

"Well, my first priority is finishing my degree. I'd like to teach a couple of years, then look for a job overseas. Ultimately, missionary work."

"Do you see marriage in your future?" *Wow, that was fast. He doesn't beat around the bush!*

"Yes, probably. I'd like to share my life with someone, and I love children. I hope it could all work together." I paused, then returned his question. "What about you? Do you want a family?"

He looked thoughtful. "Well, for years I've believed I would stay single. But that seems to be changing."

"And why is that?" I held my breath, waiting for the answer.

"I think I may have found someone who could share the life I'm called to." My heart seemed to expand as he continued. "But there are some pretty big obstacles. God would have to do some miracles to make it all work out."

Our eyes held for a few moments--his gaze was both inquiring and challenging. I needed more time to consider the implications of our conversation. I asked, "So do you see yourself as a local pastor, or on the mission field?"

"I'd enjoy short mission trips, but I don't see myself living overseas. Especially someplace like Africa. The stories in Paul and Emily's letters from Nigeria don't exactly make me yearn to live in the jungle," he chuckled.

"I could see myself living overseas," I countered. "But the most important thing for me is to be in God's will, wherever that leads." I wanted to make it clear that I had my own calling, goals and dreams, and wasn't just waiting to tag along with someone else's life.

He probed further. "If you got married, would you pursue your own goals, or your husband's?"

"I have a pretty traditional view of marriage. But I believe whoever God has for me will fit in with God's direction for my life. I wouldn't marry someone who wasn't willing to listen to God's voice and respect my goals and calling."

"I can't imagine any man not respecting you in every way." A smile defused his intensity, but there was a pulsing current between us. Beneath our words, I knew that far deeper things were being communicated.

My heart was opening to him and it was all I could do to keep from reaching for his hand. But my ingrained sense of propriety held me back. We seemed to be dancing close to something momentous, but I suddenly needed to retreat to safety.

I glanced at my watch. "It's nearly time for music practice. Let's head back to the church."

After a challenging sermon that evening, we stood together on the steps of the church in the cool night air. The rest of the congregation gradually left, the sound of their car doors disturbing the quiet of the neighborhood. The blooms in the rose garden across the street were luminous in the moonlight.

"Carolyn, would you ever consider moving to California?" Larry asked.

"Well, I'm not sure... I like San Francisco better than Los Angeles, but I'm not sure I'd like living in either place," I said teasingly.

He grinned at my sidestep. "That's not quite what I had in mind. I'd really like to get to know you better. Would you consider moving to Hanford or even Fresno, so we could spend more time together?"

"I don't think there's much chance of that for a couple of years," I said regretfully. "It wouldn't make sense financially. I have scholarships and grants for school here, and a great job. If I moved to California I'd lose all of that." My reasons came from my practical side, but my emotional side wanted to say "Yes!" I gave him the challenge. "Why don't you move to Portland?" I wanted him to know I was interested in getting to know him better, but I also needed to know whether he was willing to pursue me.

"Believe me, it's very appealing. But there's the little matter of Grace Chapel. I can't leave when I've just been installed as pastor." He shook his head. "I guess we're facing something of a dilemma."

Again I needed safe ground. "Well, let's make the most of this week. Maybe we can take another walk tomorrow afternoon."

"I'd like that," he said eagerly.

After a pause, I said. "I should probably go home."

"Yes, I guess so." He walked me to my car, appearing to share my reluctance to part. "I hope you sleep well. Goodnight, Carolyn."

"See you in the morning."

Turning onto Hawthorne Boulevard, I asked God some crucial questions.

Why are there so many obstacles, when I've found someone I could really fall in love with? We live eight hundred miles apart, and have important obligations that we can't just drop. We both want to serve you, Lord, but are our paths really compatible?

As I drove across the Hawthorne Bridge, I was oblivious to the beauty of the moon and city lights reflected in the Willamette River. I drove up Jefferson Street and Canyon Road barely aware of other cars. *What do I really know of Larry? I know a few things about him from Paul and Emily, but how much did they really know him? Is he a man I can trust with my life, to be a faithful husband and a loving father? He seems so serious and straight-laced. Do I want more fun in life? God, please, please, give me wisdom. I don't want my emotions to carry me outside your will.*

In a confused dream that night, Larry was looking at me with tender longing in his eyes. Then others crowded around, pushing us apart. Mom suddenly appeared and said, "You can't marry him, he's from California."

"I'm not going to *marry* him, Mom," I said in exasperation, "I just want to kiss him." Her shocked and disapproving look was imprinted on my mind as I woke up Wednesday morning feeling tired and agitated. I needed to talk to someone.

Later that morning I was surprised to see my parents walk into the sanctuary during the first song. They hadn't expressed an interest in the conference, but I knew they enjoyed listening to a variety of preachers. I'd mentioned that Larry was planning to be there. *Are they here to check him out?*

When the service was dismissed for mid-morning coffee break, I pulled aside my brother-in-law. "Could we talk for a few minutes?" Paul often had a perspective and wisdom that I needed.

"Sure, Carolyn." We waited until everyone had gone to the fellowship hall, and then sat on a pew in the empty sanctuary.

"Is something bothering you?" Paul's kind tone brought sudden tears to my eyes.

"I'm feeling so uncertain about the future. My direction seemed very clear, but now I'm not sure."

"Does this have anything to do with Larry?"

"Yes," I sighed. "I guess that's no big surprise."

"Are you falling in love with him?"

"I'm not sure...I think so. But what I feel for him is so different from other relationships. It's more like some irresistible force pushing us together.

It's like I don't have a choice, and that makes me uncomfortable. Don't get me wrong, I like him, a lot. But it's scary at the same time."

"Do you know how he feels?"

"I'm pretty sure he's drawn to me."

"From what I see, that's obvious." Paul chuckled

After a moment, I plunged ahead to the real issue. "But I'm not sure if our life goals are compatible. I believe God is calling me to the mission field. Larry says that's a possibility for him, but not a strong motivation. How would that work out? Following God's will is more important to me than any relationship, no matter how attractive it seems. I'm terrified of getting into a relationship that will take me away from God's purpose for my life." My tears were flowing freely.

"I don't know about all that, Carolyn. But I do know that fear isn't from God. Is it possible that Satan is trying to bring confusion, to keep you from something good that God has planned for you? If you feel it's God who is bringing you and Larry together, and you are both seeking God's will, then I believe all the details will fall into place."

I took a deep breath as I let his words soak in, then found a handkerchief in my purse and blotted my cheeks. It was a relief to share my fears and concerns, and Paul's words were reassuring. He continued when I was more composed.

"Why don't you enjoy the time you have with Larry this week, and not worry too much about the future. That's in God's hands, and you know He is working for your good."

"Yes, I know that. Thanks, Paul. I really appreciate your listening ear."

"You're welcome. You know that Em and I are praying for you. It's all going to work out."

Footsteps and voices on the stairs signaled the congregation's return. Paul stepped away to speak to Rev. Black, while I headed for the restroom to repair my makeup. I was determined to keep my emotions under control and my friendship with Larry on a safe and sensible footing.

When I entered the dining area for lunch, I saw Mom and Dad sitting across from Larry. I walked over to their table.

"Hi, Dad and Mom," I greeted them. "I was surprised to see you come in this morning. I see you've met Larry."

"Yes," said Mom. "We've been having a nice conversation."

"Don't let me interrupt; I need to get some lunch unless the food is already gone." As I walked away, I sent a mental message to my parents: *"Please like him!"*

Later, as the dining room emptied, Larry found me in the kitchen. "Can we take another walk?" he asked.

"Sure. I won't be much longer; I'll meet you in front of the church."

Thelma, a middle-aged woman working with me, gave me a knowing smile. "Need to spend more time with your beau, do you?" I blushed, wishing my relationship with Larry wasn't quite so public.

"Go on, I'll finish up here," she added. "I always like to see young people falling in love."

If it's that obvious to everyone else, why am I so uncertain?

Larry was sitting on the front steps of the church in the sunshine. "Let's walk a different direction today." I glanced quickly at him—he seemed more confident, and there was a different tone in his voice. As we stepped onto the sidewalk, he moved to the outside. "I was taught that it was the gentleman's place to be on the outside, to protect the lady," he said with a smile.

"Did you learn that from your father?"

"Not hardly. He's not much on manners and gentlemanly behavior. I don't remember where I learned it, but I do know that I want to protect you."

My heart stirred at his words, but my mind balked. "So you think I need protecting?" I bantered.

"Yes, I do. You have a very vulnerable side that you hide from most people. But I can see it, and it makes me want to protect you."

His words were much more personal today, and he reached over and took my hand. A tingle shot up my arm, and I had a sudden longing to lean against him and feel his protection. It was wonderful to be with a man who wanted to be a giver, not a taker. But we were on a public sidewalk in the middle of the day, and I was still wary. I gently withdrew my hand and gestured across the street. "Which of those houses do you like?"

"They all have interesting features," he said. "Portland houses are so different from what I'm used to in Hanford. That's one of the things I like here." He gestured at a substantial home across the street. "I love the wrap-around porch on that house. I can imagine sitting there in the morning, sharing a pot of tea with my wife."

"So now you're planning to have a wife in Portland?" I grinned mischievously at him.

"As I said, I can *imagine* sharing a pot of tea with my wife."

"Seems like you've moved a fair distance in the past couple of days from thinking you'd be single to imagining a wife in Portland."

"I think you know why," he said, with a meaningful look. "A lot of things are changing this week."

"Such as...?"

"The conference has given me a lot of spiritual food for thought. On another level, I feel like God has opened my eyes to some new possibilities for my life."

"So how will that change things when you go back to Hanford?"

"Well, I'm determined to spend more time in the Bible and in prayer. And on a practical level, I will have to either buy a lot of postage stamps or a flock of carrier pigeons." My startled look made him laugh. "You see, I plan on writing a lot of letters to a certain girl who lives in Oregon."

"Oh, really? And what makes you think you'll write a *lot* of letters?"

"Because I'm pretty sure that you'll write back." He hesitated. "You will, won't you?" His dark eyes pleaded.

"I suppose I could be persuaded to fit it into my schedule," I said, feigning reluctance. If we were going to be writing to each other, it meant that he was considering a serious relationship.

Suddenly my fear dissolved, and I reached for his hand. Surprised, he squeezed mine in return, and we stared at each other. I felt like I had just walked through a narrow gate into an open, sunny space. Wordlessly, we turned and strolled toward another fragrant rose garden.

"What if..."

"Would you..." Our thoughts spilled out at the same time, and we laughed as our words collided.

"Ladies first," he said.

I started again. "What if you end up getting drafted? What would happen with the church?" The Vietnam War was brought to our attention daily by newspapers, magazines and television.

"If God allowed that, then I believe he would have a plan to take care of the church. If I got drafted, at least it would get me out of Hanford."

"There must be an easier way," I retorted.

We walked to the end of the block before heading back towards the church, our hands intertwined, at ease again. In our silence, thoughts tripped over themselves in my mind. *What would it be like to walk with him for the rest of my life? What a lovely thought! I feel safe with him, secure.*

Maybe he'll ask me to go steady. But how do you "go steady" eight hundred miles apart?

I wish the conference were longer. The week is nearly over; it's not long enough.

"This week has gone by really fast, hasn't it?" Larry said.

Startled, I looked at him. "That's exactly what I was thinking. How did you know?"

"Great minds..." he smiled ruefully. "The conference is already half over, and I'm supposed to leave on Saturday."

"I wish you could stay longer." I couldn't keep the wistfulness out of my voice.

"Do you?" he asked softly, turning me to face him.

"Yes, I do. I'd like to spend a lot more time with you."

He looked at me intently and seemed to come to a decision. "Can we talk more tonight after the service? Right now I need to meet with Paul and Rev. Black to discuss church business. Will you save time for me tonight?"

"Of course, I'll look forward to it." We stared into each other's eyes for a few moments. He squeezed my hand and disappeared into the side door of the church.

Watching him walk away, I felt a welcome peace. My earlier doubts and fears seemed to have melted in the warm August sun. I felt enveloped by a sense of God's nearness and blessing, and knew I could trust my life into His hands. The specifics of Larry's call to ministry no longer mattered. I knew God would work out the details.

The Wednesday evening service seemed to last forever, with extra testimonies and a long sermon. Finally the last Amen was said, and people started slowly leaving the building. There were still a few stragglers in the lobby when Larry sidled up to me and said, "Let's go outside."

His hand guided me down the stairs. At the bottom, he pulled me into a shadowy doorway at the side of the building. His intensity made my heart beat wildly.

Words tumbled out as he faced me. "Carolyn, this week has been crazy for me. I feel like my whole world has turned upside down. I'm usually a very cautious, rational person, but that seems to have changed."

"What do you mean?"

He stepped closer. "I've had my life planned, willing to give up marriage and a family to do God's work. You've ruined that for me."

"Not intentionally," I murmured my pulse racing. *He smells so good up close.*

He looked at me steadily for a moment, and took a deep breath. "I know we haven't known each other very long. But I'm convinced God has brought you into my life. I've fallen in love with you, and I want to spend the rest of my life with you." His eyes searched mine with desperate hope.

My previous hesitation gave way to reckless, happy boldness. "Are you asking me to marry you?"

"Yes, I guess I am." He reached for my other hand. "Carolyn, will you marry me?"

"Oh, Larry, of course I'll marry you!" I threw my arms around his neck; his arms encircled my waist and tightened.

"You will? You'll marry me?" His voice in my ear was incredulous. "Just like that?"

"Yes, Larry, just like that," I laughed through joyful tears. "I love you!"

Chapter 10

Larry

After Carolyn said, "I love you," I pulled back so I could see her face. The joy and love in her eyes confirmed her words. She said it again, softer this time. "I love you, Larry David Wade. I want to marry you, love you, have your children. I want to grow old with you." My eyes swelled with unfamiliar moisture as I pulled her close.

"Carolyn, you have no idea how much this means to me." She snuggled closer to me, her head fitting perfectly beneath my chin.

> **Current Culture**
> **August 1966**
>
> - Lunar Orbiter 1 transmits first photos of Earth from Moon
> - *Valley of the Dolls* by Jacqueline Susann tops New York Times fiction list
> - The Beach Boys release "God Only Knows," an instant hit
> - Milk sells for 99 cents per gallon

"Well, maybe I have a little idea."

"There's something very important I need to say." I pulled slightly away so I could see her face. "If you agree to marry me, there's one thing you need to understand."

"Yes?" Her forehead furrowed.

"The woman I marry has to understand that she will never be Number One in my life." I held her gaze. "She will have to know that Jesus is Number One in my life, but she will always be Number Two." I held my breath, waiting for her response.

"Oh, Darling," she sighed. "That's the best thing you could have said to me. If you put God first, I'm totally safe. I don't want to be Number One. That's God's place."

Relief flooded through me. "Then there's just one more thing," I said softly, pulling her close again.

"What's that?"

"This." I looked deeply into her eyes while tipping up her chin with my free hand. Her lips met mine halfway, softly yielding. Our kiss was filled with sweetness and promise, sealing something momentous between us. A wave of emotion threatened my composure, and I had to step back and take a deep breath. "Oh, my Sweet, I can't believe this is happening to us."

"I know, it's like a dream, only better," Carolyn murmured. We stood with our arms around each other, absorbing each other's nearness.

"I don't want this moment to end," I said, my heart surging with happiness. "Let's never forget this date, August 31, 1966."

"We'll have many years to celebrate," she laughed. "But it's nearly midnight, and we do have tomorrow." Her words struck me with dismay. *Only tomorrow!* But I brushed the thought aside, and pulled her close for another kiss. *So this is what it feels like to kiss the woman you love!*

"Ok, Larry. We'd better stop," she said breathlessly. The look of longing in her eyes contradicted her words. But she was true to her character, and took my hand as she walked toward her car. "I'll see you in my dreams." She got in her car and drove off, blowing a kiss through the open window.

I stood under the streetlight, stunned, joyful, astounded. *Did that really just happen?*

Walking into the parsonage kitchen, I found Jesse and his dad sitting at the table talking with the Smiths. "So where have you been, Larry?" said Rev. Black.

"You look like you've seen a ghost," Jesse said. "Have a seat, there's a piece of pie left."

"No thanks, I think I'll head for bed," I said. I didn't want anything to dilute the evening's miracle.

After I turned out the bedroom light, the late evening scene replayed in my head. When I got to the part where she leaned into my embrace and I remembered the feel of her soft curves against me, my pulse quickened, and I had to shut off the film. If I kept watching that mental movie, I would violate the vow I'd made years earlier, based on the book of Job: *"I have made a covenant with my eyes, not to look with lust at a young woman."*

Instead, I concentrated on the future. The implications of the evening were enormous. I couldn't believe that I, conservative, cautious Larry Wade, had asked a girl I barely knew to marry me. It was totally insane. I didn't have a job, lived with my parents, and had the Draft hanging over my head. I was no prime prospect, but this wonderful girl had apparently also lost her mind and agreed to become my wife. It was crazy, astonishing, amazing. What she saw in me I couldn't fathom, but I wasn't going to try to figure it out.

What I did try to work out, as the hands on the clock continued to circle, was how in the world I could ever pull it off. Carolyn still had two years of college, and I didn't have a job. I tried to plan and figure everything out, but it just seemed impossible. *It's never going to work!*

Even as this thought skulked through my head, I heard a calming voice. *Trust Me. I brought you together, I can work things out.*

With those words echoing in my head, I fell asleep, only to have my dreams recreate the scene in the shadowy doorway.

When I woke up Thursday morning, the upstairs bedroom still held the previous afternoon's heat and Jesse was snoring in the bed on the other side of the room. Floating into consciousness, I suddenly remembered. *Carolyn said she would marry me!* I looked at the clock. *I'll see her in two hours.*

I was watching from the front porch of the parsonage when I saw her car. By the time she parked across from the church, I was at the curb.

"Good morning, my love," she said with a smile. Her words made me catch my breath. *Her love!*

"You look beautiful today, Carolyn," I managed to stammer.

"Thank you, Larry. You look pretty good yourself." I wanted to crush her in my arms, but it was nine o'clock in the morning, and other cars were arriving.

"Is this real?" I said, taking her hand as we crossed the street. I could do that, at least.

"I'm not sure," she said. "It seems pretty un-real to me. Did I actually agree to marry you last night?" Her tone was teasing.

"That's what I thought, but maybe that happened to some other lucky guy."

"No, it was you, Larry. You're the one I want to marry." I squeezed her hand and led her up the steps and into the lobby.

"Do you think we can keep this quiet for a little while?" I said. "I'm not sure I want everyone at the conference to know our private business."

"You mean I can't stand up during testimony time and make an announcement?" She frowned disappointedly. "You're taking all the fun out of it."

I wasn't sure if she was serious until she laughed. "I'm kidding, Darling. Of course, I want to keep it a secret for a while. After all, Paul and Emily should be the first to know. It's all because of them that this is happening."

"Them and the Lord," I said.

"Him most of all," she replied. "My heart is bursting." Tears glinted in the corners of her eyes. "Okay, I don't want to ruin my makeup, let's pretend we're just friends, okay?"

"That's going to be tough, but I'll give it my best shot."

"Can we have another long walk this afternoon? There's no service tonight, and then you'll be leaving in the morning."

"I'd like another long walk," I said. "And I might have a surprise for you."

"A surprise? Really? How do you expect me to focus on the worship and the sermon when you tell me that?"

"Think of sad things, and don't look my direction," I suggested with a grin.

"The saddest thing I can think of is that you're going back to California tomorrow." She shook her head. "There's got to be a way…"

"We'll talk this afternoon."

As the morning service was ending, I slipped away to use the phone at the parsonage. Mom was shocked to hear my voice on the phone, especially since it was daytime and the long-distance rates were highest. After I asked the operator to reverse charges, I could hear the alarm in Mom's voice. "Are you okay, Larry? Is anything wrong?"

"I'm okay, Mom," I said. "Something has come up and I need to stay in Portland through the weekend. I need you to ask Mr. Boyd to lead the service at church on Sunday. Would you ask him to just have a testimony service? He doesn't need to preach."

"Well, I guess so. Are you sure everything is okay?"

"Yes, actually, better than okay."

"Does this have something to do with Carolyn?" Mom knew me pretty well.

"You'll just have to wait until I get home to find out, Mom," I said. "Thanks for taking care of Sunday for me. I'll see you next week. Say Hi to Dad for me."

"Okay, Larry. Just don't do anything rash." *Rash? If she only knew!*

Since the conference was ending, people lingered over the lunch. It was nearly two o'clock before Carolyn and I headed for the park. As we sat down on a bench, I said, "I've changed my mind." Carolyn gasped and stared at me, looking stricken.

"No, silly, not about *us*. About leaving tomorrow." Relief replaced the shock on her face.

"Oh, Larry, I'm so glad. How much longer can you stay?"

"Well, Jesse has agreed to stay through the weekend, so we'll have several more days together."

"Oh, I can't believe it." Tears started in her eyes. "I was all braced to say goodbye this afternoon, and you've given me a reprieve." I put my arm around her shoulder and gently wiped the tears from her eyes.

"No tears today, my Sweet. This is a time for happiness." She put her head on my shoulder and we sat quietly holding hands, thrilled to be together.

"Is it okay if I tell my Dad?" she said after a while.

"Your Dad, not your Mom?" I was curious.

"Daddy first, Mom later," she said. "I need to work up to things with her."

"Shouldn't I be the one to talk to your father?" I wanted to do this the right way, but didn't know how to make it work out. "Actually, that's one of the things I wanted to talk to you about today." She turned to face me as I continued. "Being engaged usually means a ring, but everything happened so fast. I'm going to do everything I can to come back at Christmas. Then I can ask your father's permission to marry you so that we can get officially engaged."

"I'd like that," she said. "But how will that work out if you get a job? Would you fly up for a weekend?" As neither of us had ever taken a plane anywhere, this suggestion seemed out of reach.

"I'm not sure how I will work out all the details," I said. "But I'll figure out a way."

"I'm supposed to go home this afternoon, and be at the ranch until Saturday afternoon," Carolyn said. "I wish you could come with me."

"I'd love to," I replied, "but that would be awkward since I don't have a car. It might be good to have some time apart to think about everything."

"I don't know about *everything*," Carolyn said. "Mostly what I'll be thinking about is *you*."

"You know what I mean." I squeezed her shoulder. "So you'll be coming back to Portland Saturday afternoon?"

"Yes, if I can convince Mom that I have to be here for something important."

"Would a date with me be something important?"

"It would to me; I'm not sure how Mom will feel about that."

"Well, I'm asking you for a date. How about it? Can we go out for dinner and a movie or bowling or something?"

"Why yes, Mr. Wade. I'd be delighted to go out with you on Saturday," she said smiling broadly. "What time should I pick you up?"

"Why don't you pick me up at five," I said. "That should give us plenty of time."

"Okay, it's a date!"

For the next forty-eight hours, I was restless. The church and the parsonage had both emptied out, with Jesse, Rev. Black and others out of town for meetings. I walked for hours up and down Hawthorne Boulevard and through the residential neighborhood of Ladd's Addition. I found a dry cleaner, and left my suit to be cleaned. I had a long conversation with Mr. Smith at the parsonage, read my Bible, and found a musty volume of WWI history to occupy a few hours.

At four thirty Saturday afternoon, I ironed my shirt and slacks, polished my shoes, and shaved again. *My first real date with Carolyn!*

I couldn't help chuckling again at the irony. Our first date, but we were already engaged. *It's almost like an arranged marriage.*

The thought had barely floated through my mind when I heard that quiet voice. *And who do you think arranged it?*

I breathed a prayer in return. *Thank you, Lord. You're so good. Thank you for the amazing gift of Carolyn's love.* I didn't hear His voice, but in my mind I could see His smile.

When Carolyn's car pulled up at the curb, I hopped in.

Chapter 11

Carolyn

Mom and Dad's car wasn't in the driveway when I arrived at the ranch early Thursday evening. *Oh good. I'll have more time to think things through before I face them.* Instead of going into the house, I headed across the road and down the narrow path to the Sandy River. The sight and sound of water would calm my spirit and give me perspective.

> **Current Culture**
> **August 1966**
>
> - First air-conditioned subway car placed in service in New York City
> - The Beatles give final US concert performance at Candlestick Park in San Francisco, disappointed by low ticket sales
> - Cost of ticket to Beatles concert: $4.50-$6.50

A footpath meandered along the edge of the river through the fir and alder trees. As I strolled, I brushed against red huckleberry, salal, and sword ferns. A few hundred yards upstream was my favorite thinking spot—a secluded space in the washed-out roots of a huge fir tree.

I sat between sun-warmed stones, and leaned back against a smooth root. Closing my eyes, I absorbed the sounds of nature—the musical chatter of the water rushing in its stony channel, the whisper of breeze moving through the treetops, and the calls of birds discussing the end of the day. The rays of the late summer wrapped me in a comforting shawl of warmth. Every sight, sound and smell seemed magnified, filling me with a renewed sense of wonder.

After leaving Larry, my mind had been filled with anxious questions about the future. Now, as I drew green-scented river air into my lungs, deep peace filled my soul. *Thank you, Heavenly Father. Thank you!*

I thought back to my anticipation and anxiety in the days before the conference, when I wondered if the connection I'd felt with Larry back in July would actually develop into something. Since Larry had seemed conservative and cautious, the idea of a marriage proposal this week had never entered my mind. But the past few days had brought a deep conviction that this was God's plan. I could imagine Him looking down from heaven with delight at being able to thoroughly surprise me with His loving goodness.

On my stony perch, I savored the quietness and peace, examining and admiring the new treasure of our love without distraction. *Life is never going to be the same again!*

Just as that idea settled in my mind, doubts bombarded me like a cloud of gnats. *But how... What if... Are you sure?* I rubbed my hands over my face, willing the negative thoughts away.

Unaware of time, I was startled when I heard the honk of a car horn. Mom and Dad were home, and my reverie at the river ended.

"I wondered where you were," Mom said when I walked into the kitchen.

"Just down at the river, enjoying the evening."

"And did you enjoy the conference?" I could feel the unvoiced question beneath her bland words.

"Yes, I did. Everyone felt it was very successful."

"Has everyone gone home?" Again, the unspoken questions.

"Most left so they could get back home for the weekend, but a few people stayed over." Fortunately, Dad walked in at that moment. "Hi, Daddy," I said, giving him a hug.

"Hi, Sweetheart. Nice to have you home."

"Thanks. How's everything here?"

"About the same. Looks like the weather will hold through the holiday on Monday."

"That's good," I replied. "We'll have more business."

"I hope so, it's the last chance for riders and fishermen," he said.

"By the way, I'll be driving back to Portland on Saturday."

"What? But it's Labor Day weekend." Mom was obviously unhappy with my announcement.

"Don't worry, I'll be here Monday to help you."

"Why can't you just stay through the weekend?"

"Because I have a date Saturday night," I said, putting my arm around her shoulder. "Aren't you happy for me?"

"That depends," she said, frowning.

Dad said, "Who's the lucky fellow?"

"Larry Wade. He decided to stay a few more days, and isn't leaving until Monday morning."

"Well, I suppose it's okay, since it's Larry." Mom looked at me uncertainly.

"We're going bowling, so it should be fun," I smiled. Walking to the kitchen door, I added, "I'll get my things out of the car. What's for dinner?"

"We got a bite in Sandy on the way home." Mom said.

"Okay, I'll just scrounge in the fridge."

After I'd put my overnight bag in the bedroom and fixed myself a snack, Mom sat down at the kitchen table with me. "So what prompted Larry to stay over the weekend?"

"I'm not sure of all the reasons, but it will be nice to spend a little time with him. He's definitely different than the guys I'm around at school."

"Does he plan to stay in California, or is he considering moving to Portland to be part of the church here?"

"I don't think he is planning to move. He's looking for a job in Hanford, and feels responsible for the church there."

"I guess that eliminates the possibility of a romance between you," Mom said. *Do I hear regret in her voice?* The delight of my new love filled me to bursting, but I needed to protect it from her disapproval.

"Distance is definitely a problem," I answered truthfully. I walked to the sink with my dishes. "Guess I'll wash these up."

"How about playing a duet when you're finished?" Mom asked hopefully. I really wasn't in the mood for classical piano, but knew it would please her.

She'd given up a career as a pianist and music teacher to marry Dad, and loved it when one of us shared her pleasure in music.

"Sure, that would be fine." I quickly washed the dishes and left them to dry in the rack while Mom placed sheet music on the piano.

"I'm a little rusty," I warned, sitting beside her on the bench. "I haven't had much practice time."

"You'll do fine." She opened to the first measures of *Qui Vive!*, a rollicking four-handed piece that would stretch my modest skill. "Okay," she counted, "One, two, three, four!" By the time we finished, with many fumbles on my part, we were both laughing.

"Bravo," said Dad, applauding. "I always like hearing you play together."

"That did me in," I said. "It's been a long week; I think I'm going to turn in. What's on the schedule for tomorrow?"

"Blackberries are ripe, and there are some early apples ready to make sauce," Mom said.

"Okay, I'll give you a hand with that. Goodnight."

"Sleep well, pleasant dreams." Mom smiled speculatively when she added the last phrase.

Between the blackberries and apples and a couple loads of laundry hung on the backyard line, Friday was a busy day. After dinner, I followed Dad out to the barnyard. "Walk up to the pond with me?" I asked.

"Sure, Sweetheart," he said. "The horses can wait."

We walked through the barnyard and up a gentle slope. A previous owner had dug out a pond where the year-round creek flowed into the pasture. Clumps of cattails provided nesting area for ducks, and Dad bought fingerling rainbow trout each spring to stock the pond for fishermen. We sat together on a wooden bench at the water's edge.

I tucked my hand in the crook of Dad's elbow and leaned against his shoulder, feeling the corded muscles of his arm. His slight build concealed strength and toughness from years of manual labor. The only time he seemed to curb his restless energy was when he knelt with his Bible for prayer each morning.

After a few minutes of companionable silence, he smiled at me. "Something on your mind?"

"I guess you could say that." Although I'd planned what I wanted to say, now I struggled to find the right words. I watched a red-wing blackbird alight on a cattail. "This has been a pretty important week for me."

"How's that?"

"I think I've found the man I want to marry."

His eyebrows went up, and a smile pulled at his weathered cheeks. "Do I need to guess his name?"

"You probably already have," I grinned. "It's Larry Wade."

"I'm not surprised." He put his arm around me and gave me a sideways hug, then asked, "Does Larry know you want to marry him?"

"Well, actually, yes." I took a deep breath. "He proposed to me last night."

Dad blinked in surprise. "That's pretty fast work!"

"I know," I said, "I'm still in shock myself."

"So how did this happen?"

"Well, we spent hours talking together during the conference, and we both prayed about it a lot. With him going back to California and me going back to school, I think he figured it was now or never." I paused to give him a chance to absorb my words before continuing. "He wants to do things right, and ask you personally for my hand, but it didn't work out for him to come with me last night."

Dad was silent for a few minutes, staring at the surface of the pond. A trout jumped, breaking the stillness with a plop. I watched ripples flow to the bank. "Are you sure God is in this?"

"Yes, Daddy, I'm sure." I turned to face him. "This isn't like what I've felt with other guys; it's totally different. I am completely convinced that God brought us together."

"I trust you to hear God's voice." His intent gaze suddenly turned into a grin as he added, "I'm happy for you, Sweetheart."

"Thank you, Daddy. That means so much to me." I leaned against him, and we sat quietly, absorbed in our thoughts, until he broke the silence.

"Have you told Mom?"

"No, I wanted to talk to you first."

He winked at me. "Need me on your side, do you?"

"Yes, definitely."

"It'll be okay, you'll see."

Saturday morning I woke up early. I'd put a loaf of banana bread in the oven and was wiping down the cabinets when Mom came in from her bedroom.

"I hear you have some important news," she said.

"Good morning, Mom," I replied, giving her a hug. "Dad must have talked to you."

"Yes, he did," she said with an injured tone. When I didn't respond, she added, "Would you care to tell me how this happened?"

"Well, we spent lots of time between services talking. You know that ministry is my goal, and it's Larry's goal as well. We have so much in common, it just seems natural."

"But in less than a week?" Mom shook her head in disbelief. "Your father and I went together for three years before we got engaged."

"I know, Mom, but God seems to be taking my life in a different direction."

"Why didn't Larry talk to your father before he proposed?"

"He wanted to, but he's here for such a short time, and he doesn't have a car to drive out here. I told him Dad doesn't talk on the phone because of his hearing aids, so it just ended up this way. He plans to come back to Portland later to talk to Dad personally."

"Well, I guess there's no use crying over spilled milk." She shook her head and sighed. "So are you thinking you'll get married after you finish school?" I braced myself, knowing that this was a big issue.

"We haven't set a date yet."

"I certainly wouldn't have expected Larry to be so impulsive as to propose in less than a week. He seems like such a responsible and steady young man."

"I know, Mom. He told me it's definitely out of character for him. But given our circumstances, he felt like he had to take a risk." I smiled at her. "I'm glad he did!"

"Are you absolutely certain about this?"

"Yes, I am. It's strange, like I told Dad. This isn't like crushes I've had in the past. I almost feel like we are chess pieces, and God has moved us in position together. I'm certain that my destiny is with Larry."

A smile suddenly softened her face. "You know, Dear, I've done everything I could to prepare you to be a missionary or pastor's wife. Somehow this doesn't surprise me. It's just the timing that takes my breath away."

"Mine too," I agreed. "My head is still spinning."

"Well, it's going to be a busy weekend." On cue, a car pulled into the driveway. "Looks like we have customers already."

We both stood up from the kitchen table, and I gave her a hug. "Thanks, Mom."

"For what?" she asked.

"For not reading me the riot act when you found out."

"I'm not totally happy about this, but apparently my feelings won't make much difference at this point." She shook her head resignedly, and headed out the door to welcome the visitors. I gave a huge sigh of relief, grateful that our conversation hadn't been a painful verbal battle.

Thank you, Lord. You definitely prepared her heart.

When I drove up to the parsonage Saturday evening, Larry stood up from the glider on the broad porch, and started down the stone steps to my car. I greeted him through the open window. "Hi, Larry."

"You're right on time," he said, looking pleased as he got in. "Our first date," he continued with a smile. "Do you still want to go bowling?"

"Sure," I said. "There's an alley not too far from here."

"Can we get something to eat first?" Larry asked. "The house was empty today and I was on my own. I haven't eaten much."

"I'm sure there are restaurants near the bowling alley." As I pulled away from the curb and headed northwest, I suddenly felt awkward and uncertain. *I'm going to marry this man, but I barely know him!* I glanced quickly at him before turning onto busy Hawthorne Boulevard.

"Are you okay?" he asked.

Startled that he had so easily picked up my emotional state, I quickly answered "I'm fine."

"It feels a little weird, doesn't it? We're just beginning our first date, but we've already agreed to get married."

"Weird doesn't even come close to describing it," I said.

"Maybe we should just pretend we're having a normal date."

"That would work for me," I replied gratefully. Suddenly the awkwardness lifted and I relaxed. We found an Italian restaurant near the bowling alley, and talked and laughed easily through an unremarkable meal. He asked about my days at home, and I reported my conversations with my parents.

"I wish it could have worked out for me to talk to your father in person," he said.

"I know, but it was just too complicated. Just promise me that you'll come back to Portland and talk to him as soon as you can."

"Yes, I promise, my love." He grinned suddenly. "I don't want your parents to think I just sneaked up here to kidnap their baby girl. That's really not my style."

"So what is your style, Mr. Larry Wade?" I smiled back at him.

He shook his head. "I'm not sure I know any more. This week has definitely challenged my status quo. Never in a million years did I expect to go back to Hanford with a beautiful fiancée waiting in Portland."

"I'm having trouble comprehending it myself."

We finished our meal and walked to the bowling alley. After I got two strikes in the first four frames, Larry seemed to recognize that I was a serious competitor. He won two out of three games, but only by a few pins each time.

"You surprise me, Carolyn," he laughed as we changed our shoes.

"Thought I'd be a pushover, did you? That wouldn't have been any fun."

"You're right. I'd much rather win against a good competitor."

"My 7-week bowling class last quarter helped a bit."

"Now you tell me," he shook his head.

Walking back to the car I felt a thrill of connection when he took my hand. Street lights were coming on, and I didn't want the evening to end. I gathered my courage to ask a bold question.

"Are you interested in seeing the lights of the city?" I asked.

He looked surprised as he held the car door open for me. "With you, I hope?"

"Yes, with me, silly."

"I'd be very interested."

My heart raced as I headed the car toward a city park surrounding an extinct volcano. For years, I'd heard Mt. Tabor referred to as a favored "parking" spot, never thinking I'd drive there myself. But I wanted Larry to kiss me again, and feel the thrill of being in his arms. I pulled the car into an empty spot near other darkened cars, and we sat quietly for a few minutes, gazing at the city lights spread out before us like gems on a jeweler's velvet tray.

"It's beautiful, isn't it?" I murmured, leaning against his shoulder.

"Beautiful," he answered softly. "Yes, you are."

As I turned to smile at him, he gently touched my cheek. "I love you, Larry," I whispered.

We stared deeply into each other's eyes, a thousand volts of emotion flowing between us. I could feel the love in his gaze melting my core. As our lips met, I closed my eyes and slowly sank into his embrace.

We were silent on the way down the hill. When I parked in front of the parsonage, Larry reached to embrace me again, but I stopped him with a forefinger on his lips.

"I'm going to say goodnight now, Larry. I'm crazy for you, and I'd love more kisses. But we need to slow down a bit, I think."

"You're right," he said. "I respect you even more for saying that." He got out of the car and came around to my side, reached in the open window and caressed my cheek. "You have no idea how much I love you, Carolyn." His dark eyes locked with mine. "Goodnight, Sweetheart. I'll see you at church in the morning."

I turned his hand over, planted a kiss on his palm, and put the car in gear. "I'll see you in my dreams," I said as I pulled away from the curb.

First photo together, August 1966

Chapter 12

Larry

Streetlamps cast pools of light and shadow along the quiet street. I sat on the glider on the parsonage porch until long after midnight. *How is it possible that my life could be so drastically different in just one week?*

Seven days earlier, I'd arrived in Portland, wondering if there could be any possibility of a relationship with Carolyn. In a startling kaleidoscope of events, we had recognized and declared our love for each other, and now we were planning to get married!

I chuckled, thinking of the irony of proposing to Carolyn before we had a single

> **Current Culture**
> **September 1966**
>
> - NBC debuts new *Star Trek* series
> - *That Girl* with Marlo Thomas starts 5-year run on ABC
> - Willie Mays hits his 535th home run, second only to Babe Ruth
> - National airline strike ends after 42 days
> - Average cost of a new house: $14,200

date. But it was obvious to me that our romance was not going to follow a normal pattern. After our first long conversation on Monday, I'd been caught up in a journey that only God could have planned. I wasn't sure how I'd gotten on the train, and certainly didn't know what the scenery would look like in the next few months. I sat back in the glider to think of the past few hours.

When Carolyn picked me up for our date, I could sense her nervousness as soon as I got in the car. It surprised me, because she had appeared so confident and assured earlier. I felt nervous too, and was glad that our meal gave us time to talk about normal things and be together as friends.

At the bowling alley, I saw a different side of my new fiancée. Until then, she had been restrained and lady-like; suddenly she was intense and competitive. I had to concentrate on my game and work hard to beat her, but our spirited rivalry added zest to the evening. Then we drove up to Mt. Tabor to view the city lights, and I experienced another surprising dimension of her personality.

At one point in the car, she gently pulled away from me and reached for her glasses from the dashboard. "Wow! I need to catch my breath, Larry,"

"Wow is right." I sat back, trying to breathe normally.

"Can we talk a bit?" She reached for my hand.

"Of course."

"I hope you don't mind me being candid, but you need to know that I intend to be a virgin on my wedding night."

"*Our* wedding night," I corrected with a smile.

"Yes, *our* wedding night." She paused then seemed to plunge ahead. "I've never had a reason to discuss this with anyone before, but I think we need to talk about it."

"I appreciate your honesty, Carolyn. Our relationship is very important to me, and I don't want to spoil it. Thanks for bringing this up."

"I wasn't sure…" I could see that her expression was tentative in the dim light.

"If we're going to get married, we need to be able to talk about anything," I assured her.

"True, but it's still hard. Talking about personal things is difficult for me, but I feel safe with you."

"I'm glad. I will never intentionally hurt you."

"I believe that, Larry, and I'm grateful." We were quiet for a few minutes before she said, "Maybe we need to set some boundaries." She laughed, "As if we'll need them when we're eight hundred miles apart."

I chuckled. "Well we're not eight hundred miles apart tonight, and I plan on a few visits in the next twelve months!"

"Right now I just want you to hold me," she said, putting her head on my shoulder.

"Fine with me." I gently pulled her close. After a few minutes, I said, "I've been doing a lot of thinking about the future."

"I suppose we need to make some plans."

"Here's what I'm thinking. If I get the job with the county and start right away, it will be a year before I get vacation for a wedding and honeymoon."

"A whole year? How can we stand to wait that long?"

"It will be tough, but I still want to do things right. I need to be able to provide for you, and you need to finish at least one more year of college."

"I know," she sighed. "It's just that my emotional side is having a tug of war with my practical side. A one-year engagement is probably the best thing, but I don't have to *like* it."

"I don't like it either," I said, "but I don't see any other way. I've looked at the calendar, and if we got married on Labor Day weekend, it would give me an extra day off for our honeymoon. What would you say to a wedding on September 2nd? That's a year from yesterday."

"That's Priscilla's birthday! She'd like that. I can't wait to tell her!"

"Maybe we should discuss who we're going to tell, and when.

"It's not going to be too hard to keep it from the general public, since we won't be together. I'm so happy--I don't think I can keep it from my family."

"Family will probably guess, but let's not make it public for a while."

"I wish I could visit Hanford soon, Larry. I want to be able to picture you there when I think about you." Carolyn looked wistful.

"I hope you can. But at least now we have a goal to aim for, September 2nd. I like the sound of that."

"Me, too. Now that we have a date, it seems more real."

"There are some other things I want to make more real, too." I kissed her gently. "In one year, you'll be my wife, and I'll do everything in my power to make sure that we're never separated again." Her eyes glowed as I continued. "I'll be back at Christmas to put a ring on your finger."

"I'll count the days," she said wistfully.

We were silent for a few minutes, trying to imagine what our lives were going to be like. I reached for her again, wanting to capture memories--her fragrance, the taste of her lips, and her softness in my arms--for the lonely weeks ahead.

Now watching the moon rise above the house across the street I began to feel the emotions that surfaced when we shared kisses and embraces. We'd connected on a spiritual and emotional level, but the power of the physical current seemed to catch us both by surprise. The first kiss was like putting my toe in the edge of the surf; each successive kiss drew us until we were being pulled by an undertow that threatened to drag us beyond safety.

My thoughts were interrupted by footsteps in the entry hall, and the sound of a lock. I got up quickly and knocked lightly on the front door.

"Good thing you knocked," Mr. Smith said as he let me in. "You almost got locked out for the night."

"I don't think I want to sleep on the glider," I said. "Thanks for letting me in."

"G'night, see you in the morning."

I went quietly up the stairs to the room I shared with Jesse. He was sleeping soundly, but I still tried to make as little noise as possible getting ready for bed. I wasn't sure I'd be able to go to sleep, but quickly sank into dreams of Carolyn that had little resemblance to reality, but echoed the euphoric emotions of our evening together.

Sunday morning there were faint shadows underscoring Carolyn's bright blue eyes.

"Good morning, my love," I greeted her as she got out of her car in front of the church. "Did you sleep well?"

"As well as I could expect, but it was a short night."

"It was pretty late when you dropped me off."

"I don't remember much about driving home," she smiled wonderingly. "It was more like floating home on Cloud Nine."

I squeezed her hand as we entered the carved door of the church. "I'll remember last night for a very long time."

"Me too," she said, giving me a look brimming with love.

During the worship service, I was glad that the platform was small so that I could watch the song leader and see Carolyn at the same time. Every time she glanced at me, my heart surged. When she finished at the piano, she walked past her usual seat on the front row and sat down next to me. There was a discreet space between us, but I was keenly aware of her presence, and enjoyed the faint scent of her floral perfume.

In spite of the powerful distraction, I found the sermon inspiring. I would return to Hanford with fresh enthusiasm for leading my congregation. Best of all, I had the assurance of Carolyn's love and her promise for the future.

On the way to Paul and Emily's home for lunch, the road through Portland's West Hills curved through a steep, heavily forested canyon. At the top of the long ascent, Carolyn pointed out the intersection at Sylvan where her grandfather's blacksmith shop had stood, and the brick schoolhouse above it where she and her siblings had studied. A little further on, she turned off the highway onto a shady street lined with tidy bungalows and modern ranch-style homes.

"This is a nice neighborhood," I said. "It reminds me of the north end of Hanford."

"I've always loved this street," Carolyn replied. "But our house isn't quite like these. When Dad first bought the property thirty years ago, it was a two-room shack."

She pulled into an unpaved driveway and parked beside the carport attached to a modest two-story house. "Here we are," she said.

"It's definitely not a shack now."

"Several additions and remodeling over the years," Carolyn explained as we walked toward the front of her sister's home.

"Hey, just a minute," I said, catching up to her near the front door. I tipped her startled face up for a kiss. "I've been waiting to do that," I said. "In the next few hours, I plan to take advantage of every opportunity, since I'm not sure when I'll be able to kiss you again." A shadow crossed her face, and I regretted my comment. Trying to lighten the mood, I added, "How many kisses do you think we can steal this afternoon?"

"Lots, although it may be challenging," she said, glancing toward the street. Paul and Emily's car turned into the driveway and the two boys tumbled out and dashed to the front door. Their parents followed, and we were immersed in the bustle of family activity.

While Emily and Carolyn prepared lunch, Paul invited me to relax with him in their spacious living room. Sitting on a comfortable couch, I glanced around. An upright piano stood against one wall; an antique oak desk sat under a large window. French doors flanked a fireplace and looked out to a large yard bordered by tall fir trees.

We chatted about actor Ronald Reagan's bid for the California governor's office and the recent debut of a new television series, *Star Trek*.

"It won't last," Paul assured me. "It's just too far out."

"Dinner's ready!" Emily summoned us all to the table, and I was happy to be seated next to Carolyn so we could hold hands during the blessing.

"This looks great, Emily. Thank you for inviting me," I said.

"We're glad you're here, Larry. It's been a good week."

"That's an understatement," Carolyn whispered as she passed a platter of steaming corn on the cob.

"Don't take the biggest one, Larry. I want it," Gary said.

"Gary," his father admonished, "I think Larry has better manners than that. Better than yours right now, for sure!"

When Carolyn took her first bite of buttered and salted corn, I heard a sharp intake of breath. I took a bite, and understood her reaction. My lips, tenderized by last night's kisses, smarted painfully from the salt on the corn. I covered a chuckle with a cough and reached for my water glass as eyes turned toward me.

"Are you okay?" asked Emily.

"Yes, fine, thanks," I sputtered. Carolyn's knee nudged mine under the tablecloth, and I pressed back, enjoying our private joke.

The boys seemed very impatient throughout the meal. Finally Jimmy said, "Is it time yet?"

'Not yet, finish your lunch," said his mother.

"But when's the birthday cake?" Gary asked, grinning at me.

"When you clean up your plate," said Paul.

"Who has a birthday?" I asked.

"You, you," chorused the boys.

I looked at Emily in surprise. "How did you know?"

"A little bird told me."

"You mean a BIG bird, maybe by the name of Jesse?"

"Maybe. I know it's not until tomorrow, but we couldn't pass up a chance to celebrate with you." Emily went into the kitchen and returned carrying a cake with lighted candles. "The box only had twenty candles, so we're short two, but you can still make a wish and blow them out." At the last words of "Happy Birthday" I inhaled, then paused and looked at the boys.

"Blow! Blow!" said Jimmy bouncing in his chair. With an exaggerated huff, I blew out every candle.

"What did you wish for, Larry?" Gary asked.

I glanced at Carolyn and said, "It's a special wish that might not come true for a while." I smiled at the slow flush that reddened her cheeks.

Paul and Emily exchanged knowing glances before she said, "The birthday boy gets the first piece. How big, Larry?"

"Since German chocolate cake is my favorite, I'll take a big piece."

After we enjoyed the cake, Paul and I were shooed back into the living room while Emily and Carolyn cleaned up the kitchen. Paul walked over to a television set on a metal stand next to the fireplace, and fiddled with the dials and rabbit ears until the black and white image started to clear.

"I hope you don't mind some baseball," Paul said. "I sure like watching Sandy Koufax play."

"Sure," I said. While baseball wasn't my favorite, it kept me near Carolyn. While I stared at the screen, unseeing, my mind was on her and the fact that there were only a few hours before my return to Hanford.

When Carolyn came into the living room, she said, "How about a walk, Larry? I want to show you the neighborhood."

"Sounds good to me. Will you excuse me, Paul?"

"Of course, have a nice walk."

At the edge of the yard, she reached for my hand. As we strolled past well-kept homes and manicured lawns, she pointed out the homes of friends and classmates. We ended up at the school where she had spent her junior high years, and sat on the swings in the playground.

"This sure doesn't look like the school I went to in Armona," I said, nodding at the modern one-story building.

"It's only about ten years old." Her expression seemed pensive. "I had some good and some bad years here."

"What was it like?" I asked.

"Sixth grade was awful—I dreaded every day, and was sick a lot. My parents' strict rules made me feel like a total outsider. By eighth grade I had learned to focus on getting good grades and found ways to participate so I could feel included."

As we slid off the swings, I wrapped my arms around her, and said, "Thanks for sharing this part of your life with me, Carolyn."

"There's a lot more to share, if we're going to spend our lives together."

"I still can't get used to that idea."

"Oh yeah? Well, here's something else to get used to." Her eyes twinkled and she planted a playful kiss on my lips, then ran up the street. I chased her and swung her around for another kiss. *This girl is really getting under my skin!*

The rest of the afternoon was family time. Gary and Jimmy persuaded us to play *Sorry!* and I held Carolyn's hand under the table. When the game ended, Jimmy jumped on my back, Gary tugged Carolyn off her chair onto the floor, and we had a free-for-all. As we laughingly wrestled with the boys, I thoroughly enjoyed the physical contact with Carolyn.

After a late afternoon snack, we all headed back to church for the evening service. Far too soon, the meeting was over and it was time to say goodbye. As the lobby emptied, I took Carolyn's hand and led her outside to the shadowy doorway where I had proposed. Wordlessly, we embraced. I could feel tension in her body, and when I tipped up her chin to look into her eyes, I saw the shine of tears.

"I don't think I can bear it, Larry," she whispered. "My whole world has changed in the past week, and now you're leaving."

"Please don't cry, my sweet, you know I'm coming back." My throat was clogged with emotion. I pressed my cheek against her hair, wishing I could change our circumstances.

"December is *months* away," she murmured. "How will I ever make it through lectures at school when I'm thinking of you every minute?"

"Do your best, for my sake, Sweetheart. The time will pass quickly, I promise." She breathed shallowly, then stepped away slightly and looked at me intently.

"I love you, Larry David Wade. God brought us together. Don't forget that! I'll work hard at school, and you'll do your best with your job and the church. And I'll write to you every day."

"Every day?" I asked.

"Yes, every day. If we can't be together, at least we can share our lives through letters. Promise?"

"I promise, Carolyn, but I may not be very good with words."

"You've been pretty good with words this week." She smiled up at me, but as our eyes locked, a tear trickled down her cheek. "I didn't think it would hurt this much to say goodbye."

"Then don't say it." I silenced her salty lips with mine.

A few minutes later, I pulled myself away from her. "Let's not prolong the agony. You still have to drive back to the ranch tonight, and I have to get up early in the morning to leave for Hanford." I held her hand tightly as we walked to her car. We shared one last lingering kiss before I opened the door for her.

"Don't forget, Carolyn, we belong to each other. God be with you." I felt a stab of pain as the tears trailed down her cheeks. She gave me a tremulous smile, blew me a kiss and drove down the street.

Chapter 13

Carolyn

Late Sunday evening I looked around my small blue bedroom, crowded with a double bed, two dressers, Mom's sewing table, and a storage chest. *How can everything look the same, when my life has totally changed?*

Mom came to the doorway of my room. "How was your date?" she asked.

"Fun," I said. "I managed to beat him in one game of bowling."

"I hope you didn't stay out too late."

"I slept pretty well last night," I replied. Her eyes let me know she was well aware I had ignored her meaning.

> **Current Culture**
> **September 1966**
>
> - Ralph Baer begins designing the Magnavox *Odyssey*, first video game console
> - French President Charles de Gaulle calls for withdrawal of US troops in Vietnam
> - Average yearly tuition for state college: $275
> - Portable typewriter with case, $39.99

"Is he gone?" Mom continued her questions.

"He's leaving first thing in the morning."

"Well, you've had quite a week, I'd say. I hope you're up to helping out tomorrow. We've already had two reservations for trail rides."

I gave her what I hoped was a bright smile. "I'll be up early, ready to go," I assured her.

"Goodnight, Dear. Happy dreams."

" 'Night, Mom."

I closed the door behind her and sank onto the bed, giving way to my exhaustion. *In a few hours, he'll be heading back to California. How am I ever going to make it through the next few months?* Tears came and soon there was a damp circle on my pillow. Eventually I shrugged out of my clothes, tossing them to the floor beside the bed, and eased between the cool sheets. As my mind shut off, there was one predominant thought: *Larry loves me!*

As Mom predicted, Labor Day was extremely busy. The first riding customers came as we finished breakfast, and it was nearly dark when the last car left. Spice was saddled all day, and I led four groups of riders on the forest trails. Several fishermen were happy to catch fat trout in our pond. As one of them paid me for his fish, he said, "If I ever come back with my wife, please don't let on that I've been here before."

"Why?" I asked.

"She'd kill me if she knew that I spent so much for a weekend at the lake, and didn't catch anything there."

"My lips are sealed," I joked as I handed him his change.

By the time we sat down to a late dinner of leftovers, I was tired, sunburned, and saddle-sore. While Dad and Mom discussed the events of the day, my mind wandered down Interstate 5. *Where is he now? Does he miss me as much as I miss him?*

During our week together I had quickly become accustomed to Larry's presence, to the sound of his voice, to his intensity, sincerity and kindness, his gentle touch and tender kisses. Thinking of the months of separation that loomed ahead, I was suddenly flooded with sadness.

"You look a bit down tonight," said Mom across the dinner table.

"It's been a long day. I'm tired."

"I hope you didn't overdo things last week at the conference. You don't want to get sick just when you're heading back to school."

"I'm fine, Mom. It's just been a busy day."

"Maybe you should go to bed early." Dad added, expressing concern.

"That sounds like a good idea. I think I will."

"We'll save the dishes for tomorrow. It's nice to have you home, Dear." Mom patted my shoulder as she took her plate to the sink.

"Goodnight, Daddy." I paused to kiss his cheek, and he squeezed my hand.

"Goodnight, Sweetheart. Happy dreams."

I stumbled into the bathroom to brush my teeth, crept into bed, and fell into a dreamless sleep.

On Tuesday, Mom and Dad headed to Portland for the day. I put several loads of laundry in the washer and hung the clothes on the line, and I baked a cake and some cookies. My chores gave me plenty of time to think, and of course, Larry was my focus.

I thought back to the previous Wednesday night when I came in late to find Emily at her sewing machine. I knew the dress she was making was not the only reason she was up at midnight.

"It must have been a good conversation to keep you out so late." Her words were accompanied by an affectionate grin. "Is there a reason you can't stop smiling?"

"Oh, Em," I sighed happily. "My life is turning upside down!"

"I'll put water on for tea. I'm going to want plenty of details." She pulled a chair out from the kitchen table, and motioned for me to sit down.

I looked at her for a few seconds, then took a deep breath and said, "Larry proposed tonight." I giggled as her eyebrows shot up and her jaw dropped in perfect coordination. She sat down abruptly and gaped at me, speechless for a moment.

"I knew something was going on between you, but this is a shock. Isn't he rushing things a bit? It was just yesterday that you talked to Paul about your concerns."

"I know, I can't believe it myself. But Larry's here for such a short time, it's not like we have weeks and weeks to make up our minds. Believe me, I've prayed about this morning, noon, and night."

"Do I have to guess your answer?"

"Of course, I said 'Yes'. He's everything I want, Em. He loves the Lord, he treats me like a lady, and we have the same goals in life."

She got up to pour hot water on tea bags in two bone china mugs. When she brought them back to the table, she gave me a warm hug, and said, "I'm so happy for you, Carolyn. I'm not really surprised. Somehow I've known for a long time that this could happen." For another half hour, we shared happy sister-talk: the romance of the sudden proposal, the challenges of long-distance romance, and all the good things that God had ahead for us.

Now he was gone, and I was facing long weeks with only letters to connect us. When the last load of laundry was waving in the breeze and the cake was cooling on the kitchen counter, I sat down with stationery and a pen.

Dear Larry,

You've been gone less than 48 hours, but I need to "talk" to you. Labor Day was busy, as we expected, and now I need to start getting ready for school, since I leave next week. I'm doing my best to keep peace here, and not say or do anything that will create conflict. Mom hasn't asked about our plans, and I'm not offering information. I have the feeling she thinks that once we're separated, our romance will die a slow death. She doesn't know the amazing bond that God has created between us.

I wish you could really understand how you have changed my life. When I'm with you, I'm continually inspired by your dedication and insight. Everything about you is so wonderful—your way with people, the way you talk to me, the way you look at me and touch my face. There's so much joy inside me, it's hard to keep it quiet.

I love you, Larry!

Carolyn

When I finished, I found a stamp and put the letter in the mailbox so it wouldn't be around for Mom to find.

A week later, I took Spice for one last ride through the orchard, past the pond, and high up onto the hillside. *It will be a long time before I can do this again.* As excited as I was about my future life with Larry, I knew I would miss living at the ranch. Wanting one last thrill, I wheeled my horse around, nudged her with my heels, and said, "C'mon girl, let's go!" She was more than ready to jump into a gallop. By the time we skidded to a stop at the hitching post, the wind from our run had dried my tears.

The next day I stood behind Dad's car, trying to fit everything into the trunk. I'd have a private room in Todd Hall this year, and I could take a few more things to make my room feel homey. We pushed and shoved the largest item, a cedar "hope chest" until the trunk lid finally closed. I filled empty spaces with bedding and towels, and put my portable typewriter and box of dishes and cookware on the back seat. Mom came out with her arms filled with clothes on hangers, and we piled those on boxes in the back seat. "Looks like there's barely room for you back there," she said. "Are you sure you need all of this?"

"It's less than most girls have, Mom. One girl has a rocking chair in her room."

"Well, I hope you're not taking so much that you won't be able to keep your room in order."

I swallowed a retort, not wanting to start the two-hour drive to Monmouth with conflict. "I'll try to make you proud, Mom."

We were halfway between Portland and Salem when Mom turned around in her seat. "It's a little hard for me to think about you getting married when Larry hasn't talked to Father yet." She frowned and looked at me intently, while I held my breath. "But from everything we've heard, and from our conversation with him, he seems very mature." I relaxed and breathed again.

Mom patted Dad on the arm. "What do you think, Dear?"

"What's that?" Dad said.

"I asked you what you thought about Carolyn and Larry getting married next year. Maybe you should turn up your hearing aid." Dad fumbled at the controls on his glasses, while keeping his eyes on the road.

"So what do you think about a wedding next year?" Mom repeated.

"Carolyn's a big girl; she ought to know her own mind." Dad's eyes smiled at me in the rear view mirror. "And Larry doesn't seem to be a pushover."

Mom turned around again to look at me. "Don't let yourself get carried away with wedding plans. School is the most important thing for you right now, and I don't want you to be disappointed."

"What do you mean, Mom?"

"This all happened very fast, and absence doesn't always make the heart grow fonder. You may feel differently once you're back at school. I don't want you to be hurt." I stared out the window, wanting to say, 'You don't know us,' but the words stuck in my throat. When I didn't respond, she turned around and faced ahead.

Suddenly, the thought formed in my head. *Look at it from her point of view.* I sat back and took a deep breath. Mom and Dad had only seen Larry and me together for one brief interaction at the conference. He hadn't talked to them about our relationship, and with the high importance Mom placed on proper social conduct, that was a serious mark against him. *For all she knows, I could be making the whole thing up!*

I chuckled silently, and leaned forward to touch Mom's shoulder. "Thanks for your concern, Mom. I believe Larry's a man of integrity, and I hope you'll be able to see that for yourself when he comes in December."

"*If* he comes in December," she murmured, half to herself.

I refused to take the bait, and said, "I'm trusting God, Mom. I'll be fine."

As we walked up the sidewalk toward the double doors of Todd Hall, I felt eagerness and expectancy for my third year of college. I looked forward to the camaraderie of dorm life, the mental challenge of my classes, and the fulfillment I would receive from my dorm leadership role. My secret romance would add extra pleasure. *It's going to be a great year!*

Chapter 14

Larry

Driving into the outskirts of Hanford, I felt a mix of dread and excitement. I looked at Jesse, shaking my head. "After being in Oregon, the Central Valley looks like purgatory!"

"Yeah," he grunted.

"I'm looking forward to starting a job."

"And you've got a nice girl to think about."

"True," I replied briefly. It had taken self-discipline to keep from talking about Carolyn on our long drive home, but Jesse's total lack of success with girls kept me silent. "Thanks for the ride," I said as he pulled up in our driveway.

"See you around," was his terse reply.

> **Current Culture**
> **September 1966**
>
> - New Metropolitan Opera House opens in New York City, seating 3,800
> - The Soviet Union says it will provide economic and military aid to North Vietnam
> - Director John Huston released blockbuster movie: *The Bible: In the Beginning*
> - Popular comic books sell for 10 cents

Dad was watching TV, his ashtray overflowing. He glanced up when I walked in the living room. "You made it home okay."

"Looks that way. How are things here, Dad?"

"About the same, I guess. Your mom's at work." His eyes shifted back to the television, and after a moment I carried my suitcase into the bedroom. I felt grubby after the long day's drive and went into the bathroom to fill the tub. After bathing and brushing my teeth, I fell on the bed. The room was warm and stuffy, but if I opened the door to get a cross-breeze, I'd have to listen to the laugh track on Dad's comedy show.

As I turned over restlessly, the events of the past week seemed unreal, a crazy story about some other lucky guy. *I wish I had a picture of Carolyn!* Emily had taken one of us together in front of the church, but it would take time to get developed and arrive in the mail. I had to rely on my memory to visualize her face, her blue eyes, the dimple in her cheek, her smiling lips. When I finally fell asleep, my memories were replaced by dreams.

The next day I had my second interview with Kings County social services in Hanford. "We'd like to hire you, Larry," said the interviewer. "Can you start on Thursday?" When I readily accepted his offer, he continued. "Here's a list of things you'll need to do before starting." After I signed some paperwork, I walked out of the office with a light step. *My first real job! Things really are going to work out!*

Leaving the county offices, I walked across the street to the Post Office and bought ten stamps, adding the change to my flat wallet. *That just about cleaned me out. Guess I won't be calling Carolyn any time soon.*

As I drove home, I made a mental list of things to do before I started my job in two days: mow the lawn at the church, visit the shut-ins, clean out the garage for Mom. *Maybe it will help me keep my mind off the distance to Oregon.*

I managed to keep my engagement quiet until Mom was off on Thursday and home for dinner. After she asked a couple of questions, I confessed that I had proposed to Carolyn. My parents stared at me, their forks in mid-air. Dad finally said, "You WHAT?" Mom seemed unable to comprehend.

"I asked Carolyn to marry me, and she accepted," I repeated.

Mom finally found her voice. "How did you ever have the nerve to ask her so quickly?"

"I'm not sure, but that's what happened."

"I'm actually not surprised," Mom said. "I saw the way you two looked at each other back in July."

"Humph," was all Dad could muster.

When the dishes were done and the evening TV routine underway, I went to my bedroom and started a letter to Carolyn.

September 8, 1966
Dear Carolyn,
Please forgive me for not writing sooner. I got the job! In the last few days, I've been interviewed again, had a physical exam and fingerprinted, among other things. I've already worked one day.

The trip down from Portland was uneventful. Which reminds me—how long do you have off for Christmas and spring breaks? Since I can't get off work for more than two days in a row until my next vacation, do you think your mother would let you come down here at Christmas? I found out that excursion airfare is only $68 round trip!

Don't let anyone get close to hear, because I am going to whisper something in your ear. Listen closely, these are some words you'll want to hear. Get really close...I LOVE YOU!!!!

I pray for you continually, and hope a letter arrives from you soon. I love you with all my heart. You have put me in a state of euphoria.

Love, Larry

A pale blue letter finally arrived in our mailbox, with a faint fragrance that stirred my blood. She must have dabbed the envelope with her perfume, unaware of what it would do to me.

September 13, 1966
Dear Larry,
Affectionate greetings from 138 pounds of sore muscle! I think all the walking, bowling, and our little wrestling match with my nephews finally caught up with me. Ouch!

Mom keeps asking questions about us and our plans. Dad thinks you're not a push-over, and Mother thinks you're a sensible young man. Just right for their "baby," if I do say so myself! I haven't told them much about our plans, but drop hints occasionally so they'll get used to the idea.

We drove down to Oceanside to visit my aunt (Mom's sister) and while we were there, Dad and I had a lovely walk on the beach together. It was bittersweet, because I realized that there won't be too many more of those times.

I seem to be plagued by a strange illness recently which has lowered my IQ by at least 13 ½ points—I've been doing such dumb things. Lovesickness has strange symptoms. I know one thing for sure, I miss you! Write soon...

I think of you constantly.

Love, Carolyn

In my first week of work, I discovered that I was one of the few men employed by the county Social Service department, and the only male in my office. Most of the women paid no attention to me, especially since my desk was behind a partition. At times, when the conversation in the outer office got a little too personal, or the gossip was too catty, I would rattle a desk drawer or clear my throat. That would elicit giggles and comments: "Oh, I forgot, there's a man around," or "Just wait until you're married, Larry."

The busyness and novelty of my new job weren't enough to keep my mind from frequently wandering north, and the high point of my day was opening the mailbox when I got home from work. Carolyn's next letter contained unexpected news.

September 16, 1966
Hi again, from Room 309, Todd Hall.
This room is always reserved for the dorm president, and although it's small, I have it all to myself. There's even a little balcony that overlooks the street.

I heard some pretty shocking news today. Paul has been "dismissed" from the Portland church. He was told there wasn't enough money to pay his salary. Em and Paul are devastated. It makes me worry about your connection with Rev. Black through the church in Hanford.

Larry, no matter how much I love you, if marrying you involves getting into situations like this, I don't want to have any part of it. I couldn't bear to see you hurt like Paul and Emily have been. I know God has called you, and you believe your place is there. You have tremendous potential, Larry. I pray that nothing will ever change what is between us, but now is the time to get things ironed out, even if it's difficult through letters.

I know one thing. If anything ever happens to separate us, I'll be an old maid and spend my life in the South American jungle, because I could never find anyone who could take your place. You may laugh at this, but I mean it with all my heart.

I'll be praying for you.
Love, Carolyn

I read and re-read her words, feeling like I'd been slugged. I was surprised that Carolyn felt so strongly about my association with Rev. Black. While my position at Grace Chapel was reasonably secure, I had to realize that it could be taken away as easily as it had been given.

Carolyn's implied threat to break off our relationship stunned me, and as I answered her letter, my heart was heavy with anxiety and doubt.

September 20, 1966
Dearest Carolyn,

I read your letter a few minutes ago, and your distress was apparent. My love, your reaction surprises me. I know you're concerned about Paul and Emily, but I really don't think it will have that much effect on me here. Your letter sounds like you're giving me an ultimatum: you or my involvement with the church. Can't these two things be reconciled?

God has put me here, and this is where I must remain. When God releases me, I'll leave, but not before. Remember, I told you that God will always come first in my life, no matter what. Please, don't force me to a decision between you and God's will.

Carolyn, knowing you has brought peace, contentment and joy to me. I don't like even the hint of a life without you. Please write soon.

With all my love,
Larry

Chapter 15

Carolyn

Bright moonlight streamed through the open French door to my tiny balcony, laying a pale yellow pattern across my bedspread. My top-floor private room was in a prime location at the front of Todd Hall women's dormitory, overlooking the main street of the campus.

Tonight I found it difficult to appreciate the setting. The full moon and romantic music on my record player made me melancholy. When Andy Williams started crooning "Full Moon and Empty Arms," I changed the record to an upbeat Tijuana Brass album.

> **Current Culture**
> **September 1966**
>
> - *Mission: Impossible* debuts on CBS
> - U.S. Treasury Department reports that the Vietnam War costs $4.2 billion per month
> - Best-selling paperback book: *The Lord of the Rings*, by JRR Tolkien
> - Board and room at state college in Oregon: $688 per year
> - Cup of coffee in a restaurant: 10 cents

The two weeks I'd been back at college had been filled with activity: endless meetings, faculty-student discussion groups, Parent's Day, crazy dorm shenanigans and numerous other events and responsibilities. I had yet to fall asleep before midnight, and it was usually much later. In the rare quiet moments, my increasing tiredness left me depressed and sad.

I longed to hear Larry's voice and talk things over on the phone, but my budget would only allow for one phone call a month; letters would have to do. While I re-read his last letter to me, I was struck again by his integrity and was sorry that my emotional reaction had caused him anxiety.

I pulled a sheet of thin blue paper out of the box of new stationery, and reached for my favorite pen.

September 21, 1966
Dear Larry,
I'm sorry that I let myself get carried away when I told you about Rev. Black firing Paul. I shouldn't write letters when I'm upset. I didn't mean to imply that this would force a decision. You must accomplish what you are called to do, and I will never try to come between you and God. I know that would be the end of <u>us</u>. I don't understand all that's going on and how it affects you, so I guess I'm going to have to trust God to work it all out. I'm sorry it came across as such a big deal in my letter.

It's 12:30 a.m. and things are really hopping around here. There are about 400 freshmen outside running around yelling, screaming, doing calisthenics, and sweeping the streets.

I'm still not used to seeing the little brass plaque, "Dormitory President" on the door to my room. I'm glad I had a preview of this role last spring when I had to step in after the former president eloped during spring break. We have 187 girls in the dorm this year. Things will be okay once a routine is established but they need to let off steam before classes start.

I'm hoping to arrange my work schedule for eight hours a week at the Instructional Materials Center. That will give me $35.00 a month for incidentals and savings...

As I started a second sheet, I heard a soft knock on my door. June, a sophomore student I'd roomed with the year before, stood in the doorway, blinking back tears. "Can I talk to you, Carolyn?" she gulped. I motioned her into my room, casually covering the letters on my desk with a book.

"What's happening?" I asked.

"Jim just got his draft notice. He has to report in three weeks!" Her words were barely coherent and she collapsed on my bed, sobbing. I handed her some tissues and sat beside her until her sobs subsided.

"He wants to get married before he leaves," she eventually said. "But school is just starting, and we'd have hardly any time together, and then what would I do?"

"Have you talked about marriage before?" I asked.

"Well, sort of. You know how it is. But he never actually asked me to marry him until this came up."

"Do you love him?" My question brought a fresh burst of weeping.

"I don't know, Carolyn. I just don't know. I really like him, and we have fun together, but I don't know if I want to spend my whole life with him." Her sobs continued as I waited, sensing there was something more. "But what if he ends up in Vietnam?" Anguish distorted her pretty face as she took a deep breath. "He told me he can't bear the thought of going away to war without ever making love to me. But he knows I want to wait to be married for sex, so when I stalled, that's when he asked me to marry him." She wiped her eyes again. "It's all so confusing!"

We talked for a long time, and finally prayed together. As I closed the door behind her, my heart was heavy for her, but my thoughts were on Larry. *At least I don't have to worry about my boyfriend going off to war.*

Back at my desk, I continued writing to Larry.

...I've just had my third visitor in the last two hours. I'll tell you about it sometime...

Paul and Em were at the dorm when I got home from church Sunday. They are pretty upset about Paul's dismissal, but believe it's for the best in the long run. People from church have phoned them expressing concern. Apparently Rev. Black told the congregation that Paul and Em were traveling in meetings. Why didn't he tell the truth--that he fired them?

Tomorrow my freshman roomie Tricia will be arriving. She's the only one I will tell the full story about US. It will be good to be able to tell someone all about you...

My letter was interrupted again by another knock. I opened my door to see our housemother, Mrs. Anderson, looking distressed.

"I've just gotten some bad news," she said. "Would you come downstairs for a few minutes?" I followed her to her ground-floor apartment, and she closed the door after motioning me to a chair.

"My mother had a stroke." She dabbed her eyes with a crochet-edged handkerchief before continuing. "I have to leave first thing in the morning for Roseburg."

"I'm so sorry, Mrs. Anderson."

"It's bad timing, right at the beginning of the year, but I've spoken with the Dean, and he's agreed that you and a couple of seniors can take my place until I return." I blinked in surprise, my mind flooding with thoughts of all her duties.

"Here's a master key to the dorm," she continued, handing me the heavy key. "I know you'll do a good job while I'm gone. Other than locking up at night and taking turns staying in my apartment in case of emergencies, it's mostly bandaging skinned knees and soothing broken hearts." She smiled fleetingly, her eyes anxious.

I gave her a quick hug. "Please don't worry about us, we'll be fine." My confident words didn't match the apprehension I felt as I trudged slowly up the stairs. Back at my desk, I read what I'd written to Larry before adding a short ending.

...I just got a surprise. I'll be playing housemother for the weekend. Mrs. Anderson is leaving in the morning to be with her mother, who just had a stroke. This would be a challenge at any time in the year, but in the first week, it's going to be especially tricky. Fortunately I have a good team of leaders to share the responsibility!

Before this installment letter stops being coherent, I'd better close. It's 1:30 a.m. and I need to head downstairs to check in the last few stragglers before I lock the doors at 2:00.

Love and kisses, Carolyn

The following day, I earned extra money helping with registration. The lines of students with their penciled-in forms seemed endless. It took patience to deal with scared freshmen who thought their life depended on a certain schedule, and diplomacy to work with returning students who thought they could bully or sweet-talk their way into classes already closed. By the end of the day I was more than ready to head to the privacy of my room. I stopped at the mailroom just inside the dorm entrance, and was delighted to find a letter from Larry in my box.

September 22, 1966
Dear Carolyn,
Things seem to be working out great here. My job as a social service worker is very interesting. I enjoy the challenge of finding the resources for people who have significant needs. The thing I <u>don't</u> enjoy is having to dish out tax money for people who feel that the government owes them a living, and who don't seem to be trying to make their life work.

The biggest issue with the job is not getting any vacation for a year. What could I do to convince your parents to let you come here for Christmas? I can't stand the thought of not seeing you for longer than three months.

Since coming back from Portland, I've really dug into my Bible study and research. God has given me some very unusual and wonderful sermons that the congregation seems to enjoy.

There is only one thing lacking in my joy: YOU! Do you realize our wedding is still eleven months away? I'll need the patience of Job to survive. Write soon, Carolyn. Your letters are a treasure to me.

Sincerely yours, Larry Wade

PS: How's that for an ending? Try this one instead...With all my love, Larry

The following day, there was another letter in my box postmarked "Hanford, CA." Since there were several girls in the mail room, I nonchalantly put the letter in my pocket and headed upstairs to my room. As soon as the door closed, I ripped open the letter, then sat abruptly on the bed as I read the first lines.

September 24, 1966
Dear Carolyn,

I have some interesting news. My draft board has reclassified me 1-A, which means I could get drafted soon. I will appeal this, and have a good chance of winning. But in case I lose and am forced into the military, would you mind terribly marrying an Army officer?

It's tempting to be discouraged. While the job and the church are going okay, I discovered the church lawn was ruined because it hadn't been watered while I was in Portland, and the pump burned out on the church well. Fortunately, Dad and I were able to install a new pump, but it took us an entire day, and put the church treasury in the red. The lawn will take longer to recover.

I miss you! There are times that I want to be near you, just talk to you and touch you. At work I catch myself wishing I had you to go home to.

I need to close for now and finish tomorrow's sermon.

Good night, Princess. Sweet dreams.

PS. I wish it were just a few days to our wedding, rather than almost a year.

I leaned back against the wall, closed my eyes, and tried to breathe normally. *This could change everything!* While his reclassification had always been a possibility, it was the last thing I wanted to hear. Larry seemed confident that his appeal would be successful, but I had a foreboding that there might be another outcome.

In September it was easy to say that I trusted God for our future, but now that we were eight hundred miles apart, fear whispered in my ear. I thought about my recent conversation with June, and blinked back tears. *Will I face the same challenge?*

I knew that if I didn't find a distraction, I'd end up a blubbering mess, so I headed downstairs and across the campus. When I knocked on the door of my boss's office at the Instructional Materials Center, Mrs. Roberts greeted me warmly. "Welcome back, Carolyn. How was your summer?"

"Great," I replied. "Did you travel again this summer?"

"Yes, to the East Coast, to take in all the historical sights. It was wonderful." After we chatted for a few minutes, I asked her about the student work schedule

"Since you're the senior member of my staff," she answered, "you get first pick of hours to work." I quickly filled in eight slots that fit around the seventeen hours of classes I'd be taking.

At the campus bookstore, I collected the heavy stack of textbooks for my classes. *I hope this doesn't break my budget.* It was a relief to hear the student clerk say, "That will be $24.50." Financially, I'd be okay this year. Emotionally? That remained to be seen.

Back in my room, I started expressing my thoughts on paper.

September 26, 1966
Dear Larry,

So you've been reclassified 1-A? What did you do to deserve that? You know, Darling, I wouldn't mind being an officer's wife, a teacher's wife, or a ditch-digger's wife, as long as I am your *wife. If we're together, I'll be happy anywhere in the world.*

I got my first letter from Mom today. She and Dad finally heard about Paul and Emily's dismissal from the church in Portland. Mom wrote: "If you and Larry go ahead with your plans, I hope you will be able to avoid situations like what happened to Paul and Emily." She also wrote about the importance of me finishing school, a constant theme. The tone of her letter makes me think it's very unlikely that Mom and Dad would let me come to California at Christmas. But there's got to be some *way for us to be together!*

My classes (17 credits) and work schedule (8 hours a week) are going to work out well, I think. I also got a nice surprise when my textbooks cost less than I expected. I may actually be able to put some money into a savings account. I wonder if I could think of something special to save for?

I love you! (Big surprise...) I really do, Darling. I realize it more fully each day, and can't thank the Lord enough for the great blessing of our love.

With love and prayers,
Carolyn

By the last week of September, I was ready for a break, and planned to go home for the weekend. But when Tricia asked me to spend the weekend at her apartment, and Mrs. Anderson asked if I'd take care of the dorm Friday night so she could go to the campus movie, I decided to stay on campus.

While I was on duty in Mrs. Anderson's office, chatting with another lonely girl, a freshman burst into the room, looking panic-stricken. "My roommate was throwing up and now she passed out! I don't know what to do!" I spent a tense half hour trying to find the nurse on call, and finally sent a girl to the theater to get Mrs. Anderson. Once she was back on duty, I started knocking on doors to find someone to loan me a car so I could drive the sick girl to the closest doctor, several miles away in the town of Independence.

By the time the girl was treated and we got back to Monmouth, it was close to midnight. I walked the six blocks to Tricia's apartment, where I knew she'd be waiting up. After a long talk while we snacked on goodies she'd brought from home, I started writing another letter.

September 30, 1966
Dear Larry,

When I called Mom today to tell her that I wasn't coming home for the weekend, her first question was, "What about the Army?" She was obviously concerned when I told her your news. She also said Emily would be disappointed that I'm not coming home, because they are starting meetings in their home with people who have left Rev. Black's church. I'm not surprised.

I got a catalog from Fresno State today. Did you know that non-resident tuition is a mere $300 per semester? That's a fortune! How are we going to deal with that, Mr. Answer Man?

It's long after midnight, and I'm at Tricia's. It's wonderful that there's at least one person to talk to about you. But I'd rather be talking TO you. It's been just a few weeks since we said goodbye, and it seems like ages. How am I ever going to make it through the next year?

Goodnight, Sweetheart.
Love, Carolyn xxxxoooo

On Monday, I found a fat envelope in my box addressed in Larry's handwriting. Inside, I found a sheet of lined yellow paper from a legal pad, with a message at the top.

September 28, 1966
Dear Miss Cooke,
   Enclosed is a sheet of questions that must be answered promptly. They are examples of possible situations that may arise in life. Be completely honest in your answers, for a severe penalty may be exacted for incomplete or frivolous declarations.
   Thank you very much for your cooperation.
   Sincerely yours, Larry Wade

Below the message was a list of questions. I assumed he was attempting to be cute with the formal tone, but the questions seemed impersonal and very pointed. I read the questions with growing dismay. *Is he kidding? What happens if he doesn't like my answers?* Impatiently, I tossed aside the yellow paper and opened the letter.

Hi Carolyn,
   How are you doing now? Is your loneliness abating a little, or is it worse?
   I'm on break at work now, and is it ever noisy! The office is huge, and I feel almost henpecked. I've never heard so many marriage problems discussed in my life. Since the women forget I'm here, I sure get an earful of what they think of their husbands and boyfriends.
   Write soon, please!
   Larry
   PS: If you take up smoking or drinking, I'll disown you. I hate cigarettes and despise alcohol. Also, don't expect too much sympathy for your coffee habit.
   PPS: I really, do, really, really, really LOVE YOU!!

In spite of his protestations of love, the questionnaire and his comment about coffee bothered me.

Does he expect me to be perfect? I know he has high standards of character and behavior, but if these are his expectations, I don't think I can measure up.

I fell asleep that night feeling unhappy and discouraged.

·

Chapter 16

Larry

"You won't believe what my husband did last night." The voice from the other side of the welfare office was bright with laughter.

"Try me," invited another female voice. I did my best to focus on paperwork and block out the rest of the conversation.

It seemed strange that my life could settle back into a routine so quickly, after the life-altering events of September. My job kept me busy and I especially enjoyed cashing the paycheck. I was often frustrated by the endless paperwork, red tape and inane regulations, but enjoyed meeting with elderly

> **Current Culture**
> **October 1966**
>
> - Volkswagen announces that their new cars will have an optional AM Radio/8-track player
> - The Baltimore Orioles sweep the LA Dodgers in the 63rd World Series
> - 173 US aircraft bomb North Vietnam
> - Cost of Person-to-Person phone call: $1.80 per minute

clients. Most had worked hard throughout their lives, and deserved every service and benefit I could provide for them.

Opening the mailbox when I got home from work, I pulled out another pale blue letter. This time there was a pink lip-print on the back of the envelope. As I walked down the driveway, I inhaled Carolyn's fragrance and tried to visualize her face as I ripped open the envelope. If I couldn't reach out and hold her hand, the letter was a welcome substitute. *How in the world will I make it through nearly a year?*

October 3, 1966
Dear Larry,

Last night I wrote you a letter, then decided not to send it. We promised to be honest with each other, so here goes. When I got your letter yesterday I was very upset. I felt like I had to come up with just the right answers to all your questions or our engagement was off.

I realize that there are many issues that we should discuss before marriage, but we have almost a year to deal with them. Can't we just take our time and enjoy some romance right now? You said yourself that we both tend to be too serious.

It's virtually impossible to have a marriage without some disagreements or challenges. We'll face those when they come, but we have the advantage of knowing that this relationship is God's will for us.

*You'll have to be patient with me, Larry. I don't like being forced into a corner. I don't mean that **you** have forced me, but my family and people in the church wanted to have us engaged and married before we even met, and that bothered me. Once we met, I fell in love with you, but sometimes I still feel cornered. I'm trying to work through a lot of emotions. Can you give me time to do that?*

Love, Carolyn

PS: I don't think there's the slightest chance that I'll take up drinking or smoking. As for my "coffee habit," I don't consider it a habit. I can take it or leave it. But you're going to have to accept me whether my likes and dislikes coincide with yours, or we'd better not consider marriage. We can't possibly agree on everything!

When I felt the emotion behind Carolyn's words, I knew I had to splurge and make a phone call. Letters were proving to have significant limitations. Carolyn had apparently taken my questionnaire more seriously than I had intended. Whether it had arrived on a bad day, or it was simply too blunt, I needed to reassure her of my love and acceptance.

She had told me to call Person-to-Person, since the dorm phone would be answered by someone in the first-floor office, then transferred to an extension on the third floor. Whoever answered there would try to find her. The first three times I called, I waited nearly ten minutes while various girls tried to locate Carolyn. Finally on my fourth attempt, the girl who answered said, "Oh, now I remember. She's in a meeting." I reluctantly gave up my attempts to connect, and started another letter.

October 6, 1966
Dear Carolyn,

I tried to call you several times tonight, but just couldn't catch you in. I really wanted to hear your voice.

Your letter of October 3 made me realize how challenging it's going to be to communicate through letters. I appreciate your honesty about your feelings in reading the questionnaire. Please don't be afraid to tell me how you feel. Remember, above all else, I am your friend. I don't want you to hold things back and have your hurt become worse.

Please forgive me for coming across harsh or demanding. I had intended the questionnaire to be more light-hearted than it appeared to you, and I'm sorry.

On to happier thoughts. Do you have a picture of yourself that you can send me? I'll accept any photograph, snapshot, etching or carving of you. Right now I have a distinct and vivid picture of you in my mind, but I'm not sure it will stay that way.

Goodbye, Sweetheart. Don't forget the boy with the sad brown eyes.

I will love you always,
Larry

The next day, my heart thudded when I saw a long white envelope in the mailbox beneath Carolyn's blue letter. I decided to get the bad news over first, and tore open the letter from the U.S. Government. My stomach lurched when I read the summons to appear before the local draft board at 10:30 a.m.

on Monday, October 17th. At that time, the letter said, I could state my case for an appeal of my 1-A draft classification.

My first thought was to not mention the appointment to Carolyn. I quickly discarded that idea--it didn't fit with our commitment to honesty. But I was concerned about how she would take this potentially bad news when we were still working through the questionnaire fiasco.

I took Carolyn's letter to my bedroom to read in private. It was the first letter since her emotional response to my questionnaire.

October 5, 1966
Dear Larry,

My friend Carol brought your letter to me in English Lit class today. I can't tell you much about the lecture, except that the topic was "Pagan versus Christian ideals in 'Beowulf'."

Darling, I hope you understand what I was trying to get across in my last letter. I didn't mean to be critical, but things often come across harsher on paper. I've answered your questionnaire as honestly as I could, and I'm enclosing it with this letter. I hope it will open more communication between us.

I'm really pleased with all my classes. I got an "A" on the first pop quiz in English Lit. Today in Social Dance we learned the waltz, which I enjoyed. There's an international student in the class who chased me for several months last year. He thinks he's a real lady-killer, but he's rather scary. Plus, he can't dance, <u>at all</u>! It's like dancing with a scarecrow. All the girls in the class dread being paired with him. When it was my turn to dance with him, we stumbled along for a while, and then he said, "Why don't you lead, Carolyn." Unfortunately, he can't <u>follow</u> either!

Today has been hectic. After classes I had three appointments, then spent from 5:00 to 8:30 in meetings. I had hoped to relax in the TV room to watch "Breakfast at Tiffany's", but couldn't spare the time. I can't wait until next year when all my extra-curricular activities will be concerned with my favorite pastime, namely Larry Wade.

My brain is really in low gear now. It's times like this, when my mind and body are exhausted, that I wish I could have your arms around me and fall asleep with my head on your shoulder. Until then, Darling, remember that I love you more than I can say.

Carolyn

As I unfolded my questionnaire with her answers written in, I realized I was holding my breath. I exhaled slowly as I realized that my apprehension was unfounded.

Question	Answer
Are you willing to do without a home of your own and live in rented apartments or homes for a few years?	Yes, for however long the Lord wants us to live that way.
Would you be willing to stay in a place that was seemingly God-forsaken for the rest of your life if God asked it?	Yes, God would be there, no matter how it <u>seemed.</u>
What would be your reaction if you found yourself forced to remain poor all of your life. Would you be unhappy?	I would be thankful that I had been brought up to deal with less than others. I will be happy as long as I am in God's perfect will for me, regardless of how, where or what.
Would you be willing to be a sacrificing missionary all your life, even when everything is going wrong?	If this is the Lord's will, certainly. But if that is the case, I don't think that <u>everything</u> would be going wrong.
Would you be willing to live "out of a suitcase" for months on end to be with me?	Yes. A wife's place is with her husband, no matter where he is or what he is doing, unless it's physically impossible.
What do you do when someone pulls you out of bed to do something at two or three o'clock in the morning?	It depends on who pulls me out, and for what purpose.

If I were asked to play a secondary role to someone else, and never did anything "great," what would you do?	Deeds of "greatness" are not always obvious. The person who is truly great is the one who knows his place in life, does his best for his cause, and is happy no matter how small a task, whether in the shadow or in the spotlight. I will stand by you as a wife should, whatever comes.

I smiled at Carolyn's response to the question about being pulled out of bed, and sat back against my brass headboard, relieved and grateful for her honesty. Her answers couldn't have satisfied me more if I had scripted them myself, and her candor and humor gave them extra significance.

She's even more perfect for me than I thought before. Thank You, Lord, for Your amazing blessing.

"Dad," I said on Saturday, "how about if I mow the lawns at the retirement village today?" His leg was propped up on a footstool in the living room, while he stared at the TV screen. Relief followed surprise across his face.

"That'd be great, Larry. I should be back on my feet next week."

Two days earlier, doctors at a hospital in Fresno had removed a benign growth from his leg, and he was still unsteady and in pain. I knew he didn't want to lose his customers, and I was glad to have extra work to keep me busy. After mowing our own lawn, I loaded the equipment into Dad's pickup and headed toward town.

The homes at Lutheran Retirement Village had large yards, and I was hot and sweaty after three hours. Each customer gave me five dollars. After taking out tithe, I would have a nice amount for my new "Household" fund. I knew that when Carolyn and I finally got married, we'd need lots of little things to set up housekeeping.

Leaving the Village, I rolled down the windows of the truck and headed for the church. I cleaned the bathrooms, mopped the floors, mowed the lawn and trimmed some shrubs.

When I finally got home, I was surprised to see my uncle's car in the driveway. Uncle Aub and Aunt Helen lived in San Pedro, four hours away near Los Angeles. They only came to Hanford once or twice a year, so it wasn't a drop-in visit. When I walked into the house to greet them, I saw my grandmother also.

"Hi, Grandma," I said. "Hi, Uncle Aub, Aunt Helen. What's the occasion?"

"Well, I heard Monk had something cut off his leg, so it was a good excuse to talk Aub into driving me up." Grandma's voice was more gravelly than I remembered. She had aged since I'd last seen her, and the deep smoker's wrinkles in her cheeks were more pronounced.

"I'm glad you made it. Sorry Mom's not here, she's working swing shift today."

"We'll catch up with Midge tomorrow. Come and sit." She patted the empty spot on the couch beside her. "I hear you have some news."

"You might want to wait until I clean up, Grandma. I've been working out in the hot sun all afternoon."

"Well, don't take too long. Monk's already talked out and looks like he needs a nap."

I ran a shallow bath in the tub and washed the sweat and grass stains off my body. Toweling off quickly, I put on clean clothes and sat down on the couch beside my grandmother.

"What's this I hear about you getting engaged?" She didn't beat around the bush.

"It's true, Grandma. I'm going to marry a girl from Oregon."

"Couldn't you find someone around here?"

"Not like this girl. She's special." I couldn't keep the grin off my face.

"And Monk tells me you're preaching at the church now."

"That's right. I was over there working this afternoon."

"You know you come from a long line of preachers, Larry," Grandma said. "Must be in your blood somehow."

"Really? I'm not sure I know all the details. What do you mean?"

"Well, your Great-Great-Grandad preached up a storm in the Disciples of Christ revival. Then when the Methodists got going, your Great-Grandpa was a circuit-riding preacher. Later when the Nazarenes were getting started, your Great Uncle was in the middle of it." She paused, looking at me intently before finishing. "It's time we had another preacher in the family, and I guess you're it."

While I had heard bits and pieces of family history over the years, this was the first time I'd heard details of my preacher ancestors. Grandma wasn't a church-goer, but I heard pride in her voice when she talked about me carrying on the family calling. It was the closest thing to approval I'd received from her in my twenty-two years.

Dad came back into the living room and the conversation went another direction. I excused myself and went to the kitchen. Since Mom hadn't expected their visit, I'd have to figure out something to fix for dinner. In the refrigerator and pantry I found the makings of enchiladas, and got busy fixing a meal. As I worked, I thought about Grandma's information. *Thanks for including me in the lineup of Wade family preachers, Lord.*

When dinner was over and the others headed for the back patio, Dad said, "Oh, by the way, there's a blue letter here somewhere, probably for you." He rifled through some mail on the top of the bookcase, and grinned as he handed me the envelope. I shook my head at his teasing, and I headed to my room to read the latest from Carolyn.

October 8, 1966
Dear Larry,

Some noise rudely awakened me this morning from a dream about you. I tried to go back to sleep and recapture it—but it didn't work. I lay there for a long time daydreaming. Later I went downstairs and found your letter in my box. I didn't realize how much your letters mean until yesterday when I didn't get one. I felt lost all day.

An exciting thing happened today—I found out that I'm one of three finalists from our dorm for Homecoming Princess! In the next few weeks, I'll go through a series of interviews with faculty and students. I think I stand a fair chance of winning, and to be honest, I really want this. The one thing that dampens my excitement is that you're not here to share moments like this.

I don't ever tire of having you say, "I love you." I appreciate having friends here to talk with when I'm lonely, but they're a poor substitute for you. So many times I don't want to be with others, but just retreat to my room, put on some nice music and try to recall a look, a word, a tone of voice, your touch on my face or my hair, a moment shared without words.

I love you, Larry, and I hope that God is very near to you and will bless you beyond measure.

Carolyn

I stared off into space after re-reading the last lines. *How in the world did I ever deserve this?* After all my years of loneliness, Carolyn's love was no small miracle.

After church the next day, I made my usual stops to visit those who hadn't been able to attend the service. Mrs. Garland was eighty-two years old, and spent hours each week sewing dresses for girls in an orphanage in Mexico. She fit the "Grandma" stereotype perfectly, with soft wrinkled cheeks, curly white hair, and a flowered apron over her ample frame.

"I heard you have a girlfriend in Portland!" she crowed as I came through her front door.

"That's true. I guess there are no secrets in this town." I wasn't sure how she really felt about this news, as she had frequently tried to match me up with her granddaughter.

"So tell me about her," she said, her eyes twinkling.

"She's pretty, blonde and blue-eyed, plays the piano, and loves the Lord," I started. "She's in college right now, studying English. She plans to be a teacher, and maybe go to the mission field one day. She's also Emily Mueller's younger sister."

"Oh, my," exclaimed Mrs. Garland. "If she's half as good as Emily, she'll make you a wonderful wife." Her genuine pleasure and approval made me feel good the rest of the day. I gave my sermon that evening with boldness and confidence. *If only I could look out and see Carolyn smiling at me from one of the pews!*

After dinner on Monday I sat at the kitchen table and tuned out the television while I wrote an answer to Carolyn's latest letter.

October 11, 1966
Dear Princess (I hope!)

If you're not chosen Homecoming Princess, I'll demand a recount! They'd be crazy to think that anyone would be better than you. I'm excited for you, of course, but sad to think that I won't be there to escort you.

This has been a very interesting day. It started like a normal day, until a group of people from the county came to inspect our offices. The way they were peering into everything, I almost expected one of them to say, "Step away from the desk, put your hands on the top, and lean over." There's some kind of shakedown going on.

Then at 3:00 p.m. we got a surprise order to pack up all our things, as we are moving to different offices tomorrow. As you can imagine, the rest of the day was very hectic.

When I got home, the little boys down the road came over and wanted me to play croquet with them. After we finished our game, I visited a member of my congregation who is ill.

The aroma on today's letter was fantastic. Only one trouble—it wasn't on that pretty soft neck of yours. It made me stop and stare off into space and think of Portland at night, long walks, etc.

Well, Love, it's been a long day. I'm still hoping there's a way to see you at Christmas. We've got to figure out a way!

I really and truly do love you.
Larry

I woke on October 17th with a sense of dread, remembering my appointment with the draft board. I tried to look confident as I walked through the door of the recruiting office, but I didn't know what to expect. So much hinged on the results of this meeting. Before I'd met Carolyn, I had actually looked forward to doing my duty and fighting for my country, but now it was the last thing I wanted.

The presiding officer's manner was stern as he leafed through the documents on the table before him. "I see here that you're asking for a ministerial exemption."

"Yes, I'm currently the pastor of Grace Chapel."

"I see. And does the church support you financially?"

"No, not really."

"So how do you support yourself, Mr. Wade?"

"I'm a social welfare worker for Kings County."

He looked at the other two members of the review board, who both raised their eyebrows. "Really? In that case, your appeal is irrelevant."

"Why is that?" I asked in surprise.

"You can't hold another job besides your church and get a draft deferment. It's right here in the regulations."

I was stunned, speechless. *Why didn't someone tell me this?* Finally I blurted out, "Can I still continue with my appeal?"

"Only if you're not employed except by your church." He shuffled the papers in his hands, then looked up at me. "Considering what you've told us today, your 1-A classification stands. You'll need to go to Fresno later this month for your induction physical. We'll send a notice in the mail." I stood uncertainly, and he dismissed me with an impatient wave. I turned and walked out of the recruiting office, then sat in my car staring blankly ahead.

Lord, you knew this all the time. Help me trust you.

Reluctant to deal with questions from my co-workers, I drove slowly through the back streets of Hanford, thinking of Carolyn and our future. If I got drafted, it would change everything for us and delay our wedding indefinitely. She had expressed a strong faith in God's providence, but how would she handle this twist? After her emotional reaction to Paul's firing, I dreaded telling her this news. *Lord, she's going to need a lot of grace!*

I desperately wanted to talk to her, but couldn't depend on the dorm phone system. That night I sat on my bed, pen in hand, wondering how to begin my letter.

Chapter 17

Carolyn

Raindrops traced an abstract pattern on the windows of the bus, nearly obscuring the Portland streets. I was startled when the bus turned onto Hawthorne Street and then down some of the side streets where Larry and I had walked just six weeks earlier. A wave of emotion came with the poignant memories and I turned toward the window so the woman next to me wouldn't see my sudden tears. *Of all the streets between Portland and Gresham, why is the bus taking this one?*

**Current Culture
October 1966**

- LSD is declared illegal in California
- President Johnson visits troops in South Vietnam
- West Coast Airlines flight crashes near Mt. Hood, killing all 18 aboard
- Top TV shows: *Bonanza, Andy Griffith, Red Skelton*
- Kellogg's Cornflakes 12-oz package sells for 25 cents

Mom had asked me to come home for the weekend, and I didn't mind getting away from the dorm for a few days. I'd skipped a couple of Friday morning classes, caught the early bus in Monmouth, and changed in Salem to a north-bound bus. When I got to Portland I bought myself lunch and did some shopping before catching another bus to Gresham to meet Mom and Dad.

Saturday morning, my attempt to sleep in was thwarted when Mom opened my bedroom door and tossed the cat onto my bed. Sleepily, I sat up and said, "Okay, I get the message, I'll get up."

"Tea's ready in the kitchen," she said with a half-smile. I pulled on my bathrobe and carried the cat into the kitchen. While I stirred honey into my tea, Mom started filling me in on the latest neighborhood doings, her Bible study, and family news. Eventually she asked, "So what's the latest from Larry?"

"He has his appeal with the Draft Board this week. We're trusting God for a good outcome."

"Your father and I have been praying about that. I'd hate to see you as an Army wife."

"If that happens, God will give me grace. By the way, Larry's grandmother came for a visit recently, and told him about other preachers in the family."

"Really?" Mom was definitely interested.

"Apparently he comes from a long line. I don't remember all the details-- you'll have to ask him about it sometime."

"Does that mean that he's coming back for a visit soon?"

"Not likely," I said regretfully. "He won't get any vacation from his job for almost a year."

She seemed to consider the implications of this news, and as if reading my mind, she said, "Don't get any ideas about going to California to visit him. He needs to talk to your father before you can do that."

I started to reply, but kept my thoughts to myself, unwilling to let an argument spoil my short weekend at home. Fortunately, the arrival of my sister Priscilla and her family distracted us both.

"Hi, little sister. How's school?" Priscilla added a hug to her greeting.

"Pretty good. Busy, as usual.

"I hope you're getting lots of letters from California."

"There's a stack growing on my desk."

"I'm so happy for you!" she said, giving me another hug.

The rest of the weekend went by quickly, and soon it was Sunday evening, and I was back at Todd Hall.

My feet were wet from splashing rain Monday morning when I got back to the dorm after early classes. I was relieved to find a letter from Larry. My apprehension since his last letter was well-founded, and I was glad I'd waited to open my mail in the privacy of my room.

October 17, 1966
Dearest Carolyn,
The most important news must come first. I appeared before the Draft board, and guess what? I am still 1-A. I will have to take a physical in Fresno sometime this month.

It seems that there is a regulation that states, "No person shall be qualified as 4-D if he holds any position of employment besides that of a minister." Why didn't someone tell me this before? So in order to continue with my appeal to the State Board of Appeals in Sacramento, I had to terminate my job as a social worker. By the time you get this letter, I will no longer be employed.

About now you are probably screaming, "What about us?" You know, Carolyn, I have a feeling that in the long run, you and I are going to be happier because of this. Don't ask me to explain, because I can't, it's just a feeling.

God is working out something in all this, but I can't see it yet. I know he has called me to preach, and I know He is working for us and our future plans, so somehow this is all tied together.

Suppose I do get drafted? It will just make me twist your arm and make you agree to an earlier wedding date. I don't know how you feel, but the past month apart has dragged by like a slow snail on crutches. Every time I look at your picture or smell the perfume on your letters, I want to run up to Monmouth.

Goodnight, love, and please don't worry. Nothing, but nothing can destroy our love for God and our love for each other. I do love you.
Larry

I lay back on the bed, my thoughts churning. Larry's letter raised all sorts of questions. *Without a job, how can he support a wife, or even himself? If his appeal is rejected, how long will it take the military to catch up with him? Will we still be able to get married?*

It was all very well for him to write, "Don't worry," but we hadn't been able to connect on the phone to talk over feelings and concerns. The situation seemed unbearable, and I could only pray: *Lord, give me peace. Help me see Your hand in this.*

I barely had time to absorb the news before I had to meet Mrs. Anderson and another student leader for a shopping trip to spruce up the dorm for Homecoming. It was late evening before I had time to sit on my bed and answer Larry's letter.

October 20, 1966
My Darling,
Your news today set my mind spinning, as I'm sure you knew it would. This development changes things, no matter how we look at it. I know that God has a plan for us, but of course I still wonder what's going to happen. I know God put me here at school for a definite purpose, and I need to carry out my duties here. But beyond that...?

One question this raises—since you quit your job, will you come here for Christmas?

Thanks to you, I may flunk English Lit! Before you get upset, I'll explain. The class is at 11:00 a.m., which is just after our mail arrives. If I get a letter from you, it's often disastrous, because I think about you instead of listening to the lecture. Yesterday I got a "D" on a quiz because I hadn't paid attention to the lecture on "The Miller's Tale" by old Geoffrey Chaucer. It was a nasty story anyway.

It's raining out tonight. Your letter created quite an emotional upheaval. I'm restless, and in spite of being exhausted, I wish I could just put on a coat and boots and walk for a mile. Unfortunately, it's 2:00 a.m., and that's frowned upon at this hour of the night (morning?). On top of that, I just found out we're having a fire drill tonight. It's always at the worst possible time for me.

Right now, I wish more than anything else that you were here with your arms around me. I need a strong shoulder to cry on. With you, I find a peace and happiness and contentment that I didn't dream possible. I could never find this anywhere else, because I believe we were created for each other. My whole being aches to have you hold me. You are the only true reality in my life.

I love you so much, Larry. Words are truly inadequate!

Carolyn

The day after I read Larry's letter about the Draft Board, I got the news that I had lost the title of Homecoming Princess to June, my former roommate. Although I was disappointed to lose, I consoled myself that I wouldn't have to spend a whole month's budget on a formal gown, shoes, gloves, jewelry and beauty shop appointment.

On Saturday morning, I joined student officers from the other dorms to head for Nelscott, a small, faded beach town an hour away on the Oregon Coast. A slightly shabby motel that fit the college budget housed the annual leadership retreat. Horseplay on the beach with other students balanced hours of lively discussions of college issues. As I walked on the beach watching the moon playing tag with the clouds, I longed to share the beauty with Larry. *It looks like we'll have a long wait before we can share such things.*

It was Monday evening before I had enough time to write a decent letter to Larry.

October 24

Dear Larry,

Something fishy is going on around here. Yesterday when I got home from the dorm leaders' retreat, I read your letter, then put on a record and fell asleep. When I woke up three hours later, the record had been removed and the record player turned off. What do you think, Sherlock? Should I plant a mine field or install a burglar alarm? It bothers me a bit that someone would sneak into my room like that, but there's not much I can do about it.

I hate Mondays. Want to know why? 1) I have to get up at 6:30 after the weekend, 2) I usually don't get any mail, 3) I always have a quiz, (today on "The Scarlet Letter" and "Moby Dick"), 4) I have to preside over two meetings, 5) I hate <u>any</u> day without you.

I missed you so much this weekend. The room I shared with other girls at the beach was cozy with a lovely view of the ocean. It made me daydream of the possibility of a honeymoon with you in a place like that.

Today one of my friends asked if you and I had ever talked of marriage. I told her "Yes" and left it at that. It's so hard not to blurt out everything—— especially how wonderful you are!

Now to serious matters. In answer to your question about getting married earlier, I don't want to leave here until I have fulfilled my responsibilities. That said, I would be perfectly willing to marry you before summer, if the Lord worked things out so that my parents agreed, and I felt confident that my responsibilities here were finished. If we are sure that it is the Lord's will, I have absolutely no objection to getting married earlier. I'll get the money for the wedding somehow. After all, I want to get married just as much as you do!

Well, Sweetheart, I suddenly realized the lateness of the hour. I've been praying for you so much lately. Remember, no matter what happens, or when it happens, I'm waiting for you, and I love you with all my heart. Please don't be discouraged. Every day our love becomes a little more a part of me. I couldn't stop loving you now if I tried, and believe me, I'm not going to try!

Goodnight, Darling. I know I won't be able to sleep for a long time.

Carolyn

On Wednesday, I awoke feeling expectant. My birthday! Life had taken such an amazing turn in the past year!

Heading out of my room for the communal shower, I discovered that my door had been decorated during the night. Covering the bottom half was a large paper Champagne glass, with pink bubbles drifting to the top of the door that said "Happy Birthday 21." I didn't have the heart to tell the girls that I had only turned twenty.

When a beautiful bouquet of long-stemmed red roses arrived at the dorm for me that afternoon, I got many envious looks. I couldn't help smiling—it was the first time I'd been sent flowers, and they couldn't have made me happier unless Larry had delivered them in person.

The cafeteria dinner of "Spanish" meatloaf and fried potatoes didn't seem festive, so I invited a friend to join me for a juicy hamburger at one of the local cafes. Back at the dorm, I waited until I thought Larry would be home from his Wednesday night service. With a pocket full of coins, I went to the basement phone booth and dialed Larry's home in Hanford. After more than six weeks, I needed to hear his voice.

"Hi, Larry," I said when he answered the phone.

"Carolyn?" Just the sound of his voice saying my name gave me a shiver.

"Yes, it's really me. How are you?"

"I'm fine." His voice conveyed his continuing surprise. "I didn't expect you to call."

"It's a birthday present to myself."

"Yes, Happy Birthday, by the way."

"Thanks. The flowers are lovely; I'm the envy of every girl in Todd Hall."

"Good! I'm having a little trouble hearing you, could you talk louder?"

"Well, there's a little problem. The phone booth doesn't have a door, and there are lots of girls in the hall."

"Oh, okay. I hope you've had a good day."

"It's actually been a great day, but I kept wishing you were here."

"You know I'd give a lot to be there. The roses will have to take my place for now."

"I smile every time I look at them."

The telephone operator rudely interrupted with her standard line, "Your three minutes are up, do you wish to continue?"

Larry said, "I guess that's it. Take care of yourself, Carolyn, I love you."

Startled at his abrupt farewell, I said "Goodbye, I'll write" just as he hung up. Much later that evening, I wrote him more about my day.

October 26, 1966
Dear Larry,

I forgot to say the most important thing tonight when I called you: I LOVE YOU! I could say it a million times and each time I would feel it ten times stronger. Maybe I shouldn't have called, but I just wanted to hear your voice again. Now my loneliness is much worse. I'm sorry I caught you off guard. As it was, I forgot half what I wanted to say, like "I love you!"

Today has been the most wonderful birthday of my life. Nearly everyone I passed wished me happy birthday, and then when I came back from lunch, your roses had arrived. It's the first time anyone has ever sent me flowers, and they are simply beautiful. Word got out, and girls came to my room all afternoon to see them and tell me how lucky I am. Don't I know it!

After calling you, I finally got back to my room about 9:30. A few minutes later, some girls came to sing Happy Birthday at the top of their lungs, and give me presents and goodies. Then there was a commotion at my door, and about thirty girls were outside, ready to throw me in the shower (the traditional birthday prank). Fortunately, the water pressure on the third floor is pretty weak, so at first I didn't get very wet. When a girl filled the mop bucket and really soaked me, I grabbed it away from her and got her wet. Then I ran into my room and got a squirt-gun (which I had filled previously), and chased everyone down the hall.

One of my favorite gifts was from Emily—a framed photo of you and me that she took in September. I called her to thank her for her thoughtfulness, and also tell her about the beautiful roses you sent.

Thank you for making my birthday extra special. Please don't worry about me, Darling. I'm getting along fine. I'm so busy all the time I hardly have time to think about myself. It's you I'm worried about. I wish you had more to keep you occupied—you'd be happier. But the Lord knows what he is doing. He is our strength, and a very present help in time of need. Larry, I know he is going to work things out for us, and it will be more wonderful than we can think now. Look how he brought us together when we weren't expecting to fall in love.

Must go—mid-terms tomorrow. I miss you terribly. The photo of us Emily sent doesn't really help--it brings back so many memories of being with you.

I love you, Larry.

Carolyn

A couple of days after my birthday I was suddenly hit with loneliness and homesickness. I wanted to talk to Larry again, but my budget couldn't stand another inter-state call, so I called home between classes and work.

I should have known better than surprise Mom in the middle of the day. Her first words were, "You should have waited until after six o'clock when the rates are cheaper." She made a few more negative comments, and by the time I hung up the phone, I was in tears. Once more I vowed not to make myself vulnerable to her disapproval. At the same time, I knew I would eventually succumb to homesickness again, and we'd go through the same cycle once more.

Larry's letters kept me going when college life was overwhelming.

October 26, 1966
Dear Carolyn,

The roses should remind you of my love every time you see them. I asked the florist to send "Happiness" roses, and I hope they are still beautiful.

When you called, I was running bath water, and I assumed it was a pastoral call. When the operator said, "Long distance calling," I still couldn't figure it out. Then when you came on the line, you talked so softly I had trouble hearing your voice. Then my Scotch ancestry kicked in, and I didn't want you to waste money. I'm sorry if I ended the call abruptly. It was wonderful to hear your voice!

I received two letters from you today, and they are very precious to me. You make me feel more love for you than I ever thought possible. I'm going to keep every one of your letters for both of us to read in ten years or so. I pray that the feelings between us will never fade, but simply get stronger.

God is teaching me many valuable lessons in this season. I'm glad you don't have to go through all of them with me. I don't want you to have to put up with too much worry or hurt. If possible, I'll never let anything hurt you.

Last night was another full moon. Guess what (who) I thought about?

Goodnight, my beautiful Princess,
Larry

After midnight on Saturday I was half-asleep studying when there was a knock on my door. I opened it to a dorm-mate and friend from high school looking distressed and disheveled.

"Martie, what's wrong?" I asked. Her face crumpled, and she sat heavily on my bed.

"It's been a horrible evening," she said. "John took me to a party, then ignored me and got drunk. I couldn't find anyone to take me home, so I started walking, and a strange guy started following me. A friend just happened to drive by and gave me a ride back to the party, but I didn't want to go in, so he finally brought me home." She paused as a fresh outburst of tears left her sobbing. "I was hoping that he really cared for me, Carolyn."

I consoled her, but was secretly glad that John had shown his true character. At one time they'd been engaged, but he treated her like dirt. This was the first time she'd seen him since she had broken up with him. She deserved better.

By the time she left, I was too tired to write coherent thoughts, and fell into bed exhausted. Sunday evening I wrote another letter.

October 30, 1966
Dear Larry,

I have the most contented feeling tonight. After dinner, I settled in my room and put on some of my favorite classical music. The only thing that would make me happier would be, 1) if I didn't have a French mid-term tomorrow, and 2) if you were here listening to this beautiful music with me.

I decided to try a different church today, and enjoyed the most intelligent and interesting sermon I've heard in this town. Last week at the church I've been attending, the pastor preached on "the true church" and kept saying "orgasm" instead of "organism." What made it worse was that he said "I think that's the right word..." and then used it again several more times. It was inexcusable (not to mention awkward and embarrassing for all the college students present).

I'm being a good buddy and giving a friend my tickets for the Homecoming concert. I'll help my friends get all dressed up, then console myself by escaping reality in the television room. I've been trying not to feel sorry for myself because you're not here.

I'll have to cut this short. I'm exhausted, and need to study French.

Love, Carolyn

The following night, the view from my balcony included a glowing harvest-orange moon. Raucous laughter floated up from the leaf-strewn sidewalk. As I studied for my last mid-term, I enjoyed a plate of cookies someone had left in front of my door. Closing my French textbook, I leaned on my pillow for a moment, thinking of Larry, and the next thing I knew it was morning.

A few days later I got the letter Larry wrote on Halloween.

October 31, 1966
Dear Carolyn,

Did you see the Great Pumpkin tonight? Since you've been a good girl, you should have gotten a basket of goodies.

Today was peaceful, the kind of day I used to hate. My major task was doing yardwork at home and at the church. Actually, I'm chomping at the bit. If I don't have more to do soon, I'll flip my lid. I may go down and <u>join</u> the armed forces if something doesn't change. At least that would give me something to do!

Tomorrow is that fateful day when I get to stand around in the nude for several hours with dozens of other potential recruits. Such is life!

I keep getting the same message from every direction: 'Trust God, and don't get bitter.' God is teaching me some very valuable lessons. I'm glad I'm able to learn them now. Things are moving slowly, but God has a plan.

It has been less than two months since I last saw you, and it feels like two years! Carolyn, what will it be like if six months pass before we see each other again? If that should be the case, you'd better not let me catch you alone. I'll tackle you, knock you down, and tickle your feet! (Hah!)

Goodnight, Princess.
Larry
PS: I love you

Chapter 18

Larry

I tried to shake off the foreboding that clouded my mind as I turned off my alarm clock on November first. After a quick breakfast of tea and toast, I drove into Hanford. At the bus station I joined a group of apprehensive young men for a one-hour ride to Fresno for our military induction physical. The atmosphere in the bus was very subdued, nothing like the carefree high school band trips I'd enjoyed. For most of the ride, I feigned sleep. Most of the guys were recent high school graduates and I felt decades removed from them.

> **Current Culture**
> **November 1966**
>
> - Actor Ronald Reagan elected governor of California
> - Edward W. Brooke is the first African-American elected to the U.S. Senate
> - *Time* magazine cover article "What's Cooking" features Julia Child
> - Hit song, "Last Train to Clarksville" by the Monkees

At the induction center, we stood in long lines having various body parts and functions examined. The supervising doctor merely grunted when he looked over the paperwork for the guys ahead of me. But after he reviewed my paperwork and did a cursory exam he said, "Better start getting in shape."

When our tests were finished, the sergeant called out names, dividing us into two groups. I was relieved to be in the smaller group, and looked smugly across at the other guys. *Those poor suckers are the next batch of recruits.*

My relief changed to dismay when the sergeant pointed at my group and said, "Congratulations. You all passed the physical." I was stunned. *You mean all those other guys are off the hook?*

The ride home to Hanford was even worse than our morning journey. Several of the "rejects" expressed their relief by taunting the rest of us with horror stories about Vietnam. As I stared out the bus window, I pondered the changes this day's events might bring.

How will Carolyn take this news? Could the path ahead really lead to the jungles of Vietnam? How will Mom and Dad handle having two sons in the Army during wartime? My thoughts scattered in many directions, but kept coming back to the fact that I had put my life in God's hands, and believed that he would control the outcome.

As we passed cotton fields, vineyards and pastures, I considered various ways of wording my letter to Carolyn so the bad news wouldn't be too much of a shock. No matter what words I used, it was still just bad news.

Dad and Mom were just starting dinner when I got home. As I walked in the door, Mom said, "Well? How did it go?"

"I guess you raised me right, Mom. I passed with flying colors."

"Oh no, Larry, really?"

"Yep, flat feet, near-sighted and all."

"Well, I'll be darned," was Dad's only comment, but I knew from the strained silence during the meal that they were both upset and worried.

When Dad settled in the living room with the TV and his cigarette, I helped Mom do the dishes. "I can't believe it, Larry," she said. "I've been so sure you would get a deferment or something else would happen to keep you out of the war."

"I know, Mom, I'm pretty surprised myself. It's not the way I thought things would go."

Mom's voice was shaky as she said, "I really hate the thought of you and Charles both in the Army."

I patted her shoulder. "I'm not gone yet, Mom. My life is in God's hands, and who knows what He's up to?"

"When will you tell Carolyn?" asked Mom.

"Right away," I said, as I put the last glass in the cupboard and hung up the dishtowel. "I'm heading off now to write her a letter."

"I'll be praying for her. It will be a shock."

"I appreciate your prayers, Mom. I have to trust that God has been preparing her."

Wishing again it wasn't so difficult and expensive to make a phone call, I sat on my bed and started to write.

November 1, 1966
Dearest, wonderful Carolyn,

How was your day today? I hope it was as pleasant as your personality.

Now that I've flattered you, I'll tell you the bad news. I am one of the healthiest individuals the Draft Board ever examined. I was one of the select few in my group to pass the physical. Isn't that a great honor?

I know this news isn't what you were hoping to hear. I'm not sure what the Lord is doing, but I am confident that it's all going to work out.

While I was in Fresno today, I checked into Officers' Training School. In the Army it's only three months long, so it's definitely worth applying for. If I'm drafted, I'll do my best to earn a commission, since officers have far better pay and privileges than enlisted men.

Carolyn, more and more through your letters, I am realizing that you are a mature woman. Sometimes I've thought of you as a girl rather than a woman, and tried to protect you from difficult news or some of the harsh realities of life. Please forgive me. From now on, I will fully share my burdens with you, because I know you can help me carry them.

I love you, I love you, I love you. You are even more perfect for me than I imagined. I'll do my best to make up to you for all the lonely days you've had to endure.

Love, Larry

For the next few days I was grateful to be distracted by preparation for a meeting in Madera, a small dairy town about an hour north of Hanford. Our ministry had a list of about forty-five people there who might be interested in our work with an orphanage in Mexico.

On Thursday, I picked up the phone and dialed Jesse. "Can you meet me at the church to help with the invitations for the meeting?"

He hesitated and made a few excuses. Finally I said, "I'll buy you a hamburger afterwards," and he agreed to join me.

My typing skills were better than Jesse's, so I ended up writing all the letters to invite people to come to see movies of the orphanage in Mexico, asking them to bring good used clothing and to pray about a cash donation to the work.

While I typed, Jesse addressed the envelopes, then folded and inserted the letters as they were finished. It was well after noon when we dropped the letters at the Post Office and headed to Jet Burger.

Waiting for our food, I said, "You *will* talk about the orphanage when you show the movies, won't you?"

"Are you kidding me?" Jesse replied. "You know I'm not good in front of people."

"But you're the one who knows the most about the orphanage," I said. "I know you can do it, Jesse. At least give it a shot."

"Maybe...I'll think about it." His reluctance was tempered by a feeble spark of interest.

On the following Friday night, the crowd was small but responsive. Jesse surprised me by speaking enthusiastically about the children as he showed his movies. His stories and heart-warming pictures of the kids brought a very positive reaction.

We drove home late, feeling good about the evening's results. There was a large box with children's clothing in the trunk, and a nice cash offering to send to the Grahams.

The next day's letter from Carolyn lifted my spirits even more. It had obviously been written before she got my news about the draft.

November 3, 1966
Hi Darling,

Today was a big day—we hosted a faculty tea, which was a great success. The dorm living room was decorated nicely with a fire in the fireplace, candles on the mantle, flowers on the tables, and homemade cookies instead of the tasteless things we get from the cafeteria. The cookies went over really well (guess who made them?). I love entertaining like this, and I'm so proud of what "my" girls did. The faculty members thanked us and said they were impressed by our hospitality.

There's so much going on with Homecoming this weekend. In addition to the concert and crowning of the Homecoming court Friday, there's the big game and bonfire competition on Saturday.

Darling, don't even think about us not seeing each other at Christmas. I simply don't believe that will happen. Since you're not working, why can't you come up in December, even for a few days?

Maybe I'd better not let you get me alone next time we see each other. As for being tackled, knocked down and having my feet tickled, you just try it, you monster. I simply demand that the man that I marry must treat me with tender, loving care. That's why I chose you--and you'd better live up to the promise I saw in you!

These last few days I've been too tired to even daydream. But tonight somehow I feel alive again, and I miss you more than ever. Sometimes it's hard to remember all the little things about you, but this evening my memories are excruciatingly real. I have a strange sense that your arms are around me and your lips are on mine.

I must stop...Goodnight, my beloved,
Carolyn

The end of the letter turned my own thoughts to the pleasures of Carolyn's company. Her words about feeling my arms around her and my lips on hers created a painful longing in me. It was one of the many times when our separation seemed unbearable. I had to communicate my thoughts to her.

November 5, 1966
Dear Carolyn,
The full moon is starting to flatten, and it's probably a good thing. Ever since being with you in Portland, my hormones work overtime when the moon is full and the day-dreaming part of my brain is especially active.

It's been less than two months since I saw you, and it seems like two years. What will happen if six months come and go without us being together?

I've gotten several letters addressed to Mr. & Mrs. Larry Wade. How in the world did that start so quickly? I wish they reflected reality!

As you can tell, there's not much going on here. The days drag by, making me wish that <u>something</u> would happen soon.

Carolyn, I once told you that many years ago, crossing the Interstate Bridge between Oregon and Washington, I had a distinct impression that my future wife lived somewhere up that river. In the same way, God has let me know that changes are ahead for me. One of the good changes is a renewal of interest in the church among the neighbors. Then there's the end of my job, and the change in my draft status. I'm trusting that all this will work out for both of us.

Goodnight, Beautiful. I love you every minute of every day. I miss you terribly.

Larry

"There's a package and letter from Oregon for you," Mom said as I came in from my Saturday chores at the church. I'd raked leaves in the parking lot, swept and mopped the floor, and prepared the Communion elements for my congregation.

Dad came in from the back yard as I ripped open the brown paper on the square parcel.

"That's a shame," he said, looking over my shoulder.

I held a photograph that made my heart beat faster. Carolyn's lips curved in a familiar smile, and her sparkling eyes looked straight at me. But the glass of the frame had broken and scratched the photo. I was thrilled to have a good picture of her, but it was badly marred.

Mom picked up the wrapping paper from the desk and turned it over. "Look," she said, "it was insured. Maybe you can get it replaced."

"Even with the scratches, that's a mighty fine looking young woman," Dad commented.

"You're right, Dad. She's beautiful. I can't wait until you meet her in person."

I took the photo to my room and propped it on my nightstand. As I sat looking at it, I was flooded with memories of the sound of her voice and the way she felt in my arms. *This could be dangerous!*

Leaning back against the pillows of my bed, I read her letter.

November 4, 1966
Dear Larry,

Another day is history, and I'm very glad. You probably didn't realize what a versatile girl you're planning to marry. Today I was a student, a secretary, a truck driver, a common laborer, a hairdresser, and a house cleaner. In other words, I was very involved with Homecoming activities. Then tonight I went to the coronation and talent show. One of the profs sang "Autumn Leaves," which has a lot more meaning to me now...

I was up early to make sure the public areas of the dorm looked good. Our Open House was a success, and after that I went to the football game (we won!) and then fixed friends' hairdos. Todd Hall won first place in "General Dorm Appearance," so all our work was not in vain.

Larry, I really appreciated what you wrote to me recently about my deserving your trust. More than anything, I want to be able to completely share life with you. I will do everything I can to live up to your trust in me and God's plan for our lives.

I wish I could put my head on your shoulder and feel your arms around me—I would sleep like a baby. How I love you and miss you.

Goodnight,
Carolyn

I sat for a while remembering what it felt like to have her head on my shoulder and my arms around her. Finally I got out my stationery to write back to her.

November 6, 1966
Dear Carolyn,

I enjoyed your description of Homecoming activities in the dorm. It must be wonderful to be part of a large group (orgasm, you might say). I have to say I feel a twinge of envy. Seriously, I'm glad you're enjoying all the fun.

Tomorrow I'm going to look into the possibility of making a small addition to the church building. Currently the restroom doors open to the outside, facing the parking lot. I'm hoping to put up a cement block wall and add evergreen shrubs to conceal the doorways. It should look much better. Oh, yes. After Dad and I replaced the pump on the well, the roof started leaking when the rain came.

I haven't heard from Paul and Emily for a while. I hope they are doing well. They're on my mind frequently.

Goodbye, darling. I'll see you when I see you (groan). I love you, and I <u>will</u> *treat you gently, my love.*
Larry
PS: I love you

Jesse and I sat in the bleachers at the football field, my letterman sweater barely keeping me warm. We had driven to Fresno to see a game between Fresno City College and College of the Sequoias, our alma mater. We enjoyed the game, in spite of losing 26-0.

In the Student Union afterward, we ran into several former classmates. As we sat drinking sodas, the conversation drifted to the subject of who was dating whom. Several of the group announced that they were engaged, but I kept quiet about my relationship with Carolyn.

Brenda, who I knew only casually from a class at junior college, bragged about her boyfriends. "I'm engaged to Rick," she said, proudly displaying a shiny diamond ring on her left hand. "But he's away at school, so I'm enjoying dates with Bob and Jeff."

"How does that work out?" I couldn't help asking. I knew both Bob and Jeff, and wouldn't trust either of them for ten minutes with *my* girlfriend.

"Well, being with them helps strengthen my relationship with Rick," she said, with a giggle. I had to bite my tongue to keep from saying, "If you really loved Rick, you wouldn't let yourself be pawed by those other guys." I was grateful that I could trust Carolyn's character.

The next day, her letter brought more news of college life and some of her thoughts and emotions.

November 10, 1966
Darling Larry,

As you can imagine your news about passing the physical created very mixed feelings in me. On one hand, I'm glad you're healthy, but on the other hand, it means there's a greater chance that you'll actually get drafted. That's a scary prospect for me, and I have to remind myself that your life is in God's hands.

If you are drafted, then of course I'd want you to pursue whatever course will give you the best opportunities. Officers Training School sounds like it would be a good choice, but if that doesn't work out, I'll be happy married to an enlisted man, as long as that enlisted man is YOU!

I went to the library after lunch today, and stayed there doing research until after 4:00. After dinner I typed up the quotes from my research, and did some sewing. Tomorrow I'll clean my room from top to bottom, do my laundry, and go back to the library. Most of my friends are going home for the weekend, so it will be peaceful.

One of the girls in our dorm ended up in the hospital this week, diagnosed with tuberculosis. I've asked the nurse from the campus clinic to talk to the girls Monday night at our house meeting. Everyone in the dorm will need a skin test, since we've all been exposed. It's one of the risks of dorm life.

We had a pop quiz in English Lit today. Anticipating the possibility, I read the selections from Thomas More's 'Utopia' and Hooker's 'Laws of Ecclesiastical Polity' twice. Just my luck, the quiz was ten character identifications from Spenser's 'Faerie Queene.' I may have gotten five right!

I made a serious mistake yesterday. When I was in the drugstore, I sprayed a sample of "English Leather" cologne on the back of my hand. It was a vivid reminder of you, which made it very hard to concentrate on my studies. I didn't want to wash my hand the rest of the day.

I'm not sure why you feel you can't come at Christmas. Is it a financial issue, or something else? I know that you would be welcome to stay with my family, so that shouldn't be a concern.

I need you, Darling, for so many reasons. But the reasons really don't matter. The fact is we should be <u>together</u>. Larry, if we can see each other at Christmas I don't care what we do or where we go or who knows about us—I just want to be with you.

Now I'm going to bed, to sleep: perchance to dream of my darling Larry.
Carolyn

As I folded her letter, I thought, God, you know how much I want to be with her again.

Was I just being stubborn or proud in not wanting to impose on her family? I was concerned that my '58 Chevy might not make it to Portland and back. If I flew or took the bus, I would be without my own car, and hated the thought of her having to drive us around again. I wanted to be the one in charge, to squire her around, to treat her like a lady.

One thing I knew for certain, I needed to see Carolyn again soon. *There has to be a way.*

Chapter 19

Carolyn

Thoughts of Larry filled my mind on Friday afternoon as I walked from the library to my dorm. When a car pulled up at the curb beside me, I was startled to hear someone call, "Hey, Carolyn!" I bent down to see who was driving.

"Rick! What are you doing here?" I asked.

"I'm in town for the weekend, looking up friends. I'm glad I saw you."

When I was a freshman and Rick was a senior, a friend and I had double-dated with him and one of his dorm-mates. The fact that the guys weren't Christians had made me a

> **Current Culture**
> **November 1966**
>
> - Minimum mental standard for US military inductees is lowered from 16 to 10 out of a possible 100
> - President Johnson signs a bill requiring food labels to identify contents
> - 400 people die of heart attack and respiratory failure because of smog in New York City
> - Oven-ready turkeys advertised for 39 cents per pound

little uncomfortable, but I'd convinced myself that I could maintain boundaries and not let anything get serious. When Rick and his friend graduated, my concerns were resolved.

Rick reached over and opened the passenger door. "Hop in. Let's find some of the old gang." I got in the car, glad for a diversion. He parked in front of my dorm, and I ran in to find Judy, another girl from the group. We headed for the town of Dallas, eight miles away, where Stan, Rick's former roommate, taught high school. After an hour or so of catching up at Stan's apartment, we visited a nearby grocery store, and Judy and I cooked dinner as we all continued to talk and watch TV. While it was fun to be with old friends again, my life had changed dramatically since we'd been together. Listening to the guys talk, I couldn't help contrasting their casual, worldly attitudes with Larry's single-minded purpose to serve God.

It was nearly one a.m. when Rick dropped Judy and me at the dorm. In the lobby, Judy said, "I just bought the sound track for *Dr. Zhivago*. Come to my room and let's listen to it." We sat on her bed munching M&Ms and enjoying the dramatic music. When I looked at the album jacket, I was startled to see that the male lead, Omar Sharif, had liquid brown eyes like Larry's. I suddenly felt overwhelmingly lonely. I excused myself and went to my room, frustration building as I climbed the stairs. *Lord, it's so hard being separated from Larry. I don't know if I can make it through a whole year!* Crawling into bed, I cried myself to sleep.

After English Lit class on Monday, I grabbed the letter from California out of my box, and dashed up the two flights of stairs to the privacy of my room. Dumping my books on the bed, I ripped open the letter.

November 14, 1966
Dear Carolyn,

Tonight Mom and I visited three more prospects for the church. One was a Navy wife whose husband has been at sea for four months. Another is a family with three children, and the third a young couple who live just two blocks from the church. When we left their house, they said, "We may drop in some Sunday soon." I sure hope so.

Last night's church service was very enjoyable. The people seem to really like the Bible studies we're doing, and are reading the Bible more on their own. There is much more interaction among the people than even last month. The Spirit of God is more and more evident in our meetings.

The other significant thing I did today was fill in the trench for the pipe from the house to the calf trough in the cattle pen behind our back yard. After all these years, we won't have to carry water buckets!

As you know, I was hoping to come to Portland at Christmas, and although I would like to, I'm not sure it's going to be possible. Time will tell.

Here's a strange classified ad I clipped out of the "Personals" section today. I thought you might get a kick out of it: "Mama, I love you. Please hurry. Daddy"
Well, it's that time again. Adios, mi amor,
LDW

Although I was glad for the upbeat tone of Larry's letter, I was puzzled that he seemed indecisive about coming to Portland for Christmas. After studying for several hours, I expressed my feelings in a letter.

November 16, 1966
Dear Larry,
Maybe I'm thick-headed, but I don't quite understand the problem in your coming up here for Christmas. I thought that was part of our plan, but now you seem reluctant. I realize there could be a financial issue, but beyond that, I'm puzzled. I'll be climbing the walls soon if there's no definite plan for us to get together.

Today I started tutoring a high school boy in English composition. Tutoring is one of the requirements of being part of the Women's Honorary Sorority, an academic group I've been invited to join. While the assignment was interesting, I felt inadequate and a bit presumptuous. I suppose I wouldn't have been asked to do it if I weren't considered qualified.

I also had a doctor's appointment today. I've been extremely tired lately, and thought perhaps I needed iron supplements or something. The doctor thinks I'm not allowing myself enough diversion from serious college life (such as dating). I explained to him why I hadn't dated since I came back in September, and he said I shouldn't let myself be "tied down" so soon. One man's opinion!

I'll go back on Thursday for lab reports, and start a series of immunizations. I've never had any shots, since my parents didn't believe in them. But if and when I go to the mission field, I don't want to have to start from scratch. (No pun intended.)

This evening I spent some time remembering how we met and fell in love. It will be a very romantic story to tell our children someday.

After reading many of your letters again, I marvel once more at how perfect you are for me. You are simply everything I want and need.

When I really think about it, I love you because of what you are, and also for what we will be together. I know I can trust you absolutely and give myself completely, and in so doing, make you happy and bring peace and joy to my own life. What a prospect!

Goodnight, beloved. You are in my thoughts constantly.

Carolyn

I was out of breath the next morning when I reached the second floor landing of the Humanities Building. My classmates were standing around the locked door of our classroom. A sign on the door said, "No class today. Dr. MacDonald will be on leave for the next week."

"What's going on?" asked a student behind me.

"My friend Jan works at the Dean's office," said one of the girls. "She said Dr. Mac and his wife had a visit from a couple of Army officers yesterday. Apparently their son was killed in Vietnam." There was a collective gasp as the group absorbed the news. We were sobered by this glimpse of a professor's life outside the classroom, and the pain it could involve.

"I hate Vietnam," said one of the girls vehemently.

"That's dumb," said another. "You shouldn't hate Vietnam, you should hate the American warmongers."

"If *your* brother was over there, you wouldn't be so nit-picky," said the first girl, turning away with tears in her eyes. Their exchange silenced everyone, and we dispersed down the hall and the stairway.

Please, God, not Larry...

I was more grateful than ever to find another letter from Hanford in my mailbox.

November 17, 1966
Dearest Carolyn,

It's been two months and ten days since we said goodbye. It seems like only yester-year—time is going so slowly. I received your letter today asking why I can't come to Portland for Christmas. There are three reasons why I can't come.

No reliable car to get there
No place to stay when I am there
No means of transportation once I got there

Believe me, your letter made me realize how much I really want to come, but I don't know any way around the problems I've listed.

Today I got a call from someone in the church telling me about a couple whose house burned last night. They got out safely, but with only the clothes on their backs. I spent several hours making phone calls and picking up clothing and household goods to take to them.

Right now I'm listening to the FM station, currently airing a string ensemble playing Paganini. It's fantastic, but I'm distracted by thoughts of you.

You are the only thing that seems real in my life, Carolyn. Everything else is uncertain, except for God.

I love you, and want to be near you. Please believe that.
LDW

The next day I woke up dreading my 8:00 class, where the prof alternately coughed out his thoughts and took deep drags on continuous cigarettes. I turned over and fell back asleep for another hour and was nearly late for my morning shift at work. In French class after work, Dr. Girard gave a pop quiz, for which I was definitely unprepared. Since I didn't have time to go to the cafeteria, I grabbed an ice cream cone from the snack bar for lunch.

When I arrived ravenous at the dining hall that evening, the dinner agenda included the fall sports banquet. It was against campus culture to leave before the speeches and presentations were finished, so it was after 8:00 p.m. when I got back to my room to study and eventually write to Larry.

November 20, 1966
Dear Larry,

Today was one of those frustrating and depressing days. I didn't want to get out of bed to start with, and got a disappointing B on the French quiz. I knew the material, but made silly mistakes.

I set a goal of having at least three of my five major papers done before I leave Wednesday for Thanksgiving at home, but with only three more days, I may not make it. Tomorrow I have a mid-term over 'The Great Gatsby' and 'Huckleberry Finn', plus a quiz in English Lit.

This week we found out that a prof's son was killed in Vietnam. News like that brings fear and anxiety. I know we're both in God's hands, but when you're not here to reassure me of your love and I can't talk to you face to face, I worry! You have become so important to me!

My lab tests came back normal, thank God. However, it doesn't explain why I'm exhausted all the time. I've never been a high energy person, but this is ridiculous.

The roses I dried from my birthday bouquet are lovely and unusual. They turned very dark as they dried, and they look quite dramatic against the blue wall and white bookcase. It's a wonderful reminder of your love.

I was just interrupted by some very rowdy boys making merry on our front lawn. I put on my coat and went out on my balcony to see what the commotion was. When the boys saw me, they said some rude things, then ran off, tripping and falling over each other. There was some indication that they were inebriated, although I would not like to cast any aspersions on those who attend our fair institution.

Last night I had a lovely dream about you, and when I woke up, I wanted so much to reach out and touch you. How can love be so beautiful and wonderful, and yet so painful at the same time?

There is so much to say, but the books are calling. Goodnight...my prayers and thoughts are with you always.

Carolyn

Thanksgiving Day was unusually beautiful, with bright autumn sunlight shining through the bare maple branches outside the ranch house. I was grateful that my brother Dave had been able to pick me up on his way home from the University of Oregon for the weekend.

As Mom and I were peeling sweet potatoes and making salads in the morning, I mentioned that it might be possible for Larry to come for Christmas after all.

"How will that work out?" asked Mom. "I thought he couldn't get vacation from his new job."

"Well, Mom, things have changed a bit. He doesn't have that job now."

"What? Did he get fired?"

"No, he quit."

She stared at me, open-mouthed. "He quit? Why in the world would he do that? I thought he was saving money to get married next year."

"He was, but he can't get a ministerial deferment from the Draft if he's working at a secular job."

She paused, apparently thinking through the implications. "Then when will he get the deferment?"

"He has to appeal his draft classification again, now that he's unemployed."

Mom shook her head and stirred a pot of cranberry sauce on the stove. I knew more questions would come, and I'd have to be ready to defend Larry's decision.

On the way to Portland for the family dinner, we avoided the touchy subject. Instead, Mom talked about the new horses that they were boarding and their Friday night youth group. Our family time at Paul & Emily's was pleasant, with good food, games of "Rook" in the afternoon, and TV football in the evening.

The next day Dave and I drove back to Portland. Between listening to his favorite jazz on the radio, he serenaded me with songs from his choral group, the "Bitterlick Singers." I blushed at some of the lyrics, apparently popular entertainment at clubs and parties in Eugene.

In the downtown core we skirted the crowds gathered for the annual Santa Claus parade that inaugurated the holiday season. Dave had a business appointment, and I shopped for a late birthday present for Mom. I was happy to find a nice pair of lined leather gloves, which she would love but never buy for herself.

After eating left-over turkey with Paul and Emily, we sat around the kitchen table with pie and coffee. Emily excused herself and came back to the table with a box of photos from their year in Hanford. As we looked at the snapshots, I said, "These didn't have much meaning before. Now I want to know about everyone in the pictures."

"It makes a difference when you realize they'll be part of your life, doesn't it?" said Emily.

On Saturday, Dave took me to Priscilla's to babysit so she and Lauren could have a date. With four kids, their budget didn't often allow for a babysitter, and I was happy to give them a break. Faye had just turned six, and was very motherly to her younger siblings. When they were all asleep, I flopped on the couch. *I could be a mother in just a few years!* The thought was both exciting and scary. *I'm glad Larry doesn't want kids right away, we need time to really get to know each other first!* When Priscilla and Lauren came home just before midnight, I crawled into the bottom bunk with Faye, and dreamed of having a baby with dark hair and eyes like Larry.

Dave dropped me at my dorm late Sunday afternoon, and I was relieved to find letters from Larry in my box. The long holiday weekend had left me feeling very disconnected from him. In my room, I tore open the letter with the earliest postmark.

November 27, 1966
Hello Princess,

Do you realize it's only one month until Christmas? Hooray! Perhaps Santa will bring me the three things I most need right now. I won't tell you what they are...

Today I almost got the front lawn cleared of leaves. We have two medium-sized mulberry trees that have LOTS of leaves. I was nearly finished when the boys from up the road marched into the driveway. They were determined to have another round of croquet with me. My unofficial "Boys Club of America" is continuing, whether I want it to or not.

Our Thanksgiving dinner will be a little dull here, as there will only be the three of us. With Chuck in Vietnam and Joan in Pasadena, there's no family in our area. But Mom's still going all-out, even making pumpkin pie from pumpkins we grew in our garden.

Carolyn, if you only knew just how fantastically in love with you I am, you would have pity on me. How? By showing me all your faults (I wouldn't believe a word of it). Then it might ease the pain of separation a bit.

I miss you so much, especially those wonderfully tender lips of yours, your magnificent neck, your soft hair, all of you. I ache to put my arms around you.

SWAK,

Larry

A soft knock startled me out of the dreamy state Larry's letter evoked. I hoped the girl standing at my door would assume the blush on my cheeks was because my room was warm. I held Larry's letter behind my back, which made it awkward to accept the homemade cupcake she handed me. I invited her in, and we talked for a few minutes before there was another knock on my door. This time it was a girl bringing me a red felt Christmas stocking she had embroidered with my nickname: "Car", pronounced "care." I was touched by her generosity, and invited her to join us, stuffing my unopened letters under papers on my desk.

In my role as dorm president I was a big sister to many girls. While it wasn't always convenient when girls in the dorm knocked on my door, I loved talking and laughing with them, or offering a shoulder to cry on. The cupcake and Christmas stocking were tangible tokens of their appreciation.

When the girls finally left I sat on my bed propped up by pillows and read the rest of my mail. The loving, romantic things in the letters brought pleasure, but Larry's evasiveness about coming to Portland for Christmas left me frustrated. I tried to figure it out, but it just didn't make sense. *In September, he seemed so certain that he'd come for Christmas. What changed?*

I wished I could talk to Tricia, the only one at college who knew the truth about our relationship, but she was at work, and wouldn't be back at her apartment until after dorm closing hours. After rereading the letters, and praying for peace and wisdom, I decided to wait until my emotions were more stable to reply to his letters.

After taking a long walk, I was ready to answer Larry's letters.

November 29, 1966
Dear Larry,

It's nearly 11:30 already, and I was hoping to be asleep by 11. I can never get to bed at a decent hour, no matter how hard I try. I've felt blah all day, probably the result of yesterday's smallpox vaccination.

I spent the evening at the library, but after 2 ½ hours of research, I was ready to climb the walls. I went to the French lab to study, but didn't accomplish much. Today I couldn't answer the prof's questions. I just sat there looking at her, like a bump on a pickle.

Now to get down to business. You seem to think you would be a burden for my family if you came up for Christmas. The reality is that they're all looking forward to you coming. Mom always thrives on company. She was disappointed that neither Dave nor I brought anyone home for Thanksgiving. Also, Mom and Dad feel left out of our romance. It would give her a lot of pleasure if she could participate in even a small way with her last single daughter's life at this special time. Believe me, Larry, if you come and stay with us, it will be the highlight of the year for Mom. She's already planning how you can stay in the little trailer behind the house so everything will "look right."

One thing I need to let you know. Mom has frequently expressed the thought that I'm taking the initiative in my relationship with you, which is contrary to her sense of propriety. Your hesitation to come for Christmas, for reasons which appear to be based on your pride, give my parents further reason to think that our romance is one-sided.

I wanted desperately to call you tonight, but my pride wouldn't let me, and I didn't want to argue about this on the phone. Please don't make me beg you, Larry. Don't stay away for the sake of being immovable in a disagreement.

You say you need me—I'm here, waiting for you.

Carolyn

My emotions were high when I finished my letter and when I heard a commotion in the hall, I stormed out of my room.

"It's quiet hours," I said in a harsh whisper. "You're all getting demerits!" Their expressions of consternation and guilt let me know that my response was unexpected, and they scampered off to their rooms.

The next day I tackled some overdue assignments at work, hoping that busyness would lift my mood. The resource center was crowded with students trying to find instructional materials for term projects, and the phone rang frequently. When my boss came back from a staff meeting, my tasks were still unfinished. By the time my shift was over, I felt overwhelmed and exhausted. *How am I going to make it through the week if I'm this tired already? Is there something wrong with my body, or am I just too busy? And what about Larry?*

I walked back to my dorm hearing the same depressing phrases that had been running through my head for days. *Will he come? If he gets drafted, will I ever see him again?*

Chapter 20

Larry

Christmas was less than a month away, and I desperately wanted to go to Oregon to see Carolyn. I also wanted to do everything right in our relationship. I felt that good manners required an invitation from someone in her family before I could make concrete plans. I couldn't travel eight hundred miles and just drop in.

As smart as Carolyn was, she didn't seem to understand my dilemma. Each letter was more persuasive and insistent. *Do I need to spell it out for her? Does she really think I'm not dying to see her?*

I considered casting caution to the wind and buying a bus ticket, but my sense of propriety and pride held me back. I did everything I could to prepare for the possibility of seeing Carolyn, including picking out a beautiful diamond ring at a Fresno jewelry store. *When will I be able to put it on her finger?*

> **Current Culture December 1966**
>
> - *How the Grinch Stole Christmas* debuts on CBS
> - Walt Disney dies during the production of *The Jungle Book*
> - 6,000 students and faculty at UC Berkeley boycott classes in protest of U.S. Navy recruiting on campus
> - The US bombs Hanoi for the first time
> - December hit song: "I'm a Believer" by The Monkees

It was already December first when Mom handed me a note that had been included with a letter from Emily Mueller. Seeing my grin as I read the note, Mom said, "Does this mean you're heading to Portland soon?"

"Yep, it sure does. Nothing will stop me now."

"That's a relief, Larry. I'll be glad not to have you moping around here, missing your sweetheart. When will you leave?"

"Probably on the 14th or 15th. I'll come back on Christmas Eve, so I'll only miss one Sunday here."

I headed for my bedroom, anxious to write Carolyn the good news.

December 1, 1966
Carolyn,

Here's the important news. In a letter Mom received today, Emily sent and invitation for me to stay at their house if I visit. I will definitely come for Christmas. I plan to come December 15-23.

Now we can see "Dr. Zhivago" together. I'd like to see the poor guy who has eyes like mine (according to you). Also, I'd like a moonlit walk in the snow!

I've been a bundle of energy in the last couple of days, doing yard work at home and at the church. I had the privilege of picking a bowl of cherry tomatoes, but I wasn't successful in avoiding the nasty thorns of the pyracantha bush beside the house.

Only a handful came to Bible study last night. Many were home sick with the flu. Even so, there was a good spirit there, and I wasn't discouraged.

Please write soon and let me know if the dates I mentioned will work, so I can make reservations.

Sincerely,
Larry
PS: I love you, Carolyn. You're likely to have sore lips and cracked ribs soon.

When the mailman drove up a few days later, I was outside weeding Mom's iris bed and didn't waste any time heading for the mailbox. I was rewarded by an envelope postmarked "Sandy, OR 97055"—a letter from Mrs. Cooke with an invitation for me to stay with them if I could come for Christmas to visit their daughter. *Yahoo! I'm really on my way!*

On Monday I drove to town to pay the utility bills, mail a letter to Carolyn, and visit some sick parishioners. When I got home, there was another blue letter in the mailbox. I sat on the porch steps in the pale winter sunshine and read Carolyn's latest.

December 4, 1966
Dear Larry,

I am so happy! I haven't been able to concentrate since I got your letter. Only ten days until you come—I can't believe it. You really had me scared that you wouldn't come. Can you forgive me for being so dense about this? Of course, you wouldn't make definite plans until you had an invitation. Please let me know exactly when you're arriving, what bus line, etc. I can't wait, I can't wait!

I called Mom to tell her you were coming for sure, and she sounded very pleased. I would really like to spend most of our time at the ranch so you can get to know Mom and Dad better. There's so much to do there, and in the evening there's always good music and a fire in the fireplace. We can also spend some time at Paul and Emily's, and maybe see a movie in Portland.

I've been a bit under the weather because of my smallpox vaccination, a flu bug, and whatever else that's going around here. I know I'm not getting enough sleep, and I hope that's the main reason I'm sick. I refuse to believe that I'm "sickly," as I was always told growing up.

The dorm is very busy tonight. Saturday is "Dad's Day" and we need to have all our Christmas decorations up. It's a bigger deal than even Homecoming, and that's saying quite a bit. I'd probably look forward to it more if my own Dad were coming.

Tonight I've been sitting here wondering what you're doing and if you are as lonesome as I am. Spending time at my sisters' homes over Thanksgiving made me think even more about marriage (if that's possible). There's something so unique about two people working together to create a home. It's going to be a challenge to me to see if we can have a better marriage than most I've seen.

Here's a sneak preview of the cracked ribs and sore lips: OOOOOO XXXXXX

Love, Carolyn

Walking into the house, I folded the letter and added it to the growing stack in the drawer of my nightstand. I couldn't afford to think too much about the hugs and kisses at the end of Carolyn's letter. It was hard enough dealing with my own memories and daydreams, without the added fuel of her comments. I got out my Bible and concordance and started studying for my next sermon. That evening I wrote to her again.

December 7, 1966
Dear Carolyn,

I'm sorry you feel so miserable. Flu and a small pox vaccination are a nasty combination. I'd love to be there to nurse you to full recovery, but by the time I get there, you should be all better. Only a week from today I get on the bus!

Today I installed a light over the side door to the church. Now that we've started getting rain, there's often a puddle in front of that door, and people get their feet wet. The cost of parts to install the light? A grand total of thirty-one cents! Why didn't someone do this years ago?? At times I wonder how people could care so little about God's house.

Last night I went to a revival meeting at the Nazarene Church in Hanford. Tom Bradford, a high school friend, was there, and he invited me over to his parents' place for a "little talk" afterwards. Little? He really had a lot to say. His wife finally went to bed at midnight, and I didn't get away until after 2:30 this morning. He just kept talking!

By the way, you said you'd make up for all the kisses we've missed in the past three months. How many do you think that will require?

Until we meet in seven long agonizing days, au revoir, ma Cherie.
Larry

For small-town Hanford, December was especially busy with holiday events. There was barely time after our morning service for me to take Mom to the Nazarene Church to hear an excellent quartet. Afterwards, I dropped her at home so she could get ready to work swing shift, then headed to the Dutch

Reformed Church, where the community choir was performing Handel's *Messiah.*

Hearing the powerful lyrics and lush music, I thought constantly of Carolyn. Knowing she loved the music from performing it with the college choir, I felt a special connection with her.

When I read the next letter from Monmouth, I worried about Carolyn's health and constant exhaustion.

December 6, 1966
Dear Larry,

I never thought I'd get through this day. I had a fever last night, then six hours of classes without a break, including two exams and an oral report. I was exhausted at 2:00 pm. but after a short nap, I was able to get through the evening.

Last night was the dorm Christmas party, which was a lot of fun. There were skits and good food, and the six Hawaiian girls in our dorm did a hula to "White Christmas."

It was also very emotional for me. I've been quite discouraged, thinking that I'm doing a poor job as Dorm President, and wondering if it is worth all the work. But at the end of the party, they asked me to come up to the front, where they gave me a lovely gift of "Intimate" perfume. (No, I won't describe the scent, you'll just have to wait until you get here.) When I stood up, the girls clapped, whistled and cheered. Of course I started crying. Their enthusiasm washed away my discouragement and feelings of failure.

It's sheer bedlam in the hall outside my room. Some poor girl is getting thrown into the shower, and you'd think that she's being murdered. Just before that, another group of girls came through the halls singing Christmas carols and passing out candy canes.

News Flash! This message was interrupted by a fire drill. I'm always so startled when that *$)%Y+&* alarm goes off, even when I'm warned ahead of time. How would you like to climb down a fire escape in your nightgown at midnight when it's 38 degrees outside? No wonder I'm sick so much.

Let me tell you a secret before I close. I am madly and wildly in love with you. Don't tell anyone, or you will break the spell, and your bus will turn into a pumpkin. (Which probably won't hurt the bus much, but will total the pumpkin.)
Just think, at this time next week, I'll be in your arms! I'm so excited!
Goodnight, beloved.
Carolyn

Only a few days remained before I could leave for Portland and wrap my arms around Carolyn, which made letter writing both easier and harder. It was easy to be positive and light-hearted, but more difficult to write things of depth and meaning. I wanted to keep her updated on my life, but my activities seemed dull and ordinary compared to her busy dorm life.

December 8, 1966
Dear Carolyn,
I'll be on the Continental Trailways bus arriving in Portland at 5:00 p.m. on Thursday, December 15th. In case you might not recognize me, I'll be wearing a pink carnation in my right lapel, a purple tie with matching red socks and a yellow handkerchief. In case you still *don't recognize me, I'm the guy with no heart—I lost it back in September.*
Tonight I wrapped Christmas presents for my family while my parents went to Fresno today to buy gifts for their nine grandchildren. I wonder if those kids feel as excited as I did when I was their age?
My congregation seemed happy when I announced that we would not have an evening service on Christmas day. That way they can stay home with their family and friends without feeling guilty.
The bus trip should be interesting. When I made the reservation, the woman told me that they will supply two meals for us, as well as magazines, tables and table games, and even a hostess to make sure we're comfortable.
By the way, do you realize we haven't really disagreed on anything? The first time I get you alone, I plan to pick a fight. I will say very sternly, "I do too love you more than you love me," and most likely you'll say, "Shut up

and kiss me." I plan on collecting on all the kisses I've missed out on in the past ten weeks.

Would you do me a huge favor? Take good care of yourself! I'm worried about you being sick so much. Please get enough rest and try not to burn the candle at all three ends!

Seven more days, and I'll be able to tell you <u>in person</u> how much I LOVE YOU!

Larry

The phone rang while I was preparing for Bible study on Wednesday. Jesse had some unexpected news. "I just got a call from my dad," he said. "The city called him yesterday to say they would like to develop the land around the church."

"You're kidding! After all this time? We've been praying for this for years."

"Yeah, I guess it would help."

"Help?" I exclaimed. "If they put the road through and allow a subdivision in the vacant lots next door, it will increase the property value and bring in new people. This is great!"

Jesse continued. "Well, since Dad's in Portland, he wants you to attend the city council meeting for him and get more details."

"Okay, I can do that. I'm anxious to find out what they're planning, and how it will affect us."

"It could cost plenty if we have to put in sidewalks and hook up to sewer."

"But it also means more people close to the church, people we can reach out to."

"I guess so, it just sounds like a lot of work to me."

Jesse's lack of excitement did nothing to dampen my enthusiasm. This was an answer to years of prayer. God was definitely moving in our community!

Later that day, I was happy to open another blue letter from Oregon.

December 10, 1966

Dear Larry,

Only a few more days!

Yesterday I went shopping in Salem, which is especially fun at Christmas. I was hoping to find some gifts, but had trouble deciding what to buy. I haven't the faintest idea what to get for Mom and Dad.

This morning I found a breakfast tray outside my door, complete with fresh orange juice, cereal, banana, milk, toast and jelly, decorated with a red bow and a sprig of holly. Would you believe it was the first time I have eaten breakfast in two months?

Listen, Larry, how do you expect me to do better than a 3.0 GPA when I'm constantly thinking about your arrival? It will be your fault if I flunk out! Last night I lay awake for a couple of hours, thinking about you and your visit. I'm looking forward to it so much. Besides having you here, I really need a change of pace. I'm delighted at the prospect of having some unscheduled days together.

Tonight I'm running a fever and have a terrific headache. So what am I doing up after midnight? Trying to finish a project, which is proving nearly impossible, since my thoughts keep wandering across the border to a small town in California.

I got a letter from Mom today, and I can't believe how different her tone was. She's very glad you're coming, and actually said it will be okay with her if we spend part of your visit in Portland with Paul and Emily. I was shocked that she would agree to our being "unchaperoned" (at least by her). I'm amazed. I never thought we could have such a pleasant relationship.

I don't know how many kisses you should collect when you arrive, but a conservative estimate would be 3,789,413. Does that meet with your approval? It should, or you will just have to settle for 2,789,413.

I love you, Larry. Every time I say it, I mean it a little more.

Goodnight, beloved.

Carolyn

I folded the letter and stared out the dining room window. Carolyn's letters had a way of blasting every rational thought out of my brain. The next few days couldn't go fast enough to suit me.

On the 14th, Dad drove me to Fresno after dinner. He dropped me off at the bus station with time to spare before the 11:40 p.m. departure. I didn't look forward to the 17-hour journey, but what was waiting at my destination definitely made it worthwhile.

Once the bus was heading north on Highway 99, the hostess brought everyone blankets and pillows. Sleep eluded me for several hours as my thoughts raced ahead to Carolyn and the time we'd have together. The bus was swaying through the curves near Lake Shasta when I finally fell asleep, my dreams bringing haunting images of my sweetheart.

The rattle of the hostess cart woke me the next morning. Weak dawn light revealed snowy forests beside the highway. After eating cold cereal and washing down the plastic-wrapped Danish pastry with warm tea, I opened the book I'd packed to pass the time. I stared uncomprehendingly at the first few pages. While Carolyn's letters were loving and enthusiastic, I wondered if our romance was real and would endure the months of unavoidable separation. As much as I believed that God had brought us together, I still had some doubts.

I'm not exactly a hot prospect, with no job and the draft hanging over my head. I know I have potential, but right now things look bleak. Potential doesn't pay rent. What will I tell her dad if he asks how I'll support his daughter? What if Carolyn decides that a long-distance relationship is too difficult?

For what seemed to be the hundredth time, I prayed, *"Lord, you brought us together--you'll have to keep us together!"*

I was jittery with anticipation as the bus moved through rush hour traffic in the outskirts of Portland. Low gray clouds and scattered rain showers gave the city a totally different look from its summer countenance. The last few miles seemed endless, but finally the air brakes gave a sharp sigh as the bus stopped in the depot.

Through the window, I could see Carolyn's bright hair and beaming smile. When I saw the look on her face, my anxiety melted away like frost at sunrise. I impatiently waited my turn to get off the bus, and then she ran to me. I wrapped my arms around her, inhaling her fragrance, enjoying the feel of her body against me. She was laughing and crying, vibrating with joy.

"You're here, Larry. You're really here!"

Chapter 21

Carolyn

Larry and I talked non-stop on the drive from Portland the ranch. It was hard to concentrate on the road, as I wanted to stare at him, to make sure his presence wasn't just a daydream. Once we were out of busy traffic, I reached over to squeeze his hand. "I can't believe you're really here."

"Believe it, Sweetheart," he grinned. "It's me, in the flesh."

I could only smile gratefully that we'd actually made it through fourteen weeks of separation.

The savory aroma of pot roast greeted us when we walked into Mom's kitchen. "Welcome back to the ranch, Larry," she said, wiping her hands on her apron.

> **Current Culture**
> **December 1966**
>
> - "GI Joe" is the best-selling Christmas toy
> - US cargo plane crashes into Vietnamese village, killing 129 civilians
> - *Time* magazine cover features Julie Andrews, star of the major hit movie *The Sound of Music*
> - 500+ piece LEGO set, $9.97
> - Average monthly rent for a family home: $125

"Thank you, Mrs. Cooke. I'm very glad to be here," Larry replied.

"Nice to have you here, Reverend," Dad extended his hand and grinned shyly.

"Ernest, why don't you help Larry take his things to the 'guest house,' " Mom continued. "Carolyn, you can help me serve up dinner. I hope it's not overcooked--I expected you earlier."

"The bus was a little late, and traffic was heavy," I explained.

When Larry came back into the kitchen, he handed a package to Mom. "I brought you some California pecans. They're from a tree in our back yard."

"Thank you, Larry. That's very thoughtful. I'll use them for my holiday baking." Mom put the bag of nuts on the kitchen counter, and set the last dish of food on the table. "Larry, you can sit there." She pointed to the chair opposite Dad, and seated herself at Dad's left. Larry pulled out the remaining chair and made sure I was comfortable before he sat down.

We joined hands around the table while Dad read the Psalm for the day and asked God to bless our meal. It was the first time Larry had been with my parents since their casual meeting at the conference back in August, and Mom's fussing over the meal showed her nervousness.

Larry quickly put her at ease with questions about the ranch, the upcoming holidays, and her neighborhood Bible study. As usual, Dad didn't say much, but the twinkle in his eye conveyed his approval.

After dinner, Larry offered to help me wash the dishes, and we worked companionably together. The mundane task was a pleasure with him beside me, and I thought how wonderful it would be when we had our *own* house and were washing our *own* dishes together.

After the last dish was in the cupboard, we put on our coats and headed outside. The rain had stopped, and beyond the glow of the porch light, Larry pulled me close in a silent embrace. I blissfully rested my head against his shoulder and inhaled his masculine scent. After a few quiet moments, he stepped back and tipped my face up to his.

"We've waited so many weeks for this, Carolyn," he said. At first his kiss was soft and tentative, then searching and hungry. I responded, but after a few moments, I pulled back to catch my breath.

"We might have to pace ourselves, Larry. It seems like we can go from zero to sixty in about 90 seconds." I laughed ruefully. "As much as I love them, I don't want our kisses to be the focus of our time together."

"Isn't that the whole point?" he teased.

"Getting to know each other better is the whole point to me. But I'll be happy to share some kisses as part of that."

"*Some* kisses?"

"Okay, maybe a *lot* of kisses, but we also need to talk about a lot of things."

"You're right, of course, my Sweet, that's what I want too. But you still owe me for a lot of lonely days."

"Don't worry, Darling, I'll make up for those, just not all at once, okay?" I reached up to give him a brief kiss, then turned, grabbed his hand, and headed away from the house.

Stars sparkled in the dark blue gaps between scudding clouds. We leaned against the peeled-log fence of the barnyard, our breath clouding in the frosty air. The horses were shadowy shapes against the silvery weathered boards of the old barn.

"So, what wonderful adventures can I expect in the next week?" Larry asked.

"We'll stay here at the ranch for a few days, then Mom and Dad will take us to Portland to spend the rest of the time at Paul and Emily's. Mom wants our Christmas tree decorated soon, so maybe we can find one tomorrow."

"Christmas tree hunting sounds like a great idea."

"I also want to show you all the local hangouts, maybe even drive up to Timberline Lodge on the mountain."

"Just remember, I need some time to talk to your dad soon. Alone, I mean."

"Maybe tomorrow night would work."

Mom called to us from a rectangle of light at the back door. "Hot chocolate is ready!"

I looked at Larry with a wry smile. "I think Mom is going to do a fair amount of organizing our time while you're here."

"I'm sure we can work around that," he said with an answering smile.

When our cups were empty, Larry said, "If you don't mind, I'd like to excuse myself. I didn't get much sleep on the bus last night."

As we stood up from the table, Mom said, "Breakfast will be ready at 8:00 in the morning, Larry. Carolyn, you can wash up these cups." Larry looked at me with raised eyebrows, then winked and squeezed my hand before heading out the back door.

Under heavy quilts in my bedroom I tried to recall every word, look, and touch of the past few hours. With Larry just yards away in the little travel trailer under the big apple tree, sleep would be difficult. *A whole week together!*

The next morning Larry came in the back door, breathless from his dash through a cold downpour. "I may need to borrow some rain boots, Mr. Cooke," he said to Dad.

"I've got an extra pair. I hope they fit you," Dad replied.

After breakfast, we found a saw and a hatchet in the tool shed, and headed up through the pastures. "Mom wants a Christmas tree that will fit on the corner table in the living room," I said.

"That limits our options a bit," said Larry, reaching for my hand.

We walked on the dirt road through the pasture before heading toward a patch of forest. We found a few young firs, but they were either too tall or misshapen. Frequent stops for kisses prolonged our search. Eventually we heard the put-put of Dad's tractor as he came into sight over the hill.

"I thought you might need some help getting the tree home," he said with a knowing smile. "You've been gone a while."

"We haven't found the right tree yet. Any idea where should we look?" I asked.

"I think there's a good one down by the old homestead," Dad answered. We jumped into the trailer behind the tractor, and Dad bumped down the hillside to the remains of a stone fireplace, a bleak remnant of an early homestead along the Oregon Trail. The tree he remembered wasn't perfect, but decorations would fill in the gaps. Larry crawled under the branches to cut the base and helped Dad load it into the trailer.

On the way home, we couldn't talk over the noise of the tractor. Since Dad was facing forward driving the tractor, Larry wrapped his arms around me. As I leaned against him, the frustration of the past months ebbed away, and my body and soul relaxed.

That evening after dinner, I said, "Mom, could you help me wrap some gifts in my bedroom?" In our small house, there was little opportunity for a private conversation, but I had a plan.

"Well, yes, I guess I can do that. I'll get paper and ribbon from the closet," she said.

I squeezed Larry's hand, and said, "Here's your chance." His brief expression of panic made me smile. "Don't worry, Dad's already primed."

Mom seemed happy to cooperate if it meant that Larry would follow the acceptable protocol of asking Dad for my hand. After closing the bedroom door, we started cutting ribbon and paper, still able to hear every word.

"Mr. Cooke, could I talk to you?" I heard Larry say.

"What's that?"

"Could I talk to you for a few minutes?" Larry repeated louder.

"Yep." Dad's newspaper rustled as he put it down, and there was a pause. I heard a whine as he turned up the volume on his hearing aid.

"I'd like to ask you a question." Larry cleared his throat. "I'm in love with Carolyn, and would like your permission to marry her."

"That's okay with me." Dad's brief reply was followed by silence. Finally we heard Larry's voice again.

"So do I have your permission?"

"Yep." The newspaper rustled again, and everything was quiet. Mom and I looked at each other in shock. After a few more minutes of silence, we walked back into the living room. Dad was reading the newspaper, and Larry was sitting on the couch, a bemused look on his face.

Mom took charge. "Let's have dessert. I'll cut some pie."

Our conversation was awkward, and after Dad finished his last bite of pie, he said, "I think I'm going to turn in early. I've got a sore throat."

Mom added, "I've got a good book to finish, so I think I'll join your father." Dad banked the fire in the fireplace, Mom brushed her teeth and I washed up the dishes from our snack. When they closed the bedroom door, I grabbed Larry's hand, and pulled him to sit on the couch.

Larry shook his head in disbelief. "I can't believe it. I expected him to grill me, ask me questions about how I would support you. Something......anything!"

"Well, it's not like he didn't know that this was the main point of your trip."

"Yes, but..."

"Anyway, he likes you, and he knows I want to marry you. That's enough for him."

"It's not the way I'd respond if it were *my* daughter."

"Well, if you want, I can go get him out of bed and tell him he needs to give you the third degree."

"Don't you dare! It's just that I expected a tough conversation. Frankly this was very anticlimactic."

"I've told you Dad is a man of few words." I leaned against his shoulder. "But I think his words were the ones you wanted to hear, right?"

"Definitely. I'm just surprised it was over so quickly." He stood up. "I guess it's time to move on to the next thing." He walked into the hallway where he'd hung his jacket, and came back into the living room looking determined and serious. He knelt in front of me and opened a small blue velvet box. Diamonds sparkled in the firelight.

"Carolyn Lee Cooke, would you do me the great honor of becoming my wife? I love you with all my heart and want to spend the rest of my life with you."

"Yes, Larry, yes, yes!" I replied joyfully. "I love you and I can't wait to marry you."

I reached out my left hand, and he gently slid the engagement ring onto my finger.

"I can't believe I'm finally doing this, Carolyn. I'm so grateful to God for bringing us together," he said, his voice husky with emotion.

I could only smile at him, unshed tears trapping words in my throat. It was a sacred moment, a milestone on the journey of our destiny.

For the next hour, we talked of the future, holding hands in the flickering firelight. As much as we enjoyed kisses and embraces, neither of us wanted our physical hunger to distract us. When we finally said goodnight, my heart throbbed with gratefulness to the heavenly Father who had brought us together.

In the next few days, I shared ranch life with Larry. One day we rode horses into the high pastures and startled a pair of ducks on the fish pond. Later we skipped rocks on the river.

There was fresh snow at Timberline Lodge, the massive log hotel built in the 1930s at the tree line on Mt. Hood. As we wandered the corridors and warmed our feet on the stones of the massive central fireplace, Larry said, "This would be a great place for a honeymoon!" On the way home, we drove back roads so I could show him the areas still devastated by the Christmas flood two years before which had washed away two acres of our land and several neighbors' homes.

Another day we drove the opposite direction to the town of Sandy. I showed him my high school and the office where I had my very first job working for a blind Justice of the Peace. We ate lunch at the town hot-spot, Dea's In 'n Out, locally famous for their rectangular hamburgers.

"Now that you've given me the tour of your life, it's your turn to come to Hanford," Larry said, dipping his French fries in ketchup. "What about spring break?"

"Honestly, Larry, it would take a miracle to get Mom to agree to that."

"We can ask, can't we?"

"Of course, but I think it's hopeless. I'd only have seven days, and I don't know if I can afford to fly."

"Let's at least give it a shot, okay?"

Larry surprised me that evening at dinner. "Mr. Cooke," he said, "I'd like to invite Carolyn to come visit me and my family during her spring break in March."

"Well, I don't know..." Dad's eyebrows shot up, and he shook his head, frowning. Mom blinked in surprise.

"It would be only fair," Larry pleaded, "since I've had the great opportunity to get to know you and Mrs. Cooke this week, I'd like Carolyn to meet my dad and the rest of my family." He paused for a moment. "Could you give it some thought?"

"I guess so," Dad said.

Mom was anxious to add her opinion. "I'm not sure that would look right, Larry."

"If you're concerned about us being chaperoned, Mrs. Cooke, one of my parents is always at home."

"Well, we'll have to pray about it." For the time being, the subject was closed.

"There's their car," I said as Dad pulled into the Safeway parking lot on Jefferson Street in Portland. Paul and Emily had arranged to meet us and take Larry and me to their house for the remainder of his stay.

Paul opened the trunk for our suitcases, and Emily walked over to the car to greet Mom and Dad. As I pulled my garment bag out of the car, the diamond on my finger caught the light from the nearby streetlight, and Emily squealed, "Carolyn! Let me see." I held out my hand, and she examined my ring before giving me an enthusiastic hug. "I'm so happy for you!"

"What's this?" said Paul.

"Look at Carolyn's hand," laughed Emily. I proudly held out my hand, and Paul glanced at it briefly before turning to Larry. "Congratulations," he said.

Larry's smile reached both ears. "You both had a big part in this, and I'm very grateful."

In the car, Emily wanted all the details of Larry's proposal. When he described Dad's nonchalant response, Paul laughed heartily, and Emily shook her head. "You never know with Dad. When Lauren asked to marry Priscilla, Dad gave him the third degree."

Paul chuckled. "I think Larry's status as a pastor gave him a bit of an edge."

Their house was fragrant with the warm smells of fir and spices. The star on top of their Christmas tree brushed the ceiling, and the house was festive with green and gold candles. We sat at the kitchen table sipping hot tea and nibbling on homemade Christmas cookies while planning the activities for the next few days.

Gary and Jimmy were anxious to show Larry the Toyland train at Meier & Frank department store. Paul suggested a visit to Peacock Lane, where quaint Tudor-style houses glittered with lights. The familiar Portland holiday traditions had special significance as I shared them with Larry.

During the day, our interaction was comfortable and easy. But at night, when the house was quiet and we had time to ourselves, we faced an unexpected dilemma. We had naïvely believed that keeping a standard of purity was a simple matter of mental decision and verbal agreement. Now that belief was severely challenged. The strength of our desire for longer caresses and more passionate kisses took us both by surprise.

"Staying on the right side of our line is a lot harder than I thought it would be," I said one evening, sitting straighter and trying to calm my breathing.

"It's a good thing that we're not together all the time," Larry agreed. "I might have to drive us to Reno on a long weekend to make it legal." He smiled as he said it, but the heat in his gaze told me it wasn't a joking matter.

We spent our last evening together going out on the town. Larry looked especially handsome in his dark suit, and I chose a festive red dress that added a glow to my cheeks. We enjoyed the unique ambience of a popular Japanese restaurant, with private dining rooms and savory dishes cooked at our table. After dinner we walked a few blocks to the Paramount Theater on Broadway to see the current blockbuster movie, *Doctor Zhivago*.

As the drama unfolded, we were transported by the lush music and the Oscar-winning cinematography. But the themes of love and loss, war and separation were uncomfortably close to our own experience, and we were both subdued on the drive home. As he parked in Paul & Emily's driveway, Larry finally spoke, his voice low.

"You are my one true love, Carolyn. There will never be another woman for me."

"Oh, Larry, I'm so glad we found each other at the right time, and not after we were married to others." I nestled into his arms for comfort.

"It's God's gift to us, my Sweet. I promise to be faithful to you, no matter what."

"Thank you, Darling," I sighed. "I know that if we keep God at the center of our lives, we'll be secure."

Friday afternoon I was determined to hold back my tears while we waited at the depot for Larry's bus to leave. I tried to block out thoughts of the lonely weeks of separation and the uncertainty we faced.

"If you come to California for your spring break, that's only thirteen weeks away. We can manage that."

"But that's as long as we were separated before, and I don't have permission yet! And what about the Draft?"

"Let's not worry about that now, my love. God has brought us to this point, when it looked impossible, and He won't let us down now."

"I wish I had your faith, Larry. Saying goodbye this time is the hardest thing I've ever done."

"Believe me, it's not any easier for me." His eyes reflected the anguish I felt. "At least you have school to keep you busy. Until I hear about my draft appeal, things will be pretty dull for me."

A crackly voice from the loud speaker interrupted our farewell. "Bus Number 34 for Los Angeles and points south."

"That's me," Larry said, pulling me close. I clung to him silently for a few minutes before he tipped up my face for a last kiss. "God be with you, my love," he said, before turning and walking toward the open bus door. He waved and I blew him a kiss before the doors closed and the bus pulled onto Sixth Avenue, disappearing in holiday traffic.

I drove back to Emily's house, oblivious to the festive decorations along the streets. Gary and Jimmy would soon be home from school, but I was in no mood to play the cheerful Auntie. I kicked off my shoes and crawled into bed with my clothes on. Pulling the covers over my head, I turned to the wall and let the tears flow.

Chapter 22

Larry

My life seemed to shrink with every mile between Portland and Hanford. It felt like everything important remained with my blue-eyed blonde fiancée.

When the bus finally pulled into the Fresno depot, it was early Saturday morning, Christmas Eve. Dad's truck was in the depot parking lot. "How's your girlfriend?" he asked when I got in the cab.

"Wonderful," I replied. He glanced briefly at me before backing out of his parking spot. I asked, "How are things at home?"

"About the same," was his typically terse reply. I told him a few things about my trip, falling silent when he only responded with grunts. When we got home, Dad headed for the back porch to take a nap.

I looked around the empty kitchen and living room. A small artificial tree with a few red balls and strands of silver tinsel sat on an end table beside the television. Between working full time and her college exams, Mom hadn't had time to do much decorating. After my week with Carolyn and her family, our house seemed bleak and lifeless.

As I walked toward my bedroom, I noticed a paper with my name on it taped to the telephone on the kitchen wall. Mom's note said the local radio

Current Culture
December 1966

- Mattel offers new Twist & Turn Barbie for only $1.50 plus trade-in
- The Supreme Court votes 4-3 to allow the Braves to move from Milwaukie to Atlanta
- US life expectancy now 70.2 years
- 382,010 men were drafted into military service in 1966
- December 31 Dow Jones Industrial Average: 786

station asked me to come to the studio at 11:00 a.m. on December 24th to record a short Christmas message. *That's today, only a few hours from now!* I started to panic, then stopped for a brief prayer. *Help, Lord!*

I tossed my suitcase onto my bed and picked up my Thompson Chain Reference Bible, then sat quietly for a few moments. As I meditated, I knew I would speak about love, the topic uppermost in my mind. Thinking about the love I shared with Carolyn made it an easy transition to write about God's amazing love, demonstrated by His willingness to send His Son to earth to live with us, to know us, and to ultimately die for us.

Apparently my words were appropriate, because the station manager gave me a "thumbs-up" as I left the studio. After a busy afternoon, I sat at the kitchen table and expanded my thoughts into a sermon for the next day. I wasn't sure how many would make the effort to attend the Christmas morning service, but I hoped that my announcement would put them in a festive mood.

As I stood up to preach the next day, I smiled at the assembled faithful members. "I am very happy to tell you all that within the next year, there will be a pastor's wife here at Grace Chapel." After the initial intake of breath, there were smiles and applause. "Carolyn and I are officially engaged, and we hope to be married next September." When I said, "My topic today is love," there were appreciative chuckles. I quickly added, "God's love, expressed through Jesus." My faithful flock settled back to hear about the miracle of Christmas.

Since the shut-ins I normally visited on Sunday afternoon all had family in town, I spent a quiet afternoon at home. Mom left for swing shift after lunch, and I spent the afternoon buried in a biography. That evening it seemed strange to watch Sunday evening television shows with Dad instead of being at church.

At bedtime, I tried to communicate my thoughts and feelings to Carolyn.

December 25, 1966
Dearest Love,

We have been apart 53 hours and I miss you so much. My emotions have felt like molten lava since I left you. What have you done to me?

I arrived home at 7:30 yesterday morning, with no time for a nap before heading to a local radio station at 11:00 to record a Christmas message. After that, I visited several parishioners, and stopped to see a couple with a new baby before attending the wedding of a former member of our congregation.

By the way, Carolyn, you should congratulate me. I didn't think of you one single time today. Just a <u>thousand</u> times, actually. I dream about you every night. Just promise me that you won't let me get you off somewhere by myself when you're here in March. I plan to keep us both busy around other people when you're here. Unless you're the strongest-willed person in the world, you'll need that protection!

Goodnight, my beautiful princess.
Larry

On Monday, I called Jesse and invited him to shoot pool with me. As we played, I tried to find out what was going on with him.

"You're looking low lately, Jesse. What's happening?" He was silent as he lined up his shot.

"Not much," he finally grunted as a ball dropped into the pocket.

"Come on, Jesse. Something's eating you. I'm concerned."

"Why, what difference does it make to you?"

"It makes a difference to me that you're not yourself. At least tell me how I can pray."

"I don't think prayer works with families as messed up as mine."

"You can't really believe that, Jesse."

"Does it matter what I believe? Your life is going great, mine stinks."

"Whatever's happening in your family right now, nothing's impossible with God."

"Pray if you want to, I don't have faith." The closed expression on his face made it apparent that he wasn't going to open up any further, and we talked of trivial things as we finished our game.

On the way home, I pondered my relationship with Jesse. Years of perceived failure and rejection were tough to overcome. I was still thinking about him when I pulled up at the mailbox at home, but the letter in the pale blue envelope lifted my mood.

December 23, 1966
Dear Larry,

I hope you had a good trip back home. I can't believe that you have been here and are gone already. It seems like just the other day that I wasn't even sure you were coming. I'm so glad you made the trip.

If only you knew how wonderful it was for me to have you here. You open worlds for me that I could only dream about before, and give me a confidence that I've never had. I feel myself blossoming.

Larry, how I love you! To love and be loved in return is the most beautiful experience. I continually thank God for our love, and pray that I will be a worthy partner for you.

Goodnight, my darling.
Carolyn

The dull stretch between Christmas and New Year's was enlivened one evening by a visit from college friends. They had married the previous summer and were in their first year of teaching in a high school about thirty miles away. I took great pleasure in showing them photos of Carolyn and they were suitably impressed by her smile and my glowing description.

"You'll have to bring her to meet us when she comes in March, Larry," Donna said.

Ken added, "Any girl who can snag Larry Wade is someone I definitely want to meet!"

"Just wait 'til you meet her," I said. "She's even better in person."

Watching the interplay and obvious affection between my friends made me wish, for the hundredth time, that Carolyn and I didn't have to endure a long-distance romance. I could barely contain my longing as I wrote to her that evening.

December 28, 1967
Dear Carolyn,

What a day! I've been all over town, to the bank, the post office, visiting people who couldn't come to church on Sunday. As in most small towns, news travels fast, and I was congratulated on our engagement many times.

Some of the people I visited today had sad stories. One young couple had been trying to establish an evangelism ministry for several years, but ended up nearly starving. Now they're struggling with bitterness. At the post office I ran into a young woman whose husband is now in Vietnam. She really needs friends. I hope she'll come to church soon.

This evening I had a visit from some married friends from college. Donna brought me a little gift from her mother. I'm glad she and Ken seem happy. Her parents had me picked out to marry their daughter, but Donna and I were never romantically inclined. Seeing them together made me miss you terribly.

It has now been five days since I left you. The days are becoming easier, but the nights are bad. I dreamed about you again last night—this could become a detriment to my health!

It's not right for us to be separated on New Year's Eve. I hope and pray that this is the last holiday season that we will have to celebrate separately.

I love you. I wish my words could leap off the page and encircle you, to demonstrate the meaning of the words, "I love you."

Goodnight, beautiful princess,
Larry

On the last days of the year, I worked on some long overdue projects. I bought floor wax, a wax applicator, and two gallons of green paint. By the time I finished waxing the church floor, I was tired but satisfied with the gleaming results. I planned to paint the walls of the church library the following week. *A good way to start a new year!*

I felt rewarded for my efforts when I pulled another letter from Oregon out of the mailbox.

December 28, 1966
Dearest Larry,

Good morning. How is my Prince Charming on this dreary day? I hope you have more ambition than I do—I just want to curl up in a chair with a good book. But I'm babysitting two lively nephews, so that's out of the question.

My grades arrived in the mail yesterday. I got a 3.24, with two A's and the rest B's. I must have done well on the English Lit final, as I had a C- on the mid-term. What a pleasant surprise!

Last night I went with my friend Joanna to the wedding of some college classmates. The ceremony was awful, with the minister losing his place and struggling to find the right line. I also knew the bride and groom well enough to know that the words were just tradition, without real significance.

One amusing thing happened—when we were being escorted down the aisle for the ceremony, my friend Rick grabbed my hand as I walked by. I thought, "What's he doing?" Then I realized that he could feel my engagement ring through my glove. I looked back at him and he winked at me. Pretty clever way of getting the news, wasn't it?

The reception was interesting—Joanna and I drank coffee and watched our friends get high on champagne. We left the reception early, and Joanna offered to treat me at Farrell's Ice Cream Parlor to celebrate our engagement. While we were there a newlywed couple from school came in (married last week). I don't think they exchanged more than half a dozen words in the whole time they were there! He's the one who once told me that he wasn't sure he would be faithful to her if he found someone more attractive, so it wasn't surprising. What are people thinking, Larry?

That evening made me more determined than ever to remain pure in our relationship, no matter how hard it is. I'm so very grateful that you share my determination. If you didn't, we'd be in BIG trouble. Thank you for being a man of integrity and character!

Mom and I had a little disagreement last night. I was filling out the form for an engagement announcement in the local paper. When I wrote September 1967 as a probable wedding date on the information sheet, she hit the roof. She and Dad are so worried that I won't finish college. She nagged me about it until I was in tears. Things so easily go sideways when you're not here to buffer us and help adjust my perspective.

I was thinking tonight how wonderful life will be when we're always together. I wish I had a mental tape recorder to replay our conversations while you were here. I'm already forgetting things I wanted to remember. But I can recall the joy of being in your arms and the peace your presence brings me.

Goodnight again. I think of you constantly.

Carolyn

In the quiet house, as I read her letter a second time, I could almost hear her voice. *Has it only been a few days since we were together?*

Mom got home from work that evening much later than usual. "I was beginning to worry, Mom," I said. "Is everything okay?"

"You'll see," was her enigmatic answer. I waited impatiently while she went to her bedroom and changed from her nurse's uniform into her housedress. As she walked back into the kitchen, I saw headlights turn into the driveway.

"Are you expecting someone?" I asked.

"Just wait, Larry." She smiled as she walked to the window. Within a few minutes, a couple of men were hefting a large box marked Zenith Color Television onto our porch.

"Mom, you didn't!" I exclaimed.

"Yes, I did. I figured that if we can't go down to Pasadena to see the Rose Parade, the next best thing is seeing it in our own living room—in COLOR!"

"That, and the Rose Bowl game!"

"Well, you can watch the game, but I'll enjoy the parade. Maybe I'll invite the Maguire's over.

With major national New Years Day festivities postponed until Monday, there was a sense of expectation in my congregation on Sunday. The usual attenders were joined by family members visiting for the holidays. I challenged them to make a difference in their world in the coming year, and I saw tears in the eyes of several people, including Jesse. When I invited people to dedicate themselves to God's will for their lives, the entire group came to the altar. *Thank you, Lord. This is the reason I continue.*

After the service, I took communion elements to housebound Mr. and Mrs. Jackson. Their son and daughter-in-law were there, and when I asked if they would like to participate, they asked some questions. During the lengthy discussion that followed, I was able to share the entire Gospel message with them. I didn't want to pressure them into taking such an important step, but they seemed very thoughtful as I left.

Monday morning I drove into town to buy our traditional New Year's treat of donuts, which we shared with our next-door neighbors while watching the Rose Parade. The rare event of guests in our home made the day particularly enjoyable. I felt lazy spending the day eating and watching television, but when the football games were over, I quieted my conscience by typing Mom's term paper for her college Anatomy class.

Mail had been delayed by the long holiday weekend, so I was especially glad to get a letter from Carolyn on Thursday.

January 1, 1967
Dear Larry,

If this New Year's Day is any predictor of what's ahead, watch out! You won't be able to hold me down. (Well, maybe that's not strictly true...)

Seriously, it has been a very meaningful weekend, starting Sunday night at church. During a time of prayer and soul-searching, I felt the Lord pointing out bitterness. After the typical "Who, me?" reaction, I asked the Lord to expose my heart. Tears and repentance followed, as I began to recognize my resentment against my parents, my strict upbringing, and past circumstances. How easy it is to fool ourselves!

Later in the evening, a couple of women pulled me aside. They congratulated me on our engagement, and challenged me to act differently with my mother, as adult to adult, rather than as child to parent. You've been around Mom enough to understand how tough that will be. The women also prayed that I would be released from the restraints and hindrances of my childhood, and that my fear would be gone. That was especially meaningful to me.

Larry, do you have any idea what it's like to have overpowering fear, and not know what it is that you fear? It's a terrible thing, especially for a child. I am determined to trust God to remove those old fears from me.

All afternoon yesterday I prayed for a good opportunity to talk with Mom before I came back to school today. She went to bed right after dinner, so I went in and sat on the bed and did my best to talk to her as an adult about our plans, my schooling, and how I felt about her critical and negative comments. After some painful words and more than a few tears, the wall between us finally fell. By the end of our conversation, we were laughing and joking. After being afraid of her for so long, I feel <u>free</u>.

While I packed today, and on the drive down here, we actually discussed <u>wedding plans</u>! She even made a tentative guest list to see how large a church we will need to rent. This is a <u>radical</u> change for her. While you were here she was okay with the idea of our engagement, but after you left, she was NOT willing to talk about a September wedding. I'm sure my own change of attitude has improved our relationship.

It's good to be back at the dorm. Tricia came over at 11 tonight, and stayed until after 1 a.m. I'm going to be a good girl and go to bed as soon as I put this letter in an envelope.

I'll write more tomorrow. Goodnight, my beloved,
Carolyn

I sat holding Carolyn's letter, thinking about what she had written. Her admission of bitterness helped me understand some things that had puzzled me. I'd picked up an edginess in her interactions with her mother that seemed inconsistent with her behavior around other people. Her description of being plagued by fears made me want to wrap my arms protectively around her. *God, why do we have to be so far apart?*

I wanted her to know that her disclosures had made me respect her even more. Her honest sharing made me feel even closer to her, and I wished again that we could talk face to face. My meager budget prohibited a phone call, so a letter would have to do.

January 5, 1967
My lovely future bride,

Thank you for sharing your experience on New Year's Eve. I wasn't aware of the fears that you described, although I had noticed a tendency toward bitter comments about your upbringing. Your parents did what they thought was best for you, and they love you in their own way. I'm so glad your relationship with your mother is improving. Thank you for being honest with me about what you're going through—your candor makes me respect you even more, if that's possible.

Our New Year's celebration was a bit different this year. We had our usual donuts and hot chocolate (shared with our next door neighbors), but we watched the parade and the football game in <u>color</u>. I must say, it made a big difference!

It's very strange. Somehow I don't miss you quite as much as I did in the fall. Do you know why? #1, I believe I'll see you again in March——just ten weeks away, and #2, in less than a year, I'll have you beside me always. You'll be the best birthday present I'll ever receive!

Today I painted the library wall at the church. What a difference! I also installed padlocks on the doors to the bathrooms, which open to the outside. It will be a simple matter to unlock them before a service, and having them locked during the week will save lots of cleaning on Saturday.

I know this is a short letter, but not a lot is happening around here. Please pray for me and for my congregation. I have a feeling that this year is going to be challenging, and I am determined to remain true to God's purposes and his call.

Goodnight, Beautiful. As usual, I dreamed about you <u>all</u> last night. I'll see you again tonight in my dreams, I'm sure.

Au revoir,

Larry

Chapter 23

Carolyn

In spite of the drama and excitement of Christmas break, it was a relief to be back at school with a regular schedule of classes, work, and meetings. While mostly predictable, not everything in my college routine was enjoyable. Registration for the new term emptied my bank account, and my sleep was disrupted by several early-morning fire drills.

One thing I looked forward to was my "Candle-Lighting," to announce my engagement to the girls in the dorm. Until then, my diamond ring was concealed on a thin chain under my sweaters, and on my ring finger only late at night in the privacy of my room. I couldn't wait to show it off to everyone.

In my next letter, I described the ritual to Larry.

> **Current Culture**
> **January 1967**
>
> - 1966 casualties in Vietnam: 6,143, plus more than 30,000 wounded
> - President Johnson requests tax increase to fund the Vietnam War
> - First Super Bowl game played with the Green Bay Packers defeating the Kansas City Chiefs 35-10
> - Cost of a Super Bowl TV ad: $42,000
> - Zenith 20 inch color TV: $399.95

January 7, 1967
Darling,

Now everyone here knows about our engagement! Tonight was my Candle-Lighting, the traditional way we announce an engagement in the dorm.

After classes this afternoon, I borrowed a bike and rode to Independence to a florist. (I didn't want to ruin the surprise by being seen at the Monmouth florist.) For only $1.50, she decorated a white candle with three tiny red rosebuds and three baby white chrysanthemums, plus greenery and white ribbons. My ring fit on the candle just above the flowers.

A friend posted a sign in the dorm "Candle-Lighting Tonight." After closing time, everyone gathered in the lounge, with the girls on my floor sitting in the middle. The housemother lit the candle and while it was slowly passed around the circle, one of my friends read some love poems I had chosen. The second time the candle went around the circle, a friend reversed it back to me, and I blew it out, indicating that I was the lucky girl. After the gasps and applause, everyone sang the Joni Mitchell song, "My Best to You," wishing us a lifetime of love and dreams come true. It was very sweet.

Of course, the girls wanted to know how we met, since you're a "mystery man," and when I told them the story, several girls said, "It's just like a romance novel..."

I'm so glad I can talk freely about you now, and wear my engagement ring 24 hours a day, instead of just at night in my room.

You're going to get tired of hearing this, but my thoughts about you and our future are more wonderful and exciting to me every day. I love you, Larry David Wade. I love you so much I'd marry you on a moment's notice. I hate waking up each morning, because my alarm rudely pulls me out of dreams of you.

With all my love,
Carolyn

As I folded the letter and sealed the envelope, I realized that the music next door had been getting steadily louder. When I opened my door, the music quieted, but a few minutes after I closed the door, the volume went up again. My neighbors might enjoy listening to the Beatles at midnight, but I had tests the next day, and needed my sleep. I finally banged on the wall, and the music stayed low enough for me to doze off, falling into a pleasant dream about Larry.

His next letter let me know he was dreaming of me as well.

January 10, 1967
Dear Carolyn,

Nine more lousy weeks! I wish time wouldn't keep dragging until I see you again. I dreamed last night that we were both in grammar school and had to face something scary together. We both ended up smiling at the end of the dream. What do you make of that?

Thank you for the description of your candle-lighting ceremony. Are you sure you told them the way our romance actually happened? Did you throw in the detail that I proposed to you after knowing you less than a week? That puts us in the class of incurable romantics.

Jesse and I went up to Madera today to pick up some donated clothes for the orphanage in Mexico. We visited with some college friends, then stopped for pizza when we got back to Hanford. I didn't get home until 11:15.

By the way, our engagement announcement should be in the local papers next week. I'll send you a copy.

Goodnight,
Larry
P.S. I love you...you desirable woman, you!!!

After work on payday, I filled out an application for a half-fare student ID card for a major airline. While I hadn't gotten final approval from Mom and Dad for a trip to California at spring break, it wouldn't hurt to plan ahead. After mailing the form, I was late getting to the dining hall.

"Carolyn, we've been waiting," said Judy, the dorm Vice President, waving me over to her table. "There's pie for dessert tonight, and you know what that means!"

"Oh, no, I've lost my appetite," I groaned, glancing at the dorm girls gathering around me with mischievous expressions on their faces. I really didn't want to eat my dessert under the table.

"Oh, yes," said Judy. "We can't let you skip out on this tradition. It's pumpkin with whipped topping, extra messy." She handed me a slice of pie on a plate, ceremoniously removing the fork as she handed it to me. A couple of other girls moved chairs and grabbed my arms and shoulders to push me under the table.

I knew if I put up a fight they'd enjoy it more, so I tried to pull away. In the struggle, the first piece of pie landed on the floor. Judy grabbed another piece from someone at the next table, and I reluctantly crawled under the table to eat with my hands. When I stood up again holding up the clean plate, there was applause and congratulations.

At a dorm meeting later that evening, I had to give the girls ten reasons why I loved Larry. Watching their faces as I described him, I was reminded again what a treasure God had given me, and felt incredibly blessed.

My heart was bursting when I wrote to Larry that night.

January 12, 1967
Dear Larry,

Another hectic day gone, filled with thoughts of you. Last night I don't think I even dreamed--I was so tired.

This evening was hopefully the last in the line of engagement traditions. Girls from my dorm were waiting for me at dinner, ready to enforce the public dining room celebration/humiliation. After I ate a piece of pumpkin pie with whipped cream <u>with my hands</u> sitting under a table, everyone in the dining hall joined in to sing "My Best to You" again. Later, at our house meeting, it was easy to give the girls ten reasons why I love you.

I've decided to drop my Crafts class, as new policies require students to pay for their own supplies. On my limited budget, with saving for a wedding, I just can't afford the extra cost. Instead of crafts, I signed up for "Marriage and Family Life." I've heard good things about the class, and thought it might be appropriate.

I'm going to have to hoard my pennies this term. Last year, Mom would send me $10 or so once a month. This year, that hasn't happened, so I'm on my own. Unfortunately my parents didn't give me much financial education. They don't operate with a budget, at least that I'm aware of, and are *generally secretive about finances. We'll have to work on that together when we're married.*

"When we're married..." What a wonderful thought. As always, I long to be near you. I never knew before what it is to want someone so much that it's an actual physical ache. I try not to think about it, but that's really impossible, because you're as much a part of me as breathing. More so, in fact, because breathing is unconscious, and my need for you is conscious. Sometimes it's so real I can almost feel your arms around me and your lips on mine. But you're not here, and I'm alone.

I love you, darling. You are everything to me that makes life worth living. For the first time, my life has a definite goal. Everything points to the time when we'll be together, forever!

Sweet dreams, my love.

Carolyn

The next day I was glad to find a letter from Mom in my mailbox. I hadn't heard from her since Christmas break, and wondered if she or Dad were ill. The letter said the Sunday services at Paul & Emily's had been especially good. Dad was taking vitamins and feeling better. While she didn't specifically mention my wedding plans, the positive tone of her letter gave me hope that our disagreements and hurt feelings were a thing of the past.

Later that evening, I took a break from studies to join the group of girls in the basement TV lounge. The room was unusually crowded because of the celebrity stars in the evening's movie, *The Summer Place*. As I watched the story of the young lovers unfold, my aching loneliness grew. At the same time, the movie reinforced my determination to keep my desires within godly boundaries.

There was no letter in my box the following day, and I waited impatiently for the twenty-four hours before more mail was delivered. When I opened Larry's next letter, it made me smile.

January 14, 1967
Dear Carolyn,

Thank you so much for sending the wallet-size photos. I've wanted one to carry around, but hesitated to ask you to spend extra money for them. Now I can show your pretty face to everyone in sight! I am so proud of you, I just can't help wanting to brag.

By the way, I hope you don't mind if I start collecting things for our future home. Occasionally I see bargains and it's not likely that we'll be able to buy everything new when we get married. Some friends of mine are selling a couch and matching chairs that I would like to buy, if you approve. The set cost $160 a few months ago, and they are selling it for $50 because they're moving to Los Angeles and won't have room for it. Let me know what you think.

Are you as lonely on Saturday nights as I am? It seems like all the loneliness of a thousand nights weighs on me the last night of the week. And you have to endure watching other girls get dressed up and go out with their boyfriends. If only you knew how much it bothers me that I can't take you out on a date every weekend.

Tomorrow will be a busy day with morning and evening sermons and visiting shut-ins in the afternoon. Please pray for this community, Carolyn. There is a constant battle between good and evil. My church and others need to have an impact. It's time...

Goodnight, Sweetheart,
Larry

On Friday night Joanna, Martie, Tricia and I paid the 10 cent admission at the local campus theater to watch an entertaining movie, *The Wonderful World of the Brothers Grimm*. Afterward, we borrowed a car and drove to Farrell's Ice Cream Parlor in Salem. We were silly and laughed a lot until Joanna said, "You know, we won't have very many times like this again. I'll be married in less than eight weeks!"

"You're right, a lot of things will change soon," I said. "I won't be back here next year."

Tricia added, "I'm thinking of changing schools or taking a year off." We were all quiet as we paid our bill and left the restaurant.

In the car, Martie broke the silence. "We've had so much fun together, let's not end the evening on a sad note. Remember our freshman year, our rooms were all close together? That was so much fun." We spent the ride home telling stories on each other and remembering joys and heartbreaks.

The following day there was another letter from Mom that made my heart sink. I wanted to sit down right away and write to Larry, but between work and meetings after dinner I didn't get a break. I finally pulled out my stationery just after midnight.

January 16, 1967
Dear Larry,

I'd just written "Dear Larry" when our beloved fire alarm rang, summoning all of us to drag our warm bodies into the cold night air. Rumor has it that since everyone has managed to get out of the dorm in the allotted time during the last couple of drills, next time we'll be able to use the inside stairs instead of the outside fire escapes. Thank heaven for small favors!

I'm delighted that you found furniture for our future home, Larry. If it's a neutral color, I'm all for it. I think I have enough Green Stamps to get some cookware for our home. Do you like Revere Ware? I've never used it, but it's highly recommended.

On a more serious note, you might want to sit down before reading further. I got a long letter from Mom today. She gave a list of reasons why we shouldn't get married in September, ending with: "Considering your current plans, Father and I cannot give our blessing to your marriage."

So now you know where they stand. Shall I clarify my own position? I understand their concern, but I can't bear the thought of another year apart. I don't feel that I need to finish school here when I can finish in California after we're married.

We both need to pray about this. As brave as my words are, I feel caught between wanting my parents' blessing and my love (and need) for you.

Goodnight, Larry. Every thought of you, every letter I receive, is very precious to me.

Carolyn

Several nights later I was roused from my absorption in *Madam Bovary* by a loud knock. I opened the door to find a freshman girl who said, "You have a phone call downstairs." Hoping it was Larry, I dashed down the two flights of stairs to grab the phone in the mail room, where I might have a little privacy.

"Hello?" I said, breathless.

"Hi, Sweetheart. It's Larry."

"It's wonderful to hear your voice, but it has to be a big occasion for you to call me."

"I got your letter today, the one about your Mom's letter."

"Ah, that one." I sighed.

"Yes, that one. Thanks for letting me know right away. Carolyn, I'm at a serious disadvantage being here in Hanford. I'd like to talk to your parents in person."

"So what are we going to do, Larry? I know we're supposed to be together, but I don't want to get married without my parents' blessing."

"I honestly don't believe it will come to that, Carolyn. I have a very strong feeling that God is going to work out something unexpected."

"But how, Larry? You've already quit your job to stay at the church. It doesn't make sense to quit the church too."

"I don't plan on quitting the church. I can't explain why I feel so strongly, but I just know that God is working, and I'm convinced it's going to be fine. The worst thing you could do right now is waste time worrying about this. You have too many other important things to think about, like your dorm responsibilities and your grades."

"I know I shouldn't worry, but when you're so far away, and when Mom makes such a big deal about this, it's hard." Words from my mother's letter floated into my brain and brought tears to my eyes. I leaned against the wall, grateful for the comfort of Larry's voice.

"You'll just have to trust me on this, Carolyn. Look how God brought us together. Our lives are in his hands, and I know he'll pull us through." He paused, waiting for me to respond. Tears closed my throat. "Are you there, Carolyn? Are you okay?" Larry asked.

I swallowed hard. "Yes, I'm here. It's just been so hard dealing with this without you here. It's such a relief to hear your voice and have your encouragement."

The operator broke into our conversation. "Three minutes are up. Do you wish to continue?"

"I'll write," said Larry, trying to get in a few last words. "I love you." Before I could say "I love you" I heard a click, and he was gone.

Chapter 24

Larry

Heavy fog creeping around the trees created a ghostly landscape outside our kitchen window. We didn't have snow or blizzards in the San Joaquin Valley, but winter fog from marshy grasslands made driving hazardous, and I was glad Mom wasn't heading out for a night shift at the hospital.

On the table next to me was a growing pile of envelopes I'd been filling. Mondays were a let-down for me, and I assumed that most ministers had similar feelings after the concentrated effort of Sunday. I tried to schedule tasks that didn't require a lot of brain power, such as preparing letters on behalf of the orphanage in Mexico.

Current Culture January 1967
• 25,000 hippies attend "Human Be-in" at San Francisco's Golden Gate Park
• PBS begins as 70-station national educational TV network
• Three astronauts are killed during a test launch fire
• Thirteen U.S. helicopters are shot down in one day in Vietnam
• Average cost of a new car: $2,650

Mom came into the kitchen and said, "Could you help me study for my Poly-Sci exam tomorrow night? I'm worried."

"Sure, Mom, I'll quiz you. Where's your book?" I was proud of Mom's determination to earn a college education, in spite of her age and exhausting work load. In the past few years, she had gotten her GED and immediately started taking college classes. She would soon finish her Associates degree.

She handed me her textbook. "It's right here. I've been studying all morning, but I'm scared to death."

"Do you have quizzes or tests from the rest of the semester? We could start there."

She pulled out a thick notebook, and turned to a green tab. "Here they are," she said, pulling a stack of papers off the rings of the binder. "I've gone over these several times, but I just don't feel confident."

"Okay, here goes." As I began to read her the test questions, I realized that she knew the material very thoroughly, even to the textbook page number where information was found. But her brow was furrowed and she fidgeted nervously. I tried to reassure her.

"You know this better than I did when I took the class, Mom, and I pulled a B."

"But you understand it better, Larry. It just doesn't stick in my brain."

"It seems pretty well stuck in your brain from what I can tell. Don't worry about it, you'll be fine." She gave me an "easy for you to say" lifted-eyebrow look, and reached for an apron to start dinner.

I took it as an opportunity for letter-writing, and headed for my bedroom.

January 16, 1967
Dear Carolyn,

How is my beautiful love today? I hope you're in your usual good humor with a smile on your face. If not, then why not part my favorite lips into a smile right now?

For some reason, you have been on my mind more than usual today. When I woke up this morning, it was as if your presence filled the room. I only wish...

I had my usual Monday "hangover" after the extra physical and emotional energy expended yesterday. It's a day for doing even less than usual. I got some fundraising letters ready for sending out about the orphanage in Mexico. I also helped prepare Mom for her Poly-Sci exam tomorrow. While I wasn't the world's best student, I never had the kind of fear about exams that she has. She knows the material, but is still very frightened about the test.

Tomorrow I'll spend the day in the 10x10 church library, installing a new acoustic ceiling. Doesn't that sound exciting?

I'm glad you don't want to wait another eighteen months to finish school before we get married. I just couldn't wait that long. If we could marry next week, it would be too long for me! This may sound trite to you, but there are deep feelings behind each syllable. Carolyn, I need you so very, very much. When the Apostle Paul spoke of those who are able to handle the "burning," he certainly wasn't referring to me. You, my sweet, are the first temptation of any kind that I have not been able to resist. For the first time in my life, I find myself unable to control all my thoughts and emotions.

Perhaps it's not right to tell you this now, but I have a deep physical ache, both day and night. When the psychology books I read mentioned the sex drive, it had no real meaning for me, but that's no longer the case. Now I feel I'm at risk to lose the first big battle of my life. I pray to God that you don't have half the ache that I have.

The words may sound hollow, but I love you. If only I could let you know just how much. Through the coming years, I will do my best to show the depth of my love. It may take an entire lifetime, but I plan to show you. Thank you, Carolyn, for loving me.

Larry

Tuesday I hoped to finish the library ceiling project at the church, but I discovered that the salesman had miscalculated the material I needed, leaving me short eighteen squares. The materials were back-ordered, so I spent the afternoon priming and installing the new library door.

When I pulled up at the mailbox, I was pleased to see a letter postmarked "Monmouth, Oregon." I didn't even wait to change clothes before opening and reading Carolyn's letter.

January 18, 1967

Dear Larry,

Why is it that no matter how carefully I plan, I never get everything done? I'll have to really hit the books this weekend, especially to make up for the sessions I missed by joining the "Marriage and Family" class late. It's quite good, by the way. I like the prof—he's very interesting and down to earth. In the first class I attended, we watched a film about inter-faith marriage, which prompted a lively discussion.

I gave my first speech today, with shaking knees and hands like ice. I was afraid I'd stutter and stumble, but it went pretty well. However, I was so concerned about what I was saying that I didn't pay attention to <u>how</u> I said it: voice tone, facial expression, gestures, or enthusiasm. I ended up with a C-minus, but that gives me a lot of room for improvement.

In spite of the long list of books we have to read, my "Realism" class is quite enjoyable. There are only seven students, which allows for good discussions. Dr. Wolfe is very entertaining, an extreme stereotype of a professor. He has a goatee, wears his hair in a pompadour, and has an affected accent. He's basically a fake, but would be the first to admit it. He's very uninhibited and emotional when he lectures, sometimes swearing and always puffing away on his unfiltered cigarettes. I learned several new words when I took a class from him last year. Bottom line, he knows the material, and his teaching style really makes me think.

Some time, would you send me a list of your pet peeves? I'd like to have an understanding of what I might need to avoid after we're married.

It's already past midnight, which means that all good girls named Carolyn Lee Cooke should be in bed dreaming about Larry David Wade. I'll have to get right to it.

Love and kisses,
Carolyn

As so often happened, I had mixed emotions reading Carolyn's letter. I was happy to hear about her life, but sad that I couldn't share it.

The following week was blessed with unusually warm weather for January, so I did some yard work for Mom. She asked me to move a crepe myrtle shrub and plant a rose bush from the local nursery. In the middle of those projects, I noticed standing water in a place that should have been dry.

Further investigation revealed the likelihood of a broken pipe somewhere between the house and the well, a mere seventy-five feet.

In the next few days, my digging gave me sore shoulders and an aching back, and I was grateful for the early winter sunsets. In the evenings, I let Carolyn know what was happening in the San Joaquin Valley.

January 24, 1967
Dear Carolyn,

Look at the date! Time is going faster than I expected. It's already more than half-way through January!

I'm sorry I didn't write yesterday, but I've worked the last few days digging a trench and laying pipe between the house and the well. Late in the afternoon today I drove over to the church to finish installing the ceiling, since the additional tiles had arrived. After dinner, I went to visit a parishioner who is now home from the hospital.

Sunday's services went very well, by the way. One woman who often sleeps during sermons declared, "That was the best sermon I've heard in a long time. It was just what I needed." While I appreciated her comments, it made me wonder if she's actually heard any of my other sermons.

My efforts at updating the church are starting to pay off. It looks better than it has in years. Members of the congregation are starting to comment and take a sense of pride in keeping it clean and orderly.

The news about your Marriage and Family Class is good. When I told Mom and Dad that you had dropped a class, Mom said, "She deserves three units of extra credit anyway, for letter-writing!" How very true!

By the way, I've been able to collect quite a selection of household goods. We now have a teapot, some salt and pepper shakers, an iron skillet, and a clever measuring cup. I hope you don't mind if I pick up some things for our house.

<u>Our house</u>. You know, that phrase means a very exciting change in my thinking, from 'me' and 'mine' to 'we' and 'our.' I don't know how people exist without someone to share life with.

When I took the engagement notice to the local paper, the society editor looked at your picture, she said, "Why, she's pretty." How about that? It's about time the rest of the world sees that. And I know that your beauty is more than skin deep.

On that note, I'll say goodnight, Princess. I really do love you, even if I do skip writing to you occasionally.

Larry

P.S. Please make the next eight weeks hurry by, will you? I want you here soon.

When the weekly local paper was delivered, I searched every page, but none of the three engagement announcements in the local news section was mine. I finally found it in the "Social and Community News" section. Apparently the editor thought my ministerial occupation rated a different treatment. I just hoped my friends wouldn't miss it. Later that day, I drove to the newspaper office and purchased eight copies. Mom wanted to send the clipping to several relatives, and I wanted to send one to Carolyn as well.

On Tuesday I drove Dad to the hospital in Fresno. His doctor believed that Dad's hearing could be significantly improved by a fairly simple operation. Needing to kill time after Dad checked in, I found a pay phone and called a friend who had commuted to Fresno State with me. When we met at a local coffee shop, her haggard appearance shocked me.

"What's going on, Lenore? Are you okay?"

"Not really. It's been a rough year so far, Larry. Sometimes I think I'm going to crack up."

"I'm so sorry. What's happening?"

"My job isn't going well, and I'm thinking about breaking up with my boyfriend. He doesn't really act like he cares about me, and sometimes I even wonder if God even cares about me."

"I believe that He does, Lenore, but I know that it's hard to understand when things are rough. What's happening with your job?"

For the next hour, she unloaded her frustration and fears about her job and her boyfriend. I tried to be a good listener, and not frustrate her with pat answers. Finally she said, "Well, enough about me. How are you doing? You look happier than the last time I saw you."

"Well, last time we saw each other was graduation, and we were both worn to a frazzle. Since then, a lot has happened. The biggest thing is that I'm engaged!"

"What?" she exclaimed. "You're kidding. Anyone I know?" I told her about Carolyn and how we had met.

She tilted her head and smiled. "It's about time you met the right girl. You're the only guy I've ever met who would actually make a good husband."

When I checked back at the hospital, Dad was in the recovery room, still groggy from anesthesia. The nurses said he'd be fine after a night's care at the hospital, so I headed back to Hanford.

Our mailbox contained several bills, a magazine, and a familiar blue envelope. I was always intrigued by Carolyn's pale blue stationery, tissue-thin, and often with a pressed flower or leaf between the two layers of the envelope. I was especially happy when the envelope carried the faint scent of her perfume or a lipstick print where she had "sealed with a kiss." Her latest missive didn't disappoint.

January 25, 1967

Dearest Love,

How were your services last weekend? I don't really remember the sermon at the church I attended--my mind was several hundred miles south.

Thank you for sharing your feelings about our emotional struggles, as I'm having similar struggles. Sometimes I want you so much it seems like I can't stand it. Unfortunately, surges of emotion can hit at rather inappropriate moments, like during a lecture. I have to pray or distract myself by focusing on the prof's words. Occasionally I wish we were the kind of people to whom physical intimacy is a "take it or leave it" proposition. But not for a moment would I want us to be different. It's not going to be easy in the next few months, especially when we're together.

I've never dealt with this kind of temptation either, Larry. I thought it would be a simple matter—you find the right one, fall in love, get engaged, get married, and then have sex. Until marriage, kisses should be sufficient. But I found out very quickly that kisses aren't always enough with you. What has happened to us?

We are going to have to be very, very careful when we are together in March. We have a responsibility to each other to make sure that we don't violate our consciences and God's standard. As much as I long for you <u>totally</u>, we both know we would never forgive ourselves if we crossed the line.

On a lighter subject, my Realism class was something of a breakthrough today. I was in charge of the discussion, and had to compare stories on death by Chekov and Tolstoy. I had spent quite a bit of time on them, and picked out eight parallel passages. As it happened, it was exactly what Dr. Wolfe wanted, and it turned out very well. I get so much more out of his classes than the lecture-only classes I have to sit through.

I had a funny dream early this morning. I was at church in Portland and as I shook hands with people in the lobby, I turned to find you standing there. We hugged in the aisle in front of everybody. You said you wanted to see me so much you just got on a plane and showed up without letting me know. Then the dream got confused, and my alarm went off.

It's time to put on some soft music, read my Bible, and then lay my head on my pillow so I can dream of you.

I love you,

Carolyn

Back at the hospital in Fresno the next day, I waited while Dad signed discharge forms before helping him to the car. He was unsteady on his feet, either from medication or lingering vertigo from the ear operation. When my questions and comments during the drive were met with silence, I turned up the radio and tried to ignore his occasional groans. Classical music wasn't his thing, but on this trip he didn't complain.

I knew I owed Carolyn a letter that evening

January 30, 1967
Hello Beautiful,
Yesterday started a wee bit earlier than the average day. I got up at 6 a.m. and headed directly over to the church to turn on the heat. At 9:00 I picked up a young man I'm working with, and we went back to the church to open up all the rooms and set things up. Then at 9:30 I left to pick up other people who needed rides.

The service was pretty good, although several regulars were missing, including Jesse and his mother. It's amazing how empty seats stand out in a small congregation. Somehow, you were on my mind so strongly I almost expected to see you smiling up at me.

Today I received the book you sent, "The Art of Loving." I'll send it back tomorrow, as I already read it straight through. It was a rainy Monday, after all. While I didn't agree with everything he said (especially about God), he had many excellent points. I was interested in the few marks you made in the book. If you want to understand my childhood, page 83 describes what I experienced: adequate "milk," but no "honey." Good meals and a clean home were far more important than silly little things like affection. My parents never showed affection in front of us—maybe that's why I have a tendency to stay detached from people.

You asked me to send a list of pet peeves, so here are a few:
1. *Anyone who makes me late.*
2. *Being taken for granted.*
3. *A girl who won't allow me to treat her like a lady (opening doors, helping her with her coat, etc.)*
4. *A woman who ignores her mate in public.*
5. *A woman who belittles her husband to others.*
6. *A girl who tries to dominate others.*
7. *A woman who doesn't kiss and hug her husband at least forty-five times a day.*

Now that you've seen the start of my list, are you still willing to marry me? I look forward to receiving your list soon.

Do you realize it's been nearly five months since that wonderful September night when I proposed to you? That was one of the wisest moves I ever made!

I didn't get a letter today, which means I should have the pleasure of two tomorrow. That will be wonderful. If only you knew how much they mean to me. Thank you for your faithfulness in writing to me.

I worry about you, Carolyn. You may sometimes feel like a squirrel on a treadmill, but please don't give up hope. When you have your diploma in your hand, you will be very glad that you finished.

In March when you come here, you'll need to bring a tape recorder, with a pre-recorded tape that says, "No, no, no, no..." If you don't, my feelings might get the best of me, and we may end up in Reno for a quick wedding.

The thing I miss most right now is saying "I love you" face to face. Please hurry the weeks until March.

Larry

The following day found me back at the church again, ready to finish my work on the library. I dragged out the ladder and tools and installed molding between the ceiling and walls.

When I got home, the afternoon paper had arrived, but the mailbox was empty. Disappointed, I browsed casually through the newspaper. In the classified ads I saw a bedroom set for sale for $35. I jumped in my car and drove to the address listed, but it was such a bargain someone else had beat me to it and was carrying it out to their truck. I consoled myself with the thought that if there was one bargain, there was likely to be another eventually.

With no mail delivery on Sunday, I had to wait another day before Carolyn's next letter arrived. It was worth waiting for.

January 30, 1967

Dear Larry,

It didn't rain today. Other than that, I don't know what good thing I can say. In case you're wondering, it was Monday. It started out wrong and isn't ending much better. I haven't felt well, and spent a couple hours in bed trying to shake off a cold. The Vice-President took over the dorm meeting because I felt so lousy.

Earlier today, Joanna came over and took me down to her apartment to see her wedding dress. Since her wedding is only six weeks away, she picked out her china and silver last weekend, and also her trousseau suit. I'm happy for her, but wouldn't like what they're facing. They won't have a honeymoon, and she goes back to school a week after their wedding. That's not what I want! I want plenty of time with just <u>you</u> on my mind.

By the way, thanks for sending the clipping of our engagement announcement. It's on my bulletin board, along with other assorted treasures.

Today in "Marriage and Family" we discussed companionship and roles in marriage. While the prof was digressing onto the topic of "mate selection" he said it wasn't necessarily realistic to have a checklist of qualities to look for. When he was in seminary he and his friends had to be careful who they dated, because "being a minister's wife is the toughest position a woman can have." He glanced at me when he said it. Sometime I'll have to tell him about the list you had before we met—I think he'd appreciate it.

The other day I got a letter from one of the airlines I had contacted, giving me four possible itineraries from Portland to Fresno. Then tonight I got a person-to-person call from another airline, giving me all their flight times. It seems I can get to Fresno via San Francisco in 4-5 hours total time, for about $45.00. That will work for me!

Thank for your list of pet peeves. Mine are very similar—being delayed, taken for granted, etc. Here are a few more:
1. *A spouse holding back something that bothers them, then blurting it out in front of friends, or worse, in-laws.*
2. *A husband who says, "How can you be tired? You were just at home all day."*

Here are some things I LIKE.
1. *A man who tells me when I look good, smell nice, or cooked a good meal.*

> 2. *A man who treats me like a lady.*
> 3. *A man who doesn't mind just sitting quietly and enjoying my company.*
>
> *I spent time consoling my friend Ellen today. She's really having a rough time with her fiancé. He was supposed to come home at Christmas, but didn't get leave. Then he was supposed to be here this weekend, but was sent to Georgia instead. She hasn't seen him since July. And we think we have it bad! I don't know how they can stand it.*
>
> *I had a hard time going to sleep last night, even though I wasn't feeling great. I had some music on, but finally turned it off because it was interfering with my thoughts (of you).*
>
> *Goodnight, love. May the days fly until I can be in your arms.*
>
> *Carolyn*

Reading her last line over again, I sat back and imagined how it felt to have my arms around her. Within moments, the familiar ache of loneliness seeped into my body like a chilly fog.

Six more weeks of separation!

Chapter 25

Carolyn

"You could take out a short-term loan," said the clerk at the registrar's office. Seeing my look of consternation, she added quickly, "You can borrow up to ninety-eight dollars with no red tape or interest, just a fifty-cent carrying charge. You have until the end of the term to pay it back."

She chuckled at my relieved expression, and handed me a one-page application. I only needed another $50.00 to pay my board and room on time, but my grant money wouldn't arrive for another thirty days. The short term loan would solve my financial problems for another month.

Current Culture February 1967
• American Basketball Association is born
• 2,500 women storm the Pentagon in protest of the Vietnam war
• The U.S. government commits 25,000 soldiers to new battle near Cambodian border
• Federal minimum wage is increased to $1.40 per hour
• Carolyn's hourly wage, $1.60

My step was lighter as I headed back to the dorm, and my spirits ballooned even higher when I saw the letter in my box.

February 1, 1967
Dear Carolyn,
Today there were two letters from you in the mailbox, and I devoured them. You have no idea how welcome they were today.

It was a day for menial, seemingly pointless tasks such as mowing the lawn. Yes, I do have to keep mowing the lawn even in winter here, since our climate is so mild. At least it helps pass the time.

Tonight's mid-week service was really very nice. Everyone seemed to be blessed by it, and there was a wonderful spirit of love in the congregation. At times like this my efforts seem especially worthwhile.

I realized today that if we do everything that's on my list when you're here for spring break, we won't have any time to ourselves. Something on the schedule will have to go. Why should you fly all the way down here for me to take you to visit people I can see any time? That would be the height of insanity.

In case you haven't guessed, I'm pretty excited about you coming. You'll see the real me, in my true setting. Actually, I'm planning to make sure all the skeletons are carefully hidden away before you arrive. If you have to live out of your suitcase because all the closet doors are locked, you'll understand why.

That's enough nonsense for one letter. I hope your dreams are sweet tonight.

Larry

P.S. Do you know how much I love you? I won't try to tell you; there just isn't enough ink or paper. I'll just have to show you.

I read the letter again, sighed, and added it to the stack on my bookshelf. Larry's P.S. brought up memories and images that were very distracting. But the pile of books on my desk was a reminder of why I was spending money on college. Trying to prioritize, I finally settled back on my pillows with one of the required novels on the *Realism in Literature* booklist.

We never knew quite what to expect in that class. The language and immorality in some of the required books took me beyond my comfort zone. I often wished I could scrub my brain after reading some of the explicit scenes. On the other hand, I found the class intellectually challenging, and it was definitely broadening my horizons, although in ways my parents wouldn't approve.

Wednesday's class was no exception. After his usual glance around the room to see who was absent, Dr. Wolfe lit the first of his cigarettes. As the wisps of smoke reached us, he said, "Today we're going to talk about sentimentalism and moral values in literature." *Moral values? There wasn't much morality in today's assigned reading!*

Dr. Wolfe continued. "Let me ask you a question. Does an immoral character in immoral situations make a novel immoral?" As usual, the guy at the end of the row shot his hand up immediately, and spouted off his typically unconsidered response. The professor listened with raised eyebrows but heard him out, and then glanced at the rest of us. "Anyone else have an opinion?" The resulting twenty-minute discussion was heated. Someone commented about the increase of eroticism in American literature, which started Dr. Wolfe on an off-topic rant about euphemisms. "Why not call a dirty book a dirty book, instead of 'erotic literature'?" he asked.

Not for the first time, I wished that I could bring a tape recorder to class so Larry could enjoy our lively debate. I knew he had read some of the same books for his English degree, and wondered if his classes had been as challenging.

After my last afternoon class, I headed for dinner, then to the library. I had just enough time to do an hour's research at the library for my next speech before heading to work for my Wednesday evening shift. Between the library and the office, I ran into my dorm to grab Larry's letter out of my box and read it outside the Resource Center.

February 10, 1967
Dear Carolyn,

In case you hadn't noticed, February is the month for lovers. Watch out! You may enjoy it this year.

Today I spent quite a bit of time at the church. I had planned to buy more materials to update the building, but when I looked into a storage space under the platform today, I found nearly everything I need. There were several cans of good paint, electrical parts, and tile for the library floor.

Let's hear it for God's perfect planning! The building will be enhanced, and the work will keep me off the streets.

All of this will help keep my mind off the fact that each day when I wake up, you are hundreds of miles away. The days are lonely, but the nights are worse. Because of our growing closeness, my dreams have become much more vivid. And that's if and when I actually fall asleep. I toss and turn most nights, longing for you. I keep telling myself, "It's all in your mind," but unfortunately that's not strictly true. Waking up from a dream about you, I could only cry out, "God, help me!"

In your letters you've implied that you're going through similar things. I'm sorry you have to go through all of this, but perhaps it will make our reunion all the sweeter, if that's possible. When we are together, I find the only peace and contentment I've ever known. When I put my arms around you, the rest of the world fades, and only that moment of time has any meaning.

I thank God for July 3, 1966, the day we met. Have courage--there are only six more weeks until we see each other!

I love you, Carolyn. Always remember that.

Larry

I folded the letter, hoping the blush on my cheeks would subside before anyone came to my desk with a question. As I walked by a study table I heard a student say, "Do you have your skis here? I heard it might snow this weekend." The comment lifted my spirits; snow would be a welcome break from the endless rain of our typical Oregon winter. I couldn't remember the last day we'd seen the sun or even a spot of blue in the thick gray cloud canopy above the campus. I was glad that I had broken out of my conservative mold and bought a bright pink raincoat; wearing it lifted my spirits on the gloomy days.

Coughs and sniffles were background noise in every lecture hall, and there were empty seats in the dining hall and absences in every class. At least the days were getting a little longer, and it was now still light when I left work at five o'clock.

Avoiding the colds that were constantly passed around in the dormitory wasn't as much of a concern to me as other physical issues. In the last few months it had been increasingly difficult to maintain my normal schedule and keep up with all my responsibilities during my monthly cycle.

On Wednesday morning, I dragged myself out of bed and barely made it to my early morning French class. My misery must have been apparent, because the girl next to me leaned over and said, "Are you okay, Carolyn? You look awful."

"Thanks a lot," I replied with a rueful smile. "Just that time of the month."

"Oh, I'm sorry." She gave me an understanding glance as I tried to concentrate on Dr. Girard's increasingly rapid French, feeling more ill by the moment. Suddenly I was hit by an intolerable wave of nausea, and bolted out of the room. As I ran toward the restroom, I heard Dr. Girard call uncertainly, "Carolyn?"

After a prolonged episode of dry heaves, I sat on the cold granite floor, grateful for the coolness of the tile wall against my cheek. *God, help me, this is the worst yet. I can't live this way.*

When my body had calmed, I walked back to my dorm, glad that the sidewalks were mostly empty with classes still in session. I dragged myself up the three flights of stairs to my room and crawled back into my unmade bed, laying huddled to ease the cramps, praying for relief. Footsteps in the hallway and slamming doors were receding noise as I slipped into a restless doze.

It was noon when I woke up, feeling slightly better. I tried to remember what day it was, and what my afternoon schedule held. Lunch was out of the question, but I could probably conceal my misery enough to work my two-hour shift. I stumbled across the hall to the bathroom and tried to salvage my hair and makeup before heading across the campus.

"Under the weather today, Carolyn?" Mrs. Roberts, my boss, looked at me kindly as she passed my desk.

I gave her a weak smile. "Just temporary. I'll be fine." Her raised eyebrows indicated doubt, but she shrugged and returned to her office. Once she closed her door, I made a quick phone call to schedule an appointment at the Student Health Center for 4:15. I'd just make it there after my last class of the day.

After the appointment, I went straight to the dining hall. Weakness from not eating all day was more pressing than potential nausea. I found an empty seat with some girls from the dorm, and tried to be social, but the doctor's unexpected words were blaring in my mind, crowding out all thoughts and conversation. This was one night I wouldn't wait until the end of the evening to write to Larry. As my future husband, he deserved to know about my disquieting conversation with the doctor.

February 3, 1967
Dear Larry,

Marriage and Family class was the one bright spot in my day. We spent most of the hour discussing incompatibility and divorce. Some of the examples the prof told us were quite amusing. For instance, he knew of a couple who had been married for fifty years, but hadn't spoken to each other for the last twenty. When absolutely necessary, they would communicate through their cats. She would say, "Patches, would you tell Mr. Jones to..." That would never work for us, since you don't like cats!

One very important thing happened that you need to know about. I hope you don't mind me being completely frank, but I want you to know what's been going on with me. I went to the doctor today because I get extremely sick each month during my period—terrible cramps, nausea, and vomiting. This has been going on for years, but today was the worst ever. I was so sick during French class I had to leave abruptly and run down the hall to the restroom.

After an exam and questions today, the doctor said that there's no specific physical reason, I just happen to be an unlucky woman. When I asked if there was anything at all that could be done, he said, "There is one thing that's become available recently--birth control pills." He must have realized this wasn't what I wanted to hear, because he said, "Their original purpose was to help women like you who have adverse adverse symptoms. Preventing conception is a side benefit."

I don't know how you feel about birth-control in general, as we haven't discussed some of the more intimate aspects of marriage. You made a comment once that let me think you might not be opposed to birth control, but I know "The Pill" is VERY controversial among Christians. Please let me know how you feel about this.

After talking to the doctor, I'm willing to give it a try to see if it would keep me from being as sick as I was this week. I know a few girls who take them for this reason, and it seems to help them. For us as an engaged couple, there are other issues involved. I wish we could talk them over in person.

It's a very different experience for me to realize that my life is really not just mine any more. My words and actions, and even my thoughts, have an effect on you as well. It's amazing to me that we have been able to develop such a close relationship at such a distance

Goodnight for now, my beloved. It's lonely here, but somehow you're very near. I love you beyond words.

Carolyn

I re-read what I had written, then folded and sealed the letter. As I slipped it in the mail slot, I sent a prayer with it. *Lord, help us make the right decision!*

I was looking in the stacks for the "XYZ" volume of *Encyclopedia Britannica* when another student came up behind me, the odor of patchouli preceding him by several yards. The smell made my stomach churn and I quickly left to search in another aisle. The *Reader's Guide to Periodical Literature* gave me sources of magazine articles and the card catalog directed me to a few other books. I needed to find an interesting angle for my next speech, or my lack of enthusiasm would generate to a low grade.

With a sigh, I gathered up my pile of books and magazines, and headed for the dorm and the possibility of a letter from Larry. I wasn't disappointed, and put my books down beside a chair in the lounge while I read the latest news from my fiancé.

February 6, 1967
Dear Carolyn,

Your letter today was very sweet. You have a way of making my head spin.

I made a hospital call today before heading to the church to mop the floor and wash the windows. The man I visited seemed very happy to see me, and kept asking me to come back soon. There are so many lonely people in the world, Carolyn. One of your future jobs as my wife will be to visit some of these people. They may not always be the most beautiful specimens of humanity, but they all need God's love. I'm beginning to understand the part of the reason for my extreme loneliness growing up. I now believe it has given me a more acute understanding and compassion for people who are not surrounded by positive relationships.

I usually do my hospital visitation on Sunday, but yesterday afternoon I took Mom to a gospel concert in Tulare. During the performance they mentioned that one of the performers had been married last Wednesday, then left on Friday for the concert tour. Anyone who would leave a wife of only two days for a concert must be money-mad, or just plain mad. I sure don't plan to leave you after only two days. Enough said on that score!

The services yesterday were really good. Several people have begun to study the Bible on their own for the very first time. It's definitely making a difference in their lives.

I ran into a couple of high school friends today that had seen the engagement announcement in the paper. One of them said he didn't know I was a minister. The other guy said, "You should go hear him. He's a good preacher." The first guy said, "Larry, when you need clothes, come to the men's store where I work. I'll give you a 10% discount." God is good!

I was thinking more about pet peeves; let me add these to my list:
1. *A woman who wears clothing so skimpy that everyone knows the color of her underwear.*
2. *A wife that uses sexual favors to bribe her husband to do something.*
3. *A woman who uses all her energy doing special things for people outside the family and has nothing left for her husband or family.*

Are you still interested in me? You must be mad!
Well, my sweet, it's getting very late. Goodnight, and pleasant dreams.
Larry

Monday's skies were clear, and I watched the sunrise through the doors of my balcony as I dressed for the day. By 8:30 I was ready to join my boss for the opening session of the "Second Language Media" seminar our office was hosting. In my speech class later that day, I chuckled as I opened the slip of paper containing the topic for my next assignment: "What is the purpose of being engaged?" I could definitely generate more enthusiasm for that subject than history or politics.

Still thinking about how I could approach that topic, I pulled Larry's letter from the mailbox.

February 10, 1967
Ma Cherie,

How is my most wonderful love today? Your letter today was very surprising. Somehow I never would have thought you would be subject to cramps and illness. It must have been very difficult all these years.

In answer to your questions, I don't disapprove of you using the pills. If you need them, then you should use them. One of my concerns is that I've read that women should only use them for two years. We've talked about not starting a family for a few years. That would mean that we'd have to use other methods of birth control at some point. From what I've read and heard, they all have short-comings or potential side-effects.

My biggest concern, of course, is your health. If you start taking the pills and have unusual symptoms <u>of any kind</u>, please see your doctor immediately. If anything happened to you, what would I do?

You may think me ignorant, but there are many things about birth control pills that I don't understand. I have some general ideas from the scant things I have read, but would like more details so that I can understand better what you're going through. If you have any books or pamphlets you could recommend, I would be very grateful.

I will say one thing more. You are everything I ever wanted in a wife. You are able to discuss potentially awkward things with me without being ashamed or crude. I hope you know that I also want to be open and honest with you. If you ever have questions about men or me in particular, just ask. I promise to answer your questions honestly, even if it embarrasses me.

I love you, Carolyn, cramps and all. Here is a hug and kiss for you. OX
Larry

Reading his kind and sincere words, I felt a huge sense of relief and hope. *Maybe I can get through this after all.*

Later I opened a letter from my brother Roger and felt a pang of homesickness, missing his humor and companionship. He wrote about some of his art projects and the classes he was enjoying at Art Center College of Design in Pasadena, California. The letter communicated his loneliness with typical dry humor: "I'd sure like to drop in on you sometime, but it's a long walk."

I put both letters on my desk, and took a brief nap before writing to Larry.

February 13, 1967
Dear Larry,

If only you knew how much your letter today means to me. Being able to talk openly and freely about everything will be a huge asset to our marriage. Somehow the tone of your letter brought tears to my eyes. Thank you for your understanding and compassion.

Regarding the length of time I can take the pills, according to the doctor, this particular prescription can be taken indefinitely, since it's a very low dose of hormones. A month's prescription costs $1.75, and if I buy a 4-month supply, it will be even less. I'll try to send you more information after I see the doctor again.

Today was sunny, and it feels like spring. My room smells lovely, thanks to some sprigs of daphne in a little vase on my desk. I'll give you fair warning—if there are flowers in the neighborhood, I'll find a way to have them in our house.

In Marriage and Family class this afternoon, we had a discussion of sexual standards before marriage. We watched a film and then took an attitude survey regarding kissing, petting, and intercourse in four types of relationships: casual or pick-up, steady dating, strong affection and love, and engagement. Next week the prof will have the results tabulated and we'll be able to see the profile of the class. We'll also do a follow up survey of actual behavior and see how that compares to attitudes. From the side comments of the guy next to me, he's a firm believer in the double standard. He wants to fool around, but wants his fiancée to be pure and untouched! Definitely not my type of guy.

If you're trying to scare me off with your lists of pet peeves, you're not succeeding. I agree with each one. Most of them I share with you. Here are more of mine: a husband who thinks his wife belongs only at home and isn't fit company for him in public. Or, a man who makes smart remarks in public about last night's burned biscuits or this morning's rubbery eggs. (Hopefully you'll never have any reason to comment negatively on my cooking!)

Today at work I got the best news in a long time. I'm going to get an honorarium for my work on a language workshop, and my boss told me it could be $125.00! This will be a life-saver. I've been wondering where I was going to get the money I need for next term. God sure knows how to take care of us!

Goodnight, Larry. I love you. I wonder if I'll ever be able to find enough ways to show you just how much!

Carolyn

Tuesday, Valentine's Day, began with snow. It came down thick and enchanting for about 90 minutes, but then the weather changed and it rained for the rest of the day, turning the lovely landscape into miserable slush. I slogged through my classes, missing Larry on this day set aside for lovers. After dinner I headed for the basement phone booth with a pocket full of coins and made a brief call to Hanford.

"Hi Larry. Happy Valentine's Day!"

"Carolyn! It's wonderful to hear your voice."

"Thank you for the lovely card you sent, Darling."

"I wish it could have been more, you know," he said somewhat wistfully.

"There are plenty of years ahead for us to celebrate together."

"Anything new there?" he asked.

"Yes, one thing. Recently Mom made a comment about 'when you visit Hanford.' I guess that means I have permission to come visit at spring break."

"Are you serious? That's fantastic."

"That's what I think. Happy Valentine's Day to us!"

"I can't wait, I miss you so much."

"I miss you too. I'll talk to you later."

"Goodbye, Carolyn. Don't forget--I love you."

Hearing his voice seemed to scatter every thought in my mind, and after I hung up, I remembered several things I wanted to say. They would have to go in a letter.

February 14, 1967
Dear Larry,

Tonight I will allow myself the luxury of writing to you before I study. You may not believe it, but it's 11:20 and I haven't gotten anything done since I talked to you earlier.

Would you believe it only cost me 95 cents to call you tonight? I've spent much more than that calling Portland or Brightwood. Your voice sounded so close over the phone, and I ached to reach out and touch you. There was so much I wanted to say, but couldn't properly express. After I hung up the phone, the effect of your love must have shown on my face, because every girl I saw in the dorm grinned at me. I want to dance and shout and tell everyone how much I love you.

Something you said makes me laugh when I think about it. You said, "Since we're so far apart, you can be wholehearted in your schoolwork." The real story is that the only thing I'm wholehearted about is getting credits to finish this year so I can marry you!

This week's house meeting was the best we've had all year, with a guest speaker from London University. She talked informally about the differences between American and British universities. The girls really enjoyed the evening, in spite of difficulties with certain terminology. One student asked about British attitudes toward women wearing pants instead of skirts, and our guest laughed. She said that in England, "pants" refer to men's underwear. The girls kept asking her questions until I finally had to close the meeting at 11:15.

I don't know what you have planned for our itinerary while I'm visiting, but I agree with you that we'll need to stay busy, as long as we have <u>some</u> time to ourselves. I know it's going to be hard, but we need time to talk without distraction.

Your suggestion that I bring a tape of myself saying "No" repeatedly was amusing, but unfortunately not funny. (What do you think I'm going to be doing that I can't say "No" myself?) I don't know what has happened to me lately. So many things that were unquestionable and absolute are suddenly not that way. I can't understand myself at all—the mental (and even physical) turmoil is very hard sometimes. I've always accepted certain things and rejected others, but my values and standards are taking a beating right now.

I got a letter from Mom this week with a very positive tone. Among other things, she wrote, "Should I write a letter to Larry's mother?" As I've said, Mom is pretty hung up on doing things strictly by the book (as in proper etiquette), and it's her understanding that the mother of the groom should initiate contact with the mother of the bride. For all I know, your mom has written to her by now. One thing particularly pleased me in her letter—she and Dad are planning to come for Mom's Weekend on the 18th!

Darling, how I long for the weeks to pass so I can be with you again. It never ceases to amaze me that we have established so much love and rapport in the short time since we've met. To me, this shows the rightness and strength of our love.

Goodnight, beloved.

Carolyn

After I sealed the letter, I crawled into bed and tried to settle myself for sleep. My thoughts turned to a conversation with a good friend who had come to my room after a first date. While she didn't usually give details of her dates, she'd made me laugh with her description of how he tried to neck with her in the front seat of a VW bug, and how she'd followed another friend's advice by gritting her teeth to avoid a French kiss. "On your first date, when you'd had a lousy time?" I asked. "That's crazy!"

Our conversation refreshed my memories of being with Larry on a dark hilltop above Portland, and sleep eluded me for a long time.

Chapter 26

Larry

When Jesse pulled into the driveway and honked, I was standing at the window. *I hope the horn didn't wake Mom.* She'd only been home a couple of hours from her graveyard shift at the hospital. I hopped into the car, and Jesse backed out, gravel flying, and we headed to Modesto. Someone there had written that their garage was bursting with donations for the orphanage in Mexico.

**Current Culture
February 1967**

- 90-lb British model Twiggy storms US
- Teamsters Union President Jimmy Hoffa starts prison term for fraud and jury tampering
- Elvis Presley releases album *How Great Thou Art*
- Department store price for men's Oxford dress shoes: $12.95

On the trip north, I couldn't seem to get our conversation below the surface. I had done my best over the years to befriend and encourage Jesse, but he seemed to be constantly sinking under the weight of negative circumstances: chronic obesity, a broken home, his mother's mental illness, and his perception that he was a disappointment to his father. Lately, he seemed to turn more often to alcohol and other distractions to dull his pain.

On this trip, he spent a lot of time fiddling with the radio; I spent most of the ride wishing he would slow down and pay more attention to the other cars on the road. In Modesto, we loaded the car with more than three hundred pounds of donated clothing and household goods, filling the back seat.

It was mid-afternoon when Jesse dropped me off at our house. Unfortunately, all the mailbox contained was a few bills and Mom's *Decision* magazine from the Billy Graham Foundation. With the house empty and no letter from Carolyn to read, I busied myself getting ready for the church potluck scheduled for that evening. Much later, I put my thoughts on paper for Carolyn.

February 16, 1967
Dear Carolyn,

Today was unusual—I was busy the entire day. It started with a 6 hour, 250 mile round trip to Modesto with Jesse to pick up donations for the orphanage in Mexico. As usual, there wasn't much conversation. The one bright spot (besides the ample donations) was a stop for lunch at the Blueberry Hill Café, a well-known diner north of Merced. I felt like splurging, so I ordered the 'Special'--big juicy spare ribs, mashed potatoes and gravy, mixed vegetables, salad, and a small loaf of freshly baked bread, all for the princely sum of $1.29.

When I got home Mom and Dad were both gone, so it was up to me to fix something for tonight's church potluck. I baked a cake (fortunately Mom had a mix in the pantry) and also cooked a ham.

The people who came to the potluck were ready to enjoy themselves. They all joined in playing games after we ate, and there wasn't a boring moment. While we played Charades, I had to act out the song, "Someday, My Love" from Dr. Zhivago. That really brought back a rush of memories and emotions. Of course I think of you every time I hear "our" song. At least we can be happy that we met when we did. The happiness that eluded Yuri and Lara will be ours.

Thanks for sending the book from your marriage and family class. It definitely confirmed to me that I wouldn't want to tempt you to go all the way with me before marriage (as if you would let me...). The reasons for waiting certainly outweigh the reasons for premature gratification,

The discussion in the book about roles in marriage brought some questions to my mind. In March, we will need to discuss our ideas with full honesty. I'm also hoping you can help me understand your emotions at certain times. That should help me respond better when I leave the cap off the toothpaste and you hit me with a skillet. It may not ease the knot on my skull, but at least I might recognize why you did it.

Goodnight, Carolyn. I'm waiting to wrap my arms around you and kiss you again. I love you!

Larry

A few days later, Jesse and I went to Fresno to visit some college friends. We caught up on what everyone was doing, and no one batted an eye when I said I was the pastor of a church. One of the girls asked me about the size of the congregation, and I said, "Small, but growing."

She smiled and replied, "It should grow with you there, because you draw people to you." I was surprised at her comment and her boyfriend's nod of agreement.

The following day I drove to the church to repair the ceiling of a classroom and painted some door frames. As I was leaving, I glanced back at the auditorium. Seeing fresh paint, clean floors, and everything in order for Sunday's services gave me great satisfaction.

When I got home, there was a letter from Carolyn on the kitchen table.

February 17, 1967

Darling,

There was snow on the ground when I got up this morning. Unfortunately, it didn't last, but I wouldn't be surprised if it snowed again tonight.

Today I found out that my honorarium for my work with the Foreign Language Studies workshop will be $100! This means I will have money for my trip to California, plus some clothes and other things that I need, without dipping into my normal budget.

As usual, I didn't get as much done today as I had hoped. I read a somewhat startling article in February's Redbook *magazine on the changing view of the church on sexual standards. If you have a chance, you might want to read it. I also did some reading in a book* The Pastor's Wife *for my Marriage and Family class term paper. I am thoroughly convinced that I will be entering into the most demanding, difficult, exciting, challenging and rewarding career a woman can have. Because of you, I'm confident I will be a success in this venture. I believe in you, Larry, and you give me a confidence that I've never had.*

I called Mom today to see if they are coming on Saturday for Mom's Day at our college. She has a terrible cold, so unless she's a lot better, they won't be coming. I'm disappointed, of course.

Saturday night will be the "All-Campus Sing" with each dorm presenting a song and skit. The star of Todd Hall's skit is yours truly—portraying Miss Jessica Todd, circa 1920. This has required countless conversations, planning meetings and rehearsals several nights this week. Why can't I just learn to say "No!" to people, so my life isn't so hectic? I guess I'm just an easy mark.

It's late, beloved, and I need to close. I wish you could smell the flowers on my desk—they are so fragrant. I wish a few other things also, but...

I love you,
Carolyn

Now she's in a skit? Doesn't she ever slow down? Carolyn's constantly busy schedule worried me--I was concerned about her health as well as her grades. I wished I were close enough to help her turn down some things. Long-distance advice might not be welcome from someone who didn't really understand the whole picture. *Maybe we can talk about it when she comes to visit.*

The following week I was digging holes for some new shrubs to beautify the church parking lot when I heard a puppy barking. Eventually I followed the sound and found a large frightened pup stuck in a hole in the fence between the church property and a vacant lot. He growled at me, but when I laughed at him, he frantically squeezed out and wrapped himself around my ankles.

There were no houses nearby, so I ended up taking him home. Mom and Dad promptly named him Sam, short for Samuel, meaning "gift from God." When I sat down, he would try to scramble into my lap. If I firmly told him "NO," he flopped down beside my feet with his head on my shoe.

When I wrote to Carolyn later that evening, it was pleasant to have him next to me, with his big brown eyes looking up at me every time I moved.

February 19, 1967
Dear Carolyn,

Sunday's service seemed to lack something. There just wasn't the same spirit of enthusiasm or expectation as has been there the past few weeks. However, tonight's service was little better. I preached on how God used Joseph, Daniel and Esther for His purpose, while each was under the bondage of a foreign king. I enjoyed my research, and the Holy Spirit gave me some interesting insights to share.

The last few days have been busier than usual. On Friday I went to the planning commission to learn that our property has been re-zoned from "Urban Reserve" to "Single/Multiple Housing." This is exactly what we were hoping for as it could revitalize the neighborhood.

Speaking of the neighborhood, since I didn't want to be arrested for dog-napping, I checked with more neighbors near the church, and found the owners of Sam, a puppy I found near the church and took home a couple days ago. He had apparently wandered too far to find his way back home. I took him back to his owners this afternoon, and we miss him already. It's really surprising how quickly that puppy wormed his way into our hearts.

This afternoon I stopped by to visit one of our elderly members. Her daughter and son-in-law were there, and when they found out who I was, the daughter said, "You're her favorite, you know!" Mrs. Garland is such a wonderful woman. When you meet her next month, I know you'll love her.

I'm sending you a copy of an article I recently read in a magazine. It lists six reasons why marriages fail. We don't fit a single one of those reasons. In fact, our relationship is the exact opposite. How about that?!

Goodnight, my gorgeous doll. Just wait until we're alone. The time can't go fast enough for me.

Larry

One of the highlights of the following week was a visit from Trevor, one of my professors at Fresno State. He was only a few years older than me, and we developed a strong friendship when I took his California history class. In some ways it was an unlikely relationship, because he was a cynical "unbeliever," and I wasn't shy about sharing my faith with him. At the Imperial Dynasty, Hanford's best Chinese restaurant I was surprised when he looked at me thoughtfully, and said, "You know, Larry, recently I've been reconsidering my ideas about God."

"Really? What has prompted that?"

"I'm not sure. I've known a few people like you who have a quality of life that I envy. Maybe I should do more research."

"One thing I know for certain, Trevor. God wants you to know Him, and He's promised that anyone who truly seeks Him will find Him."

"I hope so..."

"I *know* so!" As we shook hands outside the restaurant, we promised to stay in touch.

The next day a familiar blue envelope in the mailbox made my heart beat faster.

February 21, 1967
My Love,

Today the mailman brought me two letters from you. After reading them, a strange thought hit me. I wonder if we will miss writing and receiving letters after we are married? A friend recently remarked then when we finally get married we probably won't be able to communicate properly--we'll have to write letters to make ourselves understood.

On Saturday I was awakened by a loud knock on my door. The girl at the door said someone was waiting for me in the lobby. It turned out to be a florist, delivering the corsage I had ordered for my mother for Mom's Day. From then on it was hectic and non-stop. The student hostess didn't follow through with her assigned preparation. When she wasn't downstairs when the Open House started at 9:30, I sent someone to find her. She was still in bed! Needless to say, I was a bit upset with her!

Mom and Dad actually came, and we had a nice visit. After lunch, we drove out into the countryside around Monmouth and had a good talk. As usual, Mom's version of what Dad thinks is slightly different than what Dad actually communicates. He said to me, "If you want to marry Larry, go ahead, as long as you know you're in God's will." I told them that we both feel strongly that September is the right time for us to get married, and there was no argument.

I have about eighty pages of 'Babbit' left to read tonight, not to mention research for my term paper. I managed to memorize a poem in French tonight: "C'est le moment crepuscularie, J'admire, assis sous un portail," etc., etc. Rough translation: "It is the moment of twilight; I sit admiringly under a gateway...

Only four more weeks, and then a few days of bliss! Tonight I wanted you near me more than usual. How I love you, Larry. Sometimes the power of my emotions almost frightens me. Then I remind myself that we can ask God to love each other with His perfect love.

Goodnight
Carolyn

Can I love her with perfect love? It seemed an enormous but pleasant task, one I was willing to give a lifetime to accomplish.

On Friday, I busied myself around the house until late morning when the mailman arrived, leaving only a very fat issue of Newsweek in the box. Feeling let down, I drove to the church, where an unwelcome surprise awaited. Two of the large windows had jagged holes in them, apparently made by the large rocks I found on the floor when I unlocked the doors.

I called the police, and waited an hour for an officer arrived. By the time I reached Rev. Black in Portland about insurance, it was mid-afternoon. The local glass company didn't have the right size glass in stock, so I had to return to the church with plywood and nails. I wasn't happy about having the windows boarded up for Sunday services, but instead of being discouraged, I felt energized. Was it possible that this attack was because our presence was beginning to affect the spiritual atmosphere of the neighborhood?

Saturday's mail brought me a welcome blue letter.

February 24, 1967
Hi Darling,

How is my favorite human being today? I'll bet you even have a smile on your face right now!

The weather this week has made it very difficult to study. There's a lovely scent of freshly cut grass on campus, and tonight I can see a glowing full moon from my balcony.

Today I had several appointments, including one with the former Dean of Women. As part of her research on our class, she gave me an IQ test. Later this afternoon I went back to her office and she went over the test with me. Interestingly enough, my score was 13 points higher than the previous two tests I've taken. She told me, "I hope you'll get your doctorate someday, Carolyn." That used to be my ambition, but somehow since last September, it's no longer in the forefront of my mind.

Today I got back my paper on The Art of Loving *with an A- grade. After work, I finished reading 'Rabbit, Run' for Realism class. I hope I don't have to give a report on that book. While I wasn't particularly shocked by it, I found it depressing and revolting.*

Now that my trip to California is coming quickly, I almost wish time would slow down. I'm afraid that before I know it, my time with you will be over and I'll be back with my nose to the grindstone. I'm looking forward to this trip so much—my first real "fling." I used to envy classmates who went on real vacations. In our family, we were lucky if we got away for more than two days every five years. And this isn't just a vacation for me, it's time with YOU!

I've been thinking a lot about meeting your family and your congregation. I hope they will like me. I'm counting on one thing—they love you and you love me, so I hope they will love me, too! Logical, right?

Be good, Darling, and in just three weeks, something very nice will happen.

Je t'aime. Carolyn

After dinner that evening, Mom answered the phone and said, "Larry, it's for you." When I answered, I heard an unexpected voice.

"Hi, Larry." Carolyn's voice was soft and unsteady.

"Carolyn! I'm surprised to hear from you. Is everything okay?"

"Not really." Her voice quavered, and sounded like she was trying not to cry.

"What's happening, Sweetheart?"

"I got another letter from Mom today, mostly about us."

"Oh, I'm sorry, Carolyn. Can you tell me about it?" There was silence on the other end of the line, and I sensed she was fighting for composure.

"It's the same thing again, Larry. This time she wrote that if you really loved me, you would make sure that I finish school before we get married." I could hear her voice catch.

"But I thought that issue was resolved."

"I know, Larry, so did I."

"Sweetheart, listen to me," I said gently. "In spite of how you feel right now, you must believe in God's hand in our lives. He didn't bring us together to frustrate us or to cause insurmountable problems in our families. No matter what it looks like, we need to trust Him. He is working in all of this to bring about His perfect will for our lives. Can you believe that?"

Again there was silence, then a quiet sniff, and a muffled giggle. "I'm sorry, Larry. I'm standing here crying, nodding my head in agreement, as if you can see me." I heard her take a deep breath before continuing. "I know you're right. I just have to trust that God is working behind the scenes and that eventually this will all be history."

"Focus on the future, my sweet. In just a few short weeks, you'll be in my arms, and we can talk this out face to face. That's going to make a big difference, you'll see."

"I know, Larry. Being so far apart makes problems seem so much larger than they really are."

"At least your Mom isn't preventing you from coming next month."

"I know, that's the weird part in all of this.

"You're arriving on the 20th, so that's only 28 days!"

"Four weeks from today. I can't wait." Her voice sounded happier; I wished I could see her face.

"I'll be there with open arms," I said.

"Do they allow kissing in the Fresno airport?" she giggled. I was delighted to hear her humor returning.

"I don't care if they do or not. I'm sure no one will pay any attention to us, Sweetheart."

"Let's hope so. I need your strength and confidence."

"I'll see you in my dreams. I love you!"

"Love you too…"

With Carolyn's voice fresh in my ears, I put on paper a few more thoughts I'd not said on the phone.

February 21, 1967
Hello, Beautiful!

My head is in a whirl since a certain phone call this evening. I wish you were here to discuss things in person. I am totally convinced that God has a perfect plan for us, and I believe it's for us to be <u>together</u> in His will. Please continue to listen to the Holy Spirit when you pray, my love.

I will be praying with you that the conflicts with your mom will somehow stop and these problems will be resolved so we can continue with our plans.

Goodnight. I love you very much—don't forget that.

Larry

Chapter 27

Carolyn

After typing the last line, I stretched with a sigh and started proofreading my 18-page term paper for *Realism in Literature*. I corrected several errors, then wearily glanced at the clock. *Three-thirty? This may be a record!*

I'd gotten my second wind about 1 a.m., and even without coffee or No-Doz, I wasn't particularly sleepy. I knew I wouldn't be able to fall asleep if I didn't write at least a few lines to Larry, so I pulled out my stationery and wrote a brief letter.

I sealed and stamped the letter, pulled on my robe, and walked down the dark stairway to the "Out" mailbox. Back upstairs, I let my exhausted body relax in the hot shower, grateful that I had no classes or work shift in the morning, and could sleep until noon if I wanted to. *If I didn't have my trip to California to look forward to, I'd quit!*

When I went downstairs at noon the next day, my mailbox held a letter from Larry.

**Current Culture
March 1967**

- 13-day television strike frustrates viewers
- President Johnson announces draft lottery plans
- Grammy Awards go to Frank Sinatra for "Strangers in the Night" and to the Beatles for "Michelle"
- *You're a Good Man, Charlie Brown* premieres in New York City
- Good seats for a Broadway musical: $8.60

229

March 1, 1967
Hello, My Love,
There were two beautiful letters in our mailbox today. I know I've said this before, but I want to thank you again for being so considerate and consistent in your letter-writing. I appreciate it more than I can say.

Today I spent hours sanding and finishing five doors at the church. Some of them looked like they'd never been stained or varnished. I'll need to add more coats later, but even with the first coat, they look amazingly better.

Tonight's Bible study lesson was about the Cross, and what it means to us. I emphasized the seven things Jesus said from the cross, and my remarks were very well received.

Yesterday I wrote my sister and grandmother in Los Angeles about our upcoming visit, so they will be expecting us. By the way, we're still having shirt-sleeve weather here. You won't need to pack a parka when you come!

When you receive this letter, it will be only three weeks until you are here. Believe me, I will do everything I can to make your visit worthwhile. Of course, knowing you're coming soon makes me think of you more strongly every day.

I know the next few days are going to be hectic for you. Please take things in your stride, and trust God for the outcome.

Until we are face-to-face, let me say I love you!
Larry

I couldn't keep the smile off my face as I folded the letter and tucked it into my pocket. I'd gotten two other letters from California. One was from Fresno State College, answering my questions about transferring credits. By the end of spring quarter, I would have 94 of Fresno State's required 124 credits, and it might be possible to finish there in a year. I was encouraged, but knew it would be a challenge if I had to commute two hours each day.

The third letter was from Roger in Pasadena. *"I'm glad you'll be able to see Larry again, finally,"* he wrote. *"As for visiting me while you're in LA, it might be tricky. Between my classes and work, there's not a lot of empty space. I might be able to get free for half an hour on Friday."* I pictured his easy grin. I'd be happy if we could just buy him a Coke during his lunch break.

The following day, after my 8:00 shift at work, I registered for the next semester's classes and found a quiet corner to glance over the note cards for a presentation in my 11:00 Speech class. Speaking in public still made my stomach churn and my knees knock, but how could I pursue a career in teaching without becoming comfortable talking in front of others? Fortunately, my anxiety was slowly decreasing and my grades improving.

I was encouraged by the smile on my prof's face at the end of my speech. After class, I made a quick trip to the library to find reference books for my next term paper before rushing back to my dorm. There wasn't much time to pack before my ride came to take me home for the weekend. I grabbed clothes off hangers and out of drawers, and ran down the stairs when I saw my friend's car pull up in front of the dorm.

Dad and Mom's car was in the parking lot of the Rexall drugstore in Sandy when Joanna pulled in after our two-hour trip from Monmouth. Dad opened the trunk for my overnight case and gave me a hug. I leaned over the seat to kiss Mom's powdered cheek. For most of the trip home, Mom shared neighborhood news and family gossip. Dad drove the 20 minutes in silence, his hearing aid apparently turned off.

When the car stopped in our driveway, I got out and stretched, deeply inhaling the cold mountain air. Under the sharp tang of late spring snow were layers of barnyard smells, the decaying leaves that mulched Dad's roses, and the faint hint of budding greenness. I could see the dusky shapes of horses in the barnyard, with the backdrop of sagging barns and the dark bulk of the forested ridge topped with ghostly patches of snow.

"You'll want to put your things in the bedroom before dinner," Mom said as she started putting plates on the kitchen table. I walked past the stone fireplace in the living room, and nudged open my bedroom door. A dress with store tags hung on the closet door. It was rare for Mom to purchase clothes for me; her seamstress skills had provided most of my clothing growing up. I was holding the dress up to myself, looking in the mirror, when she came to the doorway behind me.

"What do you think, Dear?"

"I love it, Mom. What a nice surprise!"

"Well, it was on sale, and I thought it would be a good color for you, so I couldn't resist." I gave her a brief hug and smelled the familiar almond scent of Jergens lotion.

"Thank you, Mom." She hurried back to the kitchen, and I wondered, *Is this a peace offering?*

At dinner, Dad asked about school, then the inevitable question, "And what about Larry? Has he heard from the Draft Board?"

"No, Daddy, nothing. It's very frustrating."

"I see President Johnson wants to start a draft lottery. If Larry's still 1-A, his name will go into the pot."

"Believe me, I think about that a lot. But there's nothing more he can do at this time. We just have to trust the Lord and wait."

"It's hard for you, I know, Sweetheart." Dad patted my shoulder as he got up from the table to head outside for late evening chores.

"Mom, I've been thinking…" I paused.

"Yes? About what?"

"About this summer." I sat up straight, and took a deep breath. "I'm going to need a job to pay for wedding expenses."

"You're still determined to have a September wedding?" There was an edge to her voice.

"Yes, we are. Larry and I both believe that it's God's will for us. But last night I had a bright idea, and I think you might like it."

"Go on," she said cautiously.

"What if I live here at home during the summer, and work for you and Dad. I can cook and clean for you, and help Dad with haying and the horses. You always need extra help during the summer when things are busy, and I need money for my wedding." Mom's mouth had dropped open, and she looked like she might fall off her chair. She stared at me, her eyes wide.

"I…I'll have to let that sink in."

We sat for a few minutes looking at each other before she smiled slightly. "The other day, your father and I picked out fabric for my mother-of-the-bride dress." Tears welled in my eyes, and I started laughing.

"I guess this could be an answer to prayer for all of us," I said, reaching over to clasp her hand. She pulled a handkerchief out of her apron pocket and dabbed her eyes.

"I just can't believe it," she shook her head in amazement.

For the rest of the evening we chatted companionably about the upcoming summer, and even tentatively talked of wedding plans. When I pulled back the blue chenille bedspread and leaned back against my pillow to write Larry, my heart was full.

March 3, 1967
Dear Larry,

Now that I'm home for the weekend and the pressure is off, I feel like a rag doll with no stuffing. On the way home, there were patches of snow beside the road between Sandy and Brightwood, and there's a lot of snow still up on the ridge. And in Hanford you're in your shirtsleeves!

When I walked into my bedroom at home, there was a new spring dress hanging on the outside of the closet door. It's very unusual for Mom to buy me something like that, and I was even more pleased that I actually liked it! Wonders will never cease!

Today was such a busy day, with work followed by pre-registration for next term. I wasn't able to get archery or golf for PE, but I did manage to talk a prof into letting me join his closed English Lit class. He's known as a superior teacher, but a soft touch. I gave him a sob-story about needing the class before I transfer next year, and he finally relented. I also signed up for my work schedule--thirteen hours a week. I'll have afternoons free, but an 8:00 a.m. shift every morning! That's going to be a challenge.

My speech today went well. I had to demonstrate something, and I chose teaching reading to adults. Because of my experience from last summer's job, I was enthusiastic, and pulled a solid "B." For the final, I'll have to take the unpopular side of a controversial issue (euthanasia), and try to persuade the class to my point of view. I also have two papers due next week, so I'll be busy.

Now to the best part of the day. After dinner, Mom and I had a long talk, and I made a proposition to her that popped into my head last night. It's such a simple and satisfactory solution to my summer employment problem. I'm going to stay here and work for them, in exchange for them paying for my wedding expenses! I'll help with horseback riders, cook and do housework for Mom. If I worked somewhere else, I would need transportation, board and room, and wouldn't have time to be outdoors or relax. This way I can give them the help they need, brush up on my cooking, and be able to sew my wedding dress. As you can imagine, when I suggested it, my mother practically fainted, and that's no exaggeration!

God is so good! Mom's change of attitude still startles me. I certainly don't deserve all of this, but it's evidently in His plan.

Lately my neck and shoulders have been sore. I wish you were here to massage my back and then just hold me close. I am so looking forward to being in your arms. It's only a few more days...

Goodnight, beloved,

Carolyn

Saturday's sun rose in a cloudless sky. Through the kitchen window I could see Dad and Mom out by the barns. I spread peanut butter on a piece of toast and walked out to the fence. Spice wandered over looking for an apple. I rubbed her soft nose and scratched her ears. "How about a ride this afternoon, girl?" She whickered and nudged my arm. "I'd like to ride you for hours, but I've got a pile of books to read."

Back in the house, I made a cup of instant coffee, and opened the novel for *Realism* class. I wasn't enjoying it, with its characters in and out of immoral relationships, but it was required reading.

I still had two chapters left when I heard tires crunch on the gravel driveway. I looked out the window to see my tall, crew-cut brother-in-law unfold himself from the driver's seat, and my sister step out of the passenger side with her baby in her arms. The other kids tumbled out of the back seat,

Faye and Diane running to me for hugs, and Darrell heading for the swing set under the maple tree.

"Hi, Priscilla," I said, untangling myself from my two small nieces.

"How's my little sister?" She gave me a hug around baby Brian in her arms, and left a bright pink lip-print on my cheek.

"Great, how are you?"

"These kids run me ragged. Two in diapers is the pits," she laughed.

"I may find out someday. By the way, I have some news for you."

"What's that?"

"How would you like to be in my wedding on your birthday?"

"Oh, Carolyn, really? What a wonderful birthday present!" She gave me another hug. "I'll give you a bridal shower. It's so exciting!" We headed to the house, arm in arm, chattering about shower and wedding plans.

When they left after lunch, I headed out to the barnyard. Spice was easy to catch, and I soon had my feet in the stirrups. I loved the feel of the saddle, the smell of horsehide and leather, and the connection I had with this animal. *Wish I could take you with me, girl, but I don't think there's room for a horse in the Wades' back yard.*

Back at school late Sunday evening, my mailbox held a letter from Larry.

March 4, 1967
Dear Carolyn,

Thanks a lot...we've had a cold front from Oregon bringing us chilly weather. Before I headed to church Sunday morning, I had to scrape ice off my windshield!

Today I washed the junk off the replacement windows. The varnished doors look pretty good. I wish I had before and after pictures so that you could fully appreciate how much better the church looks now.

Thank God that you and your mother are now able to communicate. I'm sure you realize how much a compromise it is for her to talk about wedding plans. Of course, you realize that she hasn't fired her last shot, and you may still have problems up until you hear the strains of the wedding march. Just don't let it get to you.

I think the idea of you working at the ranch this summer is great. That will give you extra time with your family, and your extra cooking practice may save me from indigestion. (I'm kidding...)

Goodnight, you gorgeous doll. Two more weeks! Just wait until I get my arms around you. Then I'll tell you in person just how much I love you.

Larry

After my last class for the semester ended, I headed to downtown Monmouth to buy some things for the bridal shower we were planning for a friend from my hometown. As I walked, I mentally compared my friend's life with my own. She was marrying the older brother of a classmate, and would be living in our hometown, surrounded by family and friends. Her fiancé was exempt from the Draft, had a steady job, a new car, and an ample bank account. *She may be headed for an easy, comfortable life, but I think I prefer passion and risk.* Why else would I have accepted the marriage proposal of a young man I barely knew? *I just hope the US government stays out of our life.*

Dad's question about President Johnson's proposed changes in the Draft policy made me uneasy, and I needed to find out what Larry thought of it all.

March 9, 1967
Dear Larry,

First, a very important question. Will the new Draft policies have an effect on you? Have you been reclassified yet? It would be rather unfortunate if you got called up this summer!

The day started out pretty well, and my presentation in Realism class went okay. But I found out that we won't have time to give our final presentations in speech class, so I may have to settle for a C. That doesn't thrill me, but what really bugs me is that it's the prof's fault, not mine. If I went to talk to him about it, he'd likely say, "That's too bloody bad, dearie." Down with Mr. A!

At our house meeting this week the speaker was Mr. Watson, my Marriage and Family prof. One of the things he talked about was the concept of "sexual progression." He explained that for every couple, the relationship progresses from holding hands to kissing, French kissing, petting and intercourse.

For each individual there is also a 'point of no return' both physiologically and psychologically. He emphasized the importance of establishing a standard of behavior in the relationship if the couple wants to remain chaste. They need to decide on their 'point of no return', and then agreeing to stop before they get there. If they go beyond that point, the rational mind is no longer in control and the sexual urge takes over.

During the discussion time, a question was asked about the relationship between premarital sex and sexual adjustment after marriage, which led to a discussion of engagement standards. Several pairs of questioning eyes turned toward me. I wished I had a sign to hold up saying I AM STILL A VIRGIN!

Please don't take all this ranting seriously—it's just that the end of semester pressure is really on now, and I need to let off steam. It's time to stop before I get silly...

Goodnight, my love. At least that remains constant.
Carolyn

When the hands on the clock showed 9:00 Friday morning, I tidied my desk and left the office for my dorm. As I changed into dressy clothes, I watched out my balcony window. When I saw my parent's car pull up in front of the dorm, I ran down the stairs and joined Priscilla in the back seat.

My brother Dave was the first of two generations in our family to earn a college degree, so his graduation from University of Oregon was a big event for our family. We arrived at the campus in Eugene at noon, just in time for a luncheon for honors grads and their families. The Crab Louis luncheon was a rare treat for us. Dave gave us a tour of the campus, ending up at the auditorium where Paul and Emily joined us for the graduation ceremony.

Dave had worked for a local CPA firm while finishing his accounting degree, and his boss invited us all to join him and his wife for dinner at the Eugene Country Club. We were all on our best behavior in the posh surroundings, and I could see from Dad and Mom's body language that they were uncomfortable with such a costly dinner.

Back in Monmouth that evening, Mom gave me a large cookie tin when she hugged me goodbye. Opening it in the dorm lobby, I found brownies, oatmeal-raisin cookies, a loaf of her brown bread, and a cube of butter, all treats she had made to carry me through finals week. Our relationship had definitely improved!

The letter I found in my mailbox contained an amusing rumor that made me chuckle.

March 13, 1967
Dear Carolyn,

Today was a typical minister's Sunday, with preaching, visitation, etc.

Would you like to hear something funny? Today a woman at church asked me if your mother was coming to Hanford with you. Apparently that rumor is circulating at the church in Portland. I guess your mother's reputation for strictness is well-known.

In spite of the rain the past few days, I've been able to mow the lawn and do all the other mundane jobs required for keeping up the church.

Time is slipping by and your arrival is so close. Only eight days now. When I sit down to write you, all I can think of is that you'll be here soon, so my letters are miserably short.

I love you, Carolyn. May the days and hours go by quickly.
Larry

During finals week, I worked extra hours at the Materials Center to earn spending money for my trip. Between shifts, I sewed a spring dress for California, and studied for finals. On Tuesday, I knocked at the door of the Dean of Students.

"Enter," said his deep voice. I stepped into his office. "Ah, the girl with the long-distance romance." Dr. Wells frowned at me over his half-moon glasses and reached for his ever-present pipe. "What's the latest from the California boyfriend?"

"He's still 1-A, but I'm flying to see him next week."

"Hmmm. Well, just don't repeat your predecessor's shenanigans, Carolyn."

"Not much chance of that," I said ruefully. Last year our dorm president had eloped during spring break, and as vice-president, I'd had to step into her role.

"It's bad enough that you're not going to finish here. Don't disappoint me further." His gruff words covered a soft heart—he was well-loved by the students.

"I'll be back, Dr. Wells. Is there any chance you would help with late registration? I'm going to miss the first two days of classes."

"Come see me when you get back, and I'll waive the late fee."

"Thank you so much. I'll see you in a couple weeks."

"I'm holding you to that, Carolyn!"

Back at the dorm, I decided to change my usual routine and write to Larry before studying.

March 14, 1967
Dear Larry,

You've been in my thoughts constantly today. I don't know how I could think of you more than usual, but today I did. Perhaps it was because I didn't have quite so much to distract me. I worked six hours at the office, which was a big change from classes. I didn't have any finals today, but have two tomorrow and one on Thursday.

Priscilla and Lauren are coming to pick me up Thursday, and Tricia is coming home with me so she can attend Joanna's wedding. Friday is the rehearsal, Saturday is the wedding, Sunday is church, then on Monday, CALIFORNIA, HERE I COME!

I had a crazy dream last night. I went to see my advisor, the head of the Humanities Department. I've only seen him to get my schedule approved, but in my dream I told him I was going to take just 13 credits next semester, and he got very upset. I explained that I had a job and other responsibilities, but he got angry and said I was trying to get out of work and being childish and stupid. I got so mad I knocked a pile papers off his desk, picked up a *paperweight, smashed it on the floor, and stomped out of his office. Then I got really worried because I knew he would write a letter to Fresno State and tell them what a horrid girl I was. Thank goodness my <u>day</u> dreams are pleasant!*

I can't believe I'm actually going to be taking my first airplane flight, by myself. I'm so excited! But flying is not nearly as exciting as the fact that it will take me to YOU.

Goodnight, my darling.

Carolyn

Chapter 28

Larry

Spring breezes stirred puffs of dust beside the runway as I paced in front of the observation windows at the Fresno Air Terminal. I scanned the sky for a first glimpse of Carolyn's plane, feeling excited but nervous. Six months ago she had agreed to marry me, assuming that we would eventually live in Hanford. This would be her first taste of that possibility.

I planned to show her the best that Central California could offer, but feared it would fall short of her expectations. *Will she have second thoughts when she sees what it's really like?* The San Joaquin Valley was flat and dry, and the air was heavy with a pungent mix of alkali dust, dairy odors, fertilizer and pesticides.

Will she be comfortable in our home? My parents were good-hearted people, but their teenage marriage during the Great Depression had gradually become a battlefield, with constant bickering and occasional truces.

And what will she think of my church? In stark contrast to the traditional stone and stained-glass edifice where we'd met, Grace Chapel was a plain cement-block rectangle. I'd worked hard to beautify it inside and out, but I couldn't change the basic structure, the gravel parking lot, or its awkward location backed up to the highway.

**Current Culture
March 1967**

- ABC pays $2 million to air the movie, *The Robe* on Easter Sunday
- Anti-war protests in New York attract 100,000 marchers
- *Time* magazine cover article features controversial birth control: "The Pill"

I wondered what she would think about my congregation, the people who would be her flock if she became my wife. Many of them came to church because they loved God; others came out of duty or guilt, a few came to get a brief respite from a combative spouse. *Will my preaching inspire or bore her?* My musings were cut short as a plane with the United Airlines logo dropped toward the ground, and puffs of smoke marked the landing.

This is it! I have to leave it in your hands, Lord. If you have truly brought us together, Hanford won't scare her away.

I jogged down the stairs and stood by the glass doors leading to the tarmac, fidgeting impatiently as passengers came down the stairway. My heart thumped when I saw Carolyn's honey-blonde hair, and when she saw me, her uncertain look changed to a brilliant smile.

She ran the last few yards into my arms. We stood in a tight embrace, not speaking, while I breathed the fragrance of her hair and our hug. Other passengers smiled knowingly as they passed us, and for once I didn't care who was watching. The past three months had seemed like years, but now she was in my arms.

She tilted her face up for my kiss, then sighed against my shoulder. "It's so wonderful to see you, Larry!" The dimple in her cheek showed as she gave me a 100-watt smile. After another quick hug, we headed to baggage claim.

"Welcome to California." I squeezed her hand. "How was your flight?"

"It was wonderful! I *love* flying! The mountains were gorgeous from the air, and I saw the Golden Gate Bridge. But the San Joaquin Valley is so dry."

"You haven't seen anything yet," I chuckled. "Wait until you're here in the summer. Then you'll find out what dry really is."

In the parking lot, I opened the passenger door of my black Chevy Bel Air for her. When I got behind the steering wheel, she scooted over to the middle of the bench seat, sitting close. I reached for her, taking time to kiss her thoroughly in the privacy of the car. She pulled away after a few minutes. "I'm here for a whole week, Larry," she smiled. "We don't have to make up for lost time in the first hour." She quickly contradicted her words by wrapping her arms around my neck and kissing me again, before settling back on the seat as I pulled out of the airport parking lot.

"Okay, Mr. Wade, what's the plan for today?"

"We're going to my house tonight. Mom was cooking when I left, so dinner should be ready when we get there."

"That's sounds wonderful. I'm anxious to see her again and to meet your Dad."

Our route between Fresno and Hanford was full of novelty for Carolyn. She excitedly pointed out the fields of cotton and raisin grapes. "Look, lilacs blooming by that house! We barely have daffodils blooming at home." I grinned happily at her enthusiasm. I had a hard time keeping my eyes on the road with Carolyn next to me. I wanted to look at her, touch her, to make sure she wasn't a mirage.

"Here we are," I said eventually, pulling the car into the driveway and parking behind Dad's pickup. She slid across the seat and reached for door handle.

"Ahem," I cleared my throat, signaling her to wait for me to open her door.

"Oh, sorry, Sweetheart. I'm so used to being independent at school. It's going to take me time to get used to being treated like a lady again."

I got her bag out of the back seat and led her through the front door as Dad and Mom walked in from the kitchen. "Dad, this is Carolyn," I said proudly.

"Nice to meet you," Dad said as they shook hands. "You've got a lot to live up to, young lady. My son thinks you're God's gift to humanity." I could see a blush rise on Carolyn's cheeks. "Or God's gift to him, for sure," Dad chuckled.

"Oh, Monk, don't start in on her already," Mom chided. "She hasn't been here five minutes, and you've already made her blush." She gave Carolyn a shy hug. "It's nice to see you again. Welcome to Hanford."

"Thank you, I'm happy to be here," Carolyn said.

"I'll put your bag in the bedroom," I said, heading down the short hallway.

"Dinner will be ready in fifteen minutes," Mom said. "Larry, why don't you show Carolyn where she can freshen up?"

Carolyn followed me toward the larger bedroom and I put her suitcase on the four-poster bed. "I hope you'll be comfortable," I said. "Mom insisted that you have the best bed. She and Dad will be in my room, and I'll be sleeping on the back porch while you're here."

Stepping close, Carolyn put her arms around me. "We owe each other several hundred kisses, so we'd better take advantage of every opportunity."

"I'm so glad you're here. It's amazing to hold you again."

At the dinner table, I said, "I hope you like enchiladas. They're one of Mom's specialties. We figured you should start getting used to real California food while you're here."

"I've had tacos several times, but enchiladas are new to me. They look interesting."

While we ate, Carolyn gave news from Portland, and we asked about her flight, something neither my parents nor I had experienced. As soon as Dad finished eating, he pushed his chair back from the table and headed for the living room. "Gotta catch the end of the news," he said.

Carolyn and I stayed at the table with Mom and continued talking. Then Carolyn said, "Thank you for the delicious dinner, Mrs. Wade. Why don't you let us clean up the kitchen? Larry and I work pretty well together."

"Are you sure? You must be tired from your trip," Mom said.

"Not that tired. I'll wash, you can dry and put away, Larry."

Mom took off her apron, and with a knowing glance over her shoulder, joined Dad in the living room.

"Remember the first time we did this?" Carolyn said, handing me a soapy plate.

"I sure do," I answered. "We were in the basement of the church during the conference. It was one of the first private conversations we had."

"I guess getting into hot water isn't necessarily a bad thing," she said. I chuckled, delighted to hear her lively humor again. When the last dish was put away, we sat at the table again, holding hands and talking. Eventually we heard Dad's chair creak, and he came into the kitchen for a drink of water. "'Night, all. I'm going to bed. Hope you sleep well."

I pulled Carolyn to her feet and wrapped my arms around her. In spite of her smile, I could see fatigue in her posture and dark smudges under her eyes. "There's a whole week ahead of us, my sweet. But tonight, you need to get a good rest."

"I am tired…"

"You look exhausted. Please sleep in tomorrow. The only thing on the schedule is showing you around town, and that won't take more than a few hours."

"But I don't want to waste a moment with you."

"Trust me; there will be time for everything. I don't want you to get sick. Your mother would never forgive me."

"Well, you're not my husband yet, but I guess I'll submit," she grinned at me impishly.

I kissed her goodnight at the bedroom door. "Sweet dreams, my love."

After Mom and Dad left for work the next morning, I picked up my Bible and notebook and worked on my Easter sermon. At mid-morning I made a pot of tea, added it to a tray with one of Mom's pretty teacups and knocked lightly on the bedroom door.

When there was no response, I quietly opened the door. Putting the tray on the dresser, I sat gently on the bed beside Carolyn. Seeing her bare shoulder above the blanket and her cheeks flushed with sleep, I had a powerful desire to crawl into the bed beside her and wake her with kisses. She slowly opened her eyes, gave me a sleepy smile and reached up to me. I leaned down to kiss her and before I knew it, we were side by side and I could feel her passion rising with mine.

"This is probably not a good idea," I said, reluctantly sitting up.

"I agree." Carolyn said breathlessly. She sat up and pulled the comforter around her. "Why don't you be a good boy and sit in the chair while I drink my tea." I handed her the cup, and after a sip, she looked at me over the rim of the cup. "I love having you bring me tea in bed, but I'm not sure I can handle it every day. Maybe we could have tea together in the kitchen from now on."

"Okay, you're right," I said. The strong physical pull we were experiencing was going to challenge our self-control to the limit.

The week that followed was even better than I had imagined. I showed Carolyn my life: the little house where I was born, my elementary school, my high school. Our tour of Main Street took about five minutes, but we lingered in the public library, my childhood haven. In Fresno, she was impressed by the new pedestrian mall and surprised that the campus of Fresno State was so much bigger than her college in Monmouth.

On Wednesday evening, she got her first introduction to my congregation, meeting the faithful mid-week attenders. In the car on the way home, Carolyn said, "I really enjoyed meeting these people. They have a lot of love and respect for you."

"They don't have any choice. I'm the only pastor they've got."

"Seriously, Larry, it's obvious that they respond to your leadership. And you did a great job with the Bible study, by the way."

"Thank you. That means a lot to me." My concerns about her reaction to my life continued to fade.

Early Thursday we started the four hour drive to Los Angeles. Carolyn had never been to Disneyland, and her delight in the park was exactly what I had hoped for. Our lunch of Monte Cristo sandwiches at the Blue Bayou Café with its romantic water-side setting made us both smile.

She couldn't get over how immaculate everything was; the life-like animals on the jungle cruise amazed her. She leaned close to me as our boat tilted into the pirate's cave, and laughed delightedly at the pirate's chants. Eventually she convinced me to shed my adult respectability and enjoy the swooping Peter Pan ride and Mr. Toad's bumper cars.

As the sun set behind palm trees and a Dixieland band serenaded us, we stood on the top deck of the sternwheeler. "It's been a perfect day," Carolyn said, leaning against my shoulder. "Thank you for bringing me. It wouldn't have been nearly as much fun with someone else."

"I'm so glad I could share this with you," I said. I wrapped my arms around her and looked into her eyes. "I look forward to sharing all of life with you--perfect days like today, and the not-so-perfect days, too."

"I can't wait," she said, snuggling closer.

At my sister JoAn's home for dinner, she charmed the three kids by reading to them and trading "Knock-Knock" jokes. Later, at Grandma's house in San Pedro, she politely covered her cough when Grandma served a liquor-soaked fruitcake for a late night snack. I appreciated her willingness to sleep on a cot in Grandma's bedroom while I spent the night on the lumpy sofa.

Friday morning we drove to Pasadena to visit her brother Roger. "Hi, kids," he said as he opened the door to his tiny studio apartment. Carolyn gave him a hug.

"Are you losing weight, Rog?" Concern tinged her voice.

"Well, I don't care much for my own cooking."

"And where would you cook?" Carolyn asked, glancing around the shabby space. A small counter held a hot plate next to a miniature sink. Canvases leaned against the legs of an oilcloth-covered table littered with paint and brushes. My nose wrinkled at the odor of oils and turpentine. We sat on the rumpled single bed in the corner, while Roger sat on a paint-splattered chair by the rickety dinette table.

"Peanut butter sandwiches don't need cooking," he grinned. "Someone from church usually invites me for Sunday dinner, so I'm not starving."

"I'm not convinced," Carolyn said. "I hope this is all worth it."

"Art Center is one of the top schools in the nation, and I'm learning a lot. Here's a project I just finished." He handed us a beautifully intricate paper collage with a comic-book head in one corner.

"I see you're not losing your sense of humor," Carolyn commented.

As we left his apartment she said, "His work has definitely improved, and he seems happy, in spite of looking half-starved."

On Saturday morning I headed the car west toward Highway 1 to show Carolyn the famous beach towns of Santa Monica and Malibu. Further north, the coastline was ruggedly beautiful. "Can we stop here?" Carolyn asked as we approached a picturesque cove. I parked beside the road and we scrambled under a wire fence to head for a small secluded bay.

"I love the ocean," Carolyn sighed, as the blue breakers splashed against the headland.

"I love *you*," I said.

"And today we can have both," she smiled happily. We found a reasonably comfortable spot and leaned back against the rocks, enjoying the crash of the surf, the warm touch of the sun and soon, kisses and caresses. Our isolation stirred possibilities in my mind. My conscience battled with my body, intoxicated by her nearness. With great effort, I pulled away. We were silent for a few minutes, serenaded by raucous, swooping gulls. Carolyn sat with her arms hugging her knees.

"This is a lot harder than I expected," she said eventually.

"I can't believe I was foolish enough to think we could have a strictly platonic relationship until our wedding day."

"That was pretty silly, wasn't it? I'm glad we've set some boundaries, but to be honest, I'm tempted to move them."

"I know what you mean," I said. I turned to look her full in the face. "I want you, right now, right here." I watched emotions cross her face: desire, hope, hesitation, anguish, determination.

"Oh, Larry, I want you, too. We've talked and prayed and discussed and planned, but right now, I want to toss all that aside." We were silent again, struggling with our thoughts and shared emotions.

"I love you too much to do something we'd both regret," I finally said. "We're alone, and we can do anything we want. You're on the pill; no one would know, except God. But He's the most important One, and as much as I want to make love to you right here on this beach, I don't want to end up disappointing you, or myself, or God."

Carolyn gazed out at the pounding waves. I could see the continued struggle on her face. "As much as I want you, I know I'd regret it later if we went all the way now. I'm glad we can talk about it, and I'm glad you're just as determined as I am to stay pure. I don't think I'd have much chance if you didn't have self-control right now."

Lord, help us. We still have three days together!

Back in the car, Carolyn said, "As much as I hate to, we probably should talk about the possibility of you getting drafted."

"Do we have to?" I retorted, half teasing. Seeing the apprehension on her face I added, "You're right, we should."

"So what are your realistic chances of getting the deferment?" she asked.

"Without God's intervention, probably not that great. At one point I thought that Chuck's being in Vietnam would make a difference, but apparently that's not true. I hate feeling in limbo, and keeping you up in the air."

"It doesn't matter where you are, Larry. I'll follow you."

"To Timbuktu?" I glanced from the road to her face, hoping for a smile.

"Who knows, maybe someday." She squeezed my knee. "I know God has a plan, and it's going to be good."

"But does Uncle Sam know that?"

"Come on, Larry. You're a man of faith. You said you didn't want to stay in Hanford forever, maybe this is the way God will get you out."

"My biggest concern is how this all affects you, Carolyn. I can handle pretty much anything, but I don't want you to have to deal with uncertainty or hardship."

"I think I'm pretty resilient, Larry. After all, my mother's favorite comment when I faced a tough situation was, 'It's good training for the mission field.' Maybe it was good training for difficulties besides the mission field."

I squeezed her hand, grateful for her positive outlook. It was the perfect antidote to the negative atmosphere I'd grown up in. *Lord, thank you for bringing this woman into my life!*

In Hanford Saturday afternoon, we went to the church for last-minute preparations. While I straightened chairs and laid out hymnals, she sat at the piano practicing the song list for worship and the solo I'd asked her to sing during communion. As we left, she glanced back at the sanctuary.

"Would your church budget allow for a few Easter lilies, Pastor Wade?"

"I guess so," I said, looking around. "It looks a bit stark in here, doesn't it?"

"Just a bit," she smiled.

We stopped at a supermarket with a display of lilies by the front door. I put three in the cart, and Carolyn added a fourth. "I'll pay for that one," she said. "My gift to your mother."

I awoke on Sunday morning feeling nervous—not only was it Easter, but Carolyn would meet the full congregation for the first time. "You look wonderful," I said, when she came into the kitchen for breakfast. Her pink dress brought extra color to her cheeks.

"Thank you," she murmured. "Happy Easter." I gave her hand a quick squeeze as Mom set a plate of hot-cross buns on the table. The yeasty, fruit-studded rolls were a welcome treat.

"These look great, Mom," I said as Dad came in from the back porch. "Coming with us this morning, Dad?"

"Nah, I think I'll just stick around here," he said. "I'd just make you more nervous than you already are with your sweetheart here."

I glanced at the clock. "We need to leave in ten minutes. I'll put the lilies in the car."

As usual, the Easter congregation was larger than normal. I knew Carolyn was nervous about her solo, but she looked poised, and there were murmurs of approval after she sang. At the end of the service she was surrounded by well-wishers and curious visitors. Riding home, she sighed with relief. "I'm glad that's over. Everyone was nice, but I definitely felt on display."

I had saved a few special things for Monday, her last day. I drove to Visalia to show her around the picturesque campus of College of the Sequoias, where I studied for two years. Further east in the foothills of the Sierras, we rolled down our windows to enjoy the fragrance of orange and lemon groves.

Higher in the mountains, I knew that she would appreciate the spectacular beauty of Sequoia National Park, where I'd worked as a busboy during winter breaks in college.

Back in Hanford that afternoon, I treated her at Superior Dairy, a popular local hangout with chrome and pink vinyl booths. We sipped a thick chocolate shake through two straws.

"Thank you so much for a wonderful week, Larry. I'm so glad I was able to be here to see your surroundings, and to meet your family and your congregation. Now when I read your letters, I'll be able picture things here."

"I just wish there wasn't so much uncertainty," I said. "But I guess God will have the final say." Then I asked her an important question. I thought I knew what her answer would be, but I still wanted to hear it from her. "So, Carolyn. Now that you've seen Hanford and met my family and my congregation, are you still willing to marry me, or are you having second thoughts?"

She looked surprised. "Do you really need to ask? You know I can't hide my emotions. If I were having second thoughts, you would have known it by now."

"I just need to hear you say it."

"Okay, I'll say it. Yes, I still want to marry you, Larry Wade. I want to spend the rest of my life with you. Hanford isn't the most beautiful town on earth, and the future is uncertain. But locations and circumstances can change, and probably will." She paused, looking at me intently. "The bottom line for me is YOU, your character and integrity, your love for God, and your dedication to His people. Those are the reasons I want to marry you, not Hanford or California or your family." I squeezed her hand, my throat tight with emotion. If we hadn't been in a public place, I would have kissed her soundly.

"I really don't want to go home tomorrow, Larry," she continued.

"And you know I don't want you to leave. More than once this week I've thought about driving to Reno. It's only five hours away."

"Don't tempt me, Sweetheart. I'm afraid my resistance is at an all-time low."

"I guess I'll have to be the sensible one, then. As much as I want you here with me, I know you need to finish the school year and I don't want to cheat you out of a family wedding. You'd never forgive me."

"I'd probably forgive you, but have regrets." She played with her straw in the empty glass, looking pensive.

"I'm counting on you coming back in July, when my cousins from Illinois are here for a family reunion."

"It's going to be tough to convince Mom of that. She'll tell me that it's your turn to come to Portland."

"Well, I can't expect my family to have a reunion in Portland just to accommodate your mother," I chuckled.

"That's not what I mean. I just know it will be a fight to get her approval."

"I'll write her a letter when the time is closer and give her my best persuasive pastoral request," I said with a smile.

"Be my guest," she smiled back. "Better you than me, at this point."

When we got home, Mom was at work, and Dad was watching TV. We sat on the couch holding hands, wishing we were alone. Finally Dad got up, stretched and turned off the TV. "Good night, lovebirds. See you in the morning."

I turned to Carolyn. "You have a long day ahead of you tomorrow; you'll need a good night's sleep."

"You're probably right, but that's not really what I want tonight." Her eyes were dark with emotion. At the look on my face, she said, "Sorry, I shouldn't have said that. I don't want to make it harder on you than it already is." I smiled ruefully before taking her in my arms. Everything in me cried out for more, and her body felt especially yielding. It took every particle of self-control for me to pull her to her feet and lead her to the door of her room for a last kiss.

"It's only my love for you and my fear of ruining our relationship that keeps me from joining you in bed," I whispered.

"As much as I'd like that, I won't tempt you, Larry. I love you too much to disregard your convictions. I want to be able to respect you and myself for the rest of our lives."

Later, lying in the narrow cot on the back porch, with the waning moonlight streaming into the room, I tried to think positively about the past week, and the future. But my body was on high-alert, and my thoughts kept coming back to the feel of Carolyn in my arms, her lips on mine, her body soft and responsive.

No one else would know, and our future is so uncertain.

Don't ruin a good thing for temporary pleasure.

But we love each other, and we belong together.

True love is patient, you can wait.

Yes, but I don't want to...

Eventually I drifted off into a fitful sleep, with dreams that taunted me with the fulfilment of my desires.

Returning from the airport the following day, the house seemed desolate. I missed everything about Carolyn, her smile, her laughter, the touch of her hand, the positive cheerfulness that had transformed the atmosphere of our home. I wandered around the house, restless and looking for something constructive to take my mind off her absence. In the kitchen, the calendar caught my eye.

March has been very eventful. What will April bring?

Chapter 29

Carolyn

It was all I could do to stay in my seat with my seatbelt low and snug across my lap, as the flight attendant had instructed. I wanted to rip off the restraint and run down the aisle yelling, "Stop, I'm getting off, I can't leave!"

Every cell of my body wanted to be *with* Larry, not on a plane heading *away* from him. Our week together had been wonderful in ways I hadn't even imagined. It had been blissful seeing him every day, being able to reach out and touch him, to fit my head into the perfect space between his shoulder and his neck, to hear him say he loved me. I dreaded going back to Oregon, to my lonely dorm room and another stressful term at college.

> **Current Culture**
> **March 1967**
>
> - 10,000 hippies swarm Central Park to fly kites, blow bubbles and make smoke rings from burning banana skins
> - Muhammad Ali is stripped of his boxing championship for refusing induction into the armed services
> - Hit song: "Happy Together" by the Turtles
> - Sears recliner advertised for $60.00

"Heavy fog in San Francisco will delay our take-off." The announcement brought a groan from the passengers, and new rebellious thoughts to my mind.

Perfect. Now I have to sit here even longer. But Larry's only a short sprint away on the observation deck. I'll run back into the terminal and tell him that I've changed my mind, that we should head to Reno after all. We could be there by late afternoon and be married by dinnertime.

As quickly as those thoughts ran through my head, the tedious voice of reason contradicted.

You know he's too level-headed and responsible to do that. He wants you to finish next semester. He'd tell you to be patient, that God will work it all out.

I squirmed in my seat, chafing at the delay and the emotional struggle.

But I'm tired of being responsible, tired of being away from him, tired of always doing the right thing, tired of being the good girl. Lord, it's too hard!

My body trembled from the intense emotional conflict. I hugged my arms tightly together and wished that I had a window seat so I could turn my back on my seat-mate and pretend to be interested in the flat landscape. Instead, I covered a rising sob with a cough. My neighbor gave me an irritated look, as if I had contaminated her airspace. I pulled the airline magazine out of the seat pocket and pretended interest in the glossy pages.

Instead of reading, I replayed mental snapshots of my week in California. I pictured Larry's mother with her kind brown eyes and auburn hair in its weekly beauty shop style. I'd felt her acceptance--she'd told Larry months before that she knew I was the right one for him. An image of Larry's father came next. His silver hair had a fresh crew cut and his light blue eyes were shrewd and evaluating. Teasing seemed to be his way of communicating acceptance. I remembered his laugh when I came to breakfast barefoot. "You really are a hillbilly, aren't you?

He guffawed when I retorted, "I may live in the mountains and like my feet bare, but that doesn't make me a hillbilly."

I replayed our wonderful day at Disneyland and the drive to Sequoia National Park. Larry's pleasure in sharing the spectacular scenery with me made me smile in spite of my sadness. I pictured the little church and it's salt-of-the-earth congregation. Playing the piano for the church service and interacting with Larry's congregation had given me a taste of what it would be like to be a pastor's wife, and I was excited about our future together.

I shut off scenes from the episode on the isolated beach and our last night together. I couldn't believe how close I'd come to throwing away my caution and my conscience, and giving myself totally to Larry. The intensity of our desire had shaken us both.

"We've been cleared for take-off. Please make sure your seat belts are securely fastened."

As the plane taxied to the runway, I stared past my seatmate to the window, hoping to get one last glimpse of Larry before the plane took me out of his sight. It was silly, of course, but I thought I could glimpse his tanned face and black hair at one of the windows. Then the engines revved, and we were airborne.

I put my head back on the seat and closed my eyes, not caring if the snooty woman next to me or the bored businessman across the aisle saw the tears slowly seeping from under my eyelids. The anguish of leaving Larry pressed me down, mimicking the gravitational weight of takeoff. I was leaving, in spite of all my wild thoughts about running back into his arms. Every minute took me miles away from him, and I sank into a helpless vortex of despair.

Being unable to wail, rant or yell forced me to eventually regain self-control and perspective. By the time I was offered a soft drink and snack, I'd regained a sense of emotional equilibrium. Choosing my focus, I said a silent prayer, thanking God for the week we'd had together, and most of all, for Larry's love. Gradually my thoughts turned from the past week to what was ahead, and I determined to make Larry proud of me in my last semester in Monmouth.

While Dad watched for my suitcase at baggage claim, Mom said, "We'd like to go to a prayer meeting tonight while we're in Portland. We'll get hamburgers at Scotty's on the way there."

"That's going to make it a late night," I said. "I was hoping to get home early to get ready to head back to Monmouth tomorrow."

"Well, we've already told them we're coming," Mom replied, with a shrug. I mentally adjusted my plans, and distracted myself with thoughts of Larry. Before the prayer meeting, the hosts graciously let me use their phone to make a "Collect" phone call to Hanford.

"Hello?" Larry answered, anticipation in his voice.

"Hi, Darling. I'm home safe and sound. Well, not home, but back in Portland."

"I'm so glad. Thanks for calling to let me know." There was a pause, then we both said, "I miss you." We laughed, but I could feel tears swelling my eyelids. I swallowed over the lump in my throat.

"Thank you so much for all you did to make my visit wonderful," I said.

"I wish I could have done more."

"I don't know how you could possibly have done more. The best thing you did was to treat me like a lady, with respect and consideration." I lowered my voice. "I'm also grateful for what *didn't* happen."

"Let's not talk about that," he said ruefully. "It was a pretty close call."

"But the outcome was right," I answered. "I can't say much; there's a prayer meeting starting in the next room."

"Thanks again for calling. Goodnight, Sweetheart. I love you."

"I love you too, Larry, with all my heart. Goodbye for now."

As much as I tried to participate in the prayer meeting, I found my mind wandering to California, and I was grateful when we said our goodbyes.

It was late when we finally got home and I found some paper and an envelope.

March 28, 1967
My darling Larry,

It's midnight, and I'm finally home. After the prayer meeting ended at 9:30, Mom and Dad stayed for dessert and visiting. I'm tired, but not sleepy. I already miss you horribly.

Even though there weren't any letters from you, the mail was somewhat positive. My grades came, and I managed a 3.38 GPA, not bad considering everything. Also in the mail were two tax refund checks, totaling $90. I'll have money for my tuition, board and room, and books, and still have a little left over.

One thing Dad asked me today was, "How does Larry plan to support you?" Apparently my parents don't think "living on love" is a very practical plan. At some point, I'm sure he'll talk to you about this. Mom hasn't asked many questions about my trip. Maybe she doesn't want to know the answers?

Larry, I'm so grateful for the time I was able to spend with you. I'm also grateful for your restraint and self-discipline. I know we would have both regretted it if we had gone all the way. It just isn't possible for us to put aside the convictions of a lifetime without repercussions.

My respect and love for you has increased immeasurably, which is saying quite a lot. Your love and consideration and tenderness are beyond anything I've ever dreamed of—all the things that make a woman truly happy and able to respond to her husband. What a great gift God has given us!

I pray that God will give you peace and rest. I love you more than I ever thought possible.

Carolyn

Snow was on the ground when I woke up the next morning. *At the end of March? What a change from California!*

At breakfast, Mom told me they couldn't take me back to school until the following day. She had apparently decided that while she couldn't keep me from going to California, she could try to make me rest. Without another way to get there, I resigned myself to missing another day of classes.

In the afternoon, I decided a long horseback ride would help my attitude. After Mom and Dad left for business in Sandy, I headed to the barnyard. Spice looked scruffy when she came to the fence to greet me. *Aren't they taking care of her?* She acted jumpy when I saddled her and plodded along like a pack mule on the trails. We were in the upper pasture heading back to the barn when the low clouds burst open with hail, then drenching rain. By the time I had put the saddle away and groomed Spice, my teeth were chattering. *It's supposed to be spring!*

Back in the house, I put on dry clothes, curled up in a chair by the fireplace and stared into the flames, daydreaming about Larry. The sound of Dad's car on the gravel driveway awakened me out of an unplanned nap. Dinner was a quick meal of left-overs before Mom went to bed with a headache. I scrounged the bookcases for something I hadn't read, and had to be satisfied with an outdated volume of *Reader's Digest Condensed Books* with a neighbor's name on the flyleaf. The house was quiet, and once I settled in bed with the book, I couldn't stay awake. My dreams took me back to California and Larry's embrace.

At the dorm the next day, I was surrounded by chattering friends. "How was California?" "Why didn't you elope?" "When you didn't come back yesterday, we were sure you'd gotten married!"

"No, I didn't want to repeat history, and do what last year's President did," I said.

Later Martie came back from a class and said, "Did you hear? Tricia's not coming back!"

"What? Are you sure?" I was shocked--this was totally out of the blue for my best friend.

"Jane works in the registrar's office, and she said that they got a withdrawal request for her. Someone from her hometown said she's going to California."

"I can't believe it. I didn't know she knew anyone in California."

"Well, at least *you* came back. How was it?" Martie pulled me into her room and shoved me onto the bed. "Come on, I want all the juicy details!"

Before I'd gotten very far, there were knocks on my door, and soon a cluster of girls crammed into her room. I told them the highlights of my trip, leaving out the personal tidbits.

"It's so romantic," sighed one of the freshman girls.

"It may be romantic," I said. "But it's definitely not an easy way to have a relationship."

"At least you *have* a relationship," she retorted. "I'm still waiting."

It was several days before I got my first letter from Larry.

March 31, 1967
Dear Carolyn,

It's been a totally wasted day. All that I accomplished was paying some bills for the church and visiting the Boyds. They were disappointed that they didn't meet you on Easter Sunday. But there will be time for that later.

Thank you for your letter. I didn't expect you to write the night you got home! Your 3.38 GPA is pretty good. I'm proud of you!

I don't really have a good answer for your Dad's question about supporting you. But one way or another, something's going to happen with the U.S. Army, and I have a feeling that will resolve things for us.

After Wednesday night's service, Mrs. Clark asked me to tell you that she really enjoyed meeting you. The song you sang during communion was one of her favorites, so you got extra points.

I feel even closer to you than before. In spite of missing you dreadfully, I feel happy. You've thanked me several times for my restraint while you were here. Actually I had a selfish motive of not wanting to have anything scar our marriage. We still have something very wonderful to look forward to on our wedding night!

My love for you is deeper and stronger than ever.

Goodnight, princess.

Larry

After class one afternoon I stopped by the office of my *Marriage and Family* professor to get my term paper to send to Larry.

"Carolyn! How was your trip to California?" he asked.

"It was wonderful, of course." I gave him highlights, and told him I'd really enjoyed my day as a pastor's wife.

"And what about Larry's draft status," he asked.

"It's still up in the air," I said. "But with the war heating up, something's likely to happen soon. We just have to wait."

"Has Larry considered pre-registering at a seminary? Sometimes that helps when there's an appeal, since it shows intent to continue theological studies."

"I don't think he's considered that. I'll have to ask him." Larry's pastoral training had been "on the job" and I knew he didn't have money for seminary right now. But if it could help his appeal, maybe it would be worth a try.

Sunday afternoon provided a peaceful break for letter-writing.

April 2, 1967
Dearest Larry,

I love you! How's that for a good start? Someday maybe I'll write you a letter saying only that: it's the only really important thing I want to say to you.

The sermon at church today was challenging, but my mind kept wandering south, picturing you in your pulpit. I can't wait until I can be there, sitting on the front row, cheering you on!

After dinner I went to a park to study. I didn't stay long, because a breeze came up, but I still got some sunshine. Back in my room, I put in ear plugs and was able to get in about five hours of study (and missed dinner). At least I'm caught up now.

The other day I ran into the former Dean of Women, and she asked me about our wedding plans, if I would finish school, your education, etc. She asked me if you had a "parish." My first thought was, Does she think you're Catholic? Then I thought, that's dumb, priests don't marry. I guess I was tired.

Last night several of my friends and I went on a "nocturnal promenade." Surprisingly enough, we all came back with flowers in our hands. Now I have a lovely bouquet of daffodils on my desk.

I don't know why this day has seemed so long. The sun and the birds woke me at 5:30 this morning as usual, and now this morning's events seem like they happened last week. I think I need some extra sleep!

Goodnight, darling. The peace I'm feeling now is a very welcome change from past turmoil. I hope you're feeling the same thing. I love you, Larry.

Carolyn

By the second week of classes, I had slipped back into the routine, and my trip to California was only a pleasant memory. After a busy three-hour shift at work I felt rewarded when there was a letter from Larry in my mailbox. I tore it open and started reading as I climbed the stairs to my room. Unfortunately, the letter's contents were not what I wanted to read.

April 4, 1967

Dear Carolyn,

Greetings from your expanding fiancé. The results are in—I gained a total of five pounds while you were here. See what a poor influence you are on me? Next time we're together, I'll eat less and you'll eat more, okay?

You wrote about your prof suggesting I pre-register at a seminary for draft exemption. I can't do that. I believe it would be deceitful, since I really don't have plans (or money) for seminary at this time.

It's really a moot point now, because I got a notice from the Sacramento Draft Appeals Board saying they voted 3-0 against my appeal. With a unanimous vote, I can't appeal any higher, so I'm still 1-A.

This news may put your faith to the test, as I may very well be in the armed forces within the next ninety days. Your Dad was worried about me having a steady income--if I can't depend on the US Government, who can I depend on?

You're probably wondering why I didn't call you to tell you this, but I didn't want you to hear bad news at the hall phone with girls wandering by. The strange thing is, Carolyn, that when I got this notice, I had a calmness that was truly uncanny. It must be God's will for our lives, because this assurance is definitely from Him.

The big question is, did you really mean it when you said you would marry me even if it meant going from pillar to post with the Army? It definitely wouldn't be easy; in fact, it would be better for both of us if we waited to get married until after I served my tour of duty. Better, except for one thing—I would probably be discharged early with a "Section 8" (mental instability). Waiting that long to marry you would definitely drive me out of my mind.

The next ninety days will bring more waiting and uncertainty. I'm praying that God will give you the same peace He's given me. This may seem like a foul play at the wrong time, but I believe that God has everything under control. Just trust Him, and it will all work out. I'll wait anxiously for your reply, and continue to pray. Carolyn, I love you, and will abide by whatever you say regarding our future.

I'm enclosing a few snapshots taken while you were here. We look very happy, don't we?

Goodnight, my sweet princess,

Larry

It was hard to finish the letter through my tear-blurred eyes. I leaned against the wall of the stairwell, feeling faint. *He could be gone in ninety days? I'll be in school that whole time. What if we can't see each other before leaves?*

I appreciated Larry's consideration in not wanting me to hear the news in a busy hallway, but I barely kept myself composed on the two flights of stairs to my room. Unlocking the door to my room, I fell on the bed sobbing.

While this had been a possibility for months, I'd hoped and prayed that there would be a way of escape. With no further chance of appeal, further separation was inevitable.

Larry may have peace about this, but I'm devastated, Lord. This isn't the way it was supposed to be. I did my term paper on being a pastor's wife, not an army wife. Is this some test to see how submissive I am? If it is, I'm flunking. How could You do this?

When my tears were exhausted, I lay on the bed feeling miserable. Eventually I realized I was hungry, but couldn't bear the thought of facing other students in the dining room. I rummaged in a box under my desk and found a package of slightly stale graham crackers and a small jar of homemade blackberry jam. *Not a square meal, but it will have to do.*

When phone rates were lower, I knocked on doors along the hall and begged for change. Two phone calls in two weeks was definitely a record!

When Larry answered, I was flooded with emotion, unable to speak.

"Hello? Hello?"

"Hi Larry," I choked out.

"Carolyn, are you okay? I was afraid this would hit you hard."

"You were right. I feel like I got slugged in the stomach."

"I'm so sorry, Sweetheart. There was no easy way to give you the bad news."

"It was definitely a shock," I said, swallowing back tears. "Do you have any idea when you'll get the induction letter?"

"Not really. The notice just said within ninety days."

"That would be the end of June. I have to see you again before you leave, Larry. Maybe I could come down right after finals."

"That would be great, but I could be called up sooner."

"It better not be too soon," I said. "By the way, I want to make one thing very clear."

"What's that?" His voice sounded apprehensive.

"There's no way I would wait to marry you until you got out of the Army. I couldn't possibly wait another two years on top of the time we've already been separated."

"You have no idea how happy I am to hear you say that, Carolyn. I know Army life isn't what we had planned, but if it comes to that, we'll make the best of it."

"As long as you convince them to send us someplace fun," I said, trying to lighten the mood.

"That would take a miracle, with the war going on. But I'm glad you can see a positive side, Carolyn."

"I'm trying, but I'm still reeling."

"I wish I knew the future."

"Do your parents know?" I asked.

Larry's answer was interrupted by the operator's voice. When I had put in my last few coins, he said, "No, you're the only one who knows."

"Let me know how they take the news. And next time you write, how about some good news?"

"I'll do my best, Carolyn, you know that."

"I love you. I miss you so much."

"Not nearly as much as I miss you!" he said.

I headed back upstairs, undressed, and crawled into bed. Trying to study would be pointless.

Thinking about our situation the next day, I had to acknowledge that this could be God's way of dealing with several problems. After studying that night, I wrote another letter.

April 9, 1967
Dear Larry,

Today I feel much better about everything. My initial reaction was pretty emotional; I don't know how I managed to keep from crying on the phone. Maybe I have more strength than I think. Today, looking at things more calmly, I can see that this could be an answer to many things.

It's another big lesson in learning to depend solely on God, and will test our faith. I believe with all my heart that we're meant to be together. Let's hold on to that!

Friday I'm going to Portland on the bus, and will spend the weekend with Paul and Emily. If for some reason you want to call me, you can reach me there.

Dave called this afternoon with an interesting proposal. He's gotten a good job with a CPA firm in Portland, and is buying a newer car. He wondered if I'd like to drive his old one this summer—he'll make sure it's running well for me. It's a 1950 Chevy, and will at least get me where I need to go. That's a huge blessing for me.

By the way, thank you so much for the photos you sent. You look so good in them, I want to reach out and touch you. Of course, I showed them to everyone, and got some interesting responses. One frequent comment was, "He's a minister?" I guess they didn't expect you to be actually human. I really like the fact that we both look so happy in the pictures. Sometimes I sit and stare at them, and remember...

I picked up a copy of "Bride and Groom" magazine today when I was downtown. I got a kick out of a quiz on "How Well Do You Know Him/Her?" I think I got a score of 6 out of 40, and you probably would have done about the same. According to the quiz, that gives us a "flat flunk." Of course the questions were all trivial things that a dating couple would pick up. I believe we know each other at a much deeper level.

Well, it's midnight, and that leaves me only six hours to dream of you, so I'd better get to bed.

You are loved!

Carolyn

The following Saturday, Emily and I had just returned from a shopping trip when the phone rang. Paul answered and said, "Hi, Larry," and then handed the receiver to me.

"Hi, Darling," I said.

"Hi, Carolyn." Hearing the flat tone of his voice, I started shaking. "I got some news today."

"Yes…" I answered.

"I got a letter from Uncle Sam. I have to report for induction on May second." My breath was gone, and I couldn't answer. I sat down heavily on the chair next to the desk. "Are you there?" he asked.

"Yes, I'm here," I finally croaked out, trying to comprehend his words. "May second? But that's only two weeks away."

"It's definitely sooner than we expected."

A brutal pressure squeezed my heart as I absorbed the impact of his news. *He'll be gone in two weeks?*

"Will we be able to see each other?" I asked, dreading the answer.

"I don't see how that will be possible, Honey." His voice sounded pained as he continued. "I have a lot to do to close things out at the church. They'll have to find a new pastor quickly, and there's paperwork to do, and other business. You know I want to see you, but unless you come here, I guess it won't happen."

"I can't get money for a plane ticket on such short notice," I said. "Oh, Larry, I don't know if I can handle this."

"You're tougher than you give yourself credit for. Can you be strong for me…for us?"

"I'll try, Larry." I could barely form the words. I wanted to throw myself on the floor and pound on the carpet. *No, no, no. This can't be happening!*

"Are you still there?" Larry's voice was anxious.

"Yes, I'm here. I'm just trying absorb it all."

"I'm glad you're at Paul and Emily's. Your sister has a good shoulder to cry on."

"I'm going to need it, that's for sure."

"Well, my love, please keep believing that God will work things out for good for us."

"I'll try, but it's not easy."

"I love you, Carolyn, never forget that. In spite of what things look like now, we *will* be together, and all the waiting and uncertainty will be worthwhile."

Tears streamed down my cheeks, and I could only whisper, "I love you," before hanging up the phone. When Emily heard me put down the phone, she came into the room. "Is everything okay, Carolyn?"

"Not really," I said, my face crumpling. "I'll tell you later." I headed toward my bedroom.

"I'll be here when you want to talk, Carolyn." I nodded mutely and closed the door behind me.

Chapter 30

Larry

The Lotus Bowl, with its red-flocked wallpaper and carved black screens, was one of the most exotic locales in Hanford. I was surprised when Mom suggested that we eat there tonight, as a restaurant meal was a rare treat for us.

As I tried to enjoy chow mien with crisp noodles, we talked about Mom's work at the hospital and Dad's lawn customers at the local retirement community. I didn't want to spoil my parents' dinner, so I waited until we were in the car on the way home to break the news to them.

> **Current Culture**
> **April 1967**
>
> - *A Man for All Seasons* wins six Oscars, including Best Picture
> - Major anti-war protests draw thousands in New York and San Francisco
> - First Boeing 737 makes maiden flight
> - Smiley faces become the new pop icon
> - Ground coffee: 90 cents per pound

"I got an official letter in the mail yesterday," I said, leaning forward from the back seat so Dad could hear.

"Oh no, Larry," Mom said. "Not your Draft notice."

"Good guess, Mom. That's what it was."

"When do you leave?" asked Dad.

"May second."

I saw Dad's hands clench the steering wheel, and the car swerved slightly. "But that's only a couple of weeks away!" he said.

"I know. They didn't exactly give me advance notice."

"Does Carolyn know?" asked Mom.

"I called her last night while you were at work." We were all silent for the last mile. I couldn't tell what Dad was thinking as he stared at the road, his face set. Mom's sniffling could be from emotion or her chronic allergies.

As we pulled into the driveway, Dad voiced his constant frustration with government and bureaucracy. "If they have to totally disrupt your life, you'd think they'd have the decency to give you a little more warning."

"It's wartime, Dad. It's nothing personal, just how the machinery works."

"I still think you're getting a raw deal," he growled.

Once the television went on I settled in my room and thought about Carolyn's emotional reaction when I called her. Now, twenty-four hours later, I forced myself to put my own concerns aside while I wrote to her.

April 16, 1967
Dear Carolyn,

You have no idea how hard it was for me to give you the bad news last night on the phone. I would give anything if I could avoid making you sad. I'm not too concerned about myself, but all the sadness you've endured because of our circumstances really makes me unhappy. I wish there were a way for me to bring you happiness now in place of your tears, but I'm powerless. I promise you, Carolyn, somehow I will make up for all the tears and loneliness I have caused.

Mom and Dad took the news very hard. I know they are constantly worried about Chuck, and now with another son going to war, it's a heavy burden for them. They've been very sad all evening.

While talking to you last night, I wanted so much to put my arms around you and comfort you. But I have to release you to God's hands. He knows the future, and I pray that He will comfort and guide you during this difficult time. I only hope you feel my love surrounding you in this trial.

I love you,
Larry

When I looked out at my small congregation on Sunday morning, I fought discouragement. *Have all my efforts been pointless?* One or two faces showed anticipation for worship; the rest seemed to reflect defeat and apathy. I had started with such high hopes of infusing vision and expectation into these people, but it seemed that my prayers, study, preaching and personal care each week had achieved little.

At the end of my sermon, I announced that they would be getting a new pastor soon. There were gasps and exclamations of "Oh, no!" After my closing prayer, I was surrounded before I could step away from the pulpit.

"When did you find out?" "When are you leaving?" "What will we *do*?" "Who will be our pastor?"

"I got the letter on Friday," I said, "and I'm leaving May second. I don't know yet where I'm headed. But even though I'm leaving, God's not deserting you. I know Rev. Black will find someone to be interim pastor."

Gradually people began to drift away, clustering together to discuss the unhappy development. Eventually their growling stomachs and thoughts of lunch prevailed, and soon the building was empty.

As I locked the doors, I looked back at the sanctuary, feeling a mix of sadness and excitement.

I gave everything I could here, Lord. What new door are you opening for me?

At the Army Recruiter's office at noon on Monday, I filled out paperwork and was told to report the following day for tests to determine my placement in the Army. Afterwards I stopped to make appointments with my dentist and optometrist.

When I got home, there was a letter from Carolyn in the mailbox, obviously written before she had heard the latest news.

April 14, 1967
Darling,
(Only six more Monday nights left as President of Jessica Todd Hall. Whoopee and Yippee Skippy!)
I'm listening to the radio, and the last song was "Our Day Will Come." Yes, but when??

Today I spent some time checking things out just in case you get drafted and I end up back here next fall. I called Mrs. Morse, Tricia's landlady, who rents out a room with kitchen privileges for $50/mo. She works evenings, so I'd have plenty of quiet study time. After our conversation, she said the room is mine if I want it. Of course, I really don't want our plans to come to that, but I'd rather be prepared.

The stress of everything seems to be getting to me. I wrote a letter to Roger, wanting to include a newspaper clipping about Portland State University, where he attended last year. I sealed the letter and took it downstairs to mail. When I got back to my room the clipping was still on my desk. Worse yet, last night I reached into my drawer for astringent for my face and applied it with a cotton ball. It seemed to be a little stronger than usual, and when I looked at the label, it was nail polish remover. I'm lucky to have a face left!

I told Ellen about your 1-A classification, and she was very sympathetic. Her fiancé Jack was just deployed, and she won't see him again until they get married in December, eight months from now. I haven't told anyone else that you're 1-A now, because they will all think it's such a shame, and I don't need pity right now.

The more I think about it, the more convinced I am that we should have a small wedding. That way we could have it at the Chapel of the Hills near Mom & Dad's, and it would be so much simpler than having it in a bigger church in Portland. Let me know if you like that idea.

It doesn't seem possible that it's been four weeks since our last night together in Hanford. If time continues to pass this quickly, we may both still be sane by the time we get married.

Goodnight, beloved. I think of you all the time, and pray that if you DO get drafted, you'll have plenty of time to come up to see me and also leave things in order at home and at the church.

I love you,
Carolyn

Tuesday morning I did paperwork at the church and phoned Rev. Black to discuss the future of Grace Chapel. I'd met several ministers at conferences who might be interested in taking over the pulpit. I just hoped they would also have a heart for the people, not just the pulpit.

Apparently many other young men in Kings County had gotten draft notices, because the recruiting office was crowded that afternoon. The recruiter looked hardened and harassed, but after glancing over my paperwork, he looked up with slightly less annoyance in his eyes. "College grad, I see. That puts you ahead of the pack."

"I hope so," I said. "It was a hard slog."

"Are you interested in becoming an officer?"

"That depends on the requirements and the benefits."

"Well, more pay and a little more respect. The disadvantage is the high death rate among 2nd Lieutenants."

"I've heard about that from my brother. He's a Staff Sergeant in 'Nam."

He shook his head. "Fragging is nasty business," he said, referring to the reports of unpopular officers being killed by fragmentation grenades tossed at them by one of their own men. He shuffled the papers in his hand. "I'll see what I can do. Your tests will start in about twenty minutes."

I found a seat in the overflowing waiting room, leaned back against the wall and closed my eyes, hoping to block out the jokes and bragging of other recruits. Most of them were three or four years younger than me, and today it felt like a generation.

For the next few hours, I endured the typical standardized tests intended to help the Army assign recruits to a specialty that fit their knowledge and skills. As usual, I breezed through the grammar and administrative sections but found the mechanical and math sections challenging.

I made it home in time for dinner, and was watching a Western with Dad when the phone rang. When I answered it, I was surprised to hear Carolyn's voice.

"This is a surprise," I said happily.

"I may not have that many more chances to talk to you for a while," she said. "I worked overtime this week, and can't think of anything I'd rather use the money for than to hear your voice."

"I'm glad, although my Scottish nature thinks you should be saving your money."

"Come on, Sweetheart, you know you're glad I called."

"Of course I am. Did you have any special reason for calling tonight?"

"Just that I'm lonely, and need to talk to you." There was a pause before she continued. "I've been thinking—is there any possibility we could get married in September after all?"

"Anything could be possible, but until I'm actually enlisted and know my training schedule, I can't make any plans."

"Well, with things as up in the air as they are, I'm scaling back the wedding plans."

"That's fine with me, that's more your department than mine."

"Of course, Mom may have other ideas. Even though she says she doesn't want to talk about it, she occasionally makes suggestions about what we should or shouldn't do."

"But it's OUR wedding, Carolyn."

"Yes, I know. But I also know she overruled my sisters' wedding plans. I'm just giving you fair warning that I may have to be flexible with planning in order to keep peace in the family. But enough of that. How's it going with wrapping up everything there?"

"It's coming along. I'm going to Fresno tomorrow, and have a dental appointment on Friday."

"Fresno? What's up there?"

"I need to go to the mall for something, and I may look up some old college friends to say goodbye. How were your classes today?"

"Pretty much the usual. Professor Wolfe did his usual rant about low scores on a pop quiz. But I still enjoy his classes because he makes us think."

"Those kind of profs were rare at Fresno State. You're fortunate."

"I guess so." She paused, then said wistfully, "I can't believe you'll be gone in just a few days."

"I know. Unfortunately the days are going by very quickly."

"I love you, Larry Wade. Just don't forget that once you put on your uniform and go off to some godforsaken training base."

"The base may be godforsaken, but we're not, my love. I'm so glad we can trust God through all of this."

"Some days it's easier than others, but I know He's in charge, and He'll work it out." There was a brief silence before she said, "I guess I need to hang up before Miss Operator cuts us off."

"I love you, Carolyn. Never forget that."

Dad's Western was over, and I didn't feel like watching more TV, so I headed to the bedroom. I read for a while, then got out my stationery.

April 18, 1967
Dear Carolyn,

Thank you for calling tonight. Once I'm in Basic Training, we won't be able to talk at all. I'm glad you've gotten some extra work so the phone calls don't ruin your budget.

It rained almost the entire day. But when I was coming home from the recruiting office, there was a break in the clouds and I got a clear view of the Sierras. They were absolutely gorgeous. I'm glad that since you have been here, you can picture them as I saw them.

Today my optometrist told me he was a Navy officer in WWII. He said there were many times he wished he was just an enlisted man, because of all the headaches officers had. I'm trusting that my experience will be different.

As for a small wedding, that would be wonderful. That way we could get married on short notice, (as if you haven't already thought of it). Also, I'm not sure how I'd feel "getting hitched" in front of a huge crowd of strangers.

I'm going to write a letter to your parents as soon as I have a little more information. I want them to hear directly from me what to expect in the next few months.

In spite of my periodic discouragement with the church, I know that some things have been accomplished in the past seven months. A number of people have told me how they've grown in their walk with the Lord, and I've seen some long-standing antagonisms resolved. The building is in much better shape, and a better reflection of God's order and beauty. We are also more known in the community through contacts I've made. I'm trusting God to bring revival to this area. It would give me great satisfaction to know that my sowing and watering had a part in a fruitful harvest.

I did some banking business for the church this afternoon and showed Mom where everything is in the church building so she can help the new pastor. On our way home, we stopped by a new shopping center that was having its grand opening. For Hanford, it was a big deal, with a carousel in the parking lot, lots of sales and prize giveaways. Unfortunately, neither of us won anything, but we did get a five-cent ice cream cone at the Thrifty drugstore.

In my Bible study this morning, one passage stood out to me. Philippians 3:13-14: "Brethren, I count not myself to have apprehended: but this one thing I do, forgetting those things which are behind, and reaching forth unto those things which are before, I press toward the mark for the prize of the high calling of God in Jesus Christ." I know you understand why this was so meaningful to me.

May God comfort you at this difficult time. I only hope that you feel my love surrounding you during this time of trial and testing. If you were here, I would talk you to death, then love you back to life. I wish I could wrap my arms around you right now.

Larry

PS: I hope God allows us some time together this summer, for a few days at least!

The next day, I got an early start on my drive to Fresno, and reached the mall just as it opened. I headed directly to my destination, See's candy store, and made my purchase. Then I drove to the campus and was pleased to find several people I knew. In the student lounge, we caught up on news of mutual friends. I was sobered by the news that two guys I'd had classes with had come home from Vietnam in coffins.

Pulling up to the mailbox when I got home, I was happy to see a blue letter among the bills and grocery ads.

April 20, 1967
Greetings, My Love,

I hope you're having a sunny and warm day. Today dawned cloudless and lovely here. There's a carillon bell in a tower on campus that chimes every hour. It also plays an entire song at 7:45 in the morning, and 5:00 in the evening. This morning's song was perfect, "Oh, What a Beautiful Morning!" I've gotten a little extra sleep in the past few nights, so I woke up early and had extra time for my devotions. It was a good start to the day.

Tonight Mr. Watson (Marriage & Family prof) came over to the dorm for a discussion with the engaged girls about sexual adjustment after marriage. We didn't have a big group, but the girls who came said they really learned a lot. I was surprised at how much some of them <u>didn't</u> know. I guess I've picked up more information than I realized from my reading, because nothing we discussed was new to me.

I've thought a lot about our future. I would like very much to get married after your basic training. However, I realize that this might be running ahead of God's plan for us, and we really don't want that. The other alternative is getting married after you finish Officers' Training, if you go, which could be January or March, right? The more I think about it, the more I question coming back to school next fall, with the potential of a last-minute wedding. I'm always exhausted at the end of a term, and don't want to start marriage in that state. I guess there's not much point in going over all this until things are a little more settled, but it's constantly in my mind, and I'm sure in yours as well.

One thing in your letters that has bothered me is what you've said about causing me pain and sadness. Please don't feel that way, Darling. <u>You</u> haven't caused me any sad moments. Circumstances have been upsetting at times, but never through your actions. Larry, you have brought me more joy and happiness in the last seven months than I could ever imagine.

The reality is, I've come to peace about all of this, and I'm not anxious. We are in God's hands. Two verses have been important to me lately: Romans 8:28, "we know that all things work together for our good," and Psalm 13:5-6, "I have trusted in your mercy, my heart will rejoice in thy salvation. I will sing to the Lord because he hath dealt bountifully with me."

Please don't worry about me. I'm not despondent about our circumstances, and even though it's nice to be able to lean on you at times, I really am a big girl now.

See you in my dreams.

Carolyn

I LOVE YOU   I LOVE YOU   I LOVE YOU   I LOVE YOU

Chapter 31

Carolyn

Sounds of laughter and chattering voices slowly penetrated my sleep-drugged brain. When I opened my eyes, the green fluorescent hands on my alarm clock showed 4:00. *Why do I hear voices at this ungodly hour?*

I pulled the blankets around my shoulders, hoping that the noise would subside, but it got louder. Finally I sat up, fumbled for my robe, and opened my door. Down the hall was a cluster of girls in their nighties and hair rollers, cutting a cake.

"Hey Carolyn, come and join us!"

"Are you kidding, don't you know what time it is?"

> **Current Culture**
> **April 1967**
>
> - A student from Jackson State University dies during antiwar rioting
> - Colorado legalizes abortion in some circumstances
> - PBS debuts new children's show, "Mr. Rogers Neighborhood"
> - 100 millionth telephone connected in the US
> - Snickers candy bars sell for 5 cents

"Of course we do, that's what makes it so much fun. We figured this was a sure-fire way to surprise Janet on her birthday."

"Janet isn't the only one who was surprised," I grumbled. "Can you at least hold it down to a dull roar? Some of us need our beauty sleep."

"Don't be a party pooper," said Sally.

"How about a piece of cake?" Barbara asked. "We've got lots, and ice cream, too."

"Thanks a lot, but I had a late night. I think I'll wait for breakfast." They were having so much fun I didn't have the heart to break up the party. "See you later, girls," I said, and headed back to my room.

I crawled between my still-warm sheets, and tried to go back to sleep, but my thoughts turned to Larry. In just a few days he would be Private Wade, U.S. Army, farther away from me than ever.

When will I see him again? Will we be able to get married this year, or married at all? What if something happens and I never see him again?

In the pre-dawn darkness, I couldn't keep the negative thoughts at bay. All of the worst possibilities paraded through my mind, like a ghoulish "Day of the Dead" procession I'd seen in a movie. I tossed restlessly, feeling increasingly anxious.

He could get sent directly to Vietnam. I don't want to think about that.

There's not enough money in my bank account to visit him when he gets leave from training.

It could be months and months, even a year before I see him.

Mom will say, "I told you so..."

This is too hard, God, I can't do it.

Finally I threw off the covers and fumbled for my robe again. Switching on the light over my desk, I pulled out Larry's latest letters. I needed to "hear" his voice, to read that he loved me, to have his words reassure me that things would work out.

Wrapped in my bedspread, I read letter after letter. The words helped, but I was still agitated. Finally I took my Bible off the shelf and opened to the Psalms. My eyes fell on Chapter 131, *"Lord, my heart is not proud; my eyes are not haughty. I don't concern myself with matters too great or too awesome for me to grasp. Instead, I have calmed and quieted myself, like a weaned child who no longer cries for its mother's milk. Yes, like a weaned child is my soul within me. O Israel, put your hope in the Lord—now and always."*

The tender image spoke clearly to me, and I pictured myself leaning quietly against my Heavenly Father's shoulder, in total confidence. I took a deep breath and whispered a prayer. *I WILL trust you, Father.*

The next day brought me another letter, which made me both happy and wistful.

April 21, 1967
Hi-ya Gorgeous,

When am I ever going to have my arms around you again? I miss your beautiful face and your wonderful personality, as well as your shapely body. I can't imagine waiting months to see you again.

If things go according to schedule, I should be home on leave after Basic Training in July, just in time for our big family gathering. Do you think you could manage to come down then? I'd love to introduce you to a few more family members. I'll write to your mother to help prepare the way.

Here's some news for you. Hold on...For Basic Training I'm being sent to Fort Polk, Louisiana! Can you believe that? It's situated right in the middle of swamps with water moccasins and alligators. Oh, boy!

These days are filled with mundane things like trips to the dentist and the optometrist. We also had our weekly prayer meeting at 11:00 this morning. I wish you could have been there. In spite of everything, there was a spirit of joy in the gathering. It was wonderful!

Unfortunately, my dreams are becoming much more vivid and graphic. I hope this doesn't continue. It's not that your presence in my dreams isn't welcome, it's just that it's hard on my mind (and my body). I'm just glad you're not here right now—I doubt if I'd have any will-power at all.

I love you very much,
Larry

Late Saturday night I checked on the sleeping children I was babysitting, then settled into the comfortable chair and looked around the spacious surroundings. One wall of the blue and ivory living room was floor-to-ceiling shelves containing a stereo system and extensive collection of records and books. *Could Larry and I ever have a home like this?* It didn't seem likely if ministry was our calling.

I was babysitting for one of the doctors who worked part-time at the student health center. He'd said he needed someone level-headed since he was on call and patients might phone during the evening. The two children had fallen asleep soon after I read them bedtime stories, and by 10:00 I'd taken five calls, including two emergencies. Dr. Bailey had warned me that he and his wife would be out very late, and it was already after midnight.

As the night wore on, I read and then listened to music while I knitted. I had dozed off when Mrs. Bailey came home alone at 2:45. She chatted with me for a bit until I was fully awake, explaining that Dr. Bailey was at the hospital delivering the baby of a couple who had called earlier in the evening.

"I don't want to leave the children alone to drive you back to college, Carolyn," she said. "Stan told me to have you drive yourself back to your dorm." She handed me a set of car keys.

I hesitated. "I'm not sure I'm comfortable driving your car."

"Well, I certainly wouldn't be comfortable leaving the children alone. I think you're awake enough to drive. I'll bring Stan over to pick up the car tomorrow afternoon."

As I pulled out of the driveway of their house in the town of Independence, I began to enjoy driving their late-model Mustang. But as I approached the campus, the streets were dark, and I couldn't see lights in shops or homes. It felt very creepy, even after I remembered that there was some sort of municipal repair scheduled, and the electricity to the town and campus was shut off. I parked the car behind the dorm and ran up the sidewalk to let myself in the front door, fumbling with my key in the darkness.

I felt my way up the three flights of stairs and saw a bright line under the door next to mine. When I knocked, my neighbor was happy to bring her candle into my room until I could find my own candle to light. I carried it into the dark bathroom to brush my teeth and wash my face before tumbling into bed.

Early Sunday afternoon, Dr. Bailey came to get his car. "The kids really enjoyed having you stay with them last night," he said as he handed me a folded bill. "Would you be interested in babysitting again sometime?"

"Yes, I'd like that," I replied. "Extra cash is always helpful."

"All right, we'll call you soon."

Sunday evening I wrote to Larry about my weekend.

April 23, 1967

Hi Sweetheart,

How's my favorite draftee this morning? From what you've said about mail delivery, you should get two letters today, so that should make you smile for at least 3 ½ minutes.

This has been the most pleasant weekend in a long while (since Hanford, to be exact). I didn't have any studying to do, and had a chance to live like a real human being for a change.

Last night I babysat for one of the doctors who works at the student health center. They have a lovely house in the adjacent town of Independence. I think you'd love the way the house was decorated, and you'd definitely love their collection of books and records, which ranged from Dickens and Tolstoy to Leon Uris and James Michener, from Rachmaninoff to Tijuana Brass.

The two children were very well-behaved, and went to bed fairly early. Since Dr. Bailey and his wife didn't get home until well after midnight, I did some knitting, and started reading "Catch 22." It was an easy way to earn $5.00! I also got to drive their Mustang back to the dorm! I got a taste of what it's going to be like to be "on-call" as a minister's wife. Dr. Bailey was on call last night while they were at a medical conference party, and I got five calls between seven and midnight.

This week is the half-way point in the term. It simply doesn't seem possible. Before I know it, I'll be back with Mom and Dad at the ranch. Speaking of which, I got a letter from Mom today. She didn't comment about my letter to her saying that we were planning to get married as soon as possible, but she did ask what I meant about a "smaller" wedding.

In spite of all the upheaval of our plans, God has given me a sense of contentment. I still find myself daydreaming a lot, wondering what you're doing and what life will be like in the next months. I love you, beyond anything I ever imagined.

Carolyn

When I opened my door to the soft knock, Martie was standing there in her cafeteria uniform, looking distressed.

"Can I treat you to a soda?" she asked.

"Sounds good. I need to get away from the books for a while." We headed to the little café at the edge of the campus, and chatted about classes and the rainy weather and the usual student gossip until our drinks were in front of us. I finally said, "What's up, Martie? Something's obviously bothering you."

"Oh, Carolyn, it's John again. He's driving me crazy."

"Again? What's happening now?" John was her on-again, off-again boyfriend.

"Well, he's working at the cafeteria again, and he flirts with me constantly. He's always coming up and putting his arm around me, trying to be physical. If he'd just leave me alone, I think I could get over him."

"That's rough. It's hard enough to have to be around him, but when he does stuff like that, it's not fair."

"I know. I thought I was over him until he came back to work. When he touches me, my heart starts pounding. Tonight he came up behind me and started whispering in my ear. I wanted to slap him and hug him at the same time." She ran her fingers through her short blonde hair, looking exasperated.

"You're going to have to be strong, Martie. You know he's not right for you. He treated you like dirt, and you deserve better."

"I keep telling myself that. I see nice guys out there, and really want to connect with one of them. Then I get lonely or have a bad day, and just want to settle for a warm body."

"You know that won't work. You're better off alone than with someone like John."

"I know, I know. When I talk to you, I'm determined to make the right choices and wait for the right guy. But it's hard."

"You have it in you to do the right thing, Martie. God has someone special for you, someone who will cherish you and treat you with respect."

She sighed. "When I hear about your relationship with Larry, it gives me hope. You waited to find someone who shared your values, and now you're engaged to a great guy!"

"He was definitely worth waiting for," I smiled. "Come on, let's head back to campus. I'm on duty tonight and it's nearly closing time."

While I waited for the last few girls to straggle into the dorm just before 11:00 p.m. curfew, I re-read the letter I'd received from Larry that day.

April 25, 1967
Dear Carolyn,

This has been a day of intensive Bible study, one of the last opportunities I'll have for a while. My study was on the gifts and ministries of the Holy Spirit, and was very rewarding. Several things that I wasn't sure about became clear. I'm so glad I had this chance.

Yesterday I took the AQB exam at the recruiting office. I hoped for a higher score, but I managed 10 points above what I needed to qualify for Officer's Candidate School. Now I just have to be actually admitted to OCS. Keep praying that everything will work perfectly to change me from Private Wade to Lieutenant Wade.

In the general knowledge section of the test they asked some really pertinent questions my good college education should have helped me with. Example: "What is the best way to keep a large head from forming on a glass of beer?" My background hasn't exactly helped me with that type of question. Fortunately, I've seen enough beer commercials on TV to know the answer. I also was scheduled for a "cursory physical" which turned out to be simply a hearing test. I passed, so the Army is still on.

Tonight I would like nothing better than to hold you in my arms and tell you all about my day. That's what I miss most in being apart—being able to share things face to face.

It's getting late, so I'll say goodnight and sweet dreams.
Larry

When I got back from my early-morning French class the next day, my mail box was full. There was a thank you note from Joanna for my wedding gift, a phone message, a bill for board and room, and two letters from Larry. I ran up the stairs, past the campaign posters plastered in the stairwell and along the hallways. Dorm elections were in full swing, and this year the girls were more creative than ever.

The poster for Lynn, Shirley and Dixie, three friends running for junior rep positions, took advantage of their initials, asking people to vote for LSD. Another flyer said, "Mary Grace Snork supports J. Miller for Secretary. But then, so does a good bra."

I had nearly finished reading the second letter from Larry, when I heard running footsteps and pounding on my door.

"Carolyn, you got a big package."

"Okay, I'll be down in a bit, I'm busy right now."

"Hurry up—wait 'til you see it."

I was intrigued. A package from home was a big deal for any of us, but rarely rated a special announcement. I skimmed Larry's last words, put the letter on the shelf with the others, and headed back downstairs. There was a small cluster of girls around the desk in the mailroom.

"It's from California," one girl giggled excitedly. "And it's *heavy*."

The box was about the size of a department store shirt box, and I caught my breath at the return address. **See's Chocolates, Los Angeles, California**. I pried open the outer cardboard, and pulled out a large white box with the classic black and gold lettering, and Mary See's old-fashioned cameo in the corner. The bottom corner listed the weight: Five Pounds.

"Oh, my gosh, it's CHOCOLATES," shrieked one of the girls.

"Who's it from?" another girl asked eagerly.

"I don't know yet...oh, here's a card." I reached into the outer package and opened a small white envelope.

Sweets for the sweet. Something to remember me by. I love you, Larry

"You are SO lucky," said another girl.

They crowded around and exclaimed as I opened the box and removed the white protective paper, revealing rows and rows of perfect candies. The heady fragrance of chocolate filled the small room.

"TWO layers. I can't believe it," someone said over my shoulder.

"Are you going to share? You can't eat all those by yourself."

"If you're really nice to me, I just might share. But hands off for now," I warned, replacing the lid. I held the box tightly as I went back up the stairs. Larry's extravagant gift was an expression of his love, but also a tangible reminder that he was leaving.

April 27, 1967

Darling,

Are you trying to get me killed or something? I am the envy of every girl in Todd Hall! Chocolates are wonderful, but <u>FIVE</u> pounds of <u>See's</u> chocolates, and for no reason except "He loves me?" That's just too wonderful for the average Toddian to take in. I'm sure they're all hoping that I'll get sick or gain so much weight that you won't love me, just so that they could have a chance at you. I know you think I should gain a few pounds, and you picked a fine way to help me. I can't resist chocolates. Just remember, "a pound in the box is worth five on the hips."

THANK YOU, you darling, lovable, sweet, thoughtful, irresistible man. I keep thinking that I can't love you any more than I already do, but every day you make me love you more.

So you're going to become a swamp dweller? That should prove interesting. I found out from a friend whose boyfriend just finished Basic that you won't be able to get any mail for the first few weeks you're there. Boy, will you have a pile of letters waiting at the end of that time! Just make sure I have your address.

Before I go any further, I have a very important announcement. I LOVE YOU! Now that you've heard that, I can continue.

I'd be happy to fly down to California in July, if I can save up the money. I'm not sure how to convince Mom (she'll say, "It's his turn to visit you here."). But we'll cross that bridge later.

You mentioned that your dreams are more vivid. I'm dealing with the same thing. Sometimes I wake up and feel like I could reach out and touch you, my dreams are so vivid. You're right; will power is going to be a big issue when we are together again. As much as I want to do the right thing, sometimes I think I want you more, and that bothers me a lot. We can't let down our guard.

You've said that you worry about me. Well, I worry about you, too. You may be a big boy, but you need someone to rub your back, someone to talk to and hold close. Do you think I could fit that description?

I love you, Larry. I hope that those words can carry all the meaning that can't be expressed in other ways right now.

Carolyn

On Thursday evening I couldn't concentrate, in spite of looming mid-terms. Thinking of Larry being in Louisiana in a few days, I longed to hear his voice while he was still within reach. After reading the same page of Wordsworth repeatedly without comprehension, I dumped all the coins out of my wallet and headed for the basement phone booth.

"Hi, Mrs. Wade. It's Carolyn. How are you tonight?"

"Oh, hello, Carolyn. I'm fine, but Larry's not here. He's bowling with Jesse."

"Oh, dear." I tried to keep the disappointment out of my voice. "Well, how was your day at work?"

"Very busy, I ran all day. Lots of babies were born this week. Larry will be sorry he missed you."

"Well, I'll try again before he leaves. Please say hello to Mr. Wade for me."

"I will, Carolyn. I'm sorry you wasted your money."

"Well, it wasn't totally wasted, I got to talk to you."

"That's sweet of you to say, but I know you wanted to talk to Larry. I'll tell him you called."

"Thank you. I hope you have a nice evening."

I slumped down in the phone booth, fighting back tears. Before I could wallow in self-pity, someone knocked on the door, wanting to use the phone. I trudged back up the stairs, and by the time I reached my room, my upbeat, positive attitude had crumbled, and I felt angry and resentful.

Why does it have to be this way? I don't want him to leave. I need him. You can do anything, God. Why didn't you let his appeal go through?

I opened the door to my little balcony and stood outside in the rain. I didn't want to be sensible, responsible, strong or brave. I wanted to yell at God and tell him how disappointed I was, how afraid I was about Larry going into the Army, and probably to Vietnam.

It's just not fair, God. I've tried so hard to do the right thing, to believe in your goodness, to trust that you're taking care of us. Where has it gotten me?

The rain's chill finally penetrated my consciousness, and I turned back to my room, slamming the balcony door. I pulled the cover off the box of chocolates and stuffed one in my mouth, then another. *It will serve him right if I get fat.* I looked over the rows and picked out a white one, oblivious to the taste as I chewed. *I miss him so much. I'm afraid I'll never see him again.*

The emotions of the day caught up with me, and I couldn't hold back the sobs. I left my clothes in a heap on the floor and crawled into bed. *Who cares if I wash my face or brush my teeth? I won't see Larry again. No one else matters.*

On Larry's last night in Hanford, I borrowed coins from everyone along the hall, and dialed his number again. I was determined not to waste time with tears or sadness, but to send him off cheerfully.

"Hi Darling," I said when he answered the phone.

"Oh, Carolyn, I'm so glad you called. I'm sorry I missed you the other night."

Hearing his voice unnerved me, and I could feel emotion rising. I had to change the focus. "How was bowling with Jesse?"

"I beat him, two games out of three."

"Good job, Sweetheart. How was today's church service?"

"A bit depressing. Everyone had long faces. You'd think someone died or something."

"They're going to miss you, Larry."

"I guess...by the way, how are you doing tonight?

"Don't ask, and I won't cry."

"I wish we could say goodbye in person, Carolyn."

"That would be even harder. I don't think I'd have much will power if we were together."

"Good point. I'm afraid my resolve and determination would fly out the window." He paused, and then said, "I want you, Carolyn. My desire for you is so much more powerful than I ever imagined. Just hearing your voice on the phone makes my heart pound."

"Tell me about it," I said with a rueful laugh. "The feeling is mutual, believe me."

"We're going to have to be very careful in July, I think."

"I know. Maybe I should shop for a chastity belt." I hoped my joke would lighten our mood.

"I'm not sure that would do any good. I'm getting pretty desperate."

"Well, enough of that. Let's change the subject. When do you have to be in Fresno tomorrow?"

"8:00 a.m., which means we have to leave here before 7:00."

"You know I'll be thinking of you every minute."

"That might be dangerous for your grades. Better back it off to every other minute."

I glanced at my watch and knew our time was over.

"I love you, Larry. Please don't forget that. I'll pray for you every day, and I'll write every day too."

"I love you so much, Carolyn. Believe me, that's not going to change. God be with you, my sweet."

When I read Larry's letter a few days later, tears splashed on the page.

April 30, 1967
Dear Carolyn,

Yesterday was my last lazy day for at least two months. I read for most of the day, and also watched the Stanley Cup hockey game. It was quite exciting.

In the evening we had an 80th birthday party for one of my favorite congregation members. After that, Trevor, my friend and former professor, stopped to visit after his extension class in Visalia. It meant a lot to me that he would drive out of his way to say goodbye.

Today I got up at 6 a.m., drove to the church to turn on the heat, then returned home to review my sermon. I thought it was pretty good, but it seemed to fall flat as a pancake. At the end of the service, I had everyone come to the front and make a circle. We held hands and sang, "Blessed Be The Tie That Binds." Nearly everyone began crying (except me, of course). Afterwards Mrs. Garland came up and said, "I'm going to do something no one else has done." She grabbed me by the neck and kissed me on the cheek. Don't be jealous, she's only 80 years old!

Carolyn, I promise to write you as often as possible when I get to Louisiana. You are the world's most beautiful, wonderful, most loved woman. The second it becomes possible for us to be together, we are going to be married, even if I have to kidnap you! I love you tremendously. Every time I close my eyes, your image appears. I can't wait until July.

I love you, Babe, and don't you forget it!
Larry

Chapter 32

Larry

At 8:00 a.m., I'd joined several dozen other draftees at the Army reception station in Fresno to start our new lives as soldiers. Now, in late afternoon, after being sworn into the U.S. Army, we'd been bussed to the Fresno Air Terminal to wait for the first flight of our journey to Louisiana.

I glanced around at the gray walls, neutral carpet, and uncomfortable chairs. Ironically, we were waiting at the same gate where I had kissed Carolyn goodbye at the end of her Spring Break visit. I stared out the window, imagining her turning to wave to me, her bright pink raincoat and blonde hair imprinted in my memory. Today's circumstances were far

**Current Culture
May 1967**

- Elvis Presley marries Priscilla Beaulieu in Las Vegas
- Congress gives the President power to cancel draft deferments for most graduate students
- In the case of *Loving vs. State of Virginia*, the US Supreme Court declares state laws prohibiting interracial marriage unconstitutional
- *The Fixer* wins a Pulitzer Prize for Bernard Malamud
- New Volkswagen Beetle advertised for $1,769

different, in ways that we couldn't have predicted just six weeks ago when she'd boarded her plane. *I wish I could turn back the calendar to the week we were together.*

My reminiscence was cut short when the recruiting officer approached me. "Wade, I'm putting you in charge of the group for Fort Polk. Do you think you can handle that assignment?"

"Yes, Sergeant, I can do that."

291

"Okay, you'll need to sign some paperwork saying that you're in charge, and that you'll be responsible for the conduct of the group." After I signed the papers he handed me a packet. "This envelope has your group's airline tickets, meal vouchers, and everything you'll need for the trip to Fort Polk. The other two sealed packets are not to be out of your possession until you give them to your Commander's representative at Fort Polk."

"Okay, Sergeant, I'll take care of everything." He left, and I rejoined the other three guys in my group. Trying to get comfortable in the hard chair, I thought about my last day in Hanford. I had fulfilled the request for a short sermon for the "Pastor's Corner" of the Lemoore *Advance,* completed some church business, visited some members of my congregation, and joined Jesse for a few games of pool.

Mom had taken a day off and fixed a pot roast for dinner. Our final meal together was awkward, as our family was not skilled in sharing emotion. Eventually, I had been rescued by a phone call from Carolyn.

"Flight 81, Fresno to Los Angeles, now boarding at Gate 3." The announcement jolted me out of my reverie and I joined my group at the gate. Only one guy had flown before, and the rest of us casually tried to conceal our excitement. From my window seat I enjoyed a totally new view of the San Joaquin Valley. In the waning light the shadowy presence of the Sierra Nevada mountain range to the east provided a mysterious backdrop to the flat valley.

Our short flight arrived in Los Angeles shortly after 9 p.m. Since our next flight wouldn't leave until 1:30 a.m., I had time to write a letter to Carolyn before joining the other guys to play cards.

Between Los Angeles and Dallas I managed to doze for about an hour. There were a surprising number of people at the airport at 4:30 in the morning. Many of the passengers wandering past the shuttered shops and restaurants were young guys like myself, looking bleary-eyed and out of sorts, all of us apprehensive about the next stage of our lives.

Once in Louisiana, we were escorted to an airport limousine for the last eighty miles of our journey, and the four of us stretched out in the unexpected luxury. Louisiana was surprisingly lush and green. We rolled down the windows, and the damp green smell of the countryside was very different from Hanford. Occasional stands of pine trees reminded me of Oregon, bringing back memories of my life-altering visits there.

Inside Fort Polk, the glamour of the limousine ride quickly faded. Every man with a stripe on his sleeve seemed to have a personal goal of harassing any new recruit within barking distance. We were yelled at to get into the breakfast line, yelled at while we were given bedding, and yelled at in the lunch line. By four in the afternoon, we were each assigned a bunk in the two-story barracks built to accommodate fifty-five men. Left in relative peace until dinner time, we sat around getting acquainted, suspecting that it could be the last relaxed afternoon we'd experience in a long time.

I was standing near the head of the breakfast line on Saturday when a corporal walked up. "Okay, the first ten guys in line, head into the mess hall. You can help serve." I was irritated to have my breakfast delayed, but when I was finally on my way back to the barracks after eating, the rest of the guys from my barracks were picking up cigarette butts along the paths between the buildings. Since I had served breakfast, I was exempt from the clean-up detail. I was quickly learning to avoid being seen by anyone with stripes or brass on their uniform.

On Sunday we had time off with very little to do. The barracks were too noisy for napping, so I joined a group headed for a nearby baseball field. Our vigorous game helped relieve tension and anxiety about what might be ahead in the coming weeks.

Sweat stung my eyes as I got a better grip on the shovel. *I went to college for THIS?* Our group had been sent to a rifle range to dig trenches and stack sandbags. For several hours, we'd dug around rocks and tree roots at the edge of the range to help alleviate flooding from unpredictable rain showers. In spite of the hard menial work, I had to admit that the fresh air and exercise was a welcome change from sitting in hard wooden chairs in the olive-drab classrooms.

"Never thought I'd get punished for *not* smoking," griped the guy next to me. He nodded his head toward several of our group who had told the squad leader they needed a cigarette break. After several requests, he called them over under a tree, lit up himself, and stood shooting the breeze with the smokers. A soldier on the other side of me leaned on his shovel. The squad leader glanced over and yelled at us.

"Did I tell the rest of you ladies to stop? The sooner we get this done, the sooner we can get out of here."

While there were the usual arrogant and brash trainees and trainers, I'd also met some very nice guys. The average age in my barracks was twenty, and many of the Drill Instructors were father-figures to the youngest recruits. Most of the guys in my platoon had completed only high school, but I'd run into a few with more education, including a guy with a master's degree in Biology, and another with a doctorate in Pharmacology.

In spite of the packed schedule and minimal sleep, I missed Carolyn intensely. It was the longest period of time without communication since we'd declared our love for each other eight months earlier. I figured that she'd probably been stock-piling letters to send as soon as she got my address, but after more than two weeks without a letter, I was starting to worry. When I got my first piece of mail, it wasn't from Carolyn, but from my mother.

May 14, 1967

Dear Larry,

I was glad to finally get your address. I pray for you every day, and I hope you're doing okay in Basic Training.

I got a note from Carolyn today. After you left for the Army, she came down with pneumonia. She was so sick she had to leave school and go home. She's been home for over a week and is finally getting better. Her parents will probably take her back to college sometime this week. Now that she's better and has your address, you should hear from her soon.

Everything here is fine. The interim pastor is a pretty good preacher, but you left some very large shoes for him to fill. Every time I go to church, people ask about you.

Mom

I stood staring at the letter in my hand, my stomach clenched in anxiety. *I wish I had known that Carolyn was ill. I could have at least prayed for her!* I realized just how isolated I was from my former life, and especially from the girl I loved. At that moment I hated the Army and what it had done to my life.

"Something wrong, Wade? You don't look so good." One of the guys from my barracks looked at me with concern.

"I just found out that my girlfriend has been really sick. She even had to leave school." I shook my head in frustration. "I had no clue."

"That's the pits," he said. "You can't even call her to see how she's doing."

"I know, that's the worst part, not knowing. I feel so helpless."

"Sorry, Buddy. Hope she's better soon."

Very reluctantly, I crumpled the letter from my mom and put it in the latrine garbage can. I hated throwing it away, but the Drill Sergeant had made it very plain that any personal belongings would be permanently confiscated. *If their intent is to de-personalize us, they're doing a pretty good job.*

Even though I hadn't heard directly from Carolyn, to preserve my sanity I had to do my part to stay connected.

May 18, 1967

Dear Carolyn,

What in the world has happened to you? I just heard about your illness today in Mom's letter. It sounds like you've had a miserable time. Believe me, I'd give anything to be there to take care of you. Thank you for writing to Mom and telling her what happened. Please, please, take care of yourself. I'm so glad you could go home to get well.

Today we had a physical proficiency test, which I passed (one-third of the company didn't). Even though I passed, the Drill Sergeant says I'm fat, so he put me on a special exercise detail with the guys who failed the test. While everyone else is resting, we have to run in place, and while others are standing in the chow line, we have to do push-ups. If I'm not in great condition when you see me again, something will be wrong.

May 20th

As you can see, I had to stop writing the other night. We were told there will be a big inspection tomorrow, so we all had to get busy dusting, mopping, waxing, polishing boots, etc.

Today I got the letters you sent for Mom to forward. Some of the thoughts seemed to reflect your high fever, but once you started getting better, you obviously had time on your hands. Ten pages in one letter? I can certainly understand your concern about being able to finish the semester. If you go back to school this week, you'll only have a couple of weeks before finals. Not being able to keep up with your studies must be frustrating and worrying. I have confidence in your brain power and abilities, and I'm sure you'll manage, even if you don't get the grades you had hoped for. I'm just very grateful that you're getting well. It was horrible to find out that you'd been so sick and I didn't even know.

In one of your letters you asked about getting married when I'm on leave in July. I hesitate to say this, but as much as I would LOVE to marry you as soon as possible, July may not be the right time. I'm learning that nothing is quite as planned in this Army, and I'd hate to have you make plans that we couldn't carry through. I've heard too many stories of guys who didn't get orders, or got fouled up some other way. Besides, as hard as it is to say, I just don't think it would be God's timing for us to get married then. However, if you really believe that we should get married in July, then we'll have a July wedding.

It's nearly lights-out. Pray for me, Carolyn. I'm praying for you also.

I love you tremendously.

Larry

I folded my letter and sealed the envelope. *If we actually get the promised time off this weekend, maybe I can buy some stamps to mail this.*

Aware of my surroundings again, I glanced around the barracks. Most of the guys were sitting or lying on their bunks in their skivvies, trying to relax after a day of hard physical exertion. Living in a big open room with more than twenty other guys was definitely a challenging experience, one that was constantly shaped and directed by the Drill Sergeants. As I thought about my short life as Private Wade, I realized that one thing that I would carry away with me was the smell of the barracks. The odor of floor polish, boot polish, brass polish and sweat combined with Fort Polk's pervasive swampy stench into a mix unlike anything I'd ever known.

"Private Wade!"

"Here, Sergeant," I responded.

"Report to Headquarters, on the double."

I jumped off my bunk, straightened my fatigues, and headed out the door. "Hope you're not in trouble, Wade," one of the guys near the door called to me. When I got to the headquarters building, I sat on a hard metal chair beside another nervous-looking guy. Finally someone called my name.

"Are you still interested in becoming an officer?" the Sergeant at the desk asked.

"Yes, I am," I replied.

"Then fill out this application and bring it back to me when you're finished." He handed me a sheet of paper and a pen, and waved me back to my seat. I quickly filled out the form and returned it to his desk. He glanced over the paper and said, "This will go to the committee in a few days. You'll hear the results in a couple of weeks."

As I walked back to the barracks, I couldn't help smiling. In spite of everything I'd been through in the past few weeks, I felt God's favor.

Things are going to work out! Wait 'til I tell Carolyn!

Chapter 33

Carolyn

The Willamette Valley exuberantly displayed the lushness of late spring. I gazed out the window of my parents' car on the drive back to college, enjoying the views of tidy orchards and well-kept berry farms. I was grateful that my great-grandparents and other pioneers had endured the challenges of the Oregon Trail, risking so much for a chance to settle in this abundant land bordered by perpetually snow-capped mountains and green-forested hills.

> **Current Culture**
> **May 1967**
>
> - 70,000 supporters of Vietnam War march in New York City
> - Evel Knievel jumps his motorcycle over 16 cars
> - *Barefoot in the Park* is popular new romantic comedy
> - Eggs advertised for 38 cents per dozen

I pulled a flower-printed cotton handkerchief out of my pocket and cleared my lungs with an extended coughing spell. Mom turned around in the front seat. "You're still not totally well," she shook her head. "I think you should have stayed home one more week."

"I know, Mom. But it's so close to the end of the term I just couldn't afford another week out of school."

"Well, I'm concerned about you. You tend to wear yourself out."

"I'll try to take it easy, but it's only two weeks until finals."

She frowned at me before turning around in her seat. I sat back and replayed the events that had unexpectedly taken me home from college.

In the week Larry left for Basic Training, I'd worked many overtime hours preparing for an alumni conference our department was hosting in mid-May.

Mrs. Roberts had given me several important responsibilities and was counting on me to be available during the conference. During the week I developed a troublesome cough and felt generally lousy. Registering conference attendees Friday afternoon, I struggled to function, and Mrs. Roberts finally sent me home early.

"I don't want you spreading germs to all our guests." Her concerned expression contradicted her brusque words.

"Thank you for excusing me early. I'm going straight to bed," I replied.

When my alarm rang Saturday morning, I was feverish and shaking with chills. There was no way I could go to the conference. I staggered out into the hall, grabbed the first girl I saw, and asked her to take a message to Mrs. Roberts that I was too sick to come to work. Crawling back into bed, I fell into a restless, nightmarish doze.

The creepy guy from my social dance class was clutching my hand and trying to put his arm around me. I pushed him away saying, "No, you're not my boyfriend. I have a different boyfriend. He's from another state, not another country." He tried to grab me again, but I pulled away. He followed me, calling my name.

The voice changed to a woman's voice, still calling my name. I swam up from deep dream waters, and opened my eyes to see my mother bending over me, Emily standing beside her.

"Carolyn, what in the world happened? We came for church and Emily told us you were sick. I never imagined you would be so ill." She waited as a coughing spell shook me. "We need to get you home. Have you seen a doctor?"

"No, I didn't have time." I tried to think how I could be at my sister's home in Portland, an hour from college. Thinking made my head hurt, and I asked, "How did I get here?"

"Apparently your boss went to your room to see why you didn't show up for work, and found you feverish and delirious. She brought you here last night." I vaguely remembered hearing Mrs. Roberts come into my dorm room and then helping me to her car. Another coughing spell drained my energy, and I lay with my eyes closed.

"We need to get you to a doctor as soon as possible," Mom said. My mind registered mild surprise, as Mom and Dad generally avoided doctors. *Maybe I'm sicker than I thought.*

Mom and Emily wrapped me in blankets and settled me in the back seat of Dad's car for the long drive to the ranch. I dozed most of the way, rousing occasionally to respond to Mom's periodic questions and comments. "How long have you been coughing like that?" "You've been burning the candle at both ends, no wonder you're sick." "Does Larry know you're sick?"

"No, Mom," I replied wearily. "I can't get in touch with him."

"Well, this is a fine turn of events," she said, shaking her head.

The doctor's office wasn't open on Sunday afternoon, so Mom treated me at home with cough syrup, Vick's VapoRub and her time-honored cure of hot honey-sweetened lemonade. Once the practical things were taken care of, Dad joined Mom beside my bed and they prayed fervently for my recovery.

Monday morning I shivered under a quilt in the back seat of the car on the forty minute trip to the doctor's office. Waiting on the cold exam table, I wished I'd brought the quilt from the car.

The doctor's eyebrows shot up when he read the thermometer, and after he listened to my lungs, he turned to Mom. "She's got a whopping case of double pneumonia, Mrs. Cooke. I'll give her a shot of penicillin, and you'll need to watch her carefully. If she doesn't get better soon, I may have to put her in the hospital."

Exhausted from the trip to the doctor and the painful injection in my hip, I slept most of the afternoon.

By Wednesday, my cough had subsided slightly, but an itchy red rash decorated my torso. When I showed Mom, she picked up the phone and called the doctor. When she hung up, she woke Dad from his nap beside the fireplace.

"Carolyn may be allergic to penicillin. You'll need to drive to Sandy and get her a different medicine." Dad put on his boots and jacket, and came to the bedroom to give me a hug before heading out to the car.

It wasn't until Friday that Mom announced, "I think you're well enough to eat lunch at the table." Until then, she'd brought me food on a tray, insisting that I needed to stay in bed to regain strength. While we ate lunch, the sun came out.

"I'd like to take a walk outside," I said. "I think some fresh air would do me good."

"Let me clear the table first, then I'll walk with you," Mom replied.

The short walk to the edge of the front yard wore me out. But my soul was refreshed by the sight of the deep purple violets peeping from behind their heart-shaped leaves at the edge of Dad's rose bed. Between coughing spells, I took deep breaths of the fresh mountain air, heavy with fragrance from the lilacs blooming beside the road.

Now that I was feeling better, I worried about my schoolwork. I didn't have any of my books with me, and it was near the end of the term. If I got too far behind I wasn't sure if I'd be able to pass my courses. My biggest concern was French II, where I'd been struggling with translation assignments in *L'Etranger*, Albert Camus' existential novel. Final exams were only a few weeks away. *How can I do this, Lord?*

"I need to get back to school, Mom," I told her at lunch on Saturday. "Will you take me tomorrow?"

"We're not taking you back until you're well."

"But I'm so much better, and I really need to be there," I pleaded.

"You really need to be *here* until you're well." Mom's tone let me know that argument would be fruitless. I could only get back to school if they drove me, so I'd have to be strategic. I felt like a 10-year-old again, totally dependent on my parents, being told what to do and what not to do each day.

That evening I said, "Mom, I'd like to call Mrs. Wade and let her know what's going on."

"Larry should be the one to contact you."

"But Mom, he's in Basic Training." I shook my head in frustration. "He can't make a phone call. He doesn't know I've been sick, why would he be worried?"

"Well, it's his place to get in touch with you." When I glared at her, she added, "Don't get huffy with me, Carolyn, after all I've done to take care of you these past few days."

I turned on my heel and went back to the bedroom, shutting the door with more force than necessary. *I'm twenty years old, for heaven's sake. I didn't get sick to inconvenience her.* I flopped on the bed, feeling anxious and depressed. I needed Larry. He would calm me down, help me get the proper perspective and have the right attitude with Mom.

If I couldn't call Mrs. Wade, at least I could write a letter. I took a sheet of paper from the desk and wrote a brief message to Larry's mom, telling her what had happened, and asking her to let Larry know, if she could reach him.

The following day when Mom was in the back yard hanging laundry on the line, I found a stamp and envelope in the desk. I put the letter in plain view with other out-going mail. When Mom came back into the kitchen, I was sitting at the table with a cup of tea. She saw the letter and gave me a questioning glance. With a neutral expression I said, "I think it's a courtesy to keep in touch with her." Mom's shoulders were stiff, but she didn't retort. The next time Dad went outside, he took the envelope to the mailbox.

Even though I didn't have an address for Larry, I longed to share my frustrations with him. I wrote long pages of rambling thoughts, trying to be positive so he wouldn't worry too much. I felt imprisoned, and when I thought about the deal I'd made to work for Mom and Dad in exchange for the cost of wedding expenses, I had to push away rising panic.

I really hope we can just get married when Larry has leave in July, and avoid all the hassle.

I added that thought to my letter, folded the pages and put them aside, waiting for the time that I'd have his address.

Mom and Dad drove to Portland for church on Sunday, leaving me home with strict instructions to stay in bed. She brought me a stack of Readers Digest Condensed Books hoping they would keep me in bed.

When they got back from church mid-afternoon, they were both in a good mood, and I brought up the subject of returning to school again.

"There are only a few more weeks before finals, Mom. I'd really like to go back to school this week."

She looked at me speculatively. "Well, your cough is sounding better, and you've been taking it easy like I asked. I guess there's no point in wasting the tuition and board and room by not finishing the term. Let's see how you are in a couple of days."

"Thanks, Mom." I gave her a quick hug, and she patted my shoulder.

"I'm glad you're getting better, Dear."

Now it was Friday again, and Dad was parking the car in the loading zone in front of the dorm. As I got out of the car, the dorm Vice-President was walking out the front door.

"Carolyn, you're back!" she shrieked.

"You've been gone for ages," said the girl with her. "Are you okay?"

"Yes, I'm much better, thanks," I replied.

Walking through the front doors of my dorm was a huge relief after the nightmarish events of the past two weeks. Dad and Mom wanted to get back to the ranch before dark, so they said goodbye in the lobby. After adding a few more warnings about taking it easy, Mom gave me a peck on the cheek, and Dad gave me a hug. "See you in a few weeks, Sweetheart."

Before going upstairs, I stopped at the mailroom and retrieved my mail. Back in my familiar room, it was obvious that friends had been at work. The wads of used tissues and the stale, sick-room odor were gone. My books and papers were neatly stacked, clothes were put away, and the bed made with fresh sheets and pillowcase.

I dumped my things on the floor beside the bed, plopped down against my pillow, and excitedly ripped open the letter with the earliest postmark.

May 2, 1967, Los Angeles Airport
Dear Carolyn,

This day began early and will end late. I left Hanford as Larry David Wade, and am now Private Wade, U.S. Army. I had to get up at 5:30 this morning to get to the reception station in Fresno by 8:00 a.m., and we finally left Fresno on our journey to Fort Polk twelve hours later. Only a couple of hours were spent in actual processing and paperwork, and the rest was wasted.

The best part of the day was the flight from Fresno to Los Angeles. I could see all the lights of the valley, and even lights in the foothills of the Sierras. It was very clear, and the view was magnificent. No wonder you enjoyed flying to see me—it's an experience that could easily get into one's blood.

One thing the Army didn't schedule in our trip from Fresno to Fort Polk is sleep. Our next flight leaves at 1:30 a.m., and we have several hours to wait in Dallas until our 7:30 flight to Louisiana tomorrow morning.

Guess what? The Sergeant had to pick someone to be in charge of our group of four, and who do you think he picked? Yep, yours truly. I'm responsible for plane tickets, meal tickets, and the general conduct of our group. Fortunately, the three other guys are pretty decent and don't seem to be in a rambunctious mood, so I shouldn't have any trouble. The Sergeant told them I'm "Group Leader," but on the written orders, I'm listed as "Group Commander." Impressive, don't you think?

Even with all the activity today, my thoughts have turned to you constantly. Thank you so much for calling last night. As I said on the phone, I love you so much it hurts. It would be highly impractical and nearly impossible for us to get married when you come in July, but I can always wish!

I will send you my address as soon as possible, but I'm not sure how much or how often I'll be able to write you.

I love you immensely, more than I can ever begin to say.
Larry

Starved for his words, I didn't bother putting the letters back in the envelopes, but tore them open one after another, gorging myself, hearing his voice through the ink on the page.

May 6, 1967
Dear Carolyn,
We are having a break before supper so I have time to write. It's been a really wild day. Thursday night we had lights-out at 9:00, but I had to stay awake since I was assigned to fire-guard duty from midnight to 1:00 a.m. Then the PA system blasted reveille at 4:45 a.m. They gave us thirty minutes to wash, shave, make our bunks, sweep and mop the floors. With four showers and sinks for the twenty-six guys on my floor, you can imagine what a challenge this was.

After breakfast we were photographed and finger-printed before returning to the barracks for more cleaning. After lunch we had blood tests and haircuts (mine makes me look like an idiot), and finally got our everyday Army uniforms, better known as "fatigues," dark green cotton pants and long-sleeved shirt, plus boxers, t-shirts, ugly green socks and black high-top leather boots. My uniform fits okay, except for the pants, which are two inches too big in the waist and three inches too long.

Today was the worst so far, as we had to get up at 2:30 a.m. to report for KP (kitchen patrol) duty at 3:30. We were finally able to return to the barracks at 6:00 p.m. During the day we had a total of 40 minutes of down time, including meals. I've mopped, swept, and done dishes for several hours. You should see my dishpan hands!

Tomorrow we're supposed to be able to sleep in; they won't get us up until 5:30.

I think our Sergeant must be a Christian, since he played Christian music on the radio during KP. What a pleasant surprise! Also, I've run into a lot of nice guys here, and fewer foul mouths and dirty minds than I expected. On top of that, very few of the guys smoke. How lucky can I be?

Well, Sweetheart, my letters may be short and infrequent. I'm sorry, but our schedule here doesn't allow for much more.

It's very strange to be with only men for the past week. Why couldn't you be here? I love you, and I'm waiting anxiously to see you again.

Larry

P.S. I don't have a mailing address yet, but should have it on Wednesday.

May 7, 1967

Dear Carolyn,

We were brought to the Basic Training area yesterday and have been busy from before sun-up to way after sun-down. We don't have time for anything other than training.

We are in "Zero Week" which doesn't count toward our eight weeks of Basic Training. That means that I will be finished with training here on July 9th. Before I forget it, here is my address:

PVT Larry D Wade RA 18 825 403

E (Echo) Co., 2d Bn, 2d Tng Bde, 2d Platoon

Fort Polk, Louisiana 71459

When you send me mail, please write the address exactly as I've written it. Also, could you please write and send my address to my parents? Please don't try to send anything except letters. We can't keep any personal things here, and I'm not sure I'll even be able to keep your letters.

I'm sorry I can't write more, but I have to get busy again to meet the next deadline.

Goodnight, Hon.

Love, Larry

May 11, 1967

Dearest Carolyn,

I hope everything is going well with you.

Today we ran half a mile before breakfast, and did wind sprints before lunch. Then we were sent on a work detail, and missed the extra physical training before dinner.

In case you're wondering why I can write tonight, it's because we have been given a few minutes of free time. Army life is definitely not boring.

I heard a joke that's appropriate here: "Why is the person with the least privacy called a Private?" Amen! <u>Everything</u> *I do is observed by at least five other men. It took a little time to adjust, but I'm used to it now.*

I'll write to you again as soon as I can. I love you!

Larry

May 25, 1967
Dear Carolyn,

I'm sorry I haven't written, but it's been pretty rough for the last week. The schedule has definitely sped up. I've already lost more than ten pounds. Of two ways to lose weight, sweat it off or starve it off, I'm using both concurrently.

In case you're wondering how I have time to write, I'm on fireguard duty again tonight.

We started today by putting on a full pack (fifteen pounds), picking up our rifles (another 9.6 pounds) and running for a mile. Then we walked another three miles. All that was just to get to our first class of the day at the bayonet instruction field. You would have shuddered to hear us. The Sergeant would yell, "What's the spirit of the bayonet?" and we'd have to shout back, "To kill, Drill Sergeant!" Then we were supposed to growl loudly as we thrust our bayonet, aiming at either throat or stomach of our imaginary enemy.

Yesterday we learned a new "guerilla" exercise, pairing off with another guy for open-handed boxing. I was matched up with a big guy from the South who had longer reach than me, but I was still able to get in my share of hits. It's the first time I've done anything like this since seventh grade, and found I actually enjoyed it. (I hope you're not shocked!)

Here's some news to cheer you up. I've taken several tests for Officer's Candidate School, and I'm now eligible. Don't get your hopes up; it's still a long road ahead. I have to be invited to apply, then a committee votes on the applications.

There's something in your letters...

(May 26) I was interrupted last night by a warning that the Lieutenant was coming for a guard check, so my letter had to come to a screeching halt.

As I started to say above, there's something in your recent letters that concerns me. I know you've been sick, and are worried about being able to finish your studies when you get back, but is there something else? I feel like you're holding back, like there's something you don't want to tell me. Remember our pact of complete honesty? I'll hold you to that. I know that you've had a miserable time lately, but please don't become discouraged.

Well, it's late and I'm beat. Please write again soon. Except for a brief letter from Mom, your letters are the only mail I get.

You have no idea how much I miss you. The next time I see you I am going to give you a kiss you will never forget!

Larry

Putting the letters back in their envelopes, I left them on my pillow to read again at bedtime. Standing and stretching, I opened the French doors to let in the afternoon breeze. I lifted the lid on the big See's candy box on the desk, wondering if friends had helped themselves in my absence. But there were still candies in the top layer, and the second layer was untouched. I started to reach for a dark caramel, then put the lid back on the box. My appetite hadn't returned enough for chocolate.

I glanced at the clock. If I hurried, I'd have enough time to get my assignments from most of my professors before they left their offices for the weekend. It was going to take me every spare minute to catch up.

My first stop was my French professor's office. "Bonjour," I said, pausing in her doorway.

Miss Girard peered at me over the top of her glasses. "Bonjour, Carolyn. So you're back? I heard you were home with pneumonia."

"Yes, I was, and I didn't have my books with me. What assignments will I need to make up to pass the course?"

She pulled a notebook from an untidy stack on the edge of her desk, and leafed through it. "You've missed quite a bit in the last two weeks," she frowned. "I'm not sure you'll be able to make everything up before finals."

"I'll do my best; just let me know what assignments are necessary."

"Well, I know you've tried hard in this class, and you have a high "B" so far." She studied her grade book. "What if I drop the translation work on *L'Etranger* and have you make up the grammar and conversation assignments?"

"That would be wonderful, Miss Girard. Thank you!" I was hugely relieved that I wouldn't have to struggle with the translation. I could probably manage the other assignments and pass the course. Thanking her again, I headed to the next professor's office. By dinnertime, I had a long list of assignments. I certainly wouldn't be doing much socializing in the next two weeks, but with God's help, I might be able to pass all my courses.

At the end of the first week of June, final exams were over, and I prepared to leave Todd Hall for the last time. The past weeks had been a blur of all work and no play. Even with keeping strictly to an 11:00 p.m. bedtime, it had been an exhausting challenge to complete reading assignments, finish term papers, and cram for finals. I'd turned in my last final that morning.

"Man on the floor," I yelled as Dad and Mom followed me into the hallway. Dad picked up two boxes of books and headed down to the car.

"It's going to take several trips," Mom observed, glancing at the piles on the floor.

"Three years of my life here," I said, looking around the now-bare room. "I wonder what the next three years will bring?"

Mrs. Anderson, the house-mother, gave me a hug when I turned in my key. "Please let me know about your wedding plans, Carolyn. You have my prayers and best wishes." I turned away to hide my sudden tears. *I'll miss all of this. Thank you, Lord, for the privilege of being here. It's expanded my mind and my heart.*

Field daisies dotted the grassy pastures at the ranch. The creek that ran through the barnyard was overflowing with late spring run-off from the mountains, and tiny fruits were hiding under the leaves of the apple trees.

Getting out of the car, I stretched and headed to the barnyard gate. The horses had seen us arrive and were ambling toward the fence, looking for a handout. Spice nudged my shoulder with her soft black nose, and I patted her neck, raising a puff of dust.

"I hope you're ready for lots of exercise, girl," I warned.

"Don't take too much time with her," Mom called from the back door. "You'll need to unpack before dinner."

This could be a long, lonely summer.

Chapter 34

Larry

Fort Polk's 80 degrees felt much hotter than 100 degrees back in Hanford. I'd certainly never had to push my body like we were being pushed in Basic Training.

I was glad that most of the fifty men in my platoon worked hard to do their best. We marched or ran faster than the other platoons, seldom took breaks, and were often already in our bunks when the other platoons straggled back from maneuvers.

At the end of the first week of June, I got a packet of letters at mail call. There were cards and letters from members of my congregation, a letter from my missionary friends in Mexico, and best of all, a letter from Carolyn.

**Current Culture
June 1967**

- Emmy awards won by Lucille Ball, Don Knotts, and *Mission: Impossible*
- Estimated 400 million watch *Beatles: Our World*, first global satellite TV special
- Popular WWII movie *The Dirty Dozen* premieres
- Barbra Streisand performs *A Happening in Central Park* before 135,000 fans

May 27, 1967
Dear Larry,

Thank you for your letter. I don't take your letters for granted, since I know it's a challenge to find the time. I love hearing what's happening to you, and I'm glad Basic Training hasn't been as bad as you thought it might be. Are there snakes there, or bugs?

I've been back at school for a week, and it's grueling. I have several term papers to finish, quite a bit of reading to do, and other assignments to catch up on. I've tried to be in bed by 11 p.m., but with work and end of school activities on top of my studies, it's been hard. I'm holding my own, but pneumonia really took the stuffing out of me. At least my rash is almost gone now.

The weather has been nice this week, and I'd love to be out in the sunshine, but most of my free time is spent either at the library, or in my room at my desk. At least I can have my balcony door open and get some fresh air when I'm in my room.

Several girls have asked me to do sewing or other projects for them (for pay) but I've had to turn them down. I want to save money for our wedding, but I simply can't afford to take ANY time away from my studies. Everything is due by the end of next week, which means I may not be able to write you every day.

Larry, please pray for me in the next two weeks. It will be a miracle if I get everything finished and turned in on time and get passing grades on my finals. I hate ending my time here at such a frantic pace. I know we're not supposed to question God, but sometimes I really wonder about the way things have gone, especially when you're so far away, and our plans are so uncertain.

Well, it's 10:00 p.m., and there's a stack of note cards and a rough draft sitting beside my typewriter. If I want to get to bed before midnight, I'd better make this short.

I love you, and I miss you.

Carolyn

P.S. Are you real, or just a figment of my imagination?

Rash? What rash? My heart became heavier with each line that I read. Carolyn's illness was apparently more serious than I realized. It was bad enough to have our plans turned upside down by the Army, but her pneumonia was certainly a twist that I hadn't anticipated. I shot up an arrow prayer: *God, please take care of her—I sure can't!*

On Saturday, all three platoons in our company were assigned to guard duty. I understood the training aspect of the exercise, but it seemed silly to guard the outhouse at the bayonet range or the wire fence at the North Swamp.

The following week, we went to the rifle range each day. With just fifty minutes allotted to travel five miles on foot carrying rifles and full packs, we had to hustle, but I enjoyed shooting the weapons. On Friday, we zeroed-in our M-14 rifles, and I managed to be one of the first in our Company to achieve a tight shot group, three holes close enough to be covered by a quarter.

When we got back to the barracks, it was time to clean the latrine, mop and wax the floors, and display our personal gear in our lockers for Saturday's inspection. The Company Commander and his Executive Officer examined everything, including floors, beds, foot lockers, wall lockers, and latrines. They actually put on white gloves to check window and door ledges.

After we passed inspection, our platoon was given "post privileges" for the first time, and we were free to leave the barracks on our own. There was still KP and other duties to keep us busy, but at least I was able to get to the small Post Exchange shop to buy stamps and stationery. I sat with the Fort Polk/US Army stationery on my lap, and pulled the photo of Carolyn out of my wallet. The formal black and white portrait didn't convey the sparkle of her eyes or the music of her laughter, but it made me feel closer to her as I started my next letter.

June 5, 1967
Dear Carolyn,

What's this about a rash? Your last letter mentioned it casually, but it's the first I've heard of it. For heaven's sake, please tell me everything that's wrong with you. I need to know what's going on with the girl I love.

Your letters mean so much to me. It's very hard to drop them in the garbage can, but we're not allowed "excess" personal items. Please forgive me for not writing lately, but we have been very busy. Every day last week we ran out to the rifle range (five miles one way). Right now, I'm on middle of the night fire-guard shift. We have M-14 rifles, but no ammo. I guess if there's trouble, we drop the rifle and run. One of my recent assignments was guarding the Fort Polk golf course.

The chapel service yesterday morning was quite a let-down. It was very "high church" and unfamiliar to me. I also got a surprise during communion when the cup contained wine instead of the grape juice I'm used to. I almost gagged.

Sunday some of the guys who live near the base had visits from their girlfriends. It made me miss you so much! After being around only men for the past month, I'd almost forgotten what girls look like. It seems like forever since we were together.

Today I got called out of formation to have a physical for O.C.S. There were several men who washed out because of trick knees or something, but yours truly passed. I also found out that of 300 men in two companies, only eight of us were asked to apply for O.C.S. It could prove interesting. By the way, when I was weighed as part of the physical, I discovered I've lost 13 pounds.

Your letters sound very bleak, Carolyn. I hope that it's a reflection of the pressure you're under to finish all your schoolwork, and not something else. <u>Something</u> has to be going right for you!

I wish I could write more, but I've already been interrupted several times, and tomorrow we'll be running back to the rifle range.

Goodnight, my love. Thank you for the kiss on the envelope of your letter.

Larry

Fine mist swirled around the corners of the barracks and the light posts along the pathways. This strange fog intensified the damp rotting vegetation smell of the base as we stood in early morning formation the third week of June. "Parade rest!" yelled the Drill Instructor as Captain Medeiros, the Company Commander, came to stand in front of us. We could relax slightly from the stiff "at attention" pose.

He gave us the usual pep talk, and then announced, "Second Platoon, you've won Honor Platoon again this week for the third time. Good job, men." I wanted to cheer, but that wasn't part of the parade-rest stance. All our extra effort in staying out of trouble, keeping the barracks spotless and carefully displaying our gear had paid off. For the next week, we would be exempt from extra details, would march at the front of the company, and eat first at every meal. In addition, nearly every soldier in the platoon was granted a 24-hour pass, our first opportunity to leave the base.

Six of us shared a taxi to the neighboring town of Lake Charles. We checked into a motel, with two guys to a room. I connected with a couple other guys from California who were also non-drinkers, and we headed for the movie theater. After the show, we wandered around town, and eventually ended up in our motel rooms to watch TV, which we hadn't seen in more than a month. We turned out our lights about midnight, and I didn't wake up until 9:00 a.m., five hours past our usual time to rise and shine. It was great to feel like a "normal" person, even for 24 hours!

The following weekend I got another 24-hour pass, but since the KP rotation hit my end of the alphabet, I couldn't leave the base. I used some of my spare time to describe life as a soldier to Carolyn.

June 17, 1967
Dear Carolyn,

Honestly, Honey, the reason you haven't received any mail for the past few days is not because I didn't want to write. Training has really intensified. We did night firing at the rifle range until midnight, then marched back to the barracks. I managed to stay up long enough to polish my boots and take a shower before I fell into bed.

The next day we were taken to the gas chamber for exposure to chlorine and tear gas. The real fun was when we had to go through the tear gas without a mask. Before we could leave, we had to stop at the door and give our name, rank, and serial number. Some of the guys got really ill, but I managed to hold my breath long enough to make it.

When we got home, we had to clean the barracks for today's inspection, and pack our duffle bags. Early Monday morning, we'll be driven out in the woods for bivouac (military camp-out). We'll be there most of the week, so I'll apologize in advance for not writing to you.

One of my favorite activities this week was throwing live hand grenades. They make a huge noise and shake the ground when they explode. So much power in such a small package!

HINT: We are now allowed to receive packages from home. In case you happen to have some free time and are feeling up to it, would you consider sending me a care package? It would need to arrive after June 23 (when we return from our little expedition) and before July 7, when we graduate.

After next week, there will be only two weeks of Basic Training left! I know it sounds trite, but I really do wish you were here. I used to wonder why soldiers and sailors sometimes acted like idiots, but now I understand. If I didn't have you to wait for, I might be tempted to do something stupid myself.

Well, Carolyn, my free time is nearly over, so I'll say goodbye. I'll write as soon as I can.

I really do love you!

Larry

When the guys who had gone off-post returned, it was obvious that much of their paychecks had gone for alcohol. There was extra laughter and horseplay, and at one point, a huge fight broke out in the volleyball sand pit. By the time the MPs arrived to break it up, there were a couple dozen guys swinging punches, although no one seemed to know what the fight was about. The rest of us watched through the barracks windows while the most belligerent men were separated and shoved in the back of the MP jeep. It was definitely more of a brawl than the occasional fist-fight over whose turn it was to use the barracks washer and dryer, or the verbal sparring set off by regional or racial differences.

The next day, fifty of us were crammed onto benches in the open back of a troop carrier, and trucked to the bivouac site. After weeks in the tidy barracks area, the back country of Fort Polk was wild and beautiful, with skinny pine trees and unexpectedly lush and green underbrush.

We hadn't hiked very far into the woods when we flushed out a small herd of wild razorback hogs that scrambled away snorting and snuffling. As we went deeper into the woods, we saw raccoons, armadillos, and deer tracks. When I saw a deadly water moccasin sunning itself next to the trail, I wasn't happy that we would be sleeping on the ground.

"Hey, look at this!" called Moore, a guy ahead of us on the trail. When the rest of us reached him, we saw that he had speared an armadillo with the guidon, the fancy spear that held the company flag.

"Whadja do that for?" asked Barnes.

"Well, he was there, and I moved faster than he did."

"Too bad for him." Barnes kicked the dead armadillo so the side of the path, and we continued to our assigned meeting point.

When our platoon gathered, Lieutenant Yates called us to attention. "Ten-hut!" As we stood in front of him, he continued. "Which of you guys came in from the west?" Our team all raised their hands. "And did you happen to run into any wildlife on the way?" We all stared straight ahead, trying to look innocent. "Seems like there's an armadillo back there with a guidon-sized hole in his shell. Anyone know about that?"

"That was me, Sir." Moore reluctantly took a step forward.

We all stood nervously as Lt. Yates stared at our buddy. Then he said, "The least you can do for the poor critter is give him a decent burial. Head on back, men." We ran back along the trail until we found the armadillo. Lt. Yates pointed: "You, you, and you, start digging." The guys pulled out their folding trenching tools and dug a hole in the sandy soil.

When they thought it was deep enough, Moore said, "This okay, Lieutenant?"

"No, soldier, he's going to get a proper burial. Dig that hole six by six!"

After the hole had been dug to his specifications, Lt. Yates said, "Ok, Moore, put him in. The rest of you, stand in formation and give a proper salute to the fallen comrade." Moore carefully picked up the armadillo on his shovel, and lowered him into the hole.

We stood in rank as Lt. Yates continued. "Barnes, you can hum 'Taps'."

It was all we could do to keep our faces straight as Barnes hummed, "Ta ta DAH, ta ta DAH…"

At noon, I had my first experience with K-rations. Each kit contained a full meal and extras such as a small roll of toilet paper, four cigarettes, and chewing gum. My first box had cans of steak and fruit cocktail, plastic packets of peanut butter and bread, a chocolate bar, and of course a "P-38," the key-sized folding can opener. I kept the toilet paper, but traded the cigarettes for another chocolate bar, and put the P-38 on my dog-tag chain.

On the last day of bivouac, we ran in formation several miles to the 'infiltration' course. "On the ground, troops!" the Drill Instructor yelled. We dropped to the ground at the entrance to a 175-yard cement course strewn with sharp pebbles. "Ready, GO!"

We crawled on our knees and elbows, cradling our rifles, while live machine gun fire zipped overhead and TNT explosions rocked the ground. Our satisfaction at reaching the other end was curtailed when the DI yelled, "Back around, do it again!"

I ran back to the beginning, pulled up a reserve of energy, and dropped to my belly again. After that experience, double-timing home eight miles to the barracks, with no bullets and explosives to dodge, was a breeze.

At mail call on Wednesday, I was handed a package with a Sandy, Oregon return address. I opened the box to find brownies, oatmeal raisin cookies, and homemade toffee. Any package drew a crowd in the barracks, and I didn't have the heart to keep it all to myself.

"Wow, your girl can really cook!" was the general consensus when the guys in bunks near me had sampled the treats.

When I had some free time later that evening, I wrote to Carolyn. Our letters were the only way to feel close to her, and I wanted to keep up my end of our commitment to write in spite of the difficulties of Basic Training.

June 28, 1967
My love,

You are truly wonderful. You are the greatest woman ever created. Your beauty and intelligence are beyond comparison, and should make every other woman in the world envious. Also, you are a very good cook. (Your package arrived today!) You really know how to pack a good box of goodies. Everyone in the barracks agrees. I shared with some of my friends, and your talent was greatly appreciated. Thanks so much for sending the box!

Today we went to the bayonet assault course. I've never stuck so many rubber tires so many times in my life. We also jumped hurdles, crawled under wire fences, climbed walls and ran over log bridges. Oh, what fun! Actually it isn't too bad, as we have only two more days of regular training left.

Yesterday I was called to the Officers Candidate School office for an appointment. Because of my eyesight, I can't be sent to a school dealing with combat arms. But I can still apply for a non-combatant OCS school, such as quartermaster (supply) transportation, or ordnance (weapons).

You asked if there are insects in Louisiana. Are there blonde hairs on your head? This is the only place I've ever been where I swat mosquitos in the daytime.

In one of your letters you mentioned the problem of dreams. I can certainly relate. Unfortunately, most of my dreams are typically male, and you always have the starring role. Life is certainly not becoming any easier with our long separation. I'm wondering if we should take separate vacations in July. (You'd better not say Yes to that!) We need that time to learn more about each other. I still don't know what your favorite books are, or what you're like when you're grouchy. You've never lost your temper, never complained or clammed up on me. Eventually we'll have to have some sort of fight (and I don't mean wrestling).

Before I completely disintegrate, I'll say goodnight. Above all else, remember my love for that blonde on horseback I met last July!

With all my love,
Larry

After graduation, our company assembled on the parade ground. The First Sergeant came over to our platoon with a clipboard and stack of envelopes containing our orders.

"Private Trent!"
"Here, Sir."
"Private Unger!"
"Here, Sir."
"Private Wade!"

"Here, Sir." I stepped up to the Drill Instructor, and he handed me my orders. *Finally, I'll know how much time I'll have with Carolyn before the next phase of training.* I ripped open the envelope and took out the folded sheet. I glanced over the Army boilerplate, then read the important lines more slowly, not believing what I was seeing.

> Private Larry D Wade RA18825403
> Report to Leadership Preparation Course
> Fort Ord, California, July 8, 1967
>
> Report for Advanced Infantry Training,
> Fort Ord, California, July 24, 1967

July 8th! That's the day after we graduate here.

I found a bench and sat down to read the orders for the second time, hoping there was a mistake. I knew the Army didn't care about my personal life, but what about God? *Are you too busy somewhere else, ignoring me and Carolyn? Why are you picking on us?*

There would be no leave, no break in training, no possibility of spending any time at all with Carolyn before reporting for my next assignment. It had already been three and a half months since we'd seen each other. Without this anticipated leave our separation could stretch to six months.

Other trainees walked past, excitedly talking about heading home in a few days. I walked back to the barracks, sick with disappointment.

"You don't look so happy, Wade," said the guy above me as I flopped on my bunk.

"I'm not," I replied shortly.

"Didn't get the orders you wanted?"

"It's not the orders, I don't get any leave before I report to my next training."

"You're kidding? No leave? That's rotten."

"The only good thing about it is that I'll be heading back to California."

"I guess your folks will be happy about that."

"But my girlfriend isn't going to be happy that I won't be able to see her."

"Tough luck, buddy."

"We almost made plans to get married in two weeks."

"Good thing you didn't, that would really be terrible."

I lay on my bunk, staring at the wire mesh under the top mattress.

Okay, God, what's the deal? Why did you allow this? What could possibly be the value in more separation, more disappointment?

My questions were unanswerable, and left me feeling angry, frustrated and discouraged. Worst of all, somehow I had to communicate this bad news to Carolyn. That was a task I dreaded.

Chapter 35

Carolyn

After only two weeks back home from college I wondered if I'd made a huge mistake. Initially, the idea of working at the ranch in exchange for Mom and Dad paying for my wedding had sounded like a great solution for everyone. But they had been unwilling to give me a job description or schedule, saying that we'd take things as they came. After the structure of college life, their inclination to live on the fly kept me off balance, always wondering what was coming next.

> **Current Culture**
> **July 1967**
>
> - Dozens are killed and hundreds injured in Detroit and Newark race riots
> - *Seventeen* magazine reports that fewer than 5% of respondents to their survey approve of premarital sex
> - Cost of first-run movie ticket: $1.20

In addition, the uncertainty of Larry's situation prevented me from making plans for a wedding or for returning to school. I was in limbo, feeling insecure and emotional.

"No letter?" Mom shook her head in exasperation. "You'd think if he really loved you he'd be more consistent in writing. I hope he hasn't changed his mind."

"No, Mom, he hasn't changed his mind. He's finishing Basic Training, for heaven's sake. He's not sitting around twiddling his thumbs, wondering what to do with himself." My disappointment in not getting a letter added an edge to my voice.

"You don't need to get snappy with me, Carolyn. I'm just making an observation. I don't want you to be hurt."

"Larry's not going to hurt me. He loves me, and I trust him." Of course I had to defend Larry to Mom, but I longed for the reassurance of a letter, and anxiously waiting to hear if he was coming to visit during his leave after Basic Training. *He'll be graduating in just four days!* The thought of seeing him soon was exciting, but I had an unwelcome premonition that things might not go as we hoped.

My shoulders sagged as I walked down the hall to my bedroom, closing the door to avoid more conflict. Today's date on my calendar was circled: July 3, the anniversary of the day Larry and I met. *I sure didn't know a year ago that I'd go through all this drama! I hope the end result is worth it all.*

Nearly a week later, Mom and Dad were gone to Sandy when I finally saw a letter with Larry's handwriting in our mailbox. My hands shook as I dropped the other mail on the kitchen table and ripped open the envelope. As I read, I sat down abruptly on a kitchen chair.

July 4, 1967
Dear Carolyn,

There's no use beating around the bush, so I'll start with the important news. We will graduate in three days, on July 7th, and I am required to report to Fort Ord, California on July 8th. As you can see, I wasn't given the customary two week leave following Basic Training. This puts quite a dent in our plans, but in some ways it is better.

Obviously we won't be able to see each other this month. Please hold on to the fact that God is in control, and things WILL work out for us.

The reason I didn't get leave is that I've been assigned to the Leadership Preparation Course, preliminary training for Officers Candidate School. Hopefully that will increase my chances of getting into OCS. From what we've been told about our schedule, I may not be able to write you again until I've been at Fort Ord awhile. At least I'm being sent to the West Coast. Fort Ord isn't that far from Hanford, and I can probably hitchhike home if I need to.

I'll send you my new address as soon as possible, and I plan to call you the first chance I have. I believe we will be together again before too much longer. Please don't be upset by this news, as it could actually end up working in our favor.

Goodnight, Beautiful. Remember that I love you,

Larry

"Don't be upset..." Is he kidding? Today's the 8th--he's already at Fort Ord! Not only were our plans for time together demolished, but the future was as uncertain as ever. I put my head in my hands and sobbed in disappointment and frustration.

Eventually I wiped away my tears, headed out to the barnyard and called for Spice. When she ambled across the creek and up to the hitching post, I put on her bridle and jumped on her bare-back, feeling miserable and reckless. I didn't care that my capris would be filthy, or my backside sore the next day. I urged her into a canter and headed towards the woods. In the cool alder grove, dappled light, a gurgling creek and soft birdsong beckoned to me. I slid down, wrapped the reins around a tree, and threw myself down on a bed of moss.

Okay, God, I'm trying to trust you with all of this, but you're making it pretty difficult!

Late that evening, I wrote a short letter to Larry, needing to communicate my feelings, and hoping it would be forwarded to his new address.

July 8th, 1967

Dear Larry,

Your letter with the news about your assignment to Fort Ord and the "dent in our plans" arrived today. As you can imagine, it wasn't welcome information. Part of me wishes that you had called to tell me, but I guess I can understand, since I probably would have cried and wasted valuable phone time.

It was several hours before the sick feeling left the pit of my stomach and I could think rationally about this latest setback. I'm glad you think this could work in our favor; I'm having trouble with that right now.

How many times does God need to test our faith? Are we so lacking in trust? What if you don't get leave after the next round of training? As you can tell, I'm really struggling right now. Not getting regular letters from you, not having an address to write you, not being able to call you...sometimes I wonder if you're really real. I'm feeling lost in the wilderness without a compass.

One thing I know, I love you, and I have to cling to the belief that someday I'll see you again.

Carolyn

For the next few days, I threw myself into my chores. In addition to normal meals and cleaning, I baked huge batches of cookies so we'd have plenty in the freezer for company. I also deep-cleaned the bathroom and kitchen, weeded the garden, and practiced my most difficult piano pieces. While my hard work pleased my parents, it didn't ease the ache in my heart.

Dad was sitting at the dinette table when I came into the kitchen early one morning. He looked up from his worn Bible, marked his place with a calloused finger and gave me a smile. "You're up early."

"Couldn't sleep," I murmured.

"I know it's rough for you right now, Sweetheart, but I believe the Lord is going to work things out."

I sat down across from him. "I didn't think it would be so hard, Daddy."

"Even when we know we're in God's will, it's not always easy." He reached over to squeeze my hand, while I pulled a handkerchief from the pocket of my robe. As I wiped my eyes Dad continued with a grin. "He's worth waiting for, I think." Dad's gentle words gave me courage.

I was happy to get a brief postcard sent from the Houston Airport on Larry's way between Fort Polk and Fort Ord, but after that, I didn't hear from him. Occasionally I wrote a few pages to send when I got his new address. I tried to be positive, and not voice my doubts and fears.

July 11, 1967
Dear Larry,

It has felt strange the past couple of weeks not writing you every night, but without your new address, it seemed pointless. Don't think that because I didn't write, I wasn't thinking about you <u>constantly</u>.

Life here is a rather monotonous round of housework, laundry, cooking, and other chores, with the occasional break to guide some horseback customers or entertain drop-in visitors. Last week Gary and Jim were here all week, so I had two very lively boys to keep out of trouble.

Most of the time it was fun, but by Saturday night, I was ready to throw them in the well. Lucky for them, we don't have a well! I had hoped to spend the night at Paul and Emily's after I took the boys home on Sunday, but Mom told me I needed to be back at the ranch to help Dad cut hay on Monday. This year we have more grass than I can remember, which translates to more hay and more work.

With our antiquated equipment, haying is a two-person job. The mower or rake hitches to the back of the tractor. There's a seat for the operator (me), and hand levers and foot pedals to operate. When we mow, I have to raise the mower arm to avoid rocks or stumps, and when we rake, I have to dump the hay at just the right time so that it makes a straight line for the baling machine, which we'll rent. I'm learning coordination and using muscles I didn't know I had.

July 12th

On July 4th, I went with Dad and Mom to Kah-nee-ta, a hot-springs resort on the Indian reservation across the mountain. It wasn't too hot or too crowded, and we really enjoyed the colorful and interesting tribal dances that were part of their celebration. Unfortunately, I got terribly sunburned, which has kept me awake several nights. I'm glad you're not here to see my ugly peeling shoulders.

Mom and I have been having a continuing discussion about marriage. Things got tense today when she insisted that I wear a cowboy hat when I went outside. I told her I found it difficult to have someone telling me what to *do all the time. She said, "You'll have someone telling you what to do when you get married!" and I said, "No, I won't." She must have mentioned it to Dad, because at dinner tonight, he made some comments about wives being subject to their husbands.*

July 13th

This morning while cleaning, I turned on some music and was trying to teach myself the samba when Mom came in to say Dad needed me to work the hay rake. So there went my worldly pleasure! After we finished raking the pasture, I made my own hay in the yard with the lawnmower. You know how big our yard is—it took a couple of hours, and added another layer of sunburn.

I hope you'll describe Fort Ord for me. I keep thinking of you in swampy Louisiana, but I'm sure your new location is very different.

Larry, I wish we could have slept out in the pasture together a couple of nights ago when the grass was just cut. It smelled so lovely, the moon was just a sliver and the stars were so big. Maybe after we're married...

There are so many things I want to do and share with you, Darling. I hope life is long enough! Right now, life seems too long—time drags so. It seems ages and ages since we talked and kissed and were happy together. I find myself asking "Why, why, why?" It's hard to accept reality right now.

Goodnight, Love. I miss you terribly.

Carolyn

Nearly two weeks after I'd last heard from Larry, I got a letter from his mother mentioning that he had called home after he arrived at Fort Ord. My determination to make allowances for Larry's circumstances began to crumble, and doubts turned to panic. *If he can call his parents, why can't he call or write to me?*

When I read the letter to Mom, she shook her head and said, "It doesn't make sense. Maybe you should call Mrs. Wade and get his address. I think you need to find out what's going on. Are you sure you haven't upset him?"

I turned away, hurt that she would add insult to injury. I had to walk around outside to calm down before I could make the phone call.

"Hello, it's Carolyn," I said when Mrs. Wade answered the phone.

"It's nice to hear your voice, Carolyn. How are you?"

"Okay, I guess. Thanks for your letter." I took a deep breath and said, "I haven't heard from Larry since he left Fort Polk."

"But that's been two weeks!"

"I know. I've been worried, wondering what's happening. Would you mind giving me his address?"

"I'm sorry, Carolyn. Let me find it for you." I heard paper rustling in the background, and could picture her at the small desk under the wall phone in her kitchen. When she came back on the line, I copied down the address and repeated it back to her. "I know he's been very busy," she apologized.

"Yes, it's hard to imagine what Army life is like," I said. "How are things with you and Mr. Wade?"

"We're fine, trying to stay cool in the summer heat."

"Well, I look forward to seeing you again, whenever that is."

"I'll be praying for you, Carolyn."

"Thanks, I need it."

When I hung up, I waved the piece of paper at Mom as I headed toward my bedroom. "At least I have his address now."

I felt disappointed, hurt, and angry. I wanted to write a scathing letter to let him know how I felt. I picked up paper and pen, but after writing the date, I put the pen down. Lashing out was not my nature, and wouldn't help the situation.

I put on my pajamas and settled into bed with a new book, *The Rabbi*, hoping the conflicted love story of a Jewish rabbi and a Christian minister's daughter would take my mind off the problems of my own romance.

In the morning, I wrote a short note to put in the mailbox after breakfast.

July 19, 1967

Dear Larry,

Today is overcast and cool, so I'm taking my friend Cheryl to Kah-nee-ta. Since it's on the sunny side of Mt. Hood, we hope to escape the clouds here.

To be honest, Larry, I don't know what to write you. I've been expecting to hear from you every day since you got to Fort Ord almost two weeks ago, but evidently something is wrong somewhere. I got a letter from your mother yesterday, and she said you had called home last week, so at least I know that you got to Fort Ord safely. I called her last night and she gave me this address.

Neighbors have told us that they've had trouble getting long distance calls lately, so maybe it's a phone problem.

Please write me, at least. I love you. I don't know what else to say.

Carolyn

Before I sealed the envelope, I added a blank, stamped postcard. Walking out to the mailbox, I was too upset to enjoy the fragrance of Dad's roses next to the path. I opened the mailbox and put the letter inside without adding the usual kiss to the back of the envelope.

There's nothing more I can do. The ball's in his court now.

Chapter 36

Larry

On the weekend before Basic Training ended, I hoped for some free time to catch up on sleep and call Carolyn. But Saturday morning, fifteen of us were "volunteered" for a funeral detail. The bonus of nearly a week's pay seemed scant compensation for losing a precious day off.

Even with all the windows down, it was hot in the bus. As the sun climbed in the sky, we rode 150 miles into northern Louisiana, passing tired towns and groves of spindly pines. At the beginning of our journey, there

> **Current Culture**
> *July 1967*
>
> - 134 seamen are killed when and explosion and fire damages USS Forrestal in the Gulf of Tonkin off the coast of Vietnam
> - President Johnson averts nationwide rail strike
> - *Sergeant Pepper's Lonely Hearts Club Band* is top selling album

was a fair amount of griping and horseplay to relieve tension, but as we neared our destination, the mood became somber.

Not long after we passed the sign "Rayville, Pop. 4,052" our bus stopped in front of a white clapboard church topped by a steeple and cross. We were ushered to a reserved row at the back of the sanctuary where we listened to gospel music, several sermons, and lengthy eulogy for the soldier, a Vietnam casualty. Eventually the assembled mourners were dismissed and we climbed back on the bus for a short ride to a small country cemetery. On the way, a guy across the aisle from me shook his head. "Man, he was only 19, and he left a wife and kid!"

When we arrived at the cemetery, the Sergeant in charge divided us into two groups. To my relief, I wasn't assigned as a pall bearer, but given a weapon to fire for the customary rifle salute. I was happy to keep my distance from the flag-draped coffin. *It could easily be my brother in that box.*

The bus was mostly silent on the long ride home, with guys trying to doze or staring out the window. Even the most rowdy member of our group had been sobered by the stark reality of what the future could hold for us.

That evening Lt. Yates, the Company Executive Officer, walked into the barracks and barked "Ten-shun!" We scrambled into stiff positions in the aisle between the rows of bunks.

"You guys need some harassment," he said with a brief grin. When Pvt. Stein snickered, the Lieutenant pointed at him and said, "Give me twenty-five, soldier." Stein started to chuckle until he saw the glare on the officer's face, and quickly dropped to the floor to start the push-ups.

"Did you hear the one about the…" Lt. Yates proceeded to tell a surprisingly clean joke, and when some of the guys laughed, he had them doing push-ups as well. This continued for nearly two hours before he ended his harangue with a five-minute lecture on self-discipline.

As Yates walked out the door, the guy next to me said, "He's one Lieutenant that just might survive 'Nam."

A week later I was on my way west. *Of all the places the Army could send me, I'm ending up just a few hours from home!* On a layover between Fort Polk and Fort Ord, I tried to get comfortable in the metal and vinyl airport chair while writing a message on the back of a postcard of the Houston skyline.

July 8
Dearest Carolyn, We have a four-hour layover here at the Houston Airport. This place is really pretty in a strange sort of way. You would have enjoyed it, as you love beauty so much. Larry
    P.S. I love you

As the plane descended to the Monterey airport, my window seat gave me a panoramic view of deep blue water edged by crashing surf. Two wooden piers extended out into the bay while rows of houses climbed a hillside topped with a fringe of dark trees. "Sure looks different than Louisiana," said one of the guys from Fort Polk.

"Yeah, it's different than my home, too," I answered. By the time we were in a bus headed for Fort Ord, the sun had set and the base appeared as clusters of lights dotting shadowy hills. From the Reception Station, we were marched to a barracks and ordered to stay put until morning, when we would be assigned to our respective units.

At orientation for the Leadership Preparation Course the next day, it became apparent that we were in for a tough session. In the first week, our days extended from 4:30 a.m. to nearly midnight. We worked through the night on Friday preparing for a big inspection, and by the time the Brass were through with us, we'd been on the go for 34 hours straight. *This had better help me get into OCS!*

Our hard work earned us all a weekend pass, and all but a few guys in my unit lined up for the first bus to town. I decided to save my money, and took a nap in the quiet barracks. At dinner in the mess hall, a guy at my table said, "Wanna catch a flick tonight?"

"What's on?" I asked.

"War movie—*The Dirty Dozen.* I've heard it's pretty good."

"Sure, why not?" I figured spending two bits wouldn't hurt, and we could walk to the base theater. Watching a tense war movie in a room full of soldiers was a powerful experience, and adrenaline was running high by the closing credits. Most of the guys headed for the on-post beer hall, but I joined the few walking back to the barracks. An idea had been growing in my mind, and I was anxious to write to Carolyn.

July 16, 1967, Fort Ord, California
My Love,

Please forgive me for not writing more. We got to Fort Ord late on the 8th, and I started the Leadership Preparation Course the next day. After another week of LPC, I'll start Advanced Infantry Training. This means, of course, that I won't be able to come to Oregon until September. I'm promised two weeks of leave then.

Here's where my wild, crazy idea comes in. I don't have all the money in the world, and it could be rough on both of us, but why don't we get married in September as we originally planned? That way, you could join me without complications after I finish officers training. It would give us a week or more together as husband and wife, then you could go back to school and finish one more term while I'm at OCS.

If you don't like this idea, please tell me. But if you agree to this, send me a letter starting with "YES!"

My new address is: Pvt. Larry D. Wade RA 18825403, Co A (Alpha), 4th Battalion, 2nd Brigade, Fort Ord, California 93940.

I'm going to try to call you as soon as possible. Remember that above all else, I love you. Also remember that the first word of the next letter should be "YES!" Goodbye for now, my love.

Larry

While I anxiously awaited Carolyn's response to my letter, I did some research on the benefits of being an officer. I was pleased to discover that base pay for the lowest rank of officers was $461.00 per month. Once we were married, we'd be given an additional housing allotment of $110.00. Since I was currently earning $98.00 a month as a Private, it seemed like a princely sum.

The down side of becoming an officer was that even if we were married, Carolyn would not be able to visit me during the three months of training. I continued to weigh the options while waiting for her reply to my risky idea. *Please let the answer be "Yes!"*

When her letter finally arrived, I held my breath as I tore open the envelope.

July 19, 1967 Evening

Darling,

YES!!!!

Yes, Yes, Yes!! Oh, Larry, I'm so happy. I've never been so glad to get a letter as that one. Ever since I found out you were going to Fort Ord, I've hoped that this might be a possibility. It's a good thing you wrote your new address on the inside of the letter, because I mangled the return address ripping open the envelope.

My parents weren't too surprised at your suggestion, and are quite agreeable (miracles still happen). They know I've been miserable this summer, especially when I didn't hear from you regularly. Mom concluded that you'd gotten cold feet and were backing out. I knew that wasn't the case, but sometimes her comments and questions made me anxious. Now that's all in the past, and I have a million things to do. This means we'll be married in just eight weeks!

I'll be happy to go back to Monmouth in the fall. After all we've been through I know I can handle a mere thirteen weeks of separation while you're at OCS. At least we'll be married!

Please disregard my recent short letter. It was written under pressure from my parents, who told me it was probably my fault that I hadn't heard from you. I can't believe that in only two months we'll be married!

I LOVE YOU.

Carolyn

Chapter 37

Carolyn

No matter what I do, it's wrong! Pleasing my mother was an impossible task. The previous week, I'd spent several days cutting hay with Dad and ended up with sore muscles and flaming sunburn. Instead of thanks, I'd gotten complaints because dinner wasn't ready at exactly 5:00 p.m.

"Your father and I don't feel that you're putting in a full day's work," Mom said after dinner on Monday night. I clenched the dish towel in my hand, trying to resist the impulse to fling it at her. *One, two, three, four...*

> **Current Culture**
> **August 1967**
>
> - Hit song: "Respect" by Aretha Franklin
> - China announces that it will aid North Vietnam
> - Final episode of *The Fugitive* is viewed by 78 million
> - U.S. unemployment figure reaches 3.8%
> - Wedding dress ordered from major department store: $150.00

After I'd counted to ten and taken a deep breath I said, "Maybe you should make me a list of what you want done tomorrow."

Mom looked at me skeptically, as if she were trying to determine if I was being sarcastic. I gazed at her without expression, and she shrugged and said, "Okay, I'll do that."

The following day I put the first load of laundry in the washer at 7:30, did two more loads of laundry, ironed Dad's shirts and Mom's blouses, harvested vegetables in the garden, cooked lunch and dinner, and guided some horseback riders on the trail in the west woods.

At dinner I mentioned that my throat was sore. Mom shook her head and said, "You're doing too much, no wonder you're getting sick!"

I wasn't in the best mood when I wrote to Larry that night.

August 3, 1967
Darling,

The summer has gone by so fast—before I know it, I'll be hitting the books again. Frankly, I'm looking forward to it. At least there won't be the constant tension that there is here. I wonder if I'll ever be satisfied with myself or meet my parents' expectations. But then, in a few weeks, I won't be responsible to them in the same way. <u>*Your*</u> *requirements will come before theirs, whether they like it or not.*

It's been such a busy summer, with the usual haying and horse care, plus horseback riders to guide and fishermen for the pond. These are always "drop-in," and everything else has to be put aside to take care of our customers. On top of that, we've had a lot of company, with my nephews Gary & Jim spending a couple of weeks (you know who was the babysitter), and my brother John and his wife and three kids for another week. I love my family, but I really didn't have time to enjoy them, since I'm the "chief cook and bottle-washer" plus farm hand. I'm sorry to complain, but when I get over-tired, my perspective is a bit off. My throat has been raw all day—which always happens when I get too tired.

Enough of that...tonight, like every other night, I would love to put my head on your shoulder and feel your arms around me. Somehow, when we're together, your strength seems to flow into my body, and your love brings me to peace with myself and those around me. I need that strength and peace so much right now, Darling.

Goodnight, my beloved. I miss you very much, and love you even more.
Carolyn

The next day, I was home alone when the screech of brakes and sputter of gravel announced the arrival of the mail carrier. I pried open Larry's letter while standing at the mailbox. *I hope he gives me a wedding date!* As I read, my heart lifted and a smile stretched my lips.

August 1, 1967
Ma Cherie,

Two letters today! How wonderful to hear from you. As for the blank postcard, I thought it was a very subtle (?) hint that I hadn't written often enough. Here's a letter instead.

First of all, I'm supposed to finish here at 1:00 p.m. on Friday, September 15th. Judging by what's happened in the past, it would be cutting it too close to schedule the wedding that weekend, so how about September 23rd? Even though that would mean less time together as husband and wife, it's less risky. What do you think of that date? Please let me know if you agree to that, so I can notify my family.

I would have preferred to phone you so we could talk this over, but coins for the pay phones are hard to come by. When I do get to a place where I can get some change, I can only get it if I buy something. Since I'm saving all my pennies for our wedding and honeymoon, I hope you will understand.

It would definitely be my preference to plan our honeymoon, but since I'm not familiar with Oregon and Washington, can you give me suggestions? I'm sorry to have to ask you, but I'd be grateful if you'd give me some ideas.

Well, Hon, time has flown again. I really do love you, even though sometimes my actions may not prove it.

Larry

September 23! I found a red marker on the desk and drew a big circle around the day on the kitchen calendar, then stood looking at it with a grin on my face and tears in my eyes. The circled date made everything more real. *I'll need to do something about a wedding dress—that date is only seven weeks away!*

I wanted to call my sisters, but decided to wait until the long distance rates went down after 7:00 p.m. In the meantime, there were local calls to make. I picked up the phone and dialed the pastor of the Chapel of the Hills to reserve the church for September 23rd.

Later, when Dad and Mom were home and Mom was putting away their purchases, I casually said, "I got a letter from Larry today."

"Anything new?" Mom asked. I pointed to the calendar with the big red circle around September 23. "He gave you a date?" Mom's voice was high with excitement.

"Yes, can you believe it? September 23rd." She walked across the kitchen to give me a hug as Dad came in from the porch.

"She has a wedding date, Ernest!" Her smile was wide, and she looked as relieved as I felt.

"I'm happy for you, Sweetheart," Dad said, joining our hug.

"Well, let's fix something easy for dinner so we can start planning." After fighting a cold for several days, Mom suddenly seemed infused with energy. From not wanting to talk about wedding plans to being excited was an abrupt switch. *She must have seriously doubted it was going to happen. I wish she could have been as certain as I was, it would have saved a lot of conflict!*

We spent the evening making lists and phoning family and friends. Emily and Priscilla were both thrilled with my news. When Dad came into the kitchen for a snack, Mom said, "You'll have to remodel the side porch right away. We'll need a dining room ready for the wedding guests."

"Yes, Ma'am," Dad gave her smile and a fake salute. "Maybe you could call George tomorrow and see when he can come to help me." Mom added to her list--Call George.

"We'll need to shop for your wedding dress first thing next week," she said. "We'll start at Meier and Frank and Berg's." I blinked in surprise, struggling to adjust to the sudden change in attitude. When I wrote Larry that night, I was in a very happy mood.

August 5, 1967
Darling,

September 23. You're going to have to remember that date for the next fifty years (I hope)!

I called Rev. Strand at the Chapel of the Hills this afternoon, and she said she would do some rearranging to give us the church for that date.

When you're here for the week before the wedding, I'm hoping to take you to some of my favorite spots, like Lost Lake and Kah-nee-ta. Maybe you could also help me move my things back down to Monmouth so I can start classes right after our honeymoon. That way you can actually visit the college and meet some of the people I've written about.

Do you think we'll really be able to cram six months of impressions, thoughts, kisses and hugs into two brief weeks before we're separated again? As much as I'm excited about marrying you on your two-week leave, I have to confess I'm not looking forward to the weeks of separation. Is it possible that God could work things out so that we wouldn't have to be separated? After all, he has worked it out for us to get married in a few weeks, when it looked totally impossible for a long time. Something to pray about!

Mom just stuck her head in my door, and told me, "It's way past your bedtime." Really? At 11:30? Good thing she doesn't know about all my late nights in the dorm!

I've learned so much about myself this summer. For one thing, I realize that conflict affects my health—I've finally figured out that it's often after we have a blow-up that I get a sore throat. This summer I've been observing my parent's relationship. Larry, if I ever resort to tears or headache to avoid dealing with a problem, you have my permission to look me in the eye and say, "Cut it out!"

On a more positive note, I long to share my life with you, really share, not just tell about or write about. Unfortunately, what I want most often to share with you is my bed. I hope I won't have a double bed when I'm back at school after our wedding. It's bad enough having an empty side now, but after we're married, it could be really tough.

What have you done to me, Larry? I tended to be unfeeling before and things didn't affect me deeply. But since the first time you said, "I love you" and kissed me so hard my lips were sore--since then, a look, a touch, a word from you, and I want to burst with joy and awareness.

Thank you, Darling, for bringing me into this wonderful, painful existence. I love you so much,

Carolyn

The red circle on the calendar put us into high gear. The days were noisy with sounds of saws and hammers as Dad and George began turning the drab, cement-floored side porch into a paneled dining room. Mom added to the guest list and wrote to Larry's parents, inviting them to stay at the ranch when they came for the wedding.

On our way to Portland to shop, Mom asked, "What style dress do you have in mind?"

"I have some ideas, but I'm not sure what will look best on me."

"Well, if we go to several stores, we should get a good idea. Who knows, maybe we'll find something ready-made that you like."

"I thought you'd want me to sew the dress," I replied, knowing it would be less expensive.

"You never know," she said cryptically.

Charles F. Berg was a boutique women's clothing store that we entered only when they had drastic sales. Even the air smelled expensive. We took the filigreed cage elevator to the second floor Bridal Salon and were graciously greeted by two immaculately-groomed saleswomen.

"Do you have a particular style in mind, Dear?" the older of the two ladies asked me.

"Something classic," I said, "but I'd like to look at several styles."

"Please have a seat, Madam, and I'll show the young lady what we have in her size." She motioned Mom to a pale blue satin chair, and gestured to me to follow her down a short hallway lined with racks of dresses. She started collecting gowns and ushered me into a fitting room.

"Let's start with this one, Miss." She helped me into a ruffled taffeta dress appliqued with lace medallions. "It's very pretty," I said neutrally as she fastened the back and I dutifully stepped into the hallway and walked to the mirror-lined display room.

Mom's smile was tremulous when she saw me. "Oh, Carolyn..." I turned slowly to give her a view of the ruffled train, and then carefully lifted the skirt to walk back to the dressing room. As I was helped out of the elaborate gown, the second saleswoman came in with another dress.

"Here's a new style that you might like," she said. She held up a fragile-looking dress that made me catch my breath. Sheer white fabric flowed in an unbroken line from shoulder to floor. Embroidered lilies of the valley adorned the neckline, sleeves, and hem, flowing onto the short train. I slipped it over my head and felt the layers of lining settle next to my skin. I didn't need to look in the mirror to feel beautiful. I floated out to show Mom.

"That's an unusual style," she said with an uncertain frown.

"But look at the embroidery," I said. "You know I've always loved lily of the valley."

She tilted her head to look me up and down. "I think it's a bit too modern for our family." She reached for the tag hanging from the sleeve, raised her eyebrows and shook her head. "It's pretty, I suppose, but we'll keep shopping."

In the dressing room, I avoided looking in the mirror as the sales lady unfastened the tiny pearl buttons. "It's the perfect dress for you," she whispered. "You'll be back."

"Maybe," I forced a smile. *Not a chance.*

After Berg's, everything else was anticlimactic. I tried on several dresses at Meier and Frank, and after lunch we sat down at the pattern counter of Mom's favorite fabric store. "Let's look at Vogue," she said, pushing aside the less expensive pattern books. I was surprised, as Vogue patterns were more stylish as well as more expensive and more complicated to sew. Knowing I'd never be able to duplicate the lily of the valley dress, I ended up choosing a simple style that was the best of what was available. We eventually stood at the cutting counter holding bolts of satin, lace, lining, netting, and buttons.

"Thank you, Mom," I said as she put the change into her wallet.

"You're welcome, Dear," she said patting my hand. "I know how important your wedding dress is to you." I smiled at her blandly. *Walking down the aisle to Larry is far more important to me than what I'll be wearing.*

On the way home Mom said, "It will take extra time to sew a Vogue dress. How about if I take over lunch duties to give you a little more time for sewing?"

"That would be great, Mom. I appreciate that."

"We'll need to come back to town next week to pick out a pattern and fabric for your sisters."

"Yes, they'll need as much sewing time as possible. We've only got a little more than a month for everything."

"I can't believe you're actually getting married next month."

"Believe it, Mom," I said emphatically. "It's going to happen!"

When we got home, there was a letter from Fort Ord on the kitchen table. As usual, I took it to the bedroom to read.

August 11, 1967
My wonderful love,

This has proved to be a most uneventful and dull afternoon. I had to supervise recruits at the bayonet assault course, where they had to jab and stab at a large rubber target. At least I didn't have to go with the group that ran the uphill training course.

Yesterday we fired the 3.5 'recoil-less' rifle (also known as a bazooka), and the M-70 Light Anti-Tank Weapon. In spite of having a fourteen-inch shell, there's less recoil than a .22 rifle. I actually managed to hit the target, an old WWII tank. That's what I call fun!

It's a little difficult to concentrate on writing right now. One guy next to me has his radio turned up loud, the guy on the other side keeps asking me questions, and everyone is generally very noisy.

Out of the twenty OCS candidates in our company, most have withdrawn their application. I can't see doing that myself--that little gold bar on my uniform means too much. Besides, the extra pay would make life a lot easier for you.

There are times when it seems like there is nothing to life except this Army base. Sometimes I have to strain to remember the sound of your voice or the way you walk. Every day I look forward to the end of my loneliness, when we're finally together again. The only thing that can cure this hopelessness is your presence.

Just a few more weeks and you'll be in my arms again.

Goodnight, my love.
Larry

I folded the letter with a happy sigh, and leaned back on my pillow. *I can't wait to be in his arms!*

Friday morning I was awake early. At breakfast, Dad said, "It's going to be a busy weekend!" Paul and Emily had planned a retreat at the ranch for their house-church members, and by dinner time, there were three large tents set up in the side yard and a camping trailer parked behind the house.

On Saturday afternoon, it was my turn to entertain the children of the group, aged six to seventeen. We played games like Simon Says and Red Rover, finishing with hide-and-seek. With an abundance of hiding places, there were whoops of laughter and mad dashes to the "safe" tree.

For the evening service, we gathered around a campfire on the riverbank. The sounds of guitars and voices floated up with the smoke of the fire, and Paul's message was uplifting. When everyone had settled for the night, I wrote to Larry.

August 13, 1967
Dear Larry,

It's been a very hectic weekend here with the retreat for Paul and Emily's group. Overall, it was a big success, with decent weather, lots of food, good meetings, and general relaxation. I know you would have enjoyed it.

I was kept busy most of the time with cooking and serving food (frying five pounds of bacon yesterday morning), and also supervising the children, and anything else that Paul and Em needed me to do.

In response to your earlier question about honeymoon destinations, several places would be nice. The closest would be the Oregon Coast, of course. Another possibility would be driving up through Washington State to the Olympic Peninsula (there's spectacular scenery there, I've been told) and then to Victoria, British Columbia, about 250 miles. Since we'd be going after the 15th of September, we'd get lower rates for motels. What do you think?

Suddenly, Dad has "found out" that we're going to be separated again a week after our wedding. He came to me very concerned about this "news." I don't know how he could have missed this tidbit of information, as Mom and I have talked about it frequently. But between his poor hearing and his tendency to "tune out" of conversations, he missed it. We ended up having a very nice conversation—he's always easy to talk to.

Some of our recent shopping excursions haven't been much fun. Mom has very definite ideas of what <u>she</u> wants for <u>our</u> wedding. She said the lettering style I chose for the invitations was too casual, and she doesn't like the napkins I picked out. I have to choose when to stand my ground, because I hate arguing. There are so many wedding details I'd like to discuss with you. Do you think you'll be able to call me soon?

Writing to you about possible destinations has gotten me even more excited about our honeymoon (I didn't mean it <u>that</u> way, Larry). I think Victoria could be a very lovely and romantic place to spend time together. Please tell me exactly what you think.

I love you, Larry David Wade, RA 18 825 403 (memorized, of course)

Carolyn

In the middle of the week, there was a flat brown envelope from Fort Ord in the mailbox. Inside was an 8 x 10 photograph of a group of young soldiers. Larry was front and center, holding the company flag. I touched his face with my finger, wishing it were skin and bone and not just paper and ink. Seeing him with the group of unsmiling men made me realize how little I really knew of his life in the Army. I looked at the rows of young faces, thinking how sad it was that most of them would soon be in Vietnam, and many would never return.

Larry's accompanying letter was short, but made me smile.

August 13, 1967

My Sweet,

What an easy day this has been. We only ran two miles today, fired an automatic rifle (M-14) for two hours, and then had classes the rest of the day.

Since you enjoy target practice at the ranch with your brothers, I wish you could fire these weapons. You would really like it. The rifle we fired today can shoot twenty rounds in 1.7 seconds. You should have seen our targets!

It sounds like you are having quite the challenge with your mother. Please don't antagonize her unnecessarily. I'm sure she is doing what she thinks is best for you. As for the battles over wedding choices, they'll be over soon. The problem is, she is forceful and you are strong-willed, so collision is inevitable. I feel very strongly that we shouldn't live near your parents until we've been married at least five years. If we lived near them sooner, she would try to control both of us, and that would really cause fireworks!

You said that your thoughts of me often include a bed. Isn't that one of the great factors for two people deciding that they can't live without each other? After all, what would marriage be without sex? Mighty, mighty dull, right?

Well, Baby, my day is now beginning. The guys I'm leading need some pushing to get started, so I need to close. Goodbye, my love. I miss you too much.

Larry

I had just finished reading Larry's letter when Mom came in my room with a letter in her hand. "Aunt Marian wrote to ask if you'd like to come down to stay with her for a few days."

"Really? That would be great." I resisted the urge to jump up and down. Mom's sister was gentle and undemanding; staying with her would be a wonderful break from the tension at home. My wedding dress was nearly finished, and the important details were settled. It was perfect timing.

"Well, I'll talk to your father, and maybe we'll go down at the end of the week. You can take a bus back to Portland when you're ready to come home."

"That sounds like a good plan, Mom," I said, trying to not sound too excited.

"Well, don't get your hopes up, I'm not sure we'll be able to get away."

Please, Lord, please, please work it out!

Chapter 38

Larry

I straightened the knot in my tie and adjusted my hat to the correct angle. I'd only worn my dress uniform a few times, and this would be the first for a civilian function. I wanted to be a good representative of the United States Army.

When Tom and Patricia's car stopped in front of the barracks, I ran down the steps and got into the back seat. Tom and his new wife had written to invite me to a Nazarene Church camp meeting in the hills above Santa Cruz, an hour's drive from Fort Ord.

> **Current Culture**
> **August 1967**
>
> - President Johnson announces plans to send 45,000 more troops to Vietnam
> - Color TV sets gain popularity as more color programming is available
> - Thurgood Marshall is first African-American appointed to the US Supreme Court

"You're looking great, Larry," Tom said. "Army life must agree with you."

"Thanks, it's not so bad."

Patricia added, "Any man looks better in a uniform, Tom."

"Let's not go there," I chuckled. "Thank you so much for picking me up. I'm really looking forward to this evening."

I had gone to high school with Tom, although we'd run in different circles. A couple years into college, he had stopped by our house one evening to tell me that he had turned his life over to Jesus Christ. "Your example in high school always stayed with me," he explained. "When I hit bottom, I thought about how you lived your life by godly principles. I want to live the same way."

On the drive around Monterey Bay, we caught up on our lives. "So you're really going to marry this mystery woman you proposed to when you barely knew her? This doesn't sound like the conservative Larry that Tom's told me about." Patricia's skepticism was obvious.

"Yep, no question about it. We've set the date, September 23rd."

"Where's the wedding?

"At a log chapel near Mt. Hood. She has a big family so it makes sense to get married up there."

"Oh, Tom, can you get vacation in September? I'd love to go to the wedding. I've never been to Oregon."

"I guess I could try," Tom said. "I wouldn't mind seeing Larry get hitched."

"That would be great," I said. "The church is going to look pretty lopsided, with all of Carolyn's family and friends on one side, and my side basically empty."

We got to the campground in time for dinner, and joined a long line to get our trays of food. As we slowly moved toward the servers, I noticed an older man step away from his spot near the front of the line and walk toward us. As he approached, Tom straightened up expectantly. Other people near us seemed to be watching.

"Welcome, soldier," the man said to me. "We're glad you're here tonight. I'd like you to take my place in line. Your friends can join you, too."

"Thank you, but I don't want special treatment," I said.

"I insist. You're serving our country, it's the least I can do." He took my arm and escorted me to his recently-vacated spot. I made sure that Tom and Patricia were following me.

As the man went to the end of the line, Tom whispered, "Do you know who that was?"

"No, I haven't a clue."

"That was the District Superintendent. He's the VIP here tonight."

"Well, that was unexpected," I replied. "I guess it's going to be a very good evening."

It was a pleasure to be in a spiritual atmosphere and away from the restrictive and worldly surroundings of the base. The fervent participation of those in my generation was especially gratifying. One difficult aspect of the evening was seeing Tom and Patricia together, their words and actions demonstrating their enjoyment of marriage. There was also a girl in the choir who could have been Carolyn's twin. *I sure wish Carolyn was sitting beside me!* The next day I tried to communicate my feelings to her in my letter.

August 14, 1967

Dearest Carolyn,

I didn't think it would be possible, but I missed you more than ever this weekend. Partly it was because it's been more than twenty weeks since I held you in my arms. Also, because I was around another young couple in love—only they have the great fortune of being already married. Tom and Patricia came and took me to a camp meeting near Santa Cruz this weekend, and being around them made me ache for your presence. If I hadn't had the distraction of good singing and preaching, I would have really been a basket case!

What I'm going through now is supposed to be "Advanced" training. Lately it's been something of a joke. Today we had three hours of classes on the M-60 machine gun, one hour of physical training, and four hours of free time. It's a rough life. They either work you to death or kill you with ease. I'll suffer through this easy part somehow.

Say, just how big is this feud between you and your mom? If I'm reading between the lines correctly, you sounded desperate. Carolyn, I feel like you're hiding things from me. Isn't there any way to alleviate the situation? It isn't right for a mother and daughter to be at sword's points. I wish I could be there to help.

You mentioned feeling my presence recently. That's the way I felt all weekend, as if I could just turn and you would be there. If I had less self-control, you would have found an AWOL soldier knocking on your door.

Carolyn, I love you very much. I thank God that we have such a great love that continues to grow. Goodnight, beloved.
Larry

Tuesday was another easy day. After an hour of physical training, our group was assigned to "area beautification." As a squad leader, I helped supervise recruits trimming the lawn and weeding flower beds. It was good to be outdoors and I was proud of the diligent work of my squad. The wind had cleared away the morning fog, and brought the distant sound of the surf crashing behind the sand dunes. As the sun warmed the air, the smell of the eucalyptus grew more pungent. I'd never been around these massive trees before, and their grey-green foliage and peeling bark fascinated me.

Since I hadn't gotten a letter from Carolyn for several days, I was happy to hear my name at mail call. The envelope was so thin I wondered if she had forgotten to include the letter.

August 16, 1967
Dear Larry,

Tonight I'm in a strange mood. I guess more than anything, I just want to go to sleep and forget tomorrow, forget my tiredness, and mostly forget my loneliness and need for you. I'm afraid I'm getting to the point of numbness. Sometimes, just for a few minutes, I feel alive and aware, and then a curtain drops and I just exist. Oh Larry, I need you to make me feel alive again.

This should be a long letter to make up for not writing the last two nights, but I don't have the words right now. I wish I could hear your voice.

I think I'll be spending most of next week at my aunt's house at the beach. I badly need to get away. The last ten days have been about 85% nightmare, except for your letters.

Goodnight, darling. I wish I could write more, but the only words left are...I love you.
Carolyn

I read the letter over again, feeling anxious and frustrated. I found it hard to understand the conflict between Carolyn and her mother. I knew Mrs. Cooke tended to be controlling and manipulative, but I thought Carolyn's easy-going nature could handle it. The recent tone of Carolyn's letters worried me, and I hated being so far away and not able to talk things through with her. Her next letter made me realize that I could be part of the problem.

August 17, 1967
Darling,

You can thank your lucky stars for "second thoughts." Just be glad you didn't get the letter I wrote several hours ago, and be grateful you're not around for one of my now-daily fights with Mom.

Honestly, Larry, I am trying so hard to keep her happy, but she keeps finding fault with everything. It's at the point now that I dread getting out of bed in the morning. However, this won't go on forever, and when the next four weeks are over, I'll appreciate you even more. In just a month, you'll be here!

Yesterday I went to Portland, which was like an oven. I got a lot of wedding things finalized and paid for. It all cost less than I anticipated. By the way, the flowers that you will be paying for will cost about $25, I think.

Tonight, after our latest "misunderstanding" Mom said, "I sure wish you could talk to Larry!" Obviously she thinks that would help. I couldn't agree more. In fact, she even went so far as to suggest that I call you. Heavens! She must be desperate. I had to explain that there was no way I could reach you in the barracks. She said she just can't understand why you haven't called.

By now your defenses are up, I'm sure. I'm sorry to bring this up again, but I'm tired of mumbling weak explanations when she asks why you haven't called. You know "He can't read the numbers on the dial" or "He only gets change in pennies, and they clog up the pay phone."

Perhaps you don't realize it, but I need reassurance of love in various ways. Maybe a phone call isn't significant to you, but it would mean so much to me. You've told me how much you miss me and how much you wish you *could hear my voice. So, <u>call me</u>! Would it damage your strong-man image of yourself to bend a little and respond when I express my needs?*

I love you, Larry, and I have to believe that you love me too. If I can't believe that, then the past year has been a big joke. I resent having to beg you, but right now my need is greater than my pride. Frankly, it frightens me that I can't understand why your actions don't match your words. Is my understanding of you really so poor?

Goodnight, darling.

Carolyn

Why have I been so stupid? And all for trying to save a few lousy bucks! Just as I finished reading the letter, the Lieutenant came in.

"Troops, on your feet. We're off to the firing range." I quickly stuffed the letter into my footlocker, and join the other guys in formation in front of the barracks.

"Double-time!" yelled the Drill Sergeant, and we jogged into the hills. Feeling upset about Carolyn's letter and my insensitivity gave me extra determination. When I finished my turn firing the M-60 machine gun, I got an "Expert," ranking. I waited impatiently through the firing exercises and dinner of salad, mashed potatoes, braised steak, bread, milk, and ice cream, all served on the brush-covered hills on the far edge of the base. Because it was a sunny day and everyone seemed to enjoy firing the weapons, my buddies ignored my withdrawn silence. *I have to find time to call Carolyn tonight!*

After we double-timed back to the barracks, the Sergeant gave us a dressing-down because our platoon had come in second at the last inspection. "Were you all born in a #&)*%# barn?" he yelled. "Clean this place again, and do it right this time."

My squad was in charge of the sleeping area, and I had the guys crawling on the floor for dust, cleaning windows and baseboards. I watched the clock, hoping for a chance to get away, but the Sergeant kept every squad in the barracks until it shined from top to bottom. By the time he reluctantly yelled,

"At ease," there was no way I could get change and then find a phone booth before lights-out.

That night I dreamed I was running after Carolyn, but she kept evading me. Then suddenly I was in front of a large group of blonde girls with hair like Carolyn's, all facing away from me. Before I could pick her out of the group, the Drill Sergeant was yelling "Up, guys, everybody up!"

In the middle of another busy day, I was given a thick letter with a postmark of Brightwood. I opened it, feeling equal measures of hope and apprehension.

August 19, 1967

Larry,

The enclosed papers need to be filled out, stamped by the medical officer, and returned to me for the marriage license. One page has to be notarized, and you can't complete any of this before August 31st. (I don't know why.) Please mail it all back to me, and I'll take care of the rest.

Last night was Priscilla's bridal shower for me, and Mom and I didn't get home until after midnight. There were some really nice gifts. I'll write you more about it later.

The mailman will be here soon, so goodbye for now.

I love you, schnook!

Carolyn

At least she's still communicating! Since she sent the marriage license forms, she must still be planning to marry me. I knew I needed to do whatever I could to call her, even if it meant pulling some strings. I begged change from guys in the barracks until my pockets were full and hoped for free time after dinner.

"Corporal Wade, report to the Company Commander on the double." Praying that it was good news, I made my way to his office.

"Acting Corporal Wade reporting, Sir." I stood at attention in front of Lieutenant Jensen.

"At ease, Corporal," he said. I relaxed my pose as he continued. "We like what we've seen of you, Corporal. You've done a good job with the recruits."

"Thank you, Sir."

"How would you like to stay on as a permanent troop trainer here?" I tried to keep my face from splitting into a grin.

"I'd like that very much, Sir."

"There's just one problem. You've applied for OCS, but one of the schools just closed. That means a longer wait before you could start. In the meantime, we'd like you here."

"That would be great, Sir."

"Then I'll write up the orders for you to be assigned here after you finish Advanced Training in a few weeks. You'll have leave after graduation, then report back here."

"Thank you, Sir."

"Dismissed, Corporal."

I left his office happier than I'd been for weeks. This was great news! If Carolyn was willing to come back here with me after our wedding, we might be able to have a couple of months together before I left for OCS. But would she be willing to change her plans at this late date, not return to college, and live on my meager pay until I became an officer? That would be asking a lot. *I've got to talk to her tonight!*

I waited until seven o'clock when I would be able to talk longer for my money, and dialed her number.

"Hello?" Her voice sounded tired and strained.

"Hi, Sweetheart. It's Larry."

"Oh, Larry..." I heard her intake of breath, then what sounded like a muffled sob.

After a moment I said, "Are you okay, Carolyn?" There were some sniffs on the other end of the line, and then she spoke.

"I'm okay now, Larry. I can't believe you actually called."

"Can you ever forgive me for being such a dolt and not calling you before? I'm so sorry I hurt you."

"Of course, I forgive you. I know you can't exactly do what you want there. But I'm very glad you called tonight. I was getting pretty desperate."

"Are things really that bad?"

"If only you knew. I've only told you bits and pieces. I thought wedding preparation was supposed to be a happy time, but it's been awful. I want so much to have a good relationship with Mom, but the harder I try, the worse things get."

"I wish I could be there to buffer things for you. But I have some news you might like."

"Really? That would be nice. What is it?"

"I was called in today and told that they would like to assign me to this unit after graduation. It looks like it will be a while before a slot opens up for me at OCS, so I could be here for several months."

"So what exactly does that mean?" she asked, sounding uncertain.

"How would you like to live with me here at Fort Ord, instead of going back to college?"

"What?" she squeaked. "Are you kidding?" She started laughing, and then crying.

"If you really want to go back to college that much..." I started to tease. I heard her gulp and then take a long breath.

"I can't believe it, Larry! That would be wonderful."

"Well, don't get too excited, it wouldn't be easy. We'd have to really pinch pennies to live on the economy here. But I will get my PFC stripes at the end of this training, and once we're married, you'll get a wife's allotment."

"I'll live in a tent on the beach to be with you," she giggled.

"You haven't been to the beach here when the fog rolls in, Sweetheart. Brrrrr! But it won't come to that. I know we can find a way."

"So is this a sure thing?" I could tell that her practical mind was kicking in.

"My Commanding Officer told me today that he's writing up the orders. That's about as sure as it gets."

"Oh, Larry, I'm so excited. It's going to take some time to absorb this and figure out all I need to do. Just don't tell me we have to change the wedding date. The invitations are already ordered."

"Don't worry about that, the date can stay the same. I'll still get my two weeks leave after training, and we'll have time to get reacquainted before the wedding and our honeymoon. And it's less than a month until I can wrap my arms around you again."

"You don't know how heavenly that sounds."

"Oh, yes, I do. I can't wait. My dreams have been much too vivid lately."

"You're not the only one, Darling." I heard a door close, and Carolyn said, "Hi, Mom, Larry's on the phone." I heard a muffled voice, and Carolyn said, "Mom says to tell you it's about time."

"Tell her I'll do extra kitchen duty when I come up to try to make it up to her."

"Ha, ha, as if I'll let that happen. I want you all to myself when you get here."

"Sounds good to me…" Another soldier had been standing near the phone booth for a few minutes, and had begun making gestures to let me know it was his turn to use the phone. "I'm running out of coins and someone else wants to use the phone. I'll call again next week, Sweetheart."

"Oh, Larry, I think I just may be able to make it through the next month now. Just hearing your voice is so wonderful. I love you so much."

"I love you, Carolyn. I'll write soon."

"Goodbye, Darling." I left the phone booth with a broad smile on my face. When I got back to the barracks, I pulled out my stationery and wrote Carolyn about an idea we hadn't had time to discuss on the phone.

August 20, 1967
My love,

It certainly was wonderful to hear your beautiful voice again. Your personality always comes through when I hear your voice. I love you! If it had been possible to reach out to you, I would have hugged you to death.

The best part of our conversation is that our marriage plans seem so much more concrete now. Things have felt undefined before, but now it's all so real, it hurts. I love you! You are really something to look forward to.

Here's an idea for our honeymoon. My parents just bought a brand new Chevy pickup and a very nice camper. It has a stove, refrigerator, table, and two beds (we'd only need one, of course!). If there's a way my folks could do local sight-seeing while we're on our honeymoon, we could use the camper to go to Victoria. I don't want you cooking and washing dishes on our honeymoon, so we could still stay in motels and eat in restaurants, and just use the camper when we want to. Please write soon and let me know what you think of this. If you don't like the idea, tell me, and we'll come up with something else.

Tomorrow we have duties from 5:30 a.m. until after midnight, so I won't be able to write. Please forgive me ahead of time. I love you.

Goodnight, gorgeous.

Larry

PS: I love you!

The next day when I got back from the firing range near midnight, there was a notice on my bunk saying that OCS applicants were to report the following day to the headquarters building for a briefing. I breathed a prayer: *So much hinges on this, Lord. Please help me trust you with the outcome.*

Chapter 39

Carolyn

The smell of coffee drifted up the narrow knotty-pine stairs of my aunt's house, pulling me reluctantly out of sleep. Dad and Mom's decision to bring me here for a break seemed like a gift straight from God's hand. They were leaving today after spending the night with Aunt Marian, and I'd ride a bus back to Portland at the end of the week.

> **Current Culture**
> **August, 1967**
>
> - Hit song, "All you Need is Love," by the Beatles
> - Land area of Fort Ord: 28,000 acres
> - Pro football game tickets sell for $5.00
> - Large bag of potato chips costs 60 cents

I pulled a string and the roller blind snapped up, revealing sand, surf, dazzling blue water, and puffy white clouds above the distant horizon. I couldn't think of any place I'd enjoy more than my aunt's rustic cottage on the hill above the tiny beach community of Oceanside.

Downstairs in the kitchen, Mom and her sister were exchanging family news. As I poured myself a cup of coffee, Dad came in from an early morning walk on the beach and joined us for breakfast.

After Mom and Dad left, I followed Aunt Marian into the living room. She sat down in her chair by the big picture window facing the sea and picked up some knitting. "What would you like me to do today?" I asked.

"Whatever you want, Dear," she said, smiling.

"Really? But I'm happy to help if you need something."

"Thanks for your offer, but I get along just fine here by myself. You can do whatever you want. Consider it your vacation."

"Thank you," I said. "That's very kind." I blinked back sudden tears.

She looked at me speculatively. "I think you need time to relax. I want to hear all about your boyfriend and your wedding plans, but maybe this morning you should just take a walk on the beach."

I took a deep breath and gazed out at the glittering expanse of ocean just steps from the window. "That's a great idea."

Later I gave Larry some of the details.

August 23, 1967
Darling,

I'm sitting in my aunt's living room enjoying the ocean view and a cup of coffee. It's another beautiful day, although it was overcast when I got up. It's so restful here. Later I'll smear myself with baby oil and spend time on the sand. Then I may walk to visit a friend from school who lives in another town a couple of miles down the beach.

Last night was simply lovely. At bedtime when I looked out my window, there was a bonfire on the beach, and the lights shining from several fishing boats looked like stars reflected on the water. It would have been perfect for a long walk, but not much fun alone. I'm sending you a postcard of this beach--don't be too jealous.

I still can't believe that we're actually going to be married next month. Sometimes during the past weeks when I'd work on my wedding dress or see it hanging outside the closet door, it seemed like a cruel joke. But now all that has changed. Yikes! I just realized that our wedding date is exactly one month from today!

On the way home from the bridal shower at Priscilla's last week, Mom gave me a little talk about "the facts of life." It was nothing I didn't already know, except for her personal (actually <u>im</u>-personal) anecdotes. At least she was trying...

Evening...

I didn't finish this earlier, because the day was so beautiful and I had to be outdoors. At low tide, I climbed around the point at the north end of the beach and found an isolated niche on the face of the cliff. It was exhilarating to sit and watch the surging sea and the soaring birds. On the way back, I saw a trail of footprints, a man's and a woman's. If envy is sin, I'm guilty.

I'd love to stay for another week, but there's so much to do at home, and I can only get a ride to the bus in Tillamook on Friday. Aunt Marian has been so sweet and undemanding, I really hate to leave. My soul has been restored. If only you were here, it would be perfect!

I love you
Carolyn

"What would you like for dinner, Carolyn?" Aunt Marian peered into her refrigerator Wednesday afternoon. "I've got chicken I could fry up, and there's also some ground beef."

"Chicken, please," I replied. Meals here had been very informal, with us eating whenever and whatever we wanted, a big change from the strict mealtimes at home. We had even occasionally eaten off TV trays while watching the evening news, something Dad and Mom would never do.

The next day when I walked down the hill to the tiny post office, I was surprised to receive two letters from Larry that my mother had forwarded to my aunt's address. I took them to the bench at the edge of the sand, and opened the first one.

August 22, 1967
Dear Angry,

My, what a letter I received yesterday! You were really upset because I hadn't telephoned you for a while. Actually, I don't blame you. I'm just glad I called you over the weekend!

Baby, why didn't you come right out and tell me just how deeply you were hurt? I didn't realize this meant so much to you. Forgive me, Honey. It won't happen again. My calls will be much more frequent now. Please tell me where you'll be Labor Day weekend, as I plan to hitch-hike home and won't have to deal with a pay phone.

Yesterday all the OCS candidates were called to the Adjutant General's building. There are seven hundred of us on this post, and they gave us 20 minutes to decide whether or not we wanted to stay in the OCS program. It turns out that all but three OCS schools have been closed, so only a few of us will be picked. I was tempted to drop out, but something stopped me. Then at the end of the 20 minutes, the person in charge asked all the college grads to sign a paper, and said we could postpone our decision until later.

Now here's the best part! In three weeks, I will officially be "Permanent Party" assigned to a new company formed to train troops. This means I will be stationed here at Fort Ord for sure, until OCS. On top of that, I will be able to live off the base with you. All this *and* a future as an officer! What more could I ask for? (Well, YOU, for one thing!) In spite of how impossible things have seemed for us, it's all working out.

Some of your recent letters seemed to show that you doubted my love for you. Silly girl! Don't you realize how much I love you? If we were together, you would have absolutely no doubt.

Right now there are people all around me, but I'm still terribly lonely. Why aren't we together? "Someday, My Love..." has been our theme song. Now "someday" will be very soon. It's about time!

Goodnight, my love,

Larry

On Friday morning, a friend of Aunt Marian's arrived to take me to the bus station in Tillamook. I turned at the door to give my aunt a hug.

"You have no idea how much this has meant to me, Aunt Marian."

She stepped back from our embrace with a twinkle in her eye. "I might have a little idea." She patted my shoulder. "I've enjoyed having you here, Carolyn. I'll see you at the wedding."

"I'm so glad you'll be there!"

"I wouldn't miss it, especially now. Have a safe trip home."

The bus was already at the station when we arrived, and when I looked for a seat, I saw a girl from my dorm in the fourth row, with an empty seat next to her. Talking to Barbara made the two-hour ride go quickly.

In Portland, I waited briefly at the downtown bus station before boarding another bus to Beaverton. I got off at the Canyon Lane stop, and walked the last half mile to Emily's house.

"Tell me all the latest," she said, pouring me a glass of lemonade. We sat at the kitchen table while I told her about my visit with Aunt Marian, and of course the good news from Larry.

"So you won't be separated right after the honeymoon? Oh, Carolyn, that's such good news!" She gave me a quick hug. "It's definitely an answer to prayer."

"I know; I'm so relieved. Mom and Dad aren't too excited that I won't be going back to school in September, but they also know how miserable I've been this summer."

"Just think of all the things that have happened in the last year, and now your wedding is just a few weeks away." Her smile was wide as she grasped my hand. "Come and see the dresses, I finished mine last night." My sisters would be my attendants, and their long peacock blue crepe dresses were simple and elegant.

"They're beautiful, Em," I said. "You'll both look wonderful."

"Fran says the little girl's dresses are nearly done, too." My sister-in-law in Los Angeles had made the paler blue gowns for the two nieces who would be my flower girls.

"It's really happening, Em," I said. "And you and Paul had such a big part in it. I'll never forget that!"

"I'm so glad you're happy," she replied. "Larry is going to make a great husband, and you'll be the perfect wife for him."

On Monday, after a busy weekend, I sat in the lawn swing under the fir trees in the yard to write to Larry.

August 28, 1967
My darling,

You are the most wonderful man of the century (at least). You are intelligent, honest, handsome, gentle, responsible, strong, decisive, romantic, sincere, tender, friendly, ambitious, outgoing, articulate, compassionate, lovable, and best of all you're mine *(and vice-versa). What more could any girl ask for? How smart of me to catch you. The truth is out, finally. I let you chase me until I caught you.*

By now you probably realize how happy I am that we can be together after our wedding. It's fantastic how everything has fallen into place. I can now actually believe that we'll be married. *Before this change in plans, it was like looking forward to another too-short visit, with sex added. That may be a bit crude, but that's what it seemed like.*

I'm glad you're not dropping out of OCS. I think you might regret it later if you didn't take the chance when it was available. We can endure separation later if we have some time together now, and the extra officer's pay would make a big difference for us.

By the way, Larry, if for some reason you don't get orders or leave as promised, PLEASE let me know as soon as possible. If I have to change plans it will help to know right away.

Enough of the serious stuff. Would you like to hear some sweet nothings? Okay, here goes. "   ,"   "   ,"   "   ."

I tried to be careful in case someone was reading over your shoulder. When you get here in a few weeks, I'll be happy to fill in the blanks.

Larry, do you remember what was happening just one year ago? I wanted so terribly much for you to love me, but you had said, "I'm never going to get married." Then a few days later, everything fell together (or apart) and it was so wonderful to respond to your loving words and hold your hand. Then when we parked at Mt. Tabor and you kissed me, I could sense that the joy in your heart matched my joy. You were everything I dreamed of.

How wonderful it will be to be back in that world, inside your arms, and to feel your body strong and warm and close to mine. I love you, Larry, for all that you are and for what I am becoming because of your love.

Carolyn

"Want to go to a football game tonight?" said Dave, phoning me at Emily's house. "My date canceled at the last minute."

"Sure, Dave. Who's playing?"

"It's pre-season exhibition, New Orleans versus San Francisco."

"Sounds great. What time should I be ready?"

"I'll pick you up at 6:30." As I hung up the phone, I wished Larry could join us. He'd never get such treats in Hanford or even Fresno. I decided to take the opportunity to learn more about football, and quizzed Dave as we watched. By the end of the evening I felt like I had enough understanding to be able to enjoy a game with Larry once we were married.

As Dave dropped me off later at Paul and Emily's he said, "Oh, I forgot something." He reached into the back seat of his car, and handed me a letter from Larry. "This came today before I left the ranch."

"Thanks, Dave," I said, taking the letter gratefully. "I'm glad you invited me to the game, I really enjoyed it." I gave him a quick kiss on the cheek before heading into the darkened house. Everyone was apparently in bed, so I went straight to my room and read the letter.

August 28, 1967
Dear Carolyn,

Guess what wonderful things I got today? Hint: they were all blue. 2nd Hint: they smelled wonderful, 3rd Hint: they were from the woman I love.

Thank you so much for your frequent letters. It hasn't always been easy to communicate just through writing, and I know there's been misunderstanding at times. How on earth could we ever consider being separated for an indefinite amount of time?

Yesterday was a terrible excuse for a Sunday. I didn't get off all-night guard duty until after noon, and by that time all the chapel services were over. I took advantage of some time off to do laundry, and tried to nap between putting loads in the washer and dryer.

I'm hoping that my sister and her family will be able to come up from Pasadena for the wedding. Since Chuck won't be able to get home, I'd like to have at least a couple of family members there besides my parents.

We've been told that we won't be released for the Labor Day weekend until Saturday evening, so I may not make it home to Hanford until very late

Saturday night. Please be sure to let me know where you'll be on Sunday and Monday so I can call you.

Today we had the usual morning "house-cleaning" and chores around the barracks before running out to the rifle range. It was uphill for three miles, and wasn't so bad for me, but some of the guys fell out of formation. I guess I'm in better shape than I thought.

Later, we were taught squad defense tactics until nearly midnight. A small number of us were picked to be the aggressors (pretend Viet Cong) to attack or infiltrate the defense positions. Our group "killed" the American squad twice. It sounds grim, but it was enjoyable to use all the things we've learned over the past weeks. Next week we have several more night maneuvers, and these last weeks are supposed to be the most difficult of the training.

Beautiful girl, I love you. Just think, we'll be together SOON!

Goodnight, love

Larry

When I finally got back to the ranch after taking a bus from Portland, there was a package on my dresser containing our wedding invitations. As I held them in my hands and saw our names and the date in black and white, tears filled my eyes. Mom came in and looked over my shoulder.

"They look very nice, dear," she said.

"Yes, they do, don't they?" It was a moment without tension, and I was suddenly overwhelmed by the thought that I was soon leaving my home and family for good. "Thanks, Mom, for everything you've done for me this summer."

She looked startled for a moment, then turned away as if to conceal emotion.

"You'll always be my baby girl."

I stared at her back as she walked out into the hallway. "I love you, Mom," I called after her.

Pale moonlight filtered through the branches of the gnarled apple tree outside my window when I sat down to write to Larry the next evening.

August 29, 1967
Darling,
Just call me "Grace." Today I was really uncoordinated. At breakfast, I tipped a cup of scalding tea into my lap. Then at dinner, I spilled my milk, which promptly dripped through the crack in the middle of the table and onto my leg. Then as I cleared the table, I dropped the salt shaker and salted the floor generously.

News flash: 1) Today was our sixty-eighth day without rain, 2) Dry thunderstorms yesterday set off a hundred new forest fires, adding to the ones started last week, 3) Smokey the Bear's new slogan is: "Let's at least keep it brown, not black."

While I was at Aunt Marian's, another girl about my age stayed here to help out. It actually worked in my favor, because she definitely didn't live up to Mom's expectations. Now Mom seems to appreciate my work more, and she's made several comments about my "speed and efficiency." What a relief! Several times lately I've had dreams about arguing with Mom, and woke up tense and aching all over.

Today I went to Sandy for some sewing supplies for the latest project, and ended up flattening my wallet with "little" things, like $7.50 for 150 stamps. I hope to finish addressing the invitations tonight.

One reason I love this time of year is all the wonderful produce that is ripe. We have fresh corn, tomatoes, blackberries, apples, squash, beets, plums, pears, and more cucumbers. Would you believe we've picked over three hundred cukes? We made more pickles tonight.

For some reason, I'm falling asleep sitting up. I shouldn't be tired, as I'm in bed by 10:30 every night. But then I have weird dreams about you. They're nice, but strange. I'm sure I'll sleep better when I have dreams <u>with</u> you.
Je t'aime.
Carolyn

Mom insisted that I have a formal wedding portrait taken, even though I argued that it was *our* wedding, not just *my* wedding, and I wanted to wait for photos with Larry. "You'll have plenty of those, too, Carolyn. But you'll be glad to have a formal portrait in your wedding gown."

I'd had very few experiences in a beauty shop, but the Meier and Frank salon was highly recommended. When I told the stylist I was going to have a wedding portrait taken that afternoon, she excitedly said, "I know exactly what to do!"

After an hour with shampoo, conditioner, rollers, helmet hair-dryer and hair spray, the stylist turned me around. I stared in horror at my reflection in the mirror. My hair was fluffed, back-combed and piled on my head in large sausage curls held in place by dozens of bobby pins. *I'm paying her to make me look like this?*

Feeling sick, I settled the bill, adding what I hoped was an appropriate tip. I was sure my coolness let her know I wasn't thrilled with her work, but there was no time to make changes before my appointment at the studio.

The photographer handed me a fake bouquet and had me sit, stand, tilt my head, and hold the flowers in various positions. I tried to look like a happy bride, concentrating on how much I loved Larry and how few days were left until I would see him. When I paid the sitting fee, receptionist asked when I would like to return to look at proofs. "I'll have to get back to you," I murmured. *There's no way I'll spend more money for a permanent record of this fiasco!*

Back home, I pulled out the bobby pins and brushed all the lacquer out of my hair before I opened Larry's letter.

August 31, 1967
My Dearest Carolyn,
   Today has been another one of those wasteful days the Army is famous for. We spent the entire day learning how to fire the .50 caliber machine gun. Would you believe that I fired off approximately $25.00 worth of ammunition in just ten minutes? What a waste of taxpayer's money!

Although I've always planned that my wife would never have to work, the current circumstances may make it necessary. You might be able to work as a substitute teacher, even though you haven't finished your degree yet, as there's a big teacher shortage here in California. Otherwise, I'm sure you'll be able to get a temp job easily, with your shorthand and impressive typing speed. Once I finish OCS, things will be a lot different.

In one of your recent letters, you reminded me of those days last year when we were falling in love. Even considering the other days we've spent together, I'd have to say those were the best. Life suddenly took on new meaning and purpose, and it was exhilarating. I will always think of my decision to propose to you as the smartest one of my life. Remember how very frank and grown-up we acted, and at the same time we were terribly shy? And I didn't kiss you until <u>after</u> I proposed and you accepted.

The love that started a year ago has grown and multiplied immensely. Only a wonderful woman like you could cause love to endure and grow under such circumstances. After all, you have definitely not picked the easiest path in life. Perhaps that is just part of the reason I love you so much.

Just a few more days, and we'll be married!!!!

Goodnight. I love you!

Larry

I sighed as I folded the letter and put it on my pillow to read again before going to sleep. Tiptoeing through the hall so I wouldn't wake my parents, I went out the back door into the yard. In the silent darkness, I gazed up at the night sky. Only a sliver of moon showed, making the stars seem even brighter.

Is Larry looking at these stars and thinking of me?

Chapter 40

Larry

"It's nice to have you home, but I can't get over how different you look." Mom shook her head as she put a plate of over-easy eggs on the breakfast table Sunday morning. "What will Carolyn think?"

"Well, I hope she likes the new me," I said. "We've waited six months to see each other, and I don't want her to be disappointed."

While familiar with my reflection in the mirror at the barracks latrine, the image in

Current Culture
September 1967

- Population of Fort Ord: 40,000
- New federal law requires all cigarette packs to carry a warning: "Caution! Cigarette smoking may be hazardous to your health."
- Paperback edition of *Catch-22* costs 95 cents
- Interest on bank savings accounts is 5.25-5.75%

the medicine-cabinet mirror at Mom and Dad's startled me. My face was deeply tanned, I'd lost more than twenty pounds and my biceps were nicely defined. The short GI haircut and black Army-issue glasses completed the transformation.

Dad came in from the back porch and said, "I thought you might sleep in. You got here pretty late last night."

"Eight o'clock *is* sleeping in, Dad. I'm usually up before five. This is luxury."

"Well, I'm glad you got home safe. How was your trip?"

"Pretty good. I didn't have my thumb out for more than ten minutes between rides. The couple that brought me most of the way have a son stationed in Germany. They said they always pick up soldiers."

"Will you wear your uniform to church?" Mom asked.

"I'm planning to."

"You'll cause quite a stir. By the way, do you have any laundry for me to do?"

"No, I didn't want to waste space in my duffel bag carrying dirty clothes. Besides, you haven't done my laundry for me since I was ten years old," I chuckled.

"I'm happy to do whatever will make your weekend easier, Larry." That was about as much affection as Mom could express, and I smiled at her in appreciation. "Look at the time!" she said. "We need to leave soon." I drank the last of my tea, and headed for the bedroom to dress for church.

As Mom predicted, our entrance at church brought a flurry of comments: "You make that uniform look good!" "Army life must agree with you." It had only been four months since I'd been their pastor, but it seemed like eons. I felt like a very different person from the one who preached to these folks a few months ago.

That evening I waited impatiently for seven o'clock and lower phone rates. The phone rang only once before Carolyn answered.

"Hi, Beautiful! Waiting by the phone?"

"Hi, Larry."

"That's it? Just 'Hi, Larry'?"

"It's been an exhausting weekend already, and tomorrow's Labor Day. I'm pretty tired."

"Let me guess, your mother is in the room, listening to everything you say."

"You're pretty smart. That's one of the reasons I'm going to marry you in a few weeks."

"Are you still having a rough time? You sound like you're about to cry."

"That's a possibility."

"Okay, I won't pry any more while she's listening in. How are the final plans coming?" Carolyn paused and I heard rustling noises and a door close.

"There, I'm out on the back porch," she said. "Good thing the phone has a long cord. Now I'll have a little privacy." She took a deep breath before continuing. "Plans are coming along. The cake is ordered, the dresses are nearly finished, I bought the candles for the sanctuary...but you don't want to hear all the details.

"If it's important to you, it's important to me. I happen to be in love with you, you know."

"I'm counting on that, Larry. And you have no idea how much it helps to actually talk to you, instead of waiting for answers to letters."

"Being home makes it easy for me to call. You know, I'm really looking forward to going to Victoria for our honeymoon."

"Me, too! But to be honest, I'd be happy just to drive across the river to Vancouver to be with you. "

"Funny you should say that, I was going to suggest Vancouver for our first night. That way we'd be out of range for any pranks by your family."

"That's fine with me. By the way, how are you planning to get here on the 16th?"

"I haven't decided yet. If I drive, Mom and Dad could use my car while we use their pickup and camper for our honeymoon. That would be cheaper, but I'd rather fly and get there sooner."

"Please let me know as soon as you decide. That's only two weeks away, Larry!"

"I know. Time is zipping by. By the way, you should get the blood test paperwork on Tuesday. I mailed it on Friday right after I got it notarized."

"Good, then I'll get the marriage license in the next few days. That sounds so final—*marriage license*. Is this really happening?

"Yes, my love, it's really happening. Really and truly."

"Tell me as soon as you know when I can live with you at Fort Ord." She lowered her voice before continuing. "Being here now is bad enough, but once we're married and you're back at the base, I'm not sure I can handle it."

"Couldn't you live with Paul and Emily for awhile?"

"Maybe, but Mom wouldn't like that."

"Once we're married, we can make decisions without her input, Carolyn."

"Yes, I know that's how it should be, but you have no idea how difficult she's making things. If I'm here, and you're somewhere else in training…" Her voice trailed off hopelessly.

"Maybe it won't be an issue, Carolyn. Let's pray that things will work out so you can come right away."

"I'll be praying that morning, noon and night." Her laughter had a desperate edge. "A car just drove in--looks like we have late visitors. I may have to get off the phone."

"Do we need to discuss anything else? I don't want to lose this opportunity." I heard voices in the background.

"I don't think so. Larry, please let me know when you're coming and get here as soon as you can. Fill your pockets with change, so you can call me from a pay phone on the way."

"That bad, huh? I'm so sorry, Sweetheart. Just hold on for two more weeks, and everything will be okay."

"I'm counting on that. I love you."

"I love you too, Carolyn. More than you will ever know. Goodbye for now."

I knew things were rough for her, but her sadness and distress on the phone made my protective instincts kick in. *Please let the next two weeks go quickly!*

Back at the base Monday night, I wrote to Carolyn, hoping to cheer her up.

September 3, 1967
Dear Carolyn,

Say, who was that sad girl I talked to on the phone last night? She sounded discouraged and ready to cry. It didn't seem like the same happy girl I fell in love with. Please write and tell me what's going on. Even if I can't be there, maybe there's something I can do to help.

I'm sorry you had such a busy weekend, on top of all the wedding things. Please don't wear yourself out. It would be nice if you had some energy left for our honeymoon. Don't take that wrong, I just mean that I want you to be able to enjoy our time together.

It was a little disappointing to go to church with Mom yesterday. I hoped that the congregation would have grown over the summer with the new preacher. But the group was actually smaller. I hate to think that all my efforts were in vain. I guess I'll have to trust God with that.

It only took two rides to get back to the base, and I made it in plenty of time before lights-out. What good fortune!

Goodnight, love. I hope the rest of your weekend was better. Please hang on, it's only two more weeks until we're together!

I LOVE YOU!

Larry

The Drill Instructors were evidently trying to make up for the holiday weekend. They got us up before five, and ran us over hills and gullies on patrolling exercises all day. It was close to midnight when I got back to the barracks, washed the camouflage charcoal off my face, and took a shower. Then I settled down and read the latest letter from Carolyn, written before our phone conversation.

September 1, 1967

Darling Lar,

Where has the summer gone? It's September already, and I haven't accomplished half of what I planned. I guess some things can be done after we're married, although from the implications of your letters, I'll be spending half the time you're gone each day recuperating from you.

Today I planned to bake cookies to mail to you. After shelling some walnuts, I headed out to the back porch carrying a bucket of shells. I hit a slick spot, and ended up sprawled on the floor in a pile of sharp walnut shells. Other than nasty bruises on my left side and arm, there was no real damage. But by the time I cleaned up the mess, it was time to start lunch. You'll get the cookies eventually.

Only one more lonely weekend! It seems too good to be true—all our dreams from the past year are about to be realized, and things are working out far better than we hoped.

Tomorrow will start the last holiday weekend before school begins. We always get quite a few horseback customers and fishermen, but Mom likes to deal with them, so I'll be the one doing the extra cooking and cleaning, not to mention incidental supervision of my nieces and nephews. At least we'll be busy, and maybe Mom and I won't have time to argue over wedding plans.

As much as I have enjoyed all our letters, I can't wait to talk face to face! Goodnight, Darling.

Carolyn

A few nights later, my squad had night patrol duty. While there wasn't really any possibility of attack, it was part of the training, and we took it seriously most of the time. Patrol was enjoyable in clear weather, and this night was particularly beautiful. The stars were brilliant, and I could hear the rumbling surf in the distance. As my buddy and I sat at the guard post, talking quietly, a small buck and two does gingerly stepped into the clearing near us, sniffed the air, and then settled down to browse. *I wish Carolyn could be here to see this!*

The next day I had trouble rolling out of my bunk after only three hours sleep. On outdoor maneuvers again, I was assigned as a sniper for the "aggressors." After our company walked six miles to the training site, I crawled under some bushes and slept for several hours. At noon, another sniper and I built a small fire under a tree to heat our C-rations. In spite of the moments of beauty and the satisfaction of physical challenge, I was anxious for my training to be over.

That evening, there was a fragrant blue letter on my bunk.

September 8, 1967

Darling,

Good morning! Yesterday was quite a day. At breakfast, Mom said, "Your father doesn't think you should drive all the way to Monmouth by yourself." Talk about a last-minute monkey wrench! I won't bore you with the details of our argument, but it was pretty bad. She knew I had appointments at the campus, including one with Dr. Bailey for my pre-marital blood test. I eventually called Cheryl and just by chance, she was free to go with me. In spite of the bad start, it turned out to be a pleasant day.

During my appointment with Dr. Bailey, I told him how miserable my summer has been. As usual, he expressed concern and had some wisdom. He pointed out that your absence and the uncertainty of our situation made everything worse. He had one very specific recommendation for our honeymoon: "Don't plan too much. Go off someplace and stay put." Maybe we should reconsider our plans?

After seeing Dr. Bailey, I gave Cheryl a tour of the campus. At the Dean's office, Dr. Wells was his usual jovial self, with joking threats and insults. He said you'd better bring some buddies with you, because if you get out of line, he'll personally tear you to bits. When we left his office, Cheryl said, "I think they like you here."

On the way home, I bought a guest book for the wedding, stopped at the jewelers, and bought special paper for the wedding programs. Unfortunately, when I got home at seven, Mom didn't approve of anything I'd bought. She said, "I thought you were going to get such-and-such" and "Your father will have a fit!" There was also a sink full of dirty dishes left for me to wash. By the time our "discussion" was over, I was nauseated and had a splitting headache. Maybe now you understand why I haven't told you all the gory details earlier. There just wasn't any point, as you couldn't really do anything about it.

Please don't worry about me; I'm determined to make it through the next week in one piece. Then you'll be here, and everything will change.

Car

I tried to pray for Carolyn before falling asleep, but the day's exertion caught up with me and before I knew it, "Reveille" was playing and I had to roll out of my bunk.

Our last week of training consisted of war games from 5:00 a.m. to midnight. We ran in formation to a new area in the back of the base where there was a mock-up of a Vietnamese village. Half of the group was designated U.S. Army forces, and I happened to be part of the other half, the aggressors. Our uniforms were an odd shade of green with a strange insignia. I was given Lieutenant's bars for my collar.

While it was all a game, I was surprised that the U.S. forces did so poorly. My team had far fewer "casualties" than we inflicted on the other side. I hoped it wasn't a reflection of the real war going on in Southeast Asia.

I'd come to the field with paper and pen in my pocket, and during a lull in the "battle," I sat with my back against a tree to write a letter to Carolyn.

September 12, 1967
Dear Carolyn,

It's my last week of Advanced Infantry Training. They certainly haven't let up on us, but are trying to make it more realistic. We've been playing war games every day. Somehow I frequently end up as the "aggressor" fighting against the U.S. Army.

Yesterday we had our last physical condition test. The mile run at the end was certainly easier here in this 70 degree weather than the heat and humidity at Fort Polk. I took my time and felt great after running a 6:20 mile.

We had a "Class A" inspection today, which means we had to display all our field gear on our bunks, foot lockers and wall lockers. We had taken extra care to hide all the "illegal" stuff (civilian clothes, letters, photographs, etc.) in the attic. The inspecting Sergeant kept saying, "Where is everything? You must have something hidden somewhere!" We all snickered behind his back. As you can guess, we passed the inspection.

About two-thirds of the guys in my barracks are married (they're National Guard or Enlisted Reserve soldiers). They are all very anxious to get home to their wives. My previous image of loose-living soldiers has been shattered by this group. Not one of them has been unfaithful while they were here (and yes, there is opportunity in the neighboring town).

The faint smell of perfume and the lipstick kiss on your last letter really brought back memories. My body actually began to tingle when I smelled your perfume. If only you knew what it does to me. For your sake, don't wear that perfume until our wedding day, okay?

Goodnight, gorgeous. Soon you'll know just how much I love you.
Larry

On Friday September 15 there was great excitement in the barracks. Excessive horseplay and joking showed everyone's relief at reaching this milestone. *After graduation, we'll all be out of here!*

When the mid-morning ceremony ended, we lined up to get our orders for the next phase of our Army career. I waited impatiently for the Sergeant to get to the end of the alphabet, but he turned away without calling my name.

I hurried after him. "Sergeant Miller, do you have my orders?" He looked at his clipboard.

"No, Corporal, there's nothing here for you."

A boulder dropped into the pit of my stomach. "So what does that mean? What about my leave?"

"You don't get leave without orders."

"But I'm supposed to get married next week." I said, trying not to show my panic.

"I'm sorry, Wade, that's too bad. You'll have to go to Headquarters on Monday and try to straighten it out."

"Monday? My fiancée is expecting me in Oregon tomorrow night."

"I guess she's going to be disappointed then." His gruff demeanor softened slightly. "I hope you can work it out, Corporal."

Numb with shock, I stared at his retreating back. All our carefully organized and prayed-for plans slowly crumbled as he walked away, leaving me with nothing.

Chapter 41

Carolyn

At 11:30 Friday night, one week before our wedding day, I finally crawled into bed, my anxious mind in overdrive. *Why hasn't Larry called? Has something terrible happened? Did he get mugged while hitch-hiking?* On the slim chance he might still call, I left the bedroom door open so I could hear the phone ring.

After a night haunted by bizarre dreams, I awoke just after seven and sat alone in the kitchen with a cup of tea. Mom came in to the kitchen in her robe at eight. "Did Larry call last night? I didn't hear the phone ring."

> **Current Culture**
> **September 1967**
>
> - Soviets sign pact to send more aid to North Vietnam
> - Texas Instruments announces the development of world's first hand-held calculator, which can add, subtract, multiply and divide
> - Game show *What's My Line* ends 17-year run on TV
> - Goodyear tires sell for $37.00/pair

"No, he didn't call." I tried to keep my voice even and not let her know how frightened I was.

Her brow furrowed as she said, "Well, I'm sure he'll call soon." As she spoke, the screen door on the back porch slammed, and Roger came through the hallway and into the kitchen. He'd arrived the previous day after a bus ride from Los Angeles to be at our wedding.

"What's the matter, Sis? You look like you lost your last friend." I covered my face to hide my sudden tears.

"Larry hasn't called, and she's worried," Mom explained, heading back to her bedroom.

"Oh, I'm sorry. I didn't mean to make a bad joke."

377

"It's okay, Rog," I said. "You didn't know. What do you want for breakfast?"

"Maybe some eggs. That would be a nice change from toast and peanut butter. But you don't have to cook for me. I can fix my own breakfast," he said.

"I'll sit and have another cup of tea while you eat. You can catch me up on your exciting adventures in L.A."

As he broke four eggs into the frying pan, I looked him over. He was thin and pale and his glasses were held together with tape and a safety pin. He'd ruefully told us that he left his only suit on a bench in the Los Angeles bus station.

"I thought Larry graduated yesterday," Roger said, flipping the eggs.

"He was supposed to, and then he was going to hitch-hike home and drive up here. I expected him to call me when he got to Hanford."

Roger squeezed my shoulder. "You've sure had more than your share of ups and downs in this relationship. But I know Larry's the right one for you. It'll work out."

"Thanks, Rog. I keep telling myself that, but this morning it's a little hard to believe."

We heard tires scatter gravel in the driveway, and I stood to look out the window. A second car pulled in behind the first, and people started getting out of the cars. I went out to greet them.

"Can I help you?"

"We hear you have horses here. We'd like to ride."

"Sure, let me get someone for you." I went back into the house and knocked on the bedroom door.

"Riders, Mom. Do you want to take them out?" A few minutes later, she came out to the porch in her riding outfit, a long divided skirt and a white blouse adorned with a horse pin. She grabbed a straw hat from the hall rack.

"I'll go with you, Mom," Roger said.

On the way out the door, Mom gave me instructions. "When you finish in the kitchen, there's a load of laundry to do, and you'll want to pick more blackberries before it gets too hot."

Roger grinned at me as he followed her out the door. "Sorry to leave you with KP."

"What's new?" I muttered to his retreating back.

I really wanted to fling myself on the bed and cry, but I knew that would only make me feel worse. I washed the breakfast dishes and headed out to the back porch laundry area. It was already warming up, and clothes would dry quickly on the outside line. While I worked, faith argued with fear. *Maybe he's halfway here already, planning to surprise me. If he drove straight through from Hanford, he could get here tonight.*

But I specifically asked him to let me know as soon as he got his orders. I hate not knowing! I know he's frugal and doesn't like to spend money on phone calls, but this is ridiculous.

When Dad came in from his morning barnyard chores, he looked at me expectantly. "When's your sweetheart arriving?"

I burst into tears. "I don't know, Daddy. He hasn't called." He put his arms around me and patted my back.

"Don't worry, Sweetheart. It's all going to work out. Just trust the Lord."

"But why doesn't he call? What if something has happened? He was going to hitch-hike home yesterday."

"There's got to be an explanation. Be patient, he'll call." I sniffled and wiped my eyes as he continued. "Come out to the garden with me. Lots of tomatoes are ripe." He grabbed a small bucket from the counter, and reached for my hand. His solid faith and loving touch were comforting; the kitchen chores could wait.

By mid-afternoon, I was jumpy and restless. "Why don't you take a walk," Mom said. "Some exercise might relieve your tension."

"A phone call would relieve my tension," I retorted. Seeing the pained look on her face, I added, "Sorry, Mom, I didn't mean to snap at you. I'm just so worried."

"Well, if you're not going to take a walk, then at least sit down and play the piano or read for a while and take your mind off things." Reluctantly, I sat down at the piano and picked out a difficult piece that would force me to concentrate.

After ten minutes of playing, I closed the piano and announced, "I'm going to take a walk after all. I'll stay close in the barnyard in case the phone rings." When I went through the gate, Spice ambled over and nudged my shoulder with her black nose. I hugged her warm brown neck and scratched her ears. "Oh, Spice, it's such an awful day." She bumped her head against me and blew through her nostrils. "Maybe we'll take a ride when it cools down." I walked to the far edge of the barnyard before going back to the house. Mom was lying on the couch reading.

"I want to call the Wades, Mom."

She looked at me with a slight frown. "Well, I guess since it's Saturday, and the rates are down..." She hesitated before adding, "Ask your father first, Carolyn."

I found Dad cleaning bridles in the tack room. "Mom told me to ask you if I can call the Wades."

"You can't wait for him to call?" he asked.

"Dad, it's been twenty-four hours since he was supposed to leave the base. He's had plenty of time to call. I'm really worried."

"Okay, Honey, go ahead."

My hands shook as I dialed the Wade's number. It rang four times before Larry's father answered.

"Hi, Mr. Wade. It's Carolyn."

"Hello, Carolyn. I thought maybe it would be Larry."

"He's not there?" My heart constricted with alarm.

"No. Hasn't he called you?"

"No, he hasn't." I tried to keep my voice steady.

"Well, that beats all. I wonder what's going on?"

My anxiety mushroomed. "Is there any way you can call the base and find out if he left?"

"I think we have an emergency number around somewhere, I'll have to ask Midge," he said. "We'll try to find out something and call you back."

"Okay, thanks." I hung up and stood beside the desk, paralyzed by fear.

"What did he say, Carolyn?" Mom asked.

"They don't know anything. He didn't get home and didn't call them. Now I'm really scared." My heart pounded, and I tried not to hyperventilate.

"There's got to be a good reason." She turned to Dad, who had just walked into the house. "No one knows where Larry is."

"Sounds like we need to pray," said Dad, pulling me against his shoulder. I leaned into his arms, trying not to sob. "Father, we need your peace for our girl." His arm tightened around me. "And we need your protection for Larry, wherever he is. Keep him safe, and work everything out. In Jesus' Name, Amen." He gave me a squeeze. "Keep trusting, Sweetheart. God's not going to let you down. You'll be walking down the aisle in a few days." Dad's kindness broke the dike of my self-control, and I ran into the bedroom to sob out my fear and anxiety. I tried to pray, but my mind kept envisioning terrible scenarios, and I found myself curling into a ball of confusion and misery.

It was nearly half an hour later when the phone rang. I heard Mom answer, then call, "Carolyn, it's Mr. Wade." I ran to the kitchen.

"Hello?" I answered, breathlessly.

"Well, it took a while, but I finally got through to Larry. He didn't get any orders after graduation yesterday, so he can't leave the base. He's in a terrible funk and didn't want to call you to give you the bad news."

"Oh, no! But he's okay?"

"Yes, he's fine." Relief brought new tears, and I couldn't speak.

After a few moments, Mr. Wade said, "Stay by the phone, Carolyn. I told him he'd better call you right away, or I'll drive over there and personally wring his neck. I'm sorry about this. You let me know if you don't hear from him."

I managed to chuckle through my tears. "Thanks, Mr. Wade. I appreciate you calling me back. Let's hope we see each other at the end of next week."

When I hung up the phone I sat down on a kitchen chair, suddenly weak-kneed. Mom looked at me expectantly. "Well?"

"He's okay. He didn't get orders and he's very depressed. Apparently he didn't want to upset me with the bad news."

"Well, that's not exactly the best way to handle it, but I'm glad he's okay." She paused and I could see her mental wheels turning. "So is he coming? Are we still going to have a wedding?"

"I wish I knew, Mom," I said, my tears starting again. "He's supposed to call me soon." The words were barely out of my mouth when the phone rang. I grabbed the receiver. "Hello?"

"Hi, Carolyn." Larry's voice was low and strained. "I guess I'm really in the doghouse."

"I've been scared to death, Larry. Why on earth didn't you call me?"

"When I didn't get any orders and couldn't leave the base, everything turned upside down, and I just wanted to find a cave to crawl into. I'm sorry-- I didn't think about how worried you'd be." His voice became husky. "Can you forgive me?"

"You know I'll forgive you, Larry. I'm so relieved to hear from you. "

"I'm supposed to find out something when the offices open on Monday."

"Promise me one thing, okay?"

"What's that?"

"That you'll call me Monday night, whether it's good news or bad news. Promise? I can't go through another day like this."

"Okay, I promise. Be by the phone Monday evening after seven. I *will* call you."

"I'll be waiting," I said firmly.

"Pray for me, Carolyn. Somehow God's got to change this situation. I'm desperate."

I took a deep breath and felt my heart rate begin to slow. "I love you, Larry. I'm going to believe that next week at this time we'll be married."

"I'm glad you have faith, Carolyn. I'm having a little trouble with that right now."

"Call me Monday!"

"I will. I love you, Carolyn."

At church the next day, I could barely hold myself together to talk to anyone. Paul and Em had called people to pray, so I didn't have to explain the situation. Each sympathetic look or comment brought fresh tears, and I finally hid in the restroom, alternating between praying and pleading.

You can't let us down now, God, not after all we've been through.

Please do a miracle for us, and get Larry here on Saturday. I can't imagine what I'll do if he doesn't make it. Help, Lord! I can't handle this.

I heard footsteps, then my sister's voice. "Carolyn, are you in here?"

"Yes," I said, my voice muffled by my damp handkerchief.

"Come on out, we need to talk." I reluctantly opened the door and faced her. "Let's think this through, Carolyn. We all hope and pray that Larry will be able to be here on Saturday. But if somehow that doesn't happen, you're going to live through this." She handed me a folded handkerchief from her purse to soak up my fresh tears. "Everything's ready for your wedding, but most of it will keep a few weeks, and we can re-schedule."

"I don't want to re-schedule," I wailed. "I want to get married on Saturday."

"Of course, and I really think that's going to happen," Emily said calmly. "But whatever happens, it's not the end of the world, regardless of what you feel right now, and we're going to make the best of it. God loves you and He loves Larry, and in the end, He's not going to let you down."

"I know that," I hiccupped, "and I know I'm over-reacting. It's been so hard, and I was terrified when I thought something had happened to him."

"Well, now you know he's okay, and one way or another, things are going to work out."

"I hope so." I tried to smile as she gave me a hug.

I grabbed the phone on the first ring at one minute after seven on Monday evening. Larry's voice sounded very different than it had on Saturday night.

"Hi, Beautiful. I have some good news and some bad news."

"Give me the good news first, quick!"

"We can get married on Saturday."

"Really!" I squealed. "You're not joking?"

"I wouldn't joke about something this serious. I'll be there for the wedding."

"I'm going to cry again," I sniffled.

"But happy tears, right?"

"Definitely happy!" Then I remembered. "So what's the bad news?"

"I can only get a 72-hour pass, from Thursday evening to Sunday evening."

My mind whirled with questions. "So how will that work out?" I gulped. "That means no honeymoon…"

"Let me finish, Sweetheart. I've already talked to my parents. They will pick me up at the base on Thursday evening and we'll get to Brightwood late Friday afternoon. We'll have a whole 24 hours together before the wedding."

I sputtered with a combination of tears and laughter. "And after the wedding…?"

"Well, it depends on you, but it could be more good news. Would you be willing to buy a couple of plane tickets with our honeymoon money so we could fly back down here together Sunday? After all this, I'm definitely not going to leave you in Oregon after the wedding."

I gasped at the implications. "Are you kidding? I can fly back to California with you? Of course I'll buy plane tickets."

"And I have one more request. I hate to ask you to do this, but I don't think I can manage it from here. Would you book us a decent place to stay Saturday night after the wedding?"

All the fear and worry of the past days was turning to joy, and I could feel myself smiling widely. "Of course, I'll take care of that." New aspects of the situation popped into my mind. I waited until Larry had fed the phone with more coins and our conversation could continue. "I guess this means I probably won't be going back to school this term."

"It would be a pretty hard commute from Fort Ord to Monmouth, Sweetheart. You'll need to give the college a call too."

"We're really going to be together, Larry? I can hardly believe this. It's an amazing answer to prayer."

"Well, you'll want to let your family and friends know right away how God came through," Larry said. "I'll call you again on Wednesday evening in case there are last minute details you need to know." His voice softened. "And I'll hold you in my arms in four days!"

"I can't wait! I love you so much."

"Ditto, Sweetheart. I'll see you soon. Bye for now."

"Bye, I love you."

When I told my parents the news, Dad grinned and gave me a hug. "I knew we could trust the Lord."

Mom seemed relieved, before her eyes narrowed. "I don't know that I like the idea of my daughter heading off to some unknown Army base in the middle of war-time."

I gave her a quick hug and said, "Don't worry, Mom, be happy for us," before running out the door to tell Roger.

With the sudden change of circumstances, I had a burst of energy over the next few days. I finalized all the details for the wedding, purchased two one-way tickets from Portland to Fresno, and notified the Dean's office in Monmouth that I would not be returning to school for fall quarter.

After considering the options for our wedding night, I decided to splurge. Picturesque Timberline Lodge, high on the slopes of Mt. Hood, was less than an hour from our wedding chapel. "I'd like to book a room for Saturday night," I informed the hotel reservationist.

"Would that be for this coming Saturday?"

"Yes, the 23rd."

"We have a standard room available for $20.00." I swallowed hard. My parents had never paid more than eight dollars for a night in a motel. "Is this for a special occasion?"

"Well, sort of. A brief honeymoon," I stammered.

"We could upgrade you to a deluxe room with a fireplace for only five dollars more," the clerk suggested smoothly. "That might be more appropriate for the occasion."

"Yes, I'd like that. Please book a deluxe room for us. The name is Wade."

"Very good, Miss. I have a reservation for you for one night, September 23, in a deluxe room for $25.00 plus tax. We'll see you in a few nights."

"Thank you." I hung up the phone and took a deep breath. In spite of Larry's frugality, I didn't think he would object to this extravagance. I was counting on cash in wedding cards to cover any unexpected expenses. *And after that?* I pushed those worries away, trusting that this week's miracle wouldn't be the last.

Late Friday afternoon I checked my reflection once again in the bathroom mirror. My hair was sun-streaked and curled just above my shoulders; the new blue dress matched my eyes and fit perfectly. *It's been six months! I want to look my best.* I walked outside and paced under the big maple tree in the yard.

When the turquoise and white camper finally pulled into the driveway, Larry stepped out and crushed me in his arms. I sank into his hug, absorbing strength and peace from his embrace. Eventually I pulled back to look into his face. I got a quick glimpse of brown eyes brimming with love before he covered my lips with a passionate kiss.

When we pulled apart again, he said, "Let me look at you. Your hair is so long and beautiful. You look fabulous." Before I could reply, he pulled me into another breathtaking embrace.

"Wow, you don't know your own strength," I gasped. "I'm going to have bruised ribs." I stepped back to look him up and down. "You're so tanned and fit! With your G.I. haircut, I'm not sure I'd recognize you on the street."

His brown eyes twinkled. "Just as long as you recognize me when you walk down the aisle tomorrow." I hugged him again, blinking back tears of joy.

Roger's voice interrupted our private moment. "Okay, lovebirds, come out from behind the truck. Other people want to say hello." Holding tightly to each other, we walked around the truck and I greeted Larry's parents.

"Welcome to the ranch, everyone," Mom said. "Dinner will be ready soon. You'll probably want to wash up after being on the road all day."

I waited impatiently for Larry to put his things in the guest house, not wanting him out of my sight. At the dinner table, we sat as close as possible, knees, thighs and shoulders touching, hands clasped under the table. As conversation swirled around us, I murmured to Larry, "Roger said he'd do the dishes tonight. How about a walk along the river after dinner?"

"Whatever you say, Sweetheart, as long as it's with you." His ardent look stirred a dormant internal flame, and I felt a blush rise on my cheeks. I smiled my assent and squeezed his hand.

"And tomorrow night..." I left the sentence dangling.

Tomorrow night we'll be husband and wife!

Chapter 42

Larry

Late Friday night, I stood with my arms around Carolyn at the back door of the ranch house. After all the months of separation, holding her was an incredible pleasure.

"I don't want to say goodnight," I whispered against her hair.

"Me either," she sighed. "But tomorrow is a pretty big day for us." Her eyes had a mischievous glint as she looked up at me. "Besides, I want you to be rested up for tomorrow night." My heart beat double-time as she snuggled against me. I tightened my arms around her and kissed her the way I'd been dreaming of for months. She responded warmly, and my pulse raced. It was all I could do to keep from scooping her up in my arms and carrying her to the nearest bed.

> **Current Culture**
> **September 1967**
>
> - US median household income: $7,143
> - William Styron publishes *The Confessions of Nat Turner* (1968 Pulitzer Prize)
> - Comedy special *Rowan and Martin's Laugh-In* airs on NBC
> - McDonalds sells new Big Mac sandwich for 45 cents

"Whoa, slow down." She pulled back and took a deep breath. Then she gave me a dazzling smile and said, "Just think, after tomorrow, I won't have to say that again."

I took a step back and gazed into her blue eyes, just visible in the moonlight. "I love you, Carolyn Lee Cooke. Thank God that we're actually getting married tomorrow."

"Yes, we do have a lot to thank God for. It's been a pretty miraculous week. I hope all the excitement isn't a foretaste of things to come."

"If it is, it's taught us that God is definitely on our side."

We stood in a silent embrace for a few moments, and I savored the feel of her soft curves against me.

"Goodnight, Darling," she finally said, pulling away. "Sweet dreams."

"You know they will all be of you," I said, reluctantly releasing her.

She turned and went inside, and I headed out to the barnyard fence. I leaned on a peeled log and looked up at the dark bulk of the ridge behind the ranch, thinking about all the miracles of the past week.

There had been happy chaos in the barracks last Friday after our morning graduation from Advanced Infantry Training. Happy, that is, for everyone but me. When the Sergeant told me I didn't have orders and couldn't leave the base, he might as well have lobbed a hand grenade at me. The impact of his words shattered my world. I was dazed as I walked back to the barracks, my brain shutting down. I stood confused and despondent as the other guys grabbed duffle bags off their bunks and trotted off to the bus stop or taxi stand, heading for home. By mid-afternoon, everyone was gone and I was alone in the barracks.

All the pressure, exertion, sleeplessness and fatigue of the last five months seemed to swirl around me and suck me into a deep eddy of depression and self-pity. *Why me? After all my efforts to do the right thing, to try harder, to keep my nose clean, this is the reward I get, God?*

I lay numbly on my bunk, unable to make any sense of the devastating turn of events. When *Taps* played over the speaker at the company headquarters to signal the end of the day, I crawled under the sheet, and pulled the scratchy olive-drab wool blanket over my head. When I finally fell asleep, my dreams were confused and bizarre.

Viet Cong soldiers were chasing me past the beer hall toward the beach. Then they pulled off their uniforms to reveal US Army fatigues, and laughed at my panic.

I tried to get a bus to Oregon, but was told that all the busses had been commandeered for military use, and I'd have to have orders to get a ticket. "I don't have orders!" I yelled at them.

At the ranch, Mrs. Cooke told me that Carolyn was in the upper pasture. But after I hiked up the hill, I couldn't find her. On my way back to the ranch house, I saw her on her horse near the pond. She waved at me, then turned her horse around and galloped away from me.

When I awoke early Saturday morning, the quiet of the barracks was disorienting. Then the details of my situation pelted me like a hailstorm, and I was wide awake. *I'm a hold-over. No orders, no leave, no wedding.*

I turned over, pulled the blanket up to my shoulder, and tried to think of something besides my ruined life. Eventually I had to get up, and when I came back from the latrine, my grumbling stomach reminded me that I hadn't eaten in nearly 24 hours. I dressed in fatigues and headed out the door. Since our company had graduated, the mess hall was closed. I headed to the adjacent company, where training was still in full swing. When I showed my meal card to the corporal at the chow line, he said, "You'll have to wait until everyone else has eaten. Our Company has priority."

After eating all I could manage of my solitary meal, I went back to my Company headquarters. When I walked in, the soldier on duty pulled his feet off the desk and sat up. "How come you're still here?" he asked.

"I'm a hold-over—no orders," I replied. "I can't just sit around all day. Do you have anything for me to do?" He thought for a minute, before saying, "Well, some of the curb stripes need re-painting."

"Great, where do I get the stuff to do it?" He gave me the key to a storeroom, and I spent the rest of the day mindlessly making dingy lines white again.

After dinner, I walked for an hour past look-alike military buildings, finally returning to the empty Company rec room. I was watching a Grade-B Sci-Fi movie when a Private came in.

"Your name Wade?"

"Yes," I answered.

"I've been looking everywhere for you. You've got a phone call at Company HQ."

Oh no, is there a family emergency? Is Carolyn okay?

"Larry? What the heck is going on?" Dad's voice sounded annoyed.

"I can't leave the base; I don't have any orders."

"Well why didn't you call us? We've been worried sick."

"I don't know. I guess I was just so upset that I didn't want to talk to anyone."

"You'd better call Carolyn. She's frantic, thinking something terrible has happened to you."

"Okay, I guess I'll call her."

"Don't guess, do it. I can't believe you'd treat her like that, letting her worry."

"Okay, okay, Dad. I'll call her. But I'll have to find some change first. I don't have enough coins for the pay phone right now."

"Then either get some coins or call her 'collect;' she'll pay the charges. I'm going to call her back right now and tell her you'll be calling. Pull yourself together, Son!"

After he hung up, I stood there for a few moments with the receiver in my hand. *Now I really dread calling Carolyn. I've caused her to worry, and I have nothing but bad news for her.* My hands felt heavy as I put coins in the phone.

After a phone call with profuse apologies, promises to call Monday night regardless of the news, and repeated declarations of my love, I still felt rotten for the anxiety I'd caused Carolyn. *Loving someone is a lot harder than it looks!*

First thing Monday morning, I stood in front of the First Sergeant's desk. "What do I do now?"

Sgt. Drake shook his head. "Beats me. Sit over there while I call around to find out." He made two or three calls before motioning me back to his desk.

"Apparently the problem is your application for OCS. Another school recently shut down, so all the candidates are back-logged waiting for slots at the schools that are still open. Until a place opens up, you'll be held over here at Fort Ord."

"Doing what?"

"I'm sure we'll find something for you to do. Be grateful you're not heading for 'Nam right away."

"But what about my leave?"

"Technically, as long as you're a hold-over, you can't leave the base."

"But Sergeant, I'm supposed to get married on Saturday."

"That's a problem," He frowned, looking at me speculatively. "Give me a few hours; I'll see what I can do. Come back at one o'clock."

I grasped at the thin thread of hope. "If there's any way possible that I could get to Oregon by the end of the week, I would really appreciate it."

"Well, you're one of the better trainees we've had in the past few cycles. I'll do my best."

"Thank you, Sergeant. Thanks a lot."

I started to walk away, and he suddenly said, "Wade, can you type?"

"Yes I can, Sergeant."

"Then I have work for you," he said. He walked over to an adjacent desk, pulled out a chair, and handed me a stack of papers. "We're minus a company clerk right now. These all need to be filled in with the right dates and details."

"No problem, Sergeant."

As I started in on the stack of papers, I sent up a quick prayer. *God, please work this all out for Carolyn, if not for me!*

In the middle of the afternoon I was starting on the third stack of paperwork when Sgt. Drake got a phone call. When he hung up, he walked over to me, a rare smile on his face. "You're in luck, Wade. I think you might be able to make it to Oregon by Saturday."

"Thank you, Sergeant." *And thank you God!* "You have no idea how much this means to me."

His smile spread a little. "I might have a little idea." He raised his left hand to show me a shiny wedding ring. "We don't want to disappoint your girlfriend, do we?"

"No, Sergeant, we definitely don't."

"Here's the deal. The rules say a hold-over is only allowed a two-day pass and can't go more than two hundred miles from the base. If you keep quiet about it, I'll bend the rules and give you a 72-hour pass. If you leave Thursday evening, you should be able to get to Oregon on Friday and get married Saturday. Just be back for roll call on Sunday evening."

"That's cutting it pretty close, but I'll make it work somehow. Thanks, Sergeant. What do I do in the meantime?"

"Report to me every morning. I've got enough paperwork to keep you busy for more than a week!"

As soon as I left the office, I headed for the branch PX to get change for the phone. With the weight of despair lifted from my shoulders, I felt like I could fly. But there were still some details to work out. *Will Carolyn be willing to come back to Fort Ord with me on Sunday? It's a huge risk for her.*

I bought a pack of gum at the PX and got change for a five. As I waited for 7:00 p.m., hope chased doubt through my head. *Can I really ask Carolyn to come hundreds of miles from home to a place where she doesn't know anyone? It could be weeks or months before I have permanent orders.*

When I finally made the phone call, I was still uncertain. When I told Carolyn that we could get married on Saturday, I could feel her joy across the miles.

"Of course I'll buy plane tickets!" Her reckless enthusiasm made me grin. *This could turn out even better than we imagined!*

Even though the paperwork at the Company HQ was repetitive and boring, it made the time go quickly. I was surprised to find a familiar blue envelope from Brightwood when I sorted the mail on Wednesday.

September 18, 1967
My darling Larry,

You sounded so terribly discouraged and depressed over the phone that I wanted to cry. I longed to be there to comfort and encourage you, but in these times we have to depend on God for our strength.

Thank you for calling—it was sheer agony this weekend not hearing from you. You can't imagine all the things that went through my mind, not knowing if you were safe there, or somewhere else, or even alive! I hate having you hitch-hike anyway. But as I said on the phone, I found out how much I love you and how terrifying it can be to even think about being without you. Don't ever think that you might upset me by calling me and giving me "bad" news. That's when we need each other most—to share the hard things as well as the happy moments. If I wanted an easy life, I wouldn't be marrying you. But I've chosen YOU and I know I'm going to find great joy as your wife.

You said this is the first time things have been completely beyond your control. Maybe this is for a purpose—to teach us both what it means to depend completely on God. In the life ahead of us, there will be other times when we have to trust God, and this is just a step toward that.

We have to continue believing that God brought us together for a purpose, and He has a plan for us together. If that weren't the case, I'm certain that He wouldn't have allowed things to go this far. It doesn't matter to me about the plans we made for a honeymoon. We'll have time for that later. All that matters now is that you are going to be my husband and I will go with you wherever you are sent. Let's just live each day as it comes, and know that there is a purpose in it all.

Remember, too, Darling, that I love you, and <u>nothing</u> can change that! Goodbye for now. I'm praying for you constantly.

Carolyn

Folding the letter, I put it in my shirt pocket. Only God could have given me a woman who would love and encourage me like this. *If we can make it through this, nothing can stop us!*

That evening, I called home. "Hi Mom."

"Larry! Is everything okay?"

"Yes, everything's set for me to leave tomorrow evening. That's why I'm calling. There are a few things I need you to bring when you pick me up."

"Just a minute, let me get a pencil and paper." When she came back on the line, I gave her my list.

"I'll need my black suit and a white dress shirt, a dark tie, and some cuff links. I have casual clothes here."

"Okay, I'm writing that down." She paused, then asked, "What about shoes?"

"I'll just wear the black uniform shoes I have here, and hope people look at the bride and not my feet!"

"I'm sure they won't notice," Mom said.

"And the most important thing, Mom. Carolyn's wedding ring is in a little blue velvet box in the drawer of my nightstand, under some papers. Please bring that!"

"That's a pretty important item, Larry," Mom chuckled. "I'll put it in my purse as soon as I hang up. Where should we meet you tomorrow?"

"Write this down, Mom." I gave her specific directions to find me at the base, and asked her to read the directions back to me so I knew she'd copied them correctly. "See you tomorrow evening," I said.

"We'll be there, Larry."

On Thursday evening my stomach felt hollow and I was pacing impatiently when the pickup and camper finally pulled up at the assigned spot. Dad and Mom got out and stretched, and I was surprised when Mom broke through her normal reserve and gave me a hug.

"It's good to see you, Larry," she said.

Dad growled, "I still can't believe you left Carolyn hanging like that."

I ignored Dad's comment, saying "Let's get on the road. We've got a long drive ahead of us."

"You'll have to be in the camper by yourself," Mom apologized. "With the stick-shift, it's a little too crowded in the front seat for three of us."

"Maybe I can catch up on some sleep."

I climbed into the back of the camper and opened the small sliding windows so I'd get a breeze. Between naps on the long trip north, I worked on memorizing the vows I would say to Carolyn. We had agreed that we'd speak them directly to each other, rather than repeating them phrase by phrase after the minister. "For better or worse..." *We've already experienced some of both!*

After midnight, Dad and Mom decided to get some sleep, and pulled over into a rest area near Mt. Shasta. I tried to make myself comfortable with a pillow and blanket on the bench seat of the cab, while Dad and Mom used the camper bed for their nap. I was cold and cramped when I felt the rig shift and the camper door slam. Stars were fading as I got out and unkinked my legs. Mom put a small coffee percolator on the propane stove and heated water in a pan for my tea. Kellogg's Corn Flakes provided a quick breakfast.

During the long miles north of the Oregon border, I had plenty of time to think about the immediate future. *Did I do the right thing asking Carolyn to cancel her plans to go back to school?* It seemed very selfish to want her with me, but she certainly hadn't argued about it. *What am I getting us into?* She was emphatic about not having any more separation, and said she was willing to take a chance. *I'm glad she's adventurous, but it's a huge responsibility.* When I stripped away all my anxiety and restless thoughts, I knew that we were supposed to be together. *God, you'll help us make it work somehow.*

At a rest stop south of Portland before the last leg of the journey, we decided to squeeze into the cab together. As Dad pulled back onto the Interstate, he said, "You ready for this?"

"I'd better be," I replied with more courage than I actually felt.

When the truck swayed through the last curves on Marmot Road and the ranch house came into view, my heart was pounding. Carolyn was waiting beside the driveway and when I jumped out of the cab, she ran into my arms. We hugged tightly and I breathed in the fragrance of her hair. After all the months of separation, loneliness, ruined plans, and the unreality of Army life, the pleasure of having my arms around her was even better than I remembered.

Now, stepping away from the barnyard fence, I walked to the little trailer where I would spend the night. When I pulled back the bedspread, I found a folded piece of blue stationery on the pillow. Carolyn's message quickened my heart rate again.

Dearest Larry,

As you read this, I'm settling down for my last night as a single girl and you're only a few yards away. Thinking about you being so close and what tomorrow holds for us, I'm not sure I'll be able to sleep tonight.

I love you, Larry, and I'm so very grateful to God for the miracles that brought you here at the last minute. Just think, Darling! This is the last night we'll sleep in separate beds. I can't wait for tomorrow, tomorrow night, and what's ahead in our life together!

All my love,
Carolyn

I thought I'd have trouble going to sleep on the lumpy mattress, but before I knew it, I was awakened by unfamiliar ranch sounds. With my toe, I pushed open the curtain beside the bed, and saw that the early morning sky was cloudless. After I showered and dressed, I stepped out of the trailer and saw my father standing with Mr. Cooke at the barnyard fence.

When I joined them, Dad said, "I guess breakfast will be ready in a bit. Mrs. Cooke is trying to keep you and your bride from seeing each other until the wedding. Tradition, you know." He shook his head in amusement.

"Does she really think she can keep us apart until Carolyn walks down the aisle?" I asked.

"She'll do her best," Mr. Cooke grinned.

Chapter 43

Carolyn

Slipping out the side door of the bride's dressing room an hour before the late-afternoon ceremony, I walked down a narrow hallway to sit in the small four-row balcony overlooking the sanctuary at the Chapel of the Hills. *What a perfect setting for our wedding!*

> **Current Culture**
> **September 1967**
>
> - United Auto Workers strike against Ford Motor Company
> - CBS releases *Love is a Many Splendored Thing*, first soap opera to deal with an interracial relationship
> - New TV show *Ironside* features wheelchair-bound detective
> - US population reaches nearly 199,000,000

The church was built of peeled fir logs cut from nearby forests. Diffused light from stained glass windows on each side of the sanctuary brought out the warm patina of the polished wood. The white candles in the log candelabra would provide added glow during the ceremony. Tendrils of deep green philodendron draped down from ledges over the windows, bringing nature indoors.

It was a place where I'd frequently connected with God during my teens. Now, it was the place where I'd make a forever connection with the man I'd chosen to marry.

Heavenly Father, my heart is overflowing. You've blessed me beyond my dreams by bringing Larry into my life. Give me grace as a wife and courage for the next few months...

I sat for a few minutes, enjoying the quiet, and reflecting on the busy morning. A dozen little details had needed attention—packing my suitcase for California, getting the wedding programs printed, making sure I had addresses for thank you notes. Mom was busy preparing food for a post-wedding supper for the family, and Larry's mom pitched in to help her. By noon, my five siblings and their spouses and children were tripping over each other in the crowded ranch house.

Mom had tried to make us hold to the tradition of the bride and groom not seeing each other before the wedding, but under the circumstances, it was a lost cause. I managed to fit in a few short conversations with Larry, and even a couple of kisses. It had been a chaotic day, but now in the peace of the quiet chapel, I took some deep breaths and felt calmness come to my soul. *Thank you, God, for your grace through all of this.*

"Oh, there you are. Mom's looking for you." Emily was wearing her deep blue Matron of Honor dress when she came to the row where I sat. "Are you okay?"

"Yes, I'm fine. I just needed a few minutes to myself. I was thinking of all the ways God has worked to bring us to this day."

"It's been an exciting journey," she said.

"That's an understatement," I said. "Thank you for being obedient to God, Em. If you and Paul hadn't accepted the call to the church in Hanford, you wouldn't have met the Wades, and I would never have met Larry." I squeezed her hand gratefully.

"God worked it all out, didn't He?" she said.

"And I'll always be glad for your matchmaking," I said with a smile.

She smiled back and said, "The photographer will be here soon. You should probably put on your gown."

"Okay, I'm ready otherwise. You did a great job with my hair, Em."

"It's going to be a beautiful wedding, Carolyn. I'm so happy for you and Larry."

The small dressing room pulsed with feminine energy. Mom, Larry's mother, my two sisters, sister-in-law, and two 5–year-old nieces were all there for finishing touches. "Where have you been?" Mom asked. "The photographer's downstairs and you're not dressed."

"Give me five minutes, Mom. With all this help, I'll be ready when he's finished taking pictures of the guys."

Em slipped the satin and lace gown over my head and fastened the pearl buttons up the back, while Priscilla knelt at my feet with my white pumps. Mom handed Emily the wide satin bow that held my veil, and it was quickly fastened in place with a few bobby pins. Just then the door opened, and three of my college friends burst in, chattering excitedly. "Oh, Carolyn, how lovely." "You look beautiful!" "This chapel is amazing!"

There was a knock on the rear door of the dressing room, and the photographer entered. "Let's start with the two mothers posing with you, adjusting your veil." As we followed his instructions, I glanced at the clock on the wall. *3:20—only 40 minutes to go!*

I heard the prelude music begin in the sanctuary as my father came in just after Mom and Mrs. Wade headed downstairs. He patted my arm. "You look beautiful, Honey."

"Thanks, Daddy. Thanks for everything. I love you." I smiled back at him, determined not to let tears ruin my makeup.

"Okay," said Fran, my sister-in-law standing at the door. "Time to start." Priscilla led the way down the stairs and into the center aisle, followed by Emily. My two oldest nieces, Faye and Shelly, held hands as they walked behind their aunts toward the altar. Gary, solemn in his dark suit, carefully carried the satin ring pillow in one hand while holding the stair rail with the other.

Finally, the opening notes of Wagner's *Bridal Chorus* sounded from below. I squeezed Dad's hand and said, "That's our cue, Daddy."

He gave me a smile and a kiss on the cheek. "Let's go!"

As we rounded the curve of the stair I could see that the pews were full, but my eyes sought out Larry, waiting at the altar. He looked nervously happy, and as I walked down the aisle toward him, the loving intimacy in his eyes embraced me.

The organ notes faded, and Paul began speaking the time-honored words.

"Dearly Beloved, we are gathered here together..."

When Dad put my hand into Larry's, I was sure everyone in the chapel could feel the powerful current between us. After Paul's preliminary remarks, the organ began again, and Dave's warm baritone voice filled the chapel with the hymn we'd chosen as a prayer for our marriage.

"Savior, like a shepherd lead us, much we need thy tender care..."

I listened intently to the words, keenly aware of the sacredness of the moment and the strength of the love that flowed between us. There was only a small tremor in my voice as I began saying my vows to Larry. As he said his vows, gazing deeply into my eyes, my heart was filled with joyful gratitude. *After all this time, and all the crazy things that have happened, we're here, at the altar.* I smiled at Larry and blinked back happy tears.

When Paul pronounced us husband and wife and said, "You may kiss the bride," Larry's embrace was gentle, and our kiss was tender but passionate. It felt as if all the love in the universe focused on us, a holy lightning bolt that fused us together in a sacred covenant of love.

The reception was a happy blur. We toasted each other with blackberry punch, and carefully fed each other bites of cake while flashbulbs popped. In the reception line, I proudly introduced Larry to friends, neighbors, and extended family, most of whom he'd never met. His sister and brother-in-law had driven from Pasadena, but with the uncertainty of our plans, none of his California friends had been able to attend. He gratefully greeted the few familiar faces he knew from the Portland church.

By the time the bouquet and garter were tossed and the last photograph was taken, it was nearly 6:30. I changed from my wedding gown into my turquoise and brown trousseau suit, met Larry at the door, and we jubilantly ran out of the chapel through a shower of rice. We were laughing breathlessly as we jumped into the back seat of Dave's car, and he slowly drove us back to the ranch, giving us a welcome interlude for some happy kisses.

Cheers and hugs greeted us as we walked into the ranch house. Two dozen family members crowded into every available space.

"You two sit on the couch, and start opening gifts," Mom directed.

"You get to open all the presents now?" asked Gary.

"Yes, and you can hand them to us. Your mom's going to make a list of everything so we know what Grandma should send to us once we're settled." He grinned made a place for himself at our feet.

"And besides," I told him, "If there's money in any of the cards, we'll need it right away. And I want to write thank-you notes to people as soon as possible."

As we opened gifts, there was constant chatter, comments, and advice. "You'll need that!" and "Oh, you've got two of those now!" "Better keep that rolling pin under lock and key, Larry."

By 8:30, the last gift was opened, and Mom started putting out the food for a late dinner. Larry leaned over and whispered, "I'm starving, but do you think we could get away with excusing ourselves from the big family supper?" I looked at him uncertainly, knowing how much planning and anticipation my mother had put into this event. I hesitated, knowing it would disappoint her. But my new husband took first priority.

"Sure, let's do it," I whispered back.

I got up from the couch and made my way around the piles of gifts and wrapping paper. Rather than asking, I made a statement. "Mom, Larry and I are going to leave in about ten minutes."

With a look of consternation she said, "But you can't leave now! The food is almost ready, and we've been planning this for weeks."

"I know, Mom. Thank you for putting all this together, but it's been a very long day, and we have to travel all day tomorrow. If you'd let us go, we'd be very grateful."

Her shoulders sagged, and she gazed at me with a mixture of disappointment and understanding, and finally said, "Go, Dear. We'll see you at the airport in the morning."

Larry got the keys to the camper from his dad, and after a round of hugs and farewells, we pulled away from the ranch. I sat as close to Larry as I could on the bench seat, moving my knee when he had to shift gears.

"Can you believe it?" I asked with giddy laughter. "We're married, and headed for our one-night honeymoon!"

"It's about time," Larry said. "It's been a very long day. I've never met so many new people in one day in my entire life."

"I know," I grinned. "Wasn't it fun?"

"I guess," he replied doubtfully. "Where's the best place for us to get dinner?"

"We could try the dining room at the golf course. It's five or six miles up the mountain, on the way to Timberline."

"Sounds good to me," he said, stopping for traffic on Highway 26. As he pulled into the east-bound lane, he said, "That was one wonderful wedding you planned, Carolyn. It went off without a hitch."

"I'm glad you thought so—but there were several hitches."

"Really? Like what?"

"Well, for example, when I first saw the wedding cake, I was horrified. The color of the roses was awful, much darker than I asked for."

"It looked fine to me," he said.

"Well, it definitely wasn't the subtle color I wanted. I was upset, then realized there wasn't a thing I could do about it, so I decided to ignore it."

"Good plan. What else happened?"

"Well, something a little more critical. I arranged for the girls from college to bring china plates from the dorm for the reception."

"I saw some girls come in with a box."

"Yes, *a* box—that was the problem. I'd asked them to bring all the dessert plates, and I knew from using them for events at school that there were more than a hundred plates. When they showed up, they had about thirty."

"Uh-oh." Larry looked puzzled. "But there were plates at the reception,"

"Yes, there were—paper plates, cheap picnic paper plates from the Brightwood store! It was the only solution we could come up with less than an hour before the ceremony started. The closest shop that has nice party goods is in Gresham, and that's more than half an hour away, one-way. So Dave drove up to Brightwood and found the paper plates between the fishing tackle and the beer." I burst out laughing—it seemed so ludicrous.

"Wow, I had no idea. At least the ceremony was okay, wasn't it?" he asked hesitantly.

"Yes, it was perfect," I sighed. "Paul did a great job, Dave sang beautifully, and we both said our vows without a mistake."

"I was really sweating that one."

"I knew you could do it," I said, squeezing his arm. "You're so much smarter than you give yourself credit for."

"If you say so," he chuckled as he pulled into the parking lot at the golf resort.

When we entered the dining room, the maître d' looked us up and down before asking, "Do you have a reservation, Sir?"

"No, we don't," Larry replied.

"I'm sorry, there's a thirty minute wait for a table this evening."

We looked at each other, and I saw the plea in Larry's eyes. He'd had enough of waiting, separation, social events, and meeting strangers. "Let's go," I said, turning toward the door.

A few miles further up the highway, in the hamlet of Rhododendron, we parked at the Alpine Hut. It certainly wasn't fine dining, but neither was it crowded, and we were both ravenous. After ordering our meals, we sat in a corner booth, holding hands, relieved that we'd survived the past week, the wedding, and the family drama.

"How are you doing, Mrs. Wade?" Larry asked, looking at me intently.

I glanced around in surprise. "Is your mother here?"

"Okay, silly girl, play it straight. I'm asking about Mrs. *Larry* Wade."

"I'm feeling wonderful. What do you expect?"

"You might be just a little bit tired, after all the nonsense of the past few weeks."

"Maybe, but I'm also extremely happy that it's all in the past."

"It's hard for me to believe that you'd endure all that and still marry me!" he said, with a wry smile.

"But I love you!"

We were gazing into each other's eyes when the waitress plunked plastic bowls of green salad in front of us. We grinned, shrugged, and bowed our heads as Larry prayed.

"Father, thank you for this amazing day, for this food, and most of all, for my beautiful wife. In Jesus' name, Amen."

As we drove the last fifteen winding miles to Timberline Lodge, the moon rose over the shoulder of the mountain. We stood briefly outside the camper in the cold air, looking up at the glorious starry canopy above us. Holding hands tightly, we walked up the broad stone steps into the massive log lodge.

We'd signed the guest register and turned to go up to our room when the clerk said, "Oh, by the way, I notice you have a fireplace room. Because of the drought and forest fire danger, no fires are allowed in the hotel tonight." We looked at each other with amusement. After what we'd been through this week, it was a trivial disappointment.

Walking up the stairs, Larry said quietly, "We'll make love in front of a fire another night." I wondered if he could hear my heart pounding.

After unlocking the door to our room, Larry scooped me up and carried me across the threshold, putting me down in front of the big window facing the mountain. We stood in a close embrace for a few moments, gazing at the glorious sight of the moonlit snow on the glaciers stretching high above us.

"Carolyn, *my wife*," Larry murmured against my hair. "I love you so much. It's time…

Front L-R, Faye Hill, Shelley Cooke
Rear: L-R, Priscilla Cooke Hill, Carolyn, Emily Cooke Mueller

Wedding ceremony at the Chapel of the Hills, Brightwood, Oregon

Happy Bride and Groom

Front Row L to R: Paul Mueller, Lauren Hill holding Darrell, John Cooke, Faye Hill (standing) Jim Mueller, Gary Mueller, Dave Cooke, Roger Cooke, Jack Cornelison.
Back Row L to R: Emily Cooke Mueller, Aunt Marian Keizur, Laura Cooke, Ernest Cooke, Carolyn, Shelley Cooke McCausland (standing) Larry, Ira (Monk) Wade, Fran Miller Cooke, Mildred Wade, JoAn Wade Cornelison Stephens (Priscilla Cooke Hill is behind JoAn)

Chapter 44

Carolyn

In my dream, Larry was smiling at me, his brown eyes glowing with love. He leaned over and kissed my shoulder, then my neck. As I turned to tell him how glad I was that we were finally together, I realized that it wasn't a dream. He was actually beside me, the touch of his lips making my skin tingle. I smiled sleepily at him.

Current Culture
September 1967

- One-way airfare Portland to Fresno, $45.00
- Average price of motel room: $10.50
- Three-course meal in nice restaurant: $3.75
- *Good Housekeeping* magazine sells for 50 cents

"Good morning, Sweetheart," he said, his smile broadening to a grin. "How did you sleep?"

"Like a log."

"You don't feel like a log...*much* softer." He reached for my hand and kissed my palm, then slowly planted a row of kisses up my arm. I snuggled against him for a few blissful minutes before we were rudely interrupted by the shrill noise of the alarm clock beside the bed.

"Is it 6:30 already?" I groaned.

"Sadly, yes."

"Do we really have to leave so early?" I knew the answer, but wished for a different reality.

"Believe me, there's nothing in the world I'd like better than to stay right here," Larry said, pulling me closer in a crushing embrace. "But I don't think you want your new husband to be AWOL and thrown in the stockade the first week of our marriage."

"You're right, that would be regrettable." I slipped my feet onto the braided rug on the polished wood floor and glanced out the big multi-paned window. "It looks like another gorgeous day!" The heavy bulk of Mt. Hood above the lodge was suffused with a rosy tint in the growing dawn.

We reluctantly dressed, packed our bags, gave a longing look at the rumpled bed, and walked out of our honeymoon room.

As we drove down the mountain, the early morning light illuminated spectacular views. The golden fields of Central Oregon spread to the east, and to the south, spiky Mt. Jefferson pierced the blue sky. Around the next bend the road darkened, with the Mt. Hood National Forest crowding in on both sides.

At the ski village of Government Camp, we ordered breakfast. Fatigue and nervous anticipation had stifled our appetites the previous night, but this morning we were both ravenous. Outside the window by our table, the ski lifts looked forlorn and neglected, with only dry grass and brown shrubbery beneath them. "This must look very different in winter," Larry said.

"Yes, it's totally transformed. But it's likely to be a long time before we see that," I said. "Who knows where we'll be when the snow falls here again."

"Only God," was Larry's cryptic reply.

When the server brought our orders of the café's signature wild huckleberry pancakes, we made quick work of them, anxious to be on the next leg of our journey to California.

It wasn't long before we were passing the road signs to Brightwood, and Larry slowed as we passed the Chapel of the Hills. Except for the pastor's car, the parking lot was empty, much different than the previous afternoon, when the cars of our wedding guests had filled every space.

"You pulled off a beautiful wedding, Mrs. Wade," Larry commented.

"Thank you, Mr. Wade. I'm so glad you could make it," I smiled at him and moved a little closer. There was a honk and a wave from the driver next to us, acknowledging the "Just Married" signs my brothers had taped to the back and sides of the camper. We waved back with embarrassed smiles.

Larry shook his head. "I still can't get used to the fact that we're really married. Think of all the things God worked out for us in just the past week...it's amazing."

"I know, it's hard to take it all in. Last weekend I thought I'd be heading back to college after our honeymoon, while you headed for the East Coast. And here we are, ready to fly back to California together!"

"You're taking a big risk, Sweetheart, you know that."

"Yes, I do. You could get orders next week. But somehow, I just don't think it's going to happen that way. Maybe I'm being naïve, but I think God is going to surprise us again."

"I hope it's a good surprise." He was thoughtful for a moment, before adding, "You were such a beautiful bride, Carolyn."

"I'm glad you think so," I replied, my cheeks flushing with pleasure.

"Everyone thought so. It was the best wedding I've ever attended."

"You'd better say that!" I chuckled. We continued reminiscing about the ceremony and reception, and soon found ourselves turning from 82nd Avenue to the entrance of Portland Airport.

"It's only a little after 9:00," Larry said as he pulled into the parking garage. "We could have stayed in bed another half hour." He gave me a meaningful glance, and my cheeks warmed at the implication of his words.

"Well, at least we won't have to rush for our flight."

We were so early that there were no attendants at our gate and our family hadn't arrived yet. We stood uncertainly for a moment.

"I'm still hungry," Larry said. "Let's go back to the coffee shop. We've got time for a snack."

As we looked at the menus I said, "They have blueberry pie. I think I'm going to celebrate with a piece."

"At 9:30 in the morning? Well, why not?" He turned to the waitress and said, "Two cups of tea and two pieces of pie, please. Apple for me and blueberry for my wife." When she turned away with our order, he said, "I love saying that—my wife.

"I love hearing you say that!" We smiled at each other across the table, holding hands, relishing our nearness.

"You wouldn't happen to be newlyweds, by any chance?" asked the waitress as she put our order on the table.

"That obvious, huh?" said Larry.

"Silly grins and shiny rings—easy to spot. Congratulations!"

"Thanks," we said in unison to her retreating back.

As we took our last sips of tea, Larry looked at his watch. "Oh, wow, look at the time. 10:10—it's later than I thought. We need to head to the gate." He left a tip on the table, and we paid our bill at the cashier's stand.

A dozen family members were waiting anxiously at the gate. "There you are," said Emily, a look of relief flooding her face.

Mom looked worried, "We thought you overslept and were going to miss your flight."

We quickly explained and started giving farewell hugs. By the time we got to the desk for our seat assignments and boarding passes, there were only a few other passengers heading for the plane. "You'll be in seats 13B and 15C," the desk agent informed us.

"But we need seats together!" I said in consternation.

She glanced at her seating chart again. "I'm sorry, I don't have any adjoining seats left. That's as close as I can get you."

"Oh, well," I shrugged, turning to Larry. "At least we're on the same plane."

"Blame it on the pie," he chuckled. We gave final waves to our family, and I followed Larry through the door to the tarmac. "At least it wasn't a long farewell," he said, sounding relieved. When I didn't respond, he looked at me questioningly. I tried to smile through my tears.

"I'm okay, really," I sniffed. "I always cry when I say goodbye." Larry squeezed my hand as we started up the stairs into the plane.

My seat happened to be on the terminal side of the plane, and when I saw my family standing at the observation window, my throat constricted and my eyes welled with tears again. This wasn't just a pleasure trip to California, but in many ways, an irreversible journey from childhood to adulthood. As the plane accelerated down the runway, I felt an unexpected sense of loss and tearing away—from my parents, my brothers and sisters, my home, our beloved ranch. It didn't help that the plane flew east from Portland, retracing the route we'd just taken from the mountain to the airport. As the pilot banked the plane to head south, I got a glimpse out the window of Mt. Hood below, solid, majestic and unchanging.

I took a deep breath. *Lord, I put my trust in you. You're the One who created the mountains. You're the One who planned this life journey for me, and I know it will be good.* I turned in my seat to look back at Larry. He gave me a reassuring smile and mouthed the words, "I love you." Replying in kind, I leaned back in my seat and began to relax. *Thank you, Heavenly Father.*

We'd just ordered a light lunch in the San Francisco airport when Larry said, "Excuse me, Carolyn. I need to make a phone call." I was puzzled, but figured it had something to do with the Army. He came back into the restaurant and sat down as our food arrived.

"It's all set. Jesse will meet our plane in Fresno and take us to Hanford."

My mouth dropped open. "You mean you just now made those arrangements?" I'd assumed that he'd already made the plans for the hour's drive from Fresno to Hanford to get his car.

"Yeah, I'm glad he was home."

Questions and retorts filled my mind. *What if Jesse hadn't been home? We would have been stuck in Fresno for who knows how long. How could Larry have left this critical piece of the plan until the last minute?*

I started to voice my thoughts, but swallowed them instead. There was no point in having an argument in an airport restaurant the first day of our marriage.

"Looks like God continues to pull things together for us!" I said. Larry's smile showed his relief at my response.

On the short flight between San Francisco and Fresno, we sat close together, holding hands and watching the scenery below. When I'd made the same trip in March, the landscape was mostly green. Now, after a hot summer, the sunburned landscape was relieved only by the bright reflection of sun off the water in the irrigation canals of the broad San Joaquin Valley.

In the tiny Fresno Air Terminal we spotted Jesse quickly. He helped Larry put our suitcases in the trunk, and we headed to Hanford. Alone in the back seat, I felt a wave of weariness, and leaned my head against the window. In response to Jesse's questions, Larry gave a guy's version of the wedding, which made me smile with its terse lack of detail. I closed my eyes and I drifted into a light doze, waking when the car bumped into the Wades' driveway.

"We're here, Carolyn," Larry said. "And thanks a lot, Jesse. We really appreciate the lift."

"No problem, I didn't have anything else to do this afternoon," Jesse said. He shook hands with Larry before backing out of the driveway. "Have a nice drive to the base," he called out the open window as he drove away.

Larry unhooked a house key from its hidden spot beside the garage, and we went inside. "Let's open some windows while we're here," he said. With his parents still in Oregon, the house was stuffy and warm. "I need to get more civilian clothes and my study Bible."

In his room, he glanced around. "Oh, yes, I want to bring my record player. We'll need music wherever we are. Why don't you pick out some LPs to take?" I leafed through a stack of records on the bookshelf while he pulled shirts and slacks out of the closet. Arms full, we left the bedroom and put everything on the kitchen table.

"I hope Dad put gas in the car and made sure it would start," Larry said. He had sold his Chevy sedan when he'd gotten drafted. Soon after, his brother Chuck had driven a '57 station wagon from Texas to park in his parents' garage during his second tour in Vietnam. Knowing we could make good use of it, he'd sold it to Larry for a bargain price.

In the garage, Larry turned the key in the ignition. "Alright!" he exclaimed when the car started easily. He backed it out of the cramped single garage, and opened the back hatch of the car. When all our belongings were in the cargo space, it seemed like a pitifully small amount. As if reading my mind, Larry said, "It's not much, but it's all we need for now."

Once on the road out of Hanford, Larry asked, "Can you see if there's a map in the glove compartment? I've never driven to the base, only hitch-hiked once." I searched the small space, finding only the car registration and a tire pressure gauge.

"No luck."

"Well, I know we head up through Fresno on Highway 99, and turn west somewhere north of Madera."

"We can always stop at a gas station and ask for directions."

The fields beside the highway were empty after harvest, and the small ramshackle farm buildings reflected the hardship of farming in this arid valley. The miles went quickly as we talked about the events of the last few weeks, and what the future might hold for us. We'd been on the road a little more than an hour when we saw highway signs for Highway 152 and Monterey Peninsula.

"This is where we turn west," Larry said.

"Are there any towns along here? I'm getting hungry. Lunch in San Francisco was a long time ago."

"I think there are a couple small towns before we cross the mountains."

"Mountains?"

"Well, not like Mt. Hood. Our coast range is pretty puny compared to the Cascades."

"Oh, there's a sign that says Los Banos, 35 miles. Would that be a good place to stop? We should get there about 6:30."

"Maybe we should just get something at a drive-in. We still have about three hours to go."

"A quick meal would suit me fine. It's probably going to be dark by the time we get into the mountains."

"Well, I remember the road being pretty good."

"You're a safe driver; we'll be fine." My encouraging words demonstrated a bravery I wasn't really feeling. The road seemed endless, and I knew Larry was as tired as I was. By the time we got to Los Banos and shared a milkshake with our hamburgers and fries, the sun had gone down.

I spent time fiddling with the radio dial, trying to find some kind of lively music to keep us awake in the darkness. The road began climbing out of the flat valley, and eventually we saw a roadside sign, "Pacheco Pass, Elevation 1,299 feet."

"Puny is right," I said. "We were at nearly 6,000 feet last night at Timberline Lodge."

"Well, I took you to our big mountains on the other side of the state last March."

"Yes, Sequoia Park was beautiful, and I loved seeing where you worked during college breaks." We talked for a while about our time together in March. "If I'd had any idea back then that it would be six months before I would see you again, I don't think I would have gotten back on the plane."

"I don't think I would have let you. That was way too long to be separated."

"Yes, but aren't you glad I'm sitting here beside you tonight?"

"More than you will ever know, Carolyn. I just hope there isn't a new separation right around the corner."

"Well, if there is, we'll make it through that, just like we made it through this." I put my head on his shoulder. "I'm just happy to be able to do this tonight."

"Oh, look, there's a junction coming up. I wonder if we stay on 152 or turn onto Highway 156?"

"I have no idea, Larry. What towns are ahead?"

"It looks like Gilroy one direction and San Juan Bautista the other."

"So which one is nearest Fort Ord?"

"You got me. As I said, I've only hitch-hiked, never driven this road. But Gilroy sounds more familiar than San Juan Bautista. I think I'll stay on 152."

"Okay," I agreed hesitantly. Not knowing if we were on the right road took away my sleepiness, and I carefully watched for signs. We were still in hilly country, with occasional small homesteads tucked between oak trees in the valleys.

After another thirty minutes of winding road, Larry pulled in at a Shell station, and got out to talk to the attendant in the dimly lit office. He didn't look happy as he walked back to the car.

"Apparently we should have taken 156 back there," he said. "We're actually closer to Santa Cruz now."

"Do we have to go back up through the mountains?" My dread of dark mountain roads was amplified by fatigue.

"No, we can catch Highway 1 up ahead a few miles, and then head south." Larry pulled back onto the road from the gas station.

"How far to the base?"

"He said it's another half hour. I'm so sorry, Carolyn."

"Well, it's not your fault. If it's only 30 more minutes, that's not bad. We'll get there a little after 10:00."

"Thanks for being so understanding."

"I love you, remember?"

"Yes, but I wouldn't blame you if you were upset."

"And ruin our second night together? I don't think so." I smiled at him with more energy than I felt, and reached over to try to pick up some local music on the radio. We'd gone just a few miles on Highway 1 when the sign beside the road read *Marina 18 miles* and below that, *Carmel-by-the-Sea 30 miles*. "Are we that close to Carmel?" I said, suddenly excited.

"Yes, it's not far from the base."

"Oh, when can we go?"

"This week, I hope. It all depends on what the First Sergeant says when I check in at roll call tomorrow morning.

"What time is that?"

"Six o'clock sharp. I can't be late for that." Something in his tone made me curious.

"Why is that so important?"

Larry gave me a sidelong glance, and paused before replying. "Well, technically, right now I'm AWOL. My 72-hour pass expired at 5:00 p.m., a few hours back. I kept hoping we'd get to the base earlier, and I didn't want you to worry, so I didn't say anything."

I sat frozen in disbelief, not knowing what to think or say. Finally I said, "So what will happen?"

"I really don't know. God's done some amazing things in the past week and I know he's on our side. I bailed out the First Sergeant last week, catching up a lot of paperwork for him. He's a good guy; he might give me a break."

"Oh, Larry...I'm not sure what to think." I fought tears--it was all too overwhelming. I lay my head back on the seat and spoke aloud. "Father, we're sort of dangling out in space here. It's pretty scary. But we choose to trust that you know what's ahead for us, and you're going to do the best for us. Give Larry favor, please, God."

We were silent for several miles, lost in anxious thoughts. Gradually there were more homes and buildings beside the road, and we came to the outskirts of Marina, a town that bordered the base. The first few motels we passed had *No Vacancy* signs posted. Then we saw a sign ahead on the left: *Paradise Lodge—Vacancy.*

"What do you think, Carolyn?" Larry asked.

"Looks like we don't have a lot of choices at this time of night. Let's give it a try."

"I'll check on the price, you can stay here."

"Okay, I don't mind."

He came back a few minutes later with a key in his hand. "Room 23, just across the parking lot."

When he unlocked the door, I glanced around and said, "I guess 'Paradise' is relative." The room was plain and tired, with a faded quilted bedspread on the double bed, a chair that looked like it belonged in a dentist's waiting room, and a small black and white TV on a plastic table. I checked the bathroom quickly. "At least it's clean."

As we prepared for bed, Larry laid his uniform carefully on the chair so it would be easy to get into at 5:30. Later, wrapped in his arms, I had just murmured a sleepy "Goodnight, Darling," when I felt his body tense.

"You did set the alarm, didn't you?" he asked.

"Yes, it's right here. Do you want it on your side of the bed?"

"That's probably a good idea." I fumbled on the nightstand, and handed him the small brass clock before snuggling back on his shoulder. As soon as my eyes closed, I fell into dreamless sleep.

It seemed like only five minutes later when I felt Larry jolt off the bed. "Oh, no, it's after 6:00!" he exclaimed. "Why didn't the alarm go off?"

I shook my head to clear the sleep from my eyes. "But I set the clock last night."

He grabbed it off the nightstand and peered at it in the dim light. "The alarm hand is pointing at 6:30, not 5:30."

"Oh, Larry, I'm so sorry." Panic shook me totally awake, and I scrambled for some clothes. Larry jumped into his fatigues, taking a quick look in the bathroom mirror as he lined up the buttons of his shirt, his brass belt buckle and the fly of his trousers.

"Let's go," he said. I grabbed up the room key and my purse and followed him out to the car. Anxiety silenced us in the car. I couldn't believe that I had messed up something so important. *If he gets sent to the stockade, it would be my fault. Help, Lord!*

Larry pointed out landmarks once we were on the base. "I'm glad you have a good sense of direction, Carolyn," Larry said. "You'll have to come back this way this afternoon."

"Okay," I said uncertainly. All the buildings looked alike to me.

"You can always ask anyone you see," he said as he turned down a side street, "but I'm in Company A, 4th Battalion, 2nd Brigade. Just ask for directions to "A-4-2."

I watched more drab, one-story wooden buildings pass as he continued further into the base. There were sign posts at intersections, and the starkness of the buildings was relieved by tall eucalyptus trees and red-flowered bottle brush shrubs. I looked around carefully when he parked. A carved wooden sign identified the building across the street: *Headquarters A-4-2*

"This is it," Larry said, putting the car in Park. "Be here at 5:00 tonight. If I can't come out to you, I'll make sure that someone tells you what's going on."

I took a deep breath to quiet my fear. "I'll be waiting, Darling. I love you—God be with you!" He got out of the car and walked briskly across the street. At the door he turned and waved at me before disappearing into the building.

I sat half-paralyzed for a few minutes, then gave myself a pep talk.

God, you're in control, and I know you won't let me down. Things will look better after a few more hours sleep. This could be a great adventure, it's beautiful here!

Beyond the rows of buildings, I could see a distant line of forested hills with houses on them, and in another direction, the sun glinted off the ocean. Taking a calming deep breath, I gave a final glance at *Headquarters A-4-2*, drove carefully back to the motel, hung out the *Do Not Disturb* sign and crawled back into the bed.

It was nearly noon when I woke up. *What happened with Larry? I'm trying not to be scared, Lord.*

My stomach was growling, so I showered, dressed in clean clothes, and turned the door hanger to *Maid Service, Please*. At the café adjacent to the motel, I ordered soup and a sandwich, and ate while glancing through a copy of the *Monterey Peninsula Herald* that another customer had left on the counter. With my mind on a different track, the words didn't make much sense. *Is he okay? Did they put him in the stockade after all?*

After lunch, I browsed in a drugstore, splurged on the October issue of a women's magazine, watched an unfamiliar afternoon television show and drove a few blocks to a car wash to remove the gritty Central Valley dust from the red and white Chevy.

I arrived early at the assigned meeting place. *Please, Lord, please let him come out.*

When the five o'clock cannon boomed across the base, uniformed soldiers started pouring out of various buildings. I saw Larry bound through the door of *Headquarters A-4-2*, a broad grin on his face. I jumped out of the car and met him in the middle of the street. He wrapped me in a huge hug, lifting me off my feet. "I'm hungry," he said. "Let's get something to eat."

"Really? Thank God!" I was laughing and crying as I hugged him back. As we walked to the car with our arms around each other, I could hardly keep from jumping up and down. "So tell me, what happened?"

"Well, I went in and walked up to the First Sergeant's desk. He looked up and said, 'Morning, Wade. How was your weekend?'" Larry couldn't stop grinning.

"You're kidding! That was it?"

"Yep, that was it. I told him, 'It was very good, Sergeant,' and he said, 'Well, there's more paperwork to do. You might as well get started.'"

I handed him the car keys, and we drove back toward Marina. A block before the motel, Larry pulled into the parking lot of Mortimer's Restaurant, where we sat in a booth, holding hands.

"I can hardly believe it, Larry. I tried not to worry today, but it was hard."

"Well, you're a long way from home, a new bride, and didn't know if your husband would be coming home to you tonight."

"I'm so glad you are, Darling," I said, swallowing the lump in my throat.

"Ready to order?" asked the waitress.

After requesting two $.99 dinner specials, Larry took both my hands in his. "We need to thank God tonight, for sure."

"Definitely, please go ahead."

We bowed our heads and Larry prayed, "Heavenly Father, we're so grateful for your goodness. You've proved your love and power over and over again." I blinked back tears as he continued praying softly. "Thank you, Lord, that we got here safely, that you gave me favor with the First Sergeant, and most of all, that Carolyn is here with me." He squeezed my hands. "Help us find housing quickly, and help me get promoted to PFC soon. We know you have a plan for our lives. Please increase our faith and trust so that we can fulfill your will. In Jesus' Name, Amen."

"And thank You for the food," I added, smiling happily into my new husband's eyes.

Acknowledgements

So many people have played a part in bringing this book into being. By far the most influential was, of course, Larry. Thank you for your constant support and encouragement, for your patience when I was distracted by the words parading through my head, for your kind honesty as you read each chapter (more than once), for the numerous cups of tea, sandwiches, quick meals, loads of laundry, and all the other large and small things you did so I could finish this project. My gratitude is boundless!

Major thanks go to the faithful members of my writers group: Marion Duckworth, Carol Wilson, Linda Reinhardt, Patty Oliver, Lidia Hu and Kathy Meikle. Your thoughtful and candid critiques sharpened my writing and constantly made me think about not just my story, but my readers.

Praying friends Frank and Liz Morgan and Jerry & Teri Carbone have kept the spiritual side covered, along with Susan Palmer, Bev Swanson, Nilza Brito, and Shar Northy.

Glenda Malmin was my biggest cheerleader from the beginning. As a fellow-writer, her input was extremely valuable. Thanks for all the hours you spent reading and critiquing the first full draft, as well as the numerous tea dates and encouraging words.

Vicki Owens, messaging from Africa, was always faithful to spur me on when she sensed I was lagging on the journey.

Pamela Healea planted the seed of this book when she found out we still had the box of letters: "This is a story to share with your grandchildren!"

Linda Bryan, Sharon Riesterer, Margrit Witschi and Rosie Thomas kept me inspired to reach for "More Beyond."

Two of our daughters were involved in this project. Jennifer Bowman did an excellent job as my first proofreader, while Rebecca Malmin fulfilled my vision for the cover.

Sarah Gill (www.andafterwords.com) provided professional editing, giving valued suggestions from a twenty-something viewpoint.

Special thanks to Christie Krug, whose *Wildfire Writing* classes first gave me permission to call myself a writer. Karen Wells persuaded me to go to my first writers conference, where I met many amazing and gracious people.

John & Karen Minnis generously opened their beach home, and Dan and Becky Hanenkrat kindly gave us the keys to their mountain condo so I could have concentrated "writing retreats" and actually finish the book.

To all of you who asked "How's the book coming?" I say a huge **thank you!**

ABOUT THE AUTHOR

Carolyn and Larry have been married for fifty adventurous years. More than forty of those years have been in career ministry, fulfilling the call of God they shared with each other in those first days.

They have raised four children, and now enjoy thirteen grandchildren and two great-grandchildren. While they make their home in the Pacific Northwest, they have followed God's call to California, Uganda and Australia.